Word and Power

Word *and* Power

Is the Theology of John Wimber Compatible with Presbyterian Theology and Practice?

Gareth William David Stewart

WIPF & STOCK · Eugene, Oregon

WORD AND POWER
Is the Theology of John Wimber Compatible with Presbyterian Theology and Practice?

Copyright © 2015 Gareth William David Stewart. All rights reserved. Except for brief quotations in critical publications or reviews, no part of this book may be reproduced in any manner without prior written permission from the publisher. Write: Permissions, Wipf and Stock Publishers, 199 W. 8th Ave., Suite 3, Eugene, OR 97401.

Wipf & Stock
An Imprint of Wipf and Stock Publishers
199 W. 8th Ave., Suite 3
Eugene, OR 97401

www.wipfandstock.com

ISBN 13: 978-1-62564-590-6

Manufactured in the U.S.A.

Contents

Preface | vii
Acknowledgments | ix
Abbreviations | x

The Theoretical Foundation

1. Setting the Scene | 3
2. The Theology and Writing of John Wimber | 30
3. How the Study will Work | 103

The Contextual Applications

4. Evangelism in a Reformed Church | 123
5. Discipleship in a Reformed Church | 153
6. Ministry in a Reformed Church | 189

Conclusion | 222
Bibliography | 249

Preface

THIS BOOK DISCUSSES THE contribution made by John Wimber to the theology of evangelism, discipleship, and ministry. These contributions are contextually placed within a Reformed congregation that is part of a Confessional Presbyterian Denomination. While it does not address specifics with one congregation, the principles aim to be applicable to all such congregations. It seeks to challenge the accepted attitudes toward evangelism, the integration of new converts into the Church through discipleship, and the release of these converts into some form of ministry. This thesis argues for a re-evaluation of the power of the Holy Spirit in confirming the gospel with signs accompanying, in filling each believer with his fullness and the giving of spiritual gifts, and a release of these gifts through every member ministry as a possible methodology to be implemented in Presbyterian congregations.

This book aims to offer a middle way between Pentecostalism and Cessationist theology through the ministry philosophy of John Wimber, himself an ordained minister of the Quaker denomination. It seeks to respect the theological and historical traditions of Presbyterianism, while not being uncritical of some of its current methodologies. It also seeks to suggest that the theology of the Reformed faith is best suited to a Charismatic methodology with the emphasis on God's sovereignty, omnipotence and sacramental theology. It seeks to place the practice of evangelism, discipleship, and ministry within the context of a local congregation as that which is best suited to minister to the needs of that local community in which it is planted, and to evangelize, disciple, and train those members to meet the spiritual needs of that community. This book argues for an integration of the presence and power of the Holy Spirit in the context of a Bible and preaching-based congregation.

Acknowledgments

I WANT TO THANK my wife and best friend, Cherrie, for all her support and encouragement throughout our marriage and in the ministry to which Christ has called me. For Sebastian, my best friend, who has never spoken a word but has given me nothing but love and acceptance and who died just before the completion of this work. I also want to thank my Mum for the stable home and Christian upbringing that she and Dad provided.

I want to thank Robin Routledge for supervising me throughout this period of study, and for his encouraging and challenging comments.

Lastly, but by no means least, I want to thank my Lord and Savior Jesus Christ who saved me, called me, anointed me and, to my own amazement, continues to bless the work I do for him.

Soli Deo Gloria!

Abbreviations

ESV	*The Holy Bible, English Standard Version.*
PCI	The Presbyterian Church in Ireland.
MPC	*Maghera Presbyterian Church.*
MTS	Ministry Training Strategy
NIV	*Holy Bible: New International Version.*
NLT	*Holy Bible, New Living Translation, Second Edition.*
NKJV	*Holy Bible, New King James Version.*
WARC	World Alliance of Reformed Churches.
WCF	*Westminster Confession of Faith.*
WSC	*Westminster Shorter Catechism.*

The Theoretical Foundation

1

Setting the Scene

Introduction

ADRIAN PLASS TELLS THE story of an alien visiting St. Wilfred's Anglican Church.[1] If that same alien were to land a spacecraft in Ulster and travel along the roads of our cities, towns, villages, and hamlets, it would no doubt be surprised at the number of very odd and strange-looking buildings that seem, in some instances, very grand indeed, but are closed for the vast majority of the week. These buildings are Churches and, in Ulster, many of these buildings are Presbyterian. Not only are there a vast number of individual Churches, but there are also a significant number of Presbyterian denominations: The Presbyterian Church in Ireland (PCI), the Reformed Presbyterian Synod of Ireland (Covenanters), the Non-Subscribing Presbyterian Church of Ireland (Unitarians), the Evangelical Presbyterian Church of Ireland, the Free Presbyterian Church of Ulster, and even the Free Presbyterian Church of Scotland![2] Practices in these churches may include credobaptism and exclusive psalmody.

PCI is the largest Protestant denomination in Northern Ireland. John Dickinson notes that in 2008, PCI lost 1,994 people claiming connection, 1,223 fewer contributions to the funds of the denomination, 979 fewer people attending Communion, and 731 fewer on the rolls of our Sunday

---

1. Plass, *Alien at St. Wilfred's*.

2. For a history of Presbyterianism in Ireland please consult: Hamilton, *History of Presbyterianism in Ireland*; Holmes, *Our Irish Presbyterian Heritage*, Holmes, *Presbyterian Church in Ireland*.

Schools and Bible classes.[3] How these trends are addressed may lead the Church, according to John McIntyre, to reconsider the work of the Holy Spirit.[4] These statistics suggest that there may be a need for a fresh approach to the way in which Church is practiced in Ulster. I want to suggest that one option may be to consider the theology of John Wimber. I chose to compare Reformed theology with an example of Charismatic theology because, as Greg Odgen notes, the Christian Church has been affected through the renewal of the Holy Spirit in recent years.[5] This effect has happened through worship music and events, such as Spring Harvest,[6] that have brought Charismatic theology and practice into connection with mainstream historical denominations.

Much of the writing on Pentecostalism and Charismatic theology has emphasized the Arminian, Holiness, Methodist, Revivalist and Premillennial influences, such as Cox,[7] Dayton[8] and Synan.[9] Keith Warrington does not suggest any Reformed influences on Pentecostalism.[10] Regarding the Charismatic Movement there have been some historical studies, such as those of Andrew Walker[11] and Peter Hocken[12], and some have touched on

---

3. Dickinson, *Presbyterian Herald*, 10. There has also been some reflection within the Church of Scotland (PCI's mother Church) concerning the need for re-evaluating mission and witness. See Reid, *Outside Verdict*. Brian Stanley notes that during the 1910 Edinburgh Missionary Conference there was an assumption that Western Christianity would provide for every need of the world. Stanley, *Twentieth Century World Christianity*, 3. If the Church today feels that there is no need for change and that everything they need is provided for, while ignoring the facts, there may be a sense in which history is repeating itself.

4. McIntyre, *Shape of Pneumatology*, 1. He also cites the loss of contact with youth and the spread of secularism.

5. Odgen, *New Reformation*, 13. From this point I use the capitalized form of the noun to refer to the Charismatic Renewal/Movement and the lower case to refer to charismatic experience, which may not be limited to the Renewal.

6. Spring Harvest is a residential family conference held during the English School's Easter holidays in different locations. It is generally believed to be "charismatic" and reaches across denominational barriers. Each year it publishes a music book of the songs which are sung in the conference and which can be used as a resource for local church worship. See www.springharvest.org.

7. Cox, *Fire from Heaven*.

8. Dayton, *Theological Roots of Pentecostalism*.

9. Synan, *Holiness Pentecostal Tradition*.

10. Warrington, *Pentecostal Theology*, 2–4. He cites the following: Anabaptists, Dispensationalism, Evangelicalism, Pietism, Wesleyanism, the Holiness Movement, Keswick, the Higher Life Movement, the Healing Revival Movement, the Latter Rain Movement, Premillennialism and Black Spirituality.

11. Walker, *Restoring the Kingdom*.

12. Hocken, *Streams of Renewal*.

it in writing Pentecostal histories.[13] Hocken, however, does not mention Reformed/Presbyterian influences on the Charismatic Movement or vice versa. There have been some polemical writings concerning the inaccuracy of contemporary Charismatic phenomena from a Reformed perspective,[14] and even some attempts at harmonizing the differing views on the Holy Spirit.[15] There has been, however, a paucity of reflection from a Reformed position that positively considers Charismatic issues.[16] Considering this, I believe there is a need to re-evaluate the Pentecostal/Charismatic influence on the Reformed Churches and the Reformed influence upon the Charismatic/Pentecostal Churches. This has already been done regarding the Christian and Missionary Alliance and may benefit from being applied to a Reformed context.[17]

This would benefit, not only Reformed scholars and congregations, but also open up a new avenue of study within the Pentecostal/Charismatic world. This will improve scholarship by highlighting a gap in theological discussion, by demonstrating that being Reformed does not necessarily mean cessationist, and that the Pentecostal/Charismatic Movement may share the same Reformation source as Reformed Churches.[18] It will improve practice by allowing for a wider degree of freedom in the expression of worship in Reformed Churches by anchoring the supernatural in Word-centered Churches, and challenging the Arminian basis of much Pentecostal/Charismatic evangelism. Regarding ecclesiastical policy, this study will increase the ecumenical reach of the Pentecostal/Charismatic Movement and theology. It will aid understanding amongst Pentecostal/Charismatics and Reformed believers about why each Church has different and unique features, allowing both streams to draw on their theological resources and traditions. This will show the complementary nature of the two streams and, while their theological differences may not be resolved, something of each may be added to the other that would be absent otherwise.[19]

13. Kay, *Inside Story*, 259ff.
14. Masters and Whitcomb, *Charismatic Phenomena*; Robertson, *Final Word*.
15. Grudem, *Are Miraculous Gifts for Today?*
16. Fyall, *Charismatic and Reformed*, 1.
17. King, *Genuine Gold*.

18. Turner sees the issues of cessationism and the Pentecostal doctrine of initial evidence, specifically regarding glossolalia, to be on the "fringes" of New Testament research. Turner, "Early Christian Experience," 2–3. Despite any potential fringe nature of this research it does represent the deeply held theological convictions of two Christian streams that cannot be treated as insignificant.

19. This was an aim of symphonic theology as outlined in chapter 3. See Poythress, *Symphonic Theology*, 43 and 90.

Dickinson's statistics may also suggest a change in people's attitude toward Church. Timothy Keller notes that many people today consider themselves non- or anti-religious, being wary of any institution that exercises authority over individuals, particularly on confusing moral issues.[20] Objective truth may also be rejected, leading to narcissism and "signals the death of a culture based on objective truth and civic virtue," as Philip Graham Ryken points out.[21] With numbers leaving the Church, a desire to redress this is the focus of much thinking.[22] This desire is for the Church to be "a sign of the true kingdom," not just accepting of the way things are.[23] The Church is not simply to reflect Ulster culture, but to be a sign of the kingdom of God, and to show the spiritual reason for the Church. I want to suggest that a charismatic understanding may aid this role.

Definition of Terms

In dealing with the theological and practical identity of Churches, defining the terms being used is important. Practically, it may be difficult to distinguish between Pentecostals and Charismatics in terms of worship; however, some delineation is necessary to provide parameters for this study. I have followed the definition of Andrew Lord, who uses the term "pentecostal" to denote those Churches that trace their origin to the Pentecostal experience at the beginning of the twentieth century, and "charismatic" to denote the newer Churches that have developed since the Charismatic Renewal of the 1960s. This includes the "Third Wave," and the Vineyard, but practically these distinctions may become blurred.[24] This is more general definition

---

20. Keller, *Prodigal God*, 12.

21. Ryken, *City on a Hill*, 17–18.

22. Clowney, in reflecting upon Matt 16:13-19, calls Christ "the builder" of the Church. Clowney, *Church*, 40. The desire for Church growth is also seen in the light of an apparent decline in Presbyterian membership, but an overall increase in Pentecostal and Charismatic membership. Johnstone notes that those mainstream Churches which are charismatic are experiencing growth, like the new expressions of Church. Johnstone, *Church is Bigger Than You Think*, 112.

23. Tomlin, *Provocative Church*, 32.

24. Lord, *Spirit Shaped Mission*, 2. The term "Third Wave" comes from Wagner who defined a spectrum of belief, both within and without the traditional Churches, that emphasized the work of the Holy Spirit, but remaining broadly evangelical rather than charismatic. See Wagner, *Third Wave of the Holy Spirit*. Debate continues on how Pentecostalism can be defined. A. Anderson outlines four approaches: typological, social scientific, historical and theological. He notes the "bewildering" array of Pentecostalism. However, he argues that what really defines all of these groups, including oneness, prosperity, Assemblies of God, Church of God, Catholic Charismatics, Independent

than may be helpful because, as shall be seen, Wimber himself may not have been happy with the designation "charismatic." It does, however, allow for a degree of flexibility, specifically because the influence of Wimber went beyond the bounds of the Charismatic Renewal itself, as well as influencing many Charismatic and Pentecostal leaders and Churches.

Fyall notes that: "The words 'Charismatic' and 'Reformed' come loaded with so many associations and indeed misunderstandings, that to understand what is meant, can be difficult."[25] For the purposes of this work I will use the definitions Fyall gives as a working outline of what is meant by Charismatic and Reformed. He defines "Charismatic" as Church characterized by four things: body ministry, practicing the gifts of the Spirit, spontaneity in services and home groups.[26] I have chosen Fyall because he stands in the Reformed camp and offers a positive appreciation of charismatic spirituality.[27] Regarding Charismatic theology, he notes their biblical method—drawing theology from narrative New Testament texts, which does not consider either reason or tradition to have any formative role.[28] Fyall defines "Reformed" as characterized by four things: expository preaching, congregational responsiveness to the preaching, corporate prayer, "and a strong sense of the whole congregation as the fundamental unit."[29] It is important to understand that there is diversity within the Reformed Churches. Yet, underlying their theology is the conviction that the Bible gives "authoritative and final direction for the church concerning doctrine, discipline and worship."[30] Tradition, in the form of adherence to confessions of faith, also contributes to Reformed theology along with reason, but not experience.[31]

Churches, Word of Faith Church and even Third Wave Churches, is a "family resemblance" that emphasizes the work of the Holy Spirit and spiritual gifts. This is a broader taxonomy and may negate any delineation between the different streams. Anderson, "Varieties, Taxonomies and Definitions," 13–27.

25. Fyall, *Charismatic and Reformed*, 1.

26. Ibid.

27. There are other reformed commentators who, while applauding some charismatic leaders, believe that the whole movement is founded upon a fallacy. MacArthur believes that any who espouse a charismatic position ought to "reexamine what they believe," and for those who may respect the charismatic position to become aware that the differences between Reformed and Charismatic are not inconsequential. The implication of this statement is that there is nothing worth considering in the Charismatic position other than it errors. MacArthur, *Charismatic Chaos*, 355.

28. Buschart, *Exploring Protestant Traditions*, 242–45. Although this refers to Pentecostalism many of the same principles are seen in Charismatic reflection.

29. Fyall, *Charismatic and Reformed*, 1.

30. Buschart, *Exploring Protestant Traditions*, 98–99.

31. Ibid., 100–01.

There are elements within each that are used by the other, so they are not mutually exclusive. What is common to both systems of doctrine is a high view of biblical teaching that informs their theological reflection.

The aspects that I have chosen to consider are those highlighted in the writings of John Wimber; namely, the practice of evangelism, discipleship and ministry, and applying his suggestions to a Reformed context.[32] I propose to consider how two different streams, which seem the antithesis of each other, may complement each other in terms of missional activity.[33]

The Position of the Confessional Reformed Churches

In considering the views of PCI, it is impossible to produce one monolithic typology that defines everyone. As a study in Practical Theology, this book acknowledges such diversity of opinion and makes "its home in the complex web of relationships and experiences."[34] PCI appears to have remained a conservative denomination, theologically and practically, partly due to adherence to the Westminster Confession of Faith (WCF).[35] This theological tradition has shaped the identity of PCI as much as the culture of Northern Ireland.[36] At their ordination, all Presbyterian elders, ruling and teaching, must sign a document confirming that they agree with the doctrines put forward in the WCF. They are asked: "Do you accept the Westminster Confession of Faith . . . to be founded on and agreeable to the Word of God; as such do you acknowledge it as the confession of your faith?"[37] Unlike many Presbyterian denominations, most notably the Presbyterian Church of the USA (PCUSA), PCI has retained subscription to one confession.[38] Sean

---

32. It is worth noting that New Frontiers International has sought to combine a Reformed and Charismatic theological position. I have not chosen to use them as a focus in this book because of the prohibition of women in the eldership. Grooves, "Spiritual Authority in the Church," 11–12. This would be incompatible with the position of women in PCI where they are eligible for election to eldership on the same basis as men. *Code*, 31:1.

33. There have been other studies that demonstrate the complementary nature of two distinct streams for mutual benefit, specifically Evangelical and liberals. See Warner, *New Wine in Old Wineskins*.

34. Swinton and Mowat, *Practical Theology and Qualitative Research*, 3.

35. On the issue of Subscription to the Westminster Confession of Faith see: Hamilton, *Erosion of Calvinist Orthodoxy*; Hall, *Practice of Confessional Subscription*.

36. Anderson, "Culture and Identity," 78–79. The culture of PCI in the Irish Republic may manifest itself in a different manner because of the unique context it is in, but it is beyond the remit of this study.

37. *Code*, para. 5.IV, 101.

38. PCUSA accepts not only its revised form of the WCF but also The Heidelberg

Michael Lucas reminds us that Presbyterians are "confessional," meaning they adhere to the WCF.[39] This confessional understanding may be unique because it presents a system of theology against which all beliefs and practice are to be compared.

The question then arises over whether the WCF allows for any understanding of contemporary charismata. It states that the ways in which God had spoken to the Church previously are "now ceased."[40] This would seem to suggest that the WCF does not allow for any revelation, apart from that contained in the Bible. Charismata, therefore, would seem inconsistent with the WCF. Not everyone agrees with this assumption. O. Palmer Robertson suggests that, as the Church is always reforming, it "has come to a new and richer comprehension of the person and work of the Holy Spirit."[41] Robertson believes that the WCF is "deficient" on this matter, although this does not make him a Charismatic.[42] The reason that there is nothing specifically stated concerning spiritual gifts is one of context. The Westminster Divines were primarily interested in reforming Church government and the doctrine of salvation, not pneumatology. It cannot, therefore, with any degree of confidence be claimed, that the WCF would be against charismatic theology.

There has also been a distance from ecumenism denominationally, with the withdrawal of PCI from the World Council of Churches in 1980.[43] There have been some notable exceptions to this rule, such as Rev. David Armstrong of First Limavady and Magilligan congregations, whose ecumenism in the 1980s caused ripples in the local community and wider afield.[44] There has been the ecumenical partnership between Clonard Monastery (Fr. Gerry Reynolds) and Fitzroy Presbyterian Church (Very Rev. Dr. Ken Newell).[45] In the main, however, a pattern of wariness on issues such as ecumenism continues. The Campaign for Concerned Witness to

---

Catechism, The Belgic Confession, The Theological Declaration of Barmen and its own 1967 Confession of faith. See http://oga.pcusa.org/publications/boc.pdf.

39. Lucas, *On Being Presbyterian*, 4.

40. WCF 1:1.

41. Robertson, "Holy Spirit in the Westminster Confession," 58. Robertson would not, however, endorse charismatic theology.

42. Ibid., 94.

43. The General Assembly of 1980 voted 448 for withdrawal and 388 to remain in membership. Holmes, *Our Irish Presbyterian Heritage*, 174.

44. Armstrong and Saunders, *Road too Wide*.

45. Wells, *Courage to be Protestant*. "While Presbyterians rejoice in better relationships which are now experienced between Roman Catholics and Protestants in general . . . they do not see much evidence of the radical changes which would be necessary to make a significant reconciliation between our two Churches possible, but we must always remember that with God all things are possible." *Agreements and Disagreements*, 17.

the Reformed Faith (CCW) exercises a lobbying function within the church against ecumenical matters. There has been a desire to provide a methodology for evangelism within PCI by the Board of Mission in Ireland.[46] To provide a Reformed and Charismatic methodology for Irish Presbyterianism, drawing on resources beyond their own tradition, namely Wimber, is a hurdle which must be overcome, if a Reformed and Charismatic ministry model is to work, practically.

PCI dealt with the issue of Charismatic Renewal from 1983–85, through the Doctrine Committee of the General Assembly. First, concerning divine healing (1983), then the Ad Hoc Committee on Special Fellowships (1983–85). The Doctrine Committee report outlines the widespread practice of divine healing within Presbyterian congregations and emphasized the tension between God's will to heal and people remaining sick, while underlining their support for the medical profession.[47] Although this does not deal with the Charismatic Renewal specifically, it does indicate the widespread practice of divine healing in PCI, a practice that is one of the emphases of Wimber. The reports of the Ad Hoc Committee on Special Fellowships began as an investigation by the Presbytery of East Belfast into a Christian Fellowship that developed out of the Gilnahirk congregation and their practice of baptism and the Lord's Supper.[48] The committee evaluated what was happening in other para-church organizations and concluded, "there is much within the Renewal movement for which we are thankful to God." There was a desire to look at Presbyterian structure and assess its suitability to contain Renewal. The conclusion was that the domineering leadership and other practices, such as speaking in tongues and healing, appear "to be incompatible with Presbyterian practice per se."[49] This is significant because it is not suggesting the Renewal is incompatible with Presbyterian theology, as outlined in the WCF, but its practice may be an issue of concern.

The following year another report was received which expanded the consideration of special fellowships. The issue of music, to which younger members could relate, was raised. Theological consideration was given to the issue of subsequence in receiving the Spirit evidenced by speaking in tongues. The conclusion was that if it was a valid interpretation, then

---

46. Boyce, *Personal Evangelism for Presbyterians*, 6. This, he suggests, is because PCI is wary of anything coming in from the outside and effecting change.

47. Doctrine Committee Report 1983, 22–23.

48. Ad Hoc Committee on Special Fellowships Report 1983, 188. Special fellowships are the umbrella term given to the prayer groups which met other than on Sundays, when they attended their local congregation.

49. Ibid., 188–89.

most PCI congregations would be devoid of the Spirit.[50] This is significant because if the theology of initial evidence is factual, then the conclusion stands. While not commenting directly on Wimber's position, there does seem to be an argument of *reductio ad absurdum*. Wimber did not teach tongues as an evidence of receiving the Spirit. There may be confusion with the teaching of classical Pentecostalism. They do conclude that tongues may be a "problem for some but not all within the Presbyterian family."[51] This does not state that every Presbyterian would have problems with speaking in tongues. It could be inferred that there may be some who would not have any problems with the practice. It may also suggest that other spiritual gifts may also be accepted by Presbyterians.

A number of problems were raised: the nature of prophecy apart from the Bible, contemporary apostles and prophets, preoccupation with the sensational and specifically satanic issues, the health and wealth gospel, the subordination of women and the removal of baptismal discipline outside the remit of Kirk Sessions, which often led to re-baptism.[52] These issues remain for any who embrace Renewal yet choose to remain within PCI. Many of these issues cover a wide variety of the Renewal spectrum, and not all would be held by every Charismatic. The last report was received in 1985 and dealt with the issue of those who embrace Renewal remaining within Presbyterianism. It was stated that it is difficult to keep Renewal groups within the institutional church, but leaving for new fellowships was the "soft option."[53] Seeking to redress a drift into new expressions of Church is always high on the agenda of those ruling denominations. One of the arguments of this book is that staying may be a valid and important principle.

In Britain, the Church of Scotland has no position statement on Charismatic Renewal. There was a debate in 1997 surrounding the Toronto Blessing, but nothing was put forward as the Church's position.[54] Why the Church of Scotland has never addressed this issue is unclear, when there has been significant consideration given to rejuvenating the denomination.[55] It may be that the Charismatic Renewal has not had an impact on the Church

---

50. Ad Hoc Committee on Special Fellowships 1984, 241–42.

51. Ibid., 244.

52. Ibid., 244–45.

53. Ad Hoc Committee on Special Fellowships Report 1985, 211.

54. Email from G. Bell, Senior Media Relations Officer, Communications Department, The Church of Scotland, 121 George Street, Edinburgh, EH2 4YN, to G. Stewart on 11/10/2010. Gervais Angel believes that the Church of Scotland was one of the first "historic Protestant Churches in Britain" to embrace Charismatic Renewal. Angel, *Delusion of Dynamite*, 37.

55. See Reid, *Outside Verdict*.

of Scotland.[56] The United Reformed Church experienced some Charismatic impact, through Bob Gordon, and the establishment of the Group for Evangelism and Renewal (GEAR).[57]

Commenting on North America, John Dart outlines the history of the interaction between American Presbyterianism and the Charismatic Renewal. This came in 1963, through Louis Evans Jr. who was pastor of Bel Air Presbyterian Church in California, and gave birth to the 1966 "charismatic communion" in Oklahoma. In 1984 the Presbyterian Reformed Ministries International (PRMI) was founded by Zeb "Brad" Long. This was identified with the Third Wave of John Wimber and sought to give a Reformed theological rationale to the experience of Renewal.[58] Vinson Synan comments that the 1970 General Assembly of the United Presbyterian Church, which neither condemned nor supported the growing Charismatic Movement, but emphasized that glossolalia ought not to be seen as normative.[59]

The Orthodox Presbyterian Church (OPC), Timothy H. Gregson tells us, established the Machen Retreat and Conference Center in McDowell, VA, because Paul Cunningham perceived an apparent spiritual vacuum in his local area for a Reformed witness.[60] What is significant is the concession that some believers are going to Charismatic churches to hear Bible teaching. While this does not make any comment on the authenticity of Charismatic theology, it does offer a practical ecumenism where a respect is given to their spirituality.[61] James A. Zozzaro, writing for the OPC, argues that because of the widespread influence of "neo-pentecostalism," which he defines as "charismatic," the OPC has had to restate its opposition to any form of contemporary charismatic experience. In doing this, Zozzaro believes that some have become unbiblical in their emphasis, and so he seeks to draw out the two positions of the Holy Spirit as the gift, or the Holy Spirit as the giver of gifts. The first position means that, as all believers have

---

56. New Wine Scotland's Clan Gathering represents the charismatic stream in the Church of Scotland, with a number of their ministers serving on the leadership team. It may be that this stream represents such a small dimension in the Church of Scotland that national attention is not given to it. <http://www.clangathering.org.uk/team.php>.

57. Angel, *Delusion or Dynamite*, 40–41. *Charismatic Renewal in Britain*, 25.

58. Dart, "Charismatic and Mainline."

59. Synan, "Discerning the Charismatic Renewal." The United Presbyterian Church joined with the Presbyterian Church in the United States in 1983 to form the Presbyterian Church in the United States of America.

60. Gregson, "Renewal for the Called-out Ones."

61. Odgen, *New Reformation*, 23. "In contrast to organizational union, a sign of renewal in recent years has been an ecumenism of the Spirit that transcends denominational loyalties and has nothing to do with structures. Denominational distinctions become blurred when Christians connect with each other through the Spirit."

received the gift of the Spirit at conversion, they are, by definition, charismatic. The second position needs to be explained. The OPC does not see the sign of gifts, tongues, prophecy and healing, as the main thrust of the Spirit's work in believers. It believes that it is a mistake to identify the gifts exclusively in terms of what the New Testament outlines because this would define believers as charismatic or non-charismatic. Any gift used to build up the Church is, therefore, a charismatic gift.[62] This argument becomes one of semantics in which the OPC means one thing, by the term Charismatic, and "neo-pentecostals" mean another. Yet, the final argument is one that appears to state a biblical principle from a non- biblical foundation. The New Testament does mention certain gifts of the Spirit (1 Cor 12:8–10; Rom 12:6–8), yet he is not prepared to limit his argument to the validity of these gifts in the contemporary Church. In this sense, his argument appears to be self-defeating because the validity of the Charismatic claims to the biblical gifts of the Spirit has not been addressed. It may have been better to deal with the claims of the Charismatic rather than redefine the nature of spiritual gifts.

The Evangelical Presbyterian Church (EPC) states that they take their pneumatology from the WCF directly.[63] They do not take a uniformly cessationist position, believing that the gifts of the Spirit are given "as He sees fit," not as an evidence of a spiritual event.[64] The position statement addresses two specific questions of how the EPC views the gifts of the Spirit. They see them as being "biblically valid for today," but exercised under the authority of the Kirk Session. Whether the EPC is Charismatic is also answered. They state that they are not Pentecostal, but do not seem to like to be labeled Charismatic.[65] The reticence to be defined as specifically Charismatic may be motivated by a desire not to exclude those who share the same evangelical

---

62. Zozzaro, "Charismatic Presbyterians?"

63. This is a North American denomination not to be associated with the Evangelical Presbyterian Church in Ireland or the Evangelical Presbyterian Church in England and Wales.

64. The position of the Evangelical Presbyterian Church allows a continualist view on Spiritual Gifts: "The EPC affirms the gifts of God's Spirit as biblically valid for today, and counsels that they be exercised under the guidance of God's Word and the authority of the local Session." http://www.epc.org/about-the-epc/position-papers/the-holy-spirit/.

65. "If you mean we are Pentecostal, the answer is no. If you mean we are open to the gifts of the Holy Spirit, the answer is yes. We believe that the word 'charismatic' should not be limited to specific manifestations of the work of the Holy Spirit, such as speaking in tongues, but 'charismatic' does refer to the fact that every Christian receives a gift, or gifts, from the Holy Spirit (1 Cor 12:7, 11). http://www.epc.org/about-the-epc/position-papers/the-holy-spirit/.

beliefs but are cessationist in theology.[66] This could be seen as a wise position that does not allow charismatic issues to become an area of division; yet, allowing those who want to express their faith in a charismatic manner the freedom to do so, without any denominational interference.

The Presbyterian Church in America (PCA) formulated a position paper on the Holy Spirit at their General Assembly in 1975. This paper states that the denomination "rejoices in all evidences of new life in Christ's body," yet raises some concerns about developing an experience-centered theology. They reaffirm that Christians receive the Spirit at conversion. The ongoing experience of the Spirit, in assuring believers of their salvation, means there is to be an ongoing experience of being filled with the Spirit. Specific attention is given to the gifts of the Spirit—which must not be used as a divisive issue amongst Christians by either denoting those who may have received a "baptism" in the Spirit, or by directing believers—and to miracles which they understand in a general sense to describe the work of God in all areas of creation.[67] These positions, essentially, restate the classic Reformed position but do so in an unspecific manner, allowing members of the PCA to have a Charismatic emphasis without compromising their traditions. The focus, therefore, appears to move away from the issues of spiritual gifts and miracles to holiness and eternal security, but may benefit more from stating definitely whether they are to be pursued at all.

Reasons for Choosing John Wimber

At this stage it is important to explain why I have chosen to reflect upon Wimber and his theological views as the focus for this book. There are several places to look in the search for a model for the work of the Holy Spirit in the Presbyterian Church; however, I want to suggest that Wimber offers a unique perspective for a number of reasons.[68]

Wimber himself visited Ireland in 1985 and conducted a conference in University College Dublin. While this was almost thirty years ago, it

66. http://www.epc.org/about-the-epc/.

67. http://www.pcahistory.org/documents/pastoralletter.html.

68. I would note the traditional Pentecostal Churches - Assemblies of God, Elim Pentecostal Churches, the Apostolic Churches, Church of God (both in the UK, Ireland and USA). There are also alternative streams within Pentecostalism such as the Hillsong Leadership Network, https://hillsongnetwork.com/; C3 Church Network, http://www2.myc3church.net/. Within the Charismatic Renewal there are Pioneer, http://www.pioneer.org.uk/; Salt and Light International, http://www.saltlight.org/international/; The Groundlevel Network, http://www.groundlevel.org.uk/ website/; Abundant Life Church Network, http:// www.alm.org.uk/church/network/.

places him within the living memory of those involved in the Church in contemporary Ireland. This event marked the beginning of the first Vineyard Church in Ireland.[69] This connection with the island, along with the relatively short time in which Vineyard has been functioning on the island, may mean that people still understand him primarily as a writer rather than a denominational founder.[70] There are also a relatively few number of Vineyards in Ireland in comparison to Reformed Churches.[71] This may mean that Reformed Churches understand Wimber as someone with a theological point to make, and not as someone who instituted a new ecclesiastical system that draws members away from their own. He may, therefore, be viewed as offering principles to apply to existing denominations.

It may be asked why I have not chosen to reflect upon Pentecostal teaching and its implications for Reformed doctrine and practice? There may be an argument that Pentecostalism does not fall into the definition of "conventional Protestantism."[72] Pentecostalism may represent a fourth stream of the Christian Church: Roman Catholic, Orthodox, Protestant and Pentecostal.[73] It may also be worth noting that the Charismatic stream could also be viewed as distinct from Pentecostalism.[74] While Pentecostal teaching began the consideration of spiritual gifts, miracles, signs and wonders, Cartledge believes that Wimber's teaching "superseded" the importance of earlier Pentecostal teaching' regarding its wider ecclesiastical impact.[75] Warrington also suggests that Wimber's theology influenced Pentecostalism as much as Evangelicalism.[76] For this reason, I have chosen to consider

---

69. http://www.dublinvineyard.ie/about-us/our-story.

70. http://www.causewaycoastvineyard.com/main/who-we-are.

71. http://www.vineyardchurches.org.uk/churches/areas/ireland.html. Mentioned are: Belfast City Vineyard; Causeway Coast Vineyard, Portstewart; The Lakes Vineyard; Dublin Vineyard; Upper Bann Vineyard; Vineyard Church Dungannon; Carrickfergus Vineyard; and, Liffey Valley Vineyard.

72. Hollenweger, *Pentecostals*, 507.

73. Cox believes that Pentecostalism has not made up its mind on where it stands ecumenically at the moment regarding its position amongst the other traditions. Cox, *Fire from Heaven*, 311.

74. Spittler notes: "Somewhere in the early '70s it became clear that the classical Pentecostal churches and the Charismatic Movement are two different forces. Even though the new Charismatics drew from the traditional classical Pentecostals, for the most part they did not join them. For the classical Pentecostal, whose heritage was that of a persecuted minority, the early puzzlement soon passed to a certain aloofness. The classical Pentecostals became an establishment in their own right within seventy years." Spittler, "Preface," 8.

75. Cartledge, *Encountering the Spirit*, 24.

76. Warrington, *Teaching and Praxis Concerning Supernatural Healing*, 18–19.

Wimber and not Pentecostalism. The implications of applying Pentecostal doctrine and practice to a Reformed context may be seen as akin to asking a Reformed congregation to join the Roman Catholic or Orthodox tradition.[77] It may mean completely changing its doctrinal and historical position; whereas, applying the principles outlined by Wimber may enable a denominational congregation to maintain its traditional position, but move in the gifts of the Spirit. I want to suggest that any doctrinal approach that has become associated with a denominational emphasis becomes less useful and less likely to be adopted by other denominations and streams.

Another group that might be considered here is New Frontiers International. This grouping, led by Terry Virgo, defines itself specifically as Reformed and Charismatic.[78] It might thus appear that New Frontiers is exactly where this book is arguing that the Presbyterians Churches ought to be heading. Yet, there is one issue that may make Presbyterians in Ireland specifically reject suggestions leading toward New Frontiers International; namely, their stance on women in leadership. Their statement reads: "Elders are men." It is further laid out that there is no biblical warrant for women in the eldership and such a practice would "seem incompatible" with the texts.[79] This was one of the issues of concern raised by PCI about the Renewal movement.[80] It also clearly contradicts the law of the PCI.[81] This may cause an issue of rejection from some Presbyterians who accept the egalitarian position, before the issues of the Holy Spirit are even raised. Wimber's view on this matter appears to be more in line with that of Irish Presbyterianism. Carol Wimber[82] notes that because of their evangelical Quaker background, Wimber held a view that there was only one ministry to which everyone was ordained, the ministry of Jesus. This included both genders.[83] There has

---

77. There have been instances of individuals and congregations making such a radical change: Presbyterian to Roman Catholic—Hahn, *Rome Sweet Rome*; Non-Denominational Charismatic to Eastern Orthodox—Gillquist, *Becoming Orthodox*; a compendium of various testimonies—Gillquist, *Coming Home*.

78. Virgo, *No Well-Worn Paths*, 62; Virgo, *Spirit Filled Church*, 11.

79. http://newfrontierstogether.org/Groups/101198/Newfrontiers/Resources/ Articles_and_Papers/Theological_Papers/Spiritual_Authority_in_the/ Spiritual_Authority_in_the.aspx, page 6. The texts mentioned are 1 Tim 3 and Titus 1.

80. Ad Hoc Committee on Special Fellowships 1984, 244–45.

81. *Code*, para. 31 (1), 15: "Women shall be eligible for election on the same conditions as men." The Presbyterian Church in America maintains the position that women cannot be ordained to eldership or ministry and broke ties with the Christian Reformed Church because they agreed to sanction this. http://www.pcanet.org/general/release3.htm.

82. Carol Wimber is the widow of John Wimber.

83. Wimber, "Introduction" in *Everyone Gets to Play*, 149.

been some debate around Wimber's views on women, some claiming he believed in male eldership. Rich Nathan writes: "But when John saw that gifts of teaching and what he called "elding" were pored out upon women, he got out of the way of the Holy Spirit."[84] Wherever a Presbyterian may stand on this issue, it could become something that clouds the wider principle of the presence and power of the Holy Spirit being available for today. If the debate is to focus on pneumatology then the ordination issue may subvert that focus.

Historically, it may also have been possible to reflect upon the views of Edward Irving, who was a Presbyterian minister. Irving was the minister of the National Kirk, Regent Square, London from 1822.[85] Thomas A. Smail, in commenting on the Church of Scotland's 1974 Panel on Doctrine Report on the Charismatic Renewal, notes that Irving presents the experience of the Holy Spirit in a Reformed-Calvinist way, rather than in a Methodist-Holiness way. He affirms, however, that any experience of the Holy Spirit may affirm subsequence of reception. His conclusion is to keep the experience, but reject the theology.[86] While this may be a pragmatic option, it does not deal with whether Reformed and Charismatic theologies are complementary or not. Gordon Strachan states that Irving's views were very close, if not identical, to what the Assemblies of God, Elim Pentecostal Churches and other independent Pentecostal Churches teach. He further believes that the similarity is such that it could be assumed to be a direct connection, labeling Irving "the first Reformed-Pentecostal theologian."[87] This connection with Pentecostal beliefs meant that Irving may have been too great a leap for Presbyterians to embrace as a voice to challenge their views on the Holy Spirit, as it was noted before that Pentecostalism may represent a distinct stream of the Christian Church. To implement the views of someone whose beliefs are so closely associated with Pentecostalism may preclude acceptance. Graham McFarlane notes that there is also a theological issue. It appears Irving's views sprang from his understanding of the incarnation rather than experiencing the gifts of the Holy Spirit. In this sense his theology sought experience rather than his experience seeking theology.[88] This

---

84. Nathan, "Women in Leadership." Nathan writes: "He adopted what, in my mind, was a somewhat inconsistent view. He felt that the Holy Spirit could do whatever he wanted to do, even if it meant going beyond his view of the bounds of scripture. But he endeavored, within his empowered evangelical framework to submit to the Holy Spirit's activity."

85. Allen, *Unfailing Stream*, 82–83.

86. Smail, *Reflected Glory*, 39.

87. Strachan, *Pentecostal Theology*, 19–21.

88. McFarlane, *Edward Irving*, 10–11.

book does not begin from a position of Christological reflection but ecclesiological, and seeks to consider how the Church may experience the Holy Spirit's power in evangelism, discipleship and ministry. It is a discussion of the praxis of the Church. While Irving's theology may lend itself to this, it is not the result of direct reflection upon it. There is also the practical issue that Irving was expelled from the Church of Scotland because of what were deemed to be heretical views.[89] In chapter 3, I have outlined the research questions, one of which is remaining true to my own denominational, theological and historic views while implementing a charismatic praxis. Adopting a method that considers the theology of one who was expelled from the "mother" church for heresy may contradict ordination vows.[90] Smail's comment on setting aside the theology, but holding on to the practice, equally does not answer the theological questions that I hope this book reflects upon. For these reasons I chose not to consider the views of Irving to reflect upon as a source of possible application to a Reformed context.

There are two Reformed authors who seem to have suggested a positive appreciation for the charismatic: D. Martyn Lloyd-Jones and R. T. Kendall, who were previous ministers of Westminster Chapel, London.[91] Lloyd-Jones argued for an experience of the Holy Spirit after conversion.[92] The motivation for seeking this experience was a desire for the great blessing that characterized the early church.[93] One of the reasons why I chose not to use Lloyd-Jones, as a possible companion in the conversation, was his association with separatism. When he retired, Westminster Chapel approached Eric Alexander to fill the pulpit.[94] He declined the offer because, as a Church of Scotland minister, he did not share Lloyd-Jones' separatist

---

89. The first trial was before the London Presbytery on April 26, 1832, resulting in excommunication and being loosed from his charge because of heresy. The second trial was before his ordaining Presbytery of Annan on March 13, 1833, also resulting in expulsion. Dallimore, *Life of Edward Irving*, 145–48.

90. *Code*, para. 205 (4), 65. "Do you believe the Presbyterian form of Church government to be founded on and agreeable to the Word of God; and do you promise to adhere to and to support it, and to yield submission in the Lord to the courts of this Church?"

91. Lloyd-Jones served from 1938–68 and R. T. Kendall from 1977–2002. http://www.westminsterchapel.org.uk/aboutus/history.php.

92. Lloyd-Jones, *Joy Unspeakable*, 53. He writes: "There may be an interval between the two, sometimes short, at other times longer."

93. Ibid., 356.

94. Alexander was the Minster of St. George's Tron Parish Church, Glasgow from 1977–97. http://www.ericalexander.co.uk/biography.php. There may be some merit is seeing Lloyd-Jones' ecclesiology as having been influenced by the unique Calvinistic Methodist of Wales, that was semi-Presbyterian in polity. Ross, «Aspects of Dr. Martyn Lloyd-Jones' Legacy."

leanings.⁹⁵ The issue of Church Polity is significant to Presbyterians. In the service for ordination, installation or induction, the candidate declares their acceptance of the Presbyterian form of Church government, which was noted when discussing Irving. There have been instances of Congregational Churches being formed by seceding Presbyterians. In 1927, the ecumenical talks about forming a united Protestant Church in Northern Ireland failed because of the insistence that it must adopt Congregational polity.⁹⁶ While Lloyd-Jones may be held in a high regard amongst Presbyterians, the local issues of relations with Congregationalism may make it difficult to apply his principles. Another issue is his focus on writing about the Holy Spirit, which we have noted, was to experience a spiritual blessing. John Piper notes that his main focus was experiencing God and biblical doctrine. Yet, he notes that Lloyd-Jones opposed the claiming of spiritual gifts.⁹⁷ Lloyd-Jones was focusing on proving the theological experience of the individual believer, and while Wimber does the same, as we shall note in chapter 5, he also deals with wider issues regarding the experience of the Holy Spirit. The last issue is a practical one. Lloyd-Jones' books are manuscripts of his sermons, so they do not contain references or citations. It may be somewhat unfair to take a sermon and attempt to give academic evaluation, when that was not the purpose for which it was published.

The same criteria can be applied to some of Kendall's writings as their genesis was as sermon material. He is also associated with the believer's baptism position, devoting a chapter in his theology to proving the immersionist view.⁹⁸ This position would be contrary to that of the Westminster Confession.⁹⁹ This alone may not entirely dissuade Irish Presbyterians away from Kendall; however, it may be an issue. The bigger issue may be over his book *Once Saved, Always Saved*.¹⁰⁰ This book caused a stir amongst Conservative Evangelicals, and we have noted that Irish Presbyterianism has maintained that conservative nature. Iain Murray believes that this book suggests antinomianism.¹⁰¹ This theme was further taken up by Richard Alderson, an ex-member of Westminster Chapel.¹⁰² Murray suggests that it was Kendall's

---

95. Atherstone, et al. "Lloyd-Jones and the Charismatic Controversy," 116.
96. Coles, *I Will Build My Church*, 20, 25.
97. Piper, "Passion for Christ-Exalting Power"; Lloyd-Jones, *Joy Unspeakable*, 259.
98. Kendall, *Understanding Theology, Vol. II*, 296–306.
99. WCF 28:3–4.
100. Kendall, *Once Saved, Always Saved*.
101. I. H. Murray, "Will the Unholy be Saved?"
102. Alderson, *No Holiness, No Heaven*.

openness to the Spirit that damaged Westminster Chapel.[103] None of this claims that Wimber would be any less controversial for Reformed Christians than Kendall might be. It is that the main issue of his argument may be lost because of a preoccupation with a perceived doctrinal issue, much like Irving may be preoccupied because of heresy.

It may also not be true to the principles, outlined by Wimber, to connect him with a new ecclesiastical or denominational stream. He seemed to seek for the "radical middle," the road between Evangelicalism and Pentecostalism.[104] David Pawson notes that Wimber's pragmatic aim, to bring Evangelicals and Charismatics together in evangelism, was because of their mutual dependence upon each other.[105] This pragmatism dovetails with the pragmatic function of practical theology, but does not negate Wimber's place as a theologian.[106] Wimber's theology does not seek to reconcile different positions on pneumatology, but offers a theological praxis of action. This may be because of his own background as a practical theologian of church growth. The differences between evangelical and charismatic appear to be immense because of the conviction on both sides. Wimber focuses on what the Church is doing in practice, bypassing these issues.[107] Pawson notes: "What all this boils down to is an assurance that Evangelicals can embrace charismatic gifts without any theological adjustment."[108] The choice of Wimber, therefore, is a practical choice because it means that there may be no need to reassess or reinterpret Reformed doctrinal standards in order to implement his suggestions. His suggestions may work from any systematic or historical basis, and is truly ecumenical, without demanding a change of ecclesiastical distinctives.

Wimber may offer a system of theology and practice from a unique source. Van der Kooi suggests that the Reformed Churches have been influenced by the Charismatic Renewal and continue to be taught by it. This, he suggests, happens specifically through Wimber and the movements that

103. Murray, "Openness to the Holy Spirit," 25–32.

104. Jackson, *Quest for the Radical Middle*.

105. Pawson, *Word and Spirit Together*, 94

106. Wimber's focus was a practical one: how to see the Church grow. However, he may meet the criteria of being called a theologian, according to Dunn, who defines theologians as those who «. . . have seen it as part of their calling to articulate their faith in writing and to instruct others in their common faith, and who have devoted a considerable portion of their lives to so doing." Dunn, *Theology of the Apostle Paul*, 2.

107. One of the challenges to Evangelicals, which Wimber himself argues, is the need to codify what they believe about the Holy Spirit in a positive manner rather than polemical statements against Charismatic theology and practice. Wimber, *Kingdom of God*, 21

108. Pawson, *Word and Spirit Together*, 95.

began under his theological influence.[109] This is not saying that the influences are positive, only that they exist and have an impact on the Reformed Churches.[110] Packer draws some connections between the theology of Wimber and other Reformed thinkers; namely, Martyn Lloyd-Jones and Francis Shaeffer. Their critical challenge, when considering their Evangelical and Reformed traditions, gives a springboard for Wimber to rethink the heritage itself.[111] This may suggest that connecting Wimber with a reformed context may not be impossible. It may also suggest that there already exists a theological connection between the two streams; so, the suggestions of this book extrapolate the implications of those connections.

Wimber himself sees his theology as being "distinctly evangelical" because it closely connects the gifts of the Spirit to evangelism.[112] In this sense it may not be something that requires a theological, historical or denominational change. It may be suggested that Wimber comes from a historical position; and, while he did not remain in the historic churches, they formed his theological views. To prove this point the three contextual applications seek to discover whether his views are compatible with Reformed views. This underlines the assertion that Wimber represents a distinct strand, which is neither Pentecostal/Charismatic nor cessationist Evangelical, but somewhere in between. Taking this on board, part of the focus of this book will be to draw out some of the Evangelical elements within Wimber's theology for a contextual application in a Reformed setting. This position assumes that the Reformed Churches are Evangelical. While many would hold to this position, it is not uniformly an accurate description of every Reformed communion.

Wimber writes that there is a need to marry the balance of Evangelical theology with the "firepower" of Pentecostalism "to hit the biblical target of

109. van der Kooi, "Wonders of God," 3

110. The doctrine of *semper reformanda* may also apply to this discussion. The first mention of this was in 1674 when the Dutch Reformed Jodocus van Lodenstein launched a second Dutch reformation to see the Reformed doctrines more thoroughly applied and understood within the Church. Michael Horton notes that the verb is passive; that the Church is always being reformed by God. See Horton, "Semper Reformanda." Nicole sees this happening in the context of dry spirituality and God breathing new life into the church. See Nicole, "Ecclesiology," 160–61

111. Packer, "Intellectual," 259. Lewis suggests that one of Wimber's problems was his «radical Arminianism," which may separate him from a Reformed tradition. Lewis, " Historians Assessment," 58. Yet Wimber refers to the Christian life as climbing a mountain, and because the climber is connected to the one below, they will not fall far from the mountain and will remain connected. He identifies the climber below as Jesus. This may suggest a position of eternal security. Wimber and Springer, *Dynamics of Spiritual Growth*, 5.

112. Wimber, *Kingdom of God*, 27.

making and nurturing disciples."[113] This unification of the passion of Pentecostalism, without demanding that ecclesiastical background is forsaken, may offer a practical subtext. It may be able to complement any traditional standards of belief and practice. John Vooys agrees that the contribution of Wimber is practical as his theological reflection stands within the Evangelical tradition. It is, therefore, how that theology is outworked that is unique.[114] The emphasis that Wimber is a practical theologian, and that his discussion concerning the outworking of signs and wonders comes from the Evangelical tradition, may make him more accessible to the Reformed tradition.[115] The practical issues of how this may take place will be further considered through evangelism, discipleship, and ministry.

Wimber also helps us to focus on the foundation of Christian ministry, which is people. The focus becomes that of how people can experience God at the point of their greatest need. According to Bill Hull, this is seen in compromise and change, as sensitivity to people's needs is demonstrated. It challenges what is assumed and imposed without focusing on demonstrating care for others. Without such sensitivity, people may think that programs are more important than they are, because they are dispensable.[116] This flexibility allows a compassion for those in need and for the needs that arise around us in a pastoral context, along with a commitment to act where possible. This may demonstrate itself in offering to pray for the sick, and having God's power manifest through our witness demonstrating compassion. Wimber offers a methodology that seeks to root doctrine in practice by applying it to people's needs. While there may be other methods that seek to do the same, for the reasons stated above I want to suggest that Wimber's best fits the Reformed context. This reason roots Wimber in the local Church, the purpose of the reflection in this work.

---

113. Wimber, *Way In is the Way On*, 188.

114. Vooys, "Church Renewal for the 1980s?" 66. How Wimber uniquely works this theology out becomes the main focus for this research.

115. While not every Reformed congregation or denomination may choose to define itself as evangelical (The Non-Subscribing Presbyterian Church of Ireland, http://www.nspresbyterian.org/, subscription to the WCF may imply a certain theological position on certain things. See Ward, "Subscription to the Confession," 77–138. The issue appears to be one of perspective, as Fosdick points out. Some believe Christianity is about the "original mental frameworks," while others emphasize "abiding experiences." Fosdick, *Modern Use of the Bible*, 102.

116. Hull, *New Century Disciplemaking*, 26.

The Need for a Reformed/Charismatic Ministry Model

The two streams, of Reformed and Charismatic, appear distinct yet they have the possibility to complement each other, in theology and practice. As James K. A. Smith writes, there is quite some distance between Geneva and Azusa Street.[117] This may be a challenge to some within the Reformed tradition. However, the aims of the Deep Church Movement, through which Jim Belcher believes much can be learned from those outside our natural theological position, may have an influence.[118] This book argues for the same respect to be given to Wimber as that which is given to other influential theologies. Carnegie Samuel Calian notes that, in America, the PCUSA is suffering from the same issues with which many denominations have had to deal and has entered "survival mode" due to the loss in numbers and the erosion of confessional orthodoxy. This has led to less denominational loyalty.[119] One of the aims of practical theology is to develop healthy relationships to aid self- differentiation.[120] A solution may be, as Carnegie Samuel Calian suggests, a new openness whereby the Church becomes a "laboratory of learning within a context of common values and beliefs."[121] I suggest this openness could include Charismatic theology and experience.

Having adopted a constructivist method, and being influenced by social reconstruction, I aim to challenge the manner in which contemporary concerns shape the way the past is interpreted and are solved through reconstructing the past.[122] Wimber and the Reformed streams are different. However, I want to move the argument, not to their areas of divergence, but to those of convergence.[123] What a Reformed/Charismatic model has to offer is a fully integrated ethos of evangelism that feeds into discipleship and releases into ministry. R. Nathan and K. Wilson believe that people are looking for this. They seek solid expository preaching that neither promises victory nor delivers condemnation, but produces stability rather than

---

117. Smith, "Teaching a Calvinist to Dance."

118. Belcher, *Deep Church*, 66-67. Walker sees the Charismatic Renewal of the 1960s and 1970s as capturing "some of the character of deep church" in a prophetic way. This also roots this study within the developing field of deep church. Walker, "Recovering Deep Church," 1.

119. Calian, "Building a Visionary Church," 485.

120. Stevenson-Moessner, *Prelude to Practical Theology*, 4.

121. Calian, "Building a Visionary Church," 490.

122. Browning, *Fundamental Practical Theology*, 35.

123. Some movement has been made toward an ecumenical relationship between Pentecostals and the Reformed Churches through the dialog sponsored by the World Alliance of Reformed Churches. "Word and Spirit, Church and World."

emotionalism. This releases people who are passionate about evangelism and "fueled by the power of the Spirit."[124] This is a theme taken up by Ian Stackhouse, who believes that it is a "marriage" of Word and Spirit from the basis of a strong conviction in the authority and supremacy of the Bible, and works from a disciplined community.[125] This is a movement beyond a critique of the theology of either the Charismatic or Reformed Churches and into a practical ecumenism that draws on the strengths of both to produce a positive ministry model for the twenty-first-century Church.

Traditionally, the Reformed faith has been cessationist, seen particularly in the contribution of B. B. Warfield, Professor of Theology at Princeton Seminary (1886–1921), and his book *Counterfeit Miracles* (1918).[126] The teaching of this book has influenced the thinking of Reformed believers. There has been a degree of suspicion between the Reformed and Charismatic views, as Sam Storms notes. Charismatics and Reformed believers are often unwilling to worship together because Reformed Christians are uncomfortable with the apparent emotion, shallow theology and anthropocentrism of Charismatic worship. Charismatics often accuse Reformed Christians of quenching the Holy Spirit and theological arrogance.[127] Banister comments: "There is more than ignorance dividing Charismatics and Evangelicals. There is hostility."[128] This hostility was also raised by the Report of the International Dialog between the World Alliance of Reformed Churches (WARC) and some Classical Pentecostal Churches (1996–2000).[129] This attitude may be something that Wimber himself considered. He writes that different theological positions are not expressed with humility that leads to dialog; instead, there is a "harsh spirit" of judgment when both positions belong to each other.[130] This practical ecumenism is one of the unique elements of Wimber's theology, which enables a wider spectrum of application than others may receive. Yet, there does exist a tradition that seeks to integrate a Charismatic perspective in the context of Reformed theology. Lord George MacLeod of the Church of Scotland was a speaker at the early Fountain Trust International Conferences.[131] In the United Kingdom, there

---

124. Nathan and Wilson, *Empowered Evangelicals*, 33.
125. Stackhouse, *Gospel Driven Church*, 30.
126. Warfield, *Counterfeit Miracles*.
127. Storms, *Convergence*, 147.
128. Banister, *Word and Power Church*, 20.
129. "Word and Spirit, Church and World."
130. Wimber, *Beyond Intolerance*, 15.
131. Au, "Grassroots Unity."

is Dr. R. T. Kendall[132][133] and Terry Virgo and New Frontiers International, as previously noted.[134] Fyall also notes that Martyn Lloyd-Jones[135] and James Packer have both spoken positively, although not uncritically, about Charismatic insights.[136] In the United States of America Covenant Ministries International and C. J. Mahaney, as well as Sam Storms and J. Rodman Williams, sought to give an academic rationale for Reformed Charismaticism.[137] Amongst conservative Presbyterians, Steve Brown of the Reformed

---

132. Kendall accepts both the Evangelical and Charismatic positions: "Now with some people it has been one or the other. There are those who are well acquainted with the Scriptures. They know their Bibles. They know their doctrine. They even know their church history. They can detect heresy a mile away. And there are those who are well acquainted with the raw power of God. They have experienced the infilling of the Holy Spirit. They have experienced his gifts. They have seen healing, even miracles. And they can detect dead orthodoxy a mile away. Now what is wrong with either emphasis? Nothing at all. Each is exactly right." Cain and Kendall, *Word and the Spirit*, 23.

133. There may be remit to state that Kendall's illustrious predecessor at Westminster Chapel, Lloyd-Jones would be open to charismatic phenomena: "We disagree with those who say that these things were confined to the apostolic period; we disagree equally with those who say that all these things should always be manifest in the church. We say that it is a matter for the sovereignty of the Spirit, and clearly throughout the centuries in revival in various times in the church the Spirit has manifested this sovereignty. He has given power of utterance, power of speech, power of preaching oftentimes without some of these particular gifts. However, it is vital that we should consider these things because at any time, at any moment, the Spirit in his sovereignty may decide to give these gifts again." Lloyd-Jones, *Joy Unspeakable*, 248.

134. Buckeridge comments: «The mix of charismatic and reformed Calvinistic theology is perhaps what many find the most surprising and has led in recent years to them developing partnerships and sharing platforms with some reformed groups that would normally run a mile from anything that looked Pentecostal or charismatic." Virgo, "We've Not Seen Revival," Interview with John Buckeridge, *Christianity*, 17. Virgo writes: "I have occasionally been asked to fill in a questionnaire in which I am required to state whether I am a Charismatic or Reformed evangelical Christian. I don't want to confuse people but, like the apostle Paul, I am to be both! I believe in an awesome, sovereign God and see no reason to suppose that spiritual gifts as described in the New Testament have been withdrawn from the church." Virgo, *Spirit Filled Church*, 11. Virgo calls himself a charismatic Calvinist. Virgo, *No Well-Worn Paths*, 62.

135. Some may claim that Kendall stands in the Reformed/Charismatic stream begun by Lloyd-Jones. Sargent recounts the story of a meeting between Lloyd-Jones and Principle George Jeffreys, founder of the Elim Pentecostal Church, on a Sunday evening in the 1960s. Lloyd-Jones had been preaching on Acts 2 and Jeffreys turned to his colleague, while in the vestry, to claim that Lloyd-Jones was a Pentecostal. Lloyd-Jones told Jeffreys that he did not teach the initial evidence of Baptism in the Holy Spirit as speaking in tongues, to which Jeffreys replied that neither did he. This may suggest an early connection between Reformed theology and Charismatic Experience. Sargent, *Sacred Anointing*, 29.

136. Fyall, *Charismatic and Reformed*, 1.

137 Williams, *Renewal Theology*.

Theological Seminary, Orlando, has commented that he sees "very little biblical warrant for the cessationist view."[138] William W. Menzies believes that the Reformed influence is also seen in the Pentecostal Movement more evidently than the Wesleyan.[139] Even within the "emerging church," there is a Reformed/Charismatic dimension seen in Mark Driscoll.[140] There have been instances in America and Britain of Pentecostal/Charismatic churches becoming Reformed.[141] In this book, I want to suggest that the Church is best served through adopting a Reformed/ Charismatic methodology, affecting every aspect of the Church's worship, work and witness. To take on board some of Wimber's suggestions will require resolve and determination. Howard A. Synder comments that it is "too important to be abandoned because of controversy over a word: *Charismatic* is a good and highly biblical word."[142] When no other term has the widespread understanding that Charismatic does, then it is a term that is necessary in order to define what is meant.

---

138. Brown, *Follow the Wind*, 173.

139. Menzies believes that the Wesleyan roots of Pentecostalism were prevalent until 1910. Then, in the 1920s, the Reformed influence became significant, specifically, the Fundamentalist-Modernist debate led by J. Gresham Machen, to content for the orthodoxy of Christian doctrine, especially the person and work of Jesus. There is also similarity in the rejection of the doctrine of "entire sanctification," and the influence of John Calvin who, while not continualist in his understanding of spiritual gifts, allowed them for extraordinary circumstances. The influence of Jonathan Edwards and the revivals that happened under his ministry profoundly influenced Pentecostalism. The ministry of Edward Irving (1792-1834) at the Caledonian Chapel, Regent Square, London where spiritual gifts were being exercized a century before Azusa and Sunderland is another possible influence. In the twentieth century the writings of the Dutch Reformed author Abraham Kuyper show that he believed that spiritual gifts were necessary for the health of the Church. W. W. Menzies, " Reformed Roots of Pentecostalism," 80–93.

140. Driscoll, *Confessions of a Reformission Rev.*, 25. Driscoll admits to being Reformed in theology but also having influence in the Emerging Church Movement and in Charismatic circles.

141. Victory First Presbyterian Church, Atlantic City, NJ affiliated with PCUSA Presbytery of West Jersey, and The Word Centered Fellowship of Masury, OH affiliated with PCUSA Presbytery of Shenango. Also Lakeview Community Church, Tarpon Springs, Florida, pastored by Dr. Peyton Johnson, a Presbyterian minister. "Pentecostal Presbyterian Churches? This is NOT your father's Oldsmobile" http://what-i-see.blogspot.com/ 2005/07/pentecostal-presbyterian-churches-this.html. In Cheshire, The Emmaus Fellowship united with Wycliff United Reformed Church, Warrington. Angel, *Delusion of Dynamite*, 40–41. James Brown, Upper Octoroa Presbyterian Church, PA was encouraged by David DuPlessis to remain in the Presbyterian denomination, and to seek to bring renewal to it, after having received the Baptism in the Holy Spirit in the 1950s. Robert C. Whittaker also stayed with Presbyterianism, after having received the Baptism in the Holy Spirit in 1962. Hilborn, *Charismatic Renewal in Britain*, 23.

142. Snyder, *Community of the King*, 66.

Reformed theology connects the gospel with a physical means of demonstrating the gospel, specifically in communion.[143] This may form an understanding of signs and wonders also as illustrations of the gospel. Larry Daniel Siekawitch gives an outline of John Calvin's understanding of the work of the Spirit in the sacraments and concludes that, while Calvin could not be defined as a Charismatic, his doctrine of the Lord's Supper should be understood as a means for further encounter with the Holy Spirit.[144] I do not try to draw connections directly between the Reformed understanding of the sacraments and Wimber's theology of signs and wonders. I merely suggest that the possibility of a Reformed Church that accepts Wimber's theology could be supported by the Reformed doctrine of the sacraments. Ruthven also agrees, saying that the charismata "express and concretize the Gospel."[145] While he does not tease out the implications of this, it is significant that the same criteria given to the sacraments are applied to signs and wonders. Keith A. Mathison writes that Calvin understood sacraments as being a visible expression of the gospel, and as the Bible is preached the relevance of that expression becomes more evident.[146] Essentially, this says that what is preached about the cross is visibly displayed in the elements of the Lord's Supper. Having seen this connection, it may be possible to understand signs and wonders as confirming and illustrating the gospel. Gary S. Grieg comments: "Signs and wonders do not cheapen the gospel. They illustrate it."[147] This seems to be the same point that Mathison is making about Reformed theology. This assumption, that something clarifies, explains and demonstrates the gospel, is not an idea unfamiliar to confessional Reformed theology. To draw a line between the preaching of the gospel and the manifestations of signs and wonders, is something that appears to be comprehensible and can be understood in the Reformed context.

Brian D. McClaren writes: "Whether a church is charismatic or non-charismatic, there are certain signs and wonders that it naturally has in view and that its programs are designed to promote."[148] The Church looks for signs that demonstrate that what is being done works. While congregational attendance, increase in financial contributions, or even new building programs may be judged as success, what a Reformed/Charismatic model

---

143. WCF 27:1.

144. Siekawitch, "Calvin, Spirit, Communion and the Supper," 35.

145. Ruthven, "On the Cessation of the Charismata."

146. Mathison, *Given For You*, 270.

147. Grieg, " Purpose of Signs and Wonders," in Gregg and Springer, *Kingdom and the Power*, 160.

148. McLaren, *Church on the Other Side*, 50.

offers are signs and wonders. These point beyond the success of individual congregations and ministries to the success of the kingdom of God, which includes all believers and all congregations from all denominations—something truly ecumenical!

Grudem argues that Reformed Christians and Charismatics need each other: the former because of their understanding of doctrine and practice of doctrinal preaching, the latter because of their warmth, vitality and practice of spiritual gifts.[149] This suggests that the two streams are complementary and that where one is deficient, the emphasis of the other can make up for that deficiency. Stackhouse suggests that the lack of Reformed theology within the Charismatic Movement led to extremes of the 1990s, the Toronto Blessing in particular, as churches look for the next "key to unlock the harvest."[150] The Charismatic stream will benefit from the Reformed. The Reformed stream will also benefit from the Charismatic, with their common emphasis on the sovereignty of God. Smith states that Charismatic worship takes this foundational principle of Reformed theology very seriously, in which "you might actually be surprised by God occasionally."[151] If this is applied to Reformed spirituality, then the potential outcome will be immense. It is very easy to become entrenched in our own theologies, judging all who disagree with us and seeking to gain proselytes to our position. It will be a challenge to emphasize the sovereignty of God in the works of Wimber because some see it as a missing element in his theology.[152] The issue over the work of the Holy Spirit, however, can and must complement the views of the Reformed faith and those of the Charismatic Renewal. When one is missing, the manifestation of that becomes either cold Protestant scholasticism that lacks any love and passion, or extreme experimentalism that lacks any foundation upon which to build. When there is a focus on the principles that define Church, not simply being moved by demands placed upon it in ministry, James Emery White states, "renewal flows."[153] Addressing the foundations of our beliefs about the Holy Spirit, and how those beliefs apply to our actions, is the key issue of this research, and the outcome is the same as that hoped for by White: renewal.

---

149. Grudem, *Systematic Theology*, 1046.
150. Stackhouse, *Gospel Driven Church*, 29.
151. Smith, *Foundations of the Faith*, 130, 135–36.
152. Benn and Burkhill, "Theological and Pastoral Critique," 102.
153. White, *Rethinking the Church*, 72.

Partial Conclusion

This chapter has set the scene of the uniqueness of the Reformed context and the way in which a Charismatic methodology may be applied to congregational life. It has defined the terms that will be used throughout the book as the discussion topics for the contextual applications that follow. It has outlined the current position of the Confessional Reformed Churches toward the Charismatic Renewal's theology and practice, and suggested that it is possible to maintain a fidelity to the WCF and practice charismatic gifts. This chapter also outlined the challenge of John Wimber, specifically for the Reformed Churches, and why he is being used as a conversational partner for further discussion. Lastly, it has considered a Reformed and Charismatic ministry model, which local Reformed congregations may be able to follow, without becoming practically similar to another Christian tradition in worship style or ecclesiastical polity. It appears that Wimber is uniquely suited to enable a consideration of the research question, and this will be further explored and a possible answer given in the next chapters.

2

The Theology and Writings of John Wimber

Introduction

TO SET THE FOUNDATION for the contextual applications, I want to begin by considering the theology and writings of Wimber. This will provide an insight into his thinking, specifically on the nature of the kingdom of God and how that applies to the mission and ministry of the Church.

The Theological Review

There may be some debate surrounding whether Wimber could be understood as a theologian. *The Princeton Review* defines a theologian as someone who "concentrates on the rational study of religious history and modern day religious issues." This they do to educate leaders, who in turn educate congregations. This study is diverse, ecumenical, cross-cultural and biblical.[1] Kim Fabricius further states that a theologian is someone who is a servant of the Church, and while they may work in a university context, he or she is not "an academic but an ecclesiodemic."[2] In this sense Wimber may well fit the definition of a theologian. His theology is diverse in its sources and is focused on serving the Church practically. He seeks to take theological principles and make them applicable for congregational life. His understanding

---

1. http://www.princetonreview.com/careers.aspx?cid=212.
2. Fabricius, "Ten Propositions on being a Theologian."

of "Word-workers," who aim to apply their theological understanding to every aspect of life and practice, may also fit this definition.[3] Wayne Grudem believes that Wimber does have a theological point to make, specifically on miraculous gifts and healing, from which the wider Church can benefit.[4] Wimber's views and comments on the nature and practice of Church life, therefore, have an influence. To this end he may be understood as someone with a comment to make on theological reflection.

P. D. Jensen is one of those who argues that Wimber is not a theologian and that "his lack of theological understanding and education" is responsible for what they deem to be the issues with his theology.[5] J. I. Packer disagrees with Jensen and notes that although Wimber did not view himself as an "intellectual," someone who pioneered church planting, who was a Church Growth consultant, a seminary teacher "of embarrassing effectiveness," and a worldwide Christian leader, he ought to be viewed as such.[6] The danger of Jensen's view is that it limits theologians to being a professional caste within the Christian Church. This is not a universally accepted principle, as Jurgen Motlmann believes that every believer is a theologian.[7] It could be argued that the kind of theologian that academia reflects upon requires a degree of professional training and qualifications, which may support Jensen's view. However, simply because Wimber did not have the same academic criteria as others does not negate the impact his theology has had on the Church. To ignore him, therefore, because he does not meet a specific standard of education, does not deal with the implications of his theology.

Wimber acknowledges the importance of theology, though he also recognizes that it can be divisive. One significant point for Wimber is the interpretation of charismatic gifts.[8] This seems to suggest that Wimber is prepared to engage in contemporary debate, using theological nuances.

---

3. Wimber, *Witnesses for a Powerful Christ*, 33–34.
4. Grudem, "Power and Truth," 11.
5. Jensen, "John Wimber Changes His Mind," 11.
6. Packer, "Intellectual," 258.
7. Motlmann, "What is a Theologian?" 189.

8. Wimber and Springer, *Power Evangelism*, 246. Wimber suggests two other causes of division: fear of undermining the authority of the Bible, and a cultural barrier because of evangelicals' social standing in society. Wimber, *Power Evangelism*, 250–51. Poloma, commenting on the American Assemblies of God and the Charismatic Renewal, noted that middle- and upper-middle class social standing did bring a new enthusiasm to a "staid" Pentecostalism, and legitimized acceptance of the gifts of the spirit. Poloma, "Charisma and Institution," 933. We noted some of the concerns raised by PCI in chapter 1: the nature of prophecy apart from the Bible, contemporary apostles and prophets, preoccupation with the sensational and specifically satanic issues, the

Theological Context—Dispensationalism and Fundamentalism

Noting the context of Wimber's theology is also important. Fabricius notes that all good theology is contextual: it comes from a specific context that forms and molds what is deduced.[9] For Wimber it appears that the North American context of Evangelicalism influenced his own thinking. This may be because he came to Christianity later on in life, not having had a religious upbringing.[10] This may suggest that his influences came a lot quicker and lot more vehemently than those raised within Church. His theology was filtered through a conversion experience rather than theological tradition. I propose to consider the two traditions that were influential in twentieth-century North America and in the foundation of Fuller Seminary,[11] fundamentalism and dispensationalism.

Fundamentalism takes its name from a series of essays published 1910–15, by the Bible College of Los Angeles, edited by A. C. Dixon and R. A. Torrey. While there was a theological dynamic for fundamentalism, concerns about the perceived erosion of biblical truth considering scientific advances, it was primarily a movement about connection. G. M. Marsden and B. J. Longfield note that in defending these truths, conservative Protestants attempted to forge alliances.[12] Kevin T. Bauder underlines this thought, and suggests that the primary focus of fundamentalism is the unity and fellowship of the Church.[13] According to Brad Harper and Paul Louis Metzger, this unity and fellowship encompassed a wide number of churches and denominations and was a fellowship on certain theological axioms rather than a movement to reform ecclesiastical politics.[14] Martyn Percy defines

---

health and wealth gospel, the subordination of women and the removal of baptismal discipline outside the remit of Kirk Sessions, which often led to re-baptism. Ad Hoc Committee on Special Fellowships 1984, 244–45.

9. Fabricius, "Propositions on being a Theologian."

10. Pytches, "Man Called John," 11.

11. Wimber taught on the supernatural in the Church Growth Department in Fuller Seminary.

12. Marsden and Longfield, "Fundamentalist-Modernist Controversy," 103. Murray seeks to distinguish between the doctrines of fundamentalism, which had a wider support than those who were defined as fundamentalists, and the mindset that was often anti-intellectual. Murray, *Evangelicalism Divided*, 38.

13. Harper and Metzger, *Exploring Ecclesiology*, 15 and 275. While encompassing membership in different denominations and independent congregations, Harper and Metzger also suggest a degree of uniformity in which the different and distinct cultures that formed the churches are lost in fundamentalism.

14. Bauder, "Fundamentalism," 21.

fundamentalism as "transdenominational and transreligious."[15] This could lead to tension within denominations that are perceived to be mixed. The other issue is where the line of demarcation is to be drawn. Some would draw the line higher than others, making certain theological views as normative for any kind of fellowship. The issue of theology also comes into play with fundamentalism. J. I. Packer notes that like-minded evangelicals joined together to defend their faith, giving birth to fundamentalism.[16] George Marsden suggests that fundamentalism was a reaction to declining revivalistic evangelicalism and liberal theology.[17][18] This paints the picture of what Fuller Seminary, and wider evangelicalism, were attempting to defend in the early part of the twentieth century. In Fuller Seminary there was a tension between fundamentalism and new evangelicalism.[19] The seminary became a champion of New Evangelicalism, which Marsden describes as a "moderate form of classic Calvinist Protestantism as opposed to some of the innovations of dispensationalist Bible teachers."[20] Wimber was a divisive figure for these two camps because the implications of his theology could not be solved by the traditional fundamentalist/progressive debate.

Within the Church at large there appears to have been a backlash against fundamentalism. As Murray notes, the war they waged on modernism and denominations was countered.[21] One such counter came from Harry Emerson Fosdick who, from 1918–25, was pastor of First Presbyterian Church in the City of New York, although a Baptist cleric. Fosdick represented the liberal stream in Christianity, denying that doctrinal matters, such as the virgin birth, were essential for orthodoxy.[22] On May 21, 1922, he preached a sermon entitled "Shall the Fundamentalists Win?" It is interesting that while he does not agree with where the fundamentalists draw the

15. Percy, *Power and the Church*, 59.

16. Packer, *Fundamentalism and the Word of God*, 24

17. Marsden, *Reforming Fundamentalism*, 4. He notes eternal damnation, the virgin birth, the miracles of Christ, the bodily resurrection of Christ, the substitutionary atonement and the second coming as doctrines that had become downplayed.

18. Percy outlines five characteristics of fundamentalism: it is backward looking to legitimize current beliefs and actions; it is opposed to perceived modernist trends; it is a tendency or habit of mind which looks for absolute authority; it is the widespread opposition to liberalism; it is noetic and concerned with informational propositions. Percy, *Power and the Church*, 64–66.

19. It is interesting that E. J. Carnell, President of Fuller Seminary, encouraged the faculty to drop the term because it had become misunderstood. Murray, *Evangelicalism Divided*, 20.

20. Marsden, *Reforming Fundamentalism*, 6, 294.

21. Murray, *Evangelicalism Divided*, 17.

22. Whiteman, "Fosdick, Harry Emerson (1878–1969)," 100.

line on orthodoxy, it is their attitudes that he takes greatest exception to.[23] He argues that their aim is to drive out of the Evangelical Churches all men and women with liberal opinions. This he views as illiberal and intolerant, something which is not applicable to all conservatives, some of whom are distant from fundamentalism and liberal of spirit.[24] It seems that there was a perceived lack of graciousness amongst some fundamentalists, specifically regarding those with whom they disagreed. It appears that Wimber had to deal with the same attitude from those who disagreed with him. Jensen writes: "He may be compassionate, loving, genuine and sincere, but so was the loaded dog!"[25] Equating someone to a canine because of a disagreement over theology appears to be somewhat uncharitable. Yet Wimber never reacted to those who disagreed with him in such a manner. He was careful to point out that absence of signs, wonders and miracles does not mean that a lesser gospel is being preached.[26] He points out that his theology stands within the evangelical stream and is not something different.[27] He also points out that his views are not there to replace existing theologies, but to complement and even improve them.[28] It seems that fundamentalism may have influenced Wimber positively, through its own negativity. Wimber is not unsympathetic to a correct understanding of the fundamentals of the Christian faith. He argues that once people are converted, there is a need to understand what the gospel means. Yet, it is through experiencing what is believed, specifically power evangelism, which "is not antirational," that is essential. A duality of action is anticipated, the provision of information and the demonstration of power.[29] For Wimber, correct theology is important and cannot be dispensed with for expediency. Yet, that correct theology has to have a practical application, so what is believed is put into action. He appears to have a firm commitment to fundamentalism; however, it could also be described as a commitment to fundapraxis.

Dispensationalism appears to have developed out of fundamentalism. Buschart notes that unlike many other theological traditions, dispensationalism can be located within the fundamentalist and evangelical traditions.[30]

---

23. He says that fundamentalists are arguing over "little matters". Fosdick, "Shall the Fundamentalists Win?" 201.

24. Fosdick, "Shall the Fundamentalists Win?" 190–91.

25. Jensen, "John Wimber Changes His Mind," 11.

26. Wimber, *Power Evangelism*, 79.

27. Wimber, *Kingdom of God*, 27.

28. Wimber, *Dynamics of Spiritual Growth*, 176–77.

29. Wimber, *Power Evangelism*, 108.

30. Buschart, *Exploring Protestant Traditions*, 210.

This theology views history through various dispensations, and God relates to humanity in different ways in each dispensation. Michael J. Vlach notes that dispensationalism can trace its roots to the nineteenth century, to John Nelson Darby. Darby was a Church of Ireland minister who came to believe in a future dispensation in which all of Israel would be saved. The Scofield Reference Bible, published in 1909, popularized these views.[31][32] Marsden notes that this was one of the most influential anti-modernist doctrines of the twentieth century. They believed that the Church was currently in the sixth dispensation, which is characterized by apostasy from biblical doctrine.[33] Dispensationalism believes that every word of the Bible was perfect, and was hence connected with the King James Only Movement.[34] Keith A. Mathison notes that dispensationalism took a very literal view of the Bible, that there was no allegory.[35] Vern S. Poythress calls this "first thought meaning."[36] This connection with what the Bible says lead Lewis Sperry Chafer to note that denial of the dispensational system was a refusal to be influenced by precise study of Scripture.[37] Dispensationalism, furthermore, seems to have been distinctly cessationist. Charles H. Kraft notes that enlightenment perspectives shine through dispensationalism, leading to a rejection of supernaturalism. This is underpinned by a lack of spiritual experiences of power, and so a theology to justify that lack is drawn up.[38] Fuller Seminary appears to have sought to distance itself from fundamentalist/dispensationalism, emphasizing a more intellectual emphasis for the reform and transformation of culture, rejecting the pessimism of dispensational-

---

31. Vlach, "What Is Dispensationalism." He also notes three variations of dispensationalism. In Classical Dispensationalism, which was linked with Darby and Scofield, God is understood to be operating two purposes in redemption: one for Israel on the earth, the other for the Church in heaven. In the Revised or Modified Dispensationalism, associated with C. C. Ryrie, adherents believe that Israel and the Gentiles receive the same salvation. In Progressive Dispensationalism, all the dispensations are linked and being fulfilled today.

32. For a discussion of John Nelson Darby see: Stunt, "John Nelson Darby."

33. Ryrie outlines seven dispensations: I. Infancy—to the Deluge; II. Childhood—to Moses; III. Adolescence—to the prophets; IV. Youth—to the coming of Christ; V. Manhood—" some time after that"; VI. Old Age—" the time of man's decay" (V & VI are the church age): VII. Renovation of all things- the millennium. Ryrie, *Dispensationalism Today*, 71–74.

34. Marsden, *Reforming Fundamentalism*, 5. See White, *King James Only Controversy*.

35. Mathison, *Dispensationalism*, 6.

36. Poythress, *Understanding Dispensationalists*, 96.

37. Chafer, *Systematic Theology*, 123.

38. Kraft, *Christianity with Power*, 73.

ism. This happened through Fuller's association with Billy Graham in the 1950s.[39] Wimber also appears to have been influenced by dispensationalism in how he views the Bible. He states that the Bible gives an accurate record of God's dealings with humanity.[40] This seems to be a restatement of the literalist view of the Bible. This influence could have come through Fuller Seminary, but also through the wider American evangelicalism. Questioning the validity of the cessationist position was also raised at Fuller, through Kraft. This further opened an avenue toward codifying Wimber's theology on power evangelism. In a sense it may have been a Fuller to Wimber current, and it may also have been a Wimber to Fuller current.

Fundamentalism and Dispensationalism sought to bring a rationale to the Christian faith by emphasizing biblical doctrine and belief. This was a reaction to the apparent liberalism of those, like Fosdick, who denied that key doctrines were essential for Christianity. Yet Wimber diverges from these views, stating that the Bible is the menu and not the meal.[41] He wants to respect biblical theology, yet he wants an experiential element also. This is why he speaks of "Word-workers": those who know biblical teaching and put it into action.[42] For Wimber, the result of theological reflection was to become an active participator in the Christian Church. It would not have been enough simply to know biblical doctrine, but doctrine must lead to action. He states that it is not enough for a Christian to gather information, even about the supernatural in Scripture, but not to have it affect action, because he is an "activist."[43] Wimber speaks of a "new Pharisaism" which manifests itself in a "show-it-to-me-in-the-Word" philosophy, where correct doctrine is elevated to supremacy and practicing doctrine seen as secondary.[44] Steve Sjogren, reflecting on Wimber's statement, emphasizes the need for action as well as correct theology.[45] It seems that Wimber is concerned with correct theology, which effects correct praxis. He sees a close connection between what is believed and what is done. When what is believed is correct, it manifests itself in correct action. Underlying this view is Wimber's criticism of the methods used in seminaries to train leaders. He argues that using Bible study as the key to equipping people for ministry is not enough, something

---

39. Marsden, *Reforming Fundamentalism*, 8.
40. Wimber and Springer, *Dynamics of Spiritual Growth*, 29.
41. Wimber, *Way In is the Way On*, 99.
42. Wimber, *Witnesses for a Powerful Christ*, 33–34.
43. Wimber and Springer, *Power Evangelism*, 13.
44. Wimber, *Everyone Gets to Play*, 32.
45. Sjogren, *Conspiracy of Kindness*, 33

more is needed.⁴⁶ This model, which he calls "grammatical-historical," emphasizes, through history, linguistics, and historical theology, what God was saying through the Bible to the first-century context. He believes this moves leaders away from moral and spiritual formation to an intellectual Christianity. This can be done from any faith position, including no faith, whereas proper study ought to proceed from faith, hope, and love. This makes leaders reliant less on the Holy Spirit and more on study, resulting in a tendency to reject contemporary signs, wonders and miracles. While making educated leaders, it does not produce "a people who cause demons to tremble."⁴⁷ He also suggests that it may contribute to people abdicating responsibility for studying the Bible for themselves. This happens because the experts employ academic tools that few lay members understand, and so they simply give up.⁴⁸ Perhaps Wimber is seeing theological systems that emphasize what is important, correct doctrine, but do not connect that doctrine with practice. This is something he sees as central to his own theology, and effective for the Church at large. These influences are both positive and negative with Wimber, as he is a product of his own context. Yet, he also had a missionary influence, specifically through interacting with the faculty at Fuller Seminary, which also influenced his views.

Wimber's Context

Charles E. Fuller founded Fuller Seminary on May 13, 1947.⁴⁹ Wimber, having led the Charles E. Fuller Institute of Evangelism and Church Growth at Fuller School of World Missions, as well as being an adjunct instructor, began in 1982 to teach on miracles, signs, and wonders.⁵⁰⁵¹ Fuller grew

---

46. Wimber, *Power Evangelism*, 91.

47. Wimber and Springer, *Power Evangelism*, 191–93. He also refers to the "historical-critical" method of theological education, which he suggests leads to enlightenment thinking about the contemporary supernatural. Wimber, *Riding the Third Wave*, 25.

48. Wimber and Springer, *Dynamics of Spiritual Growth*, 46–47.

49. Marsden, *Reforming Fundamentalism*, 53.

50. Ibid., 292, http://www.vineyardusa.org/site/ about/vineyard-history. The School of World Missions was renamed the School of Intercultural Studies. Its mission statement reads: "Welcome to the School of Intercultural Studies. Our school is dedicated to equipping men and women to cross the barriers that block people from seeing, hearing, and believing the gospel. As a community of people who are engaged in the worldwide mission of God, we combine the best elements of academic and practical studies to ensure that our graduates are ready to serve God."

51. Grudem, "Power and Truth," 30. "Wimber taught in various capacities as an adjunct professor at Fuller Seminary from 1975 to 1992. He worked full time in the Fuller Evangelistic Association from 1975–77. He taught the course MC510 from

out of the Fundamentalist movement of the early twentieth century. As a seminary it sought to drive a middle line of progressive evangelicalism between the "hypernaturalism of liberalism and the hypersupernaturalism of fundamentalism."[52] It was not considered a charismatic school.[53] This led it in 1987 to issue a statement on the ministry of miraculous healing. Wagner suggests that Fuller Seminary had a formative influence on the development of the theology of the kingdom of God.[54][55] This stood against classic fundamentalism, which denied the continuance of the charismata, but also sought to warn against a central emphasis on the more spectacular miracles. There was a desire for honesty, especially when celebrating the few genuine cases of divine healing, which was felt to be emphasized out of proportion. The conclusion was that Wimber's signs and wonders course was not appropriate to the academic context of Fuller Seminary.[56]

What is significant about Fuller's influence on Wimber is that it changed his theological mindset. Bill Jackson asserts that when Wimber was a Quaker minister, and began teaching at Fuller, he held to a cessationist position. Through the influence of Chuck Kraft, and stories from missionary contexts, he began to come across stories of the contemporary moving of the Holy Spirit. This led him to read Donald Gee's book *Concerning Spiritual Gifts,* and eventually led to an openness for the charismatic.[57] It could be argued that Fuller created the Wimber that they then deemed to be inappropriate for their academic setting. It could also be surmised that if Wimber had not gone to Fuller that his theology may have remained static.

1982–85. The course was taught again from 1987–91 with C. Peter Wagner as the professor, but Wimber continued to lecture in part of the course. Up to 1992 he taught two or three day-long sessions per year as an adjunct professor in the Doctor of Ministry program.16. 1975–1992 is 17 years, longer than 'a short time.'"

52. Marsden, *Reforming Fundamentalism,* 293.

53. Wagner, *Third Wave of the Holy Spirit,* 26. He writes: "No, Fuller is not a charismatic seminary. It is simply evangelical and multi-denominational. Thus, it is neither Baptist nor Presbyterian, Calvinistic nor Wesleyan, pretrib nor post-trib, charismatic nor non-charismatic."

54. Wagner was Professor of Church Growth at Fuller Theological Seminary's School of World Missions until his retirement in 2001.

55. Wagner, *Church Growth and the Whole Gospel,* 3–4.

56. Marsden, *Reforming Fundamentalism,* 294. Smedes, *Ministry and the Miraculous.*

57. Jackson, *Quest for the Radical Middle,* 51, 54.

George Elldon Ladd

Unlike Wagner and Kraft, Ladd had not been in missionary service. His background was as a Baptist pastor, then earning a degree from Harvard University. Marsden notes that he was one of a very small number of fundamentalists who became a leader of the neo-evangelical movement.[58] R. D. Moore and R. E. Sagers suggest that Ladd was one of the key theological voices in raising the issue of the kingdom of God.[59] Despite this apparent influence, Derek Morphew believes that, in his time, Ladd was not a particularly well know theologian, but he was a credible enough scholar that his "rediscovery of the theology of the kingdom" became influential in the Conservative Evangelical theological world.[60] It is this theology of the kingdom that has specific application to Wimber's theology, for he appears to have built much of his own understanding upon it. Wimber cites Ladd's view of the kingdom of God as giving him the theological rationale for power evangelism.[61] Ladd saw biblical theology as offering a path for evangelicals out of what he saw as dispensational errors, particularly about the kingdom of God.[62] For Wimber, Ladd's theology of the kingdom allowed him to emphasize the miraculous in the present, as the kingdom was already. It also allowed him to understand why the miraculous did not always take place, because the kingdom was not yet fully present.[63] Ladd notes: "God is now the King, but he must also become King."[64][65] This already/not yet tension was a key thought in Wimber's own theology of the kingdom, which allowed for miraculous events but gave a rationale as to why they may not always happen as expected.

Ladd understood the kingdom of God as being central to the Christian hope that God has a purpose to perform, and in the Old Testament that purpose was to be fulfillled through Israel.[66] The kingdom of God was already spiritually present, through those who give their lives to the Holy Spirit, yet there was also a hope that it would come in its fullness as an

---

58. Marsden, *Reforming Fundamentalism*, 120.
59. Moore and Sagers, "Kingdom of God and the Church," 70.
60. Morphew, "Why Is the Kingdom of God so Important?"
61. Wimber, *Power Evangelism*, 12.
62. Marsden, *Reforming Fundamentalism*, 150.
63. Jackson, *Quest for the Radical Middle*, 55.
64. Ladd, *Theology of the New Testament*, 61
65. There may also be an ecumenical reach to this already/not yet tension, specifically for application in Baptist circles. Moore and Sagers, "Kingdom of God and the Church," 68.
66. Ladd, *Gospel of the Kingdom*, 14.

inheritance for God's people. This is possible because Christians are already in the kingdom.[67] The participation in the kingdom of God became a key area for Wimber and other Third Wave teachers. It is through the people of God that God elected to exercise "his rule in a new and more decisive fashion."[68] Participation in the life of the kingdom was reserved not only for healing, signs and wonders, but for confronting spiritual evil and challenging Western culture, as we shall consider. Yet Ladd did not want to connect the kingdom of God to one specific people, whether Israel or the Church. It was something wider than a physical manifestation. It represented a rule and authority that was beyond people, yet included people in its activity.[69] As Wimber reflected upon this teaching, he began to see something that was beyond a denominational or cultural manifestation of religion. It was the power of God that intersected with human lives and human needs, bringing the future into the present.

Charles H. Kraft

Charles H. Kraft served as Professor of Anthropology and Intercultural Communication at Fuller Seminary. His background was also in missions, serving in Northern Nigeria,[70] with the Brethren Church.[71] It was within the context of this missionary service that Kraft, after having been confronted by a Nigerian Church leader, moved from a position of intellectual acceptance of evil spirits to a deliverance ministry.[72] Kraft states that while they were academically and theological prepared, it was not enough to enable them to deal with what the Nigerians considered most important—their relationship to the spirit world. He notes that as a missionary he brought "an essentially powerless message to a very power conscious people."[73] He attempted to answer theological problems from his theological training, and cultural problems from his anthropological training, which did not appear

---

67. Ladd, *Gospel of the Kingdom*, 16–17; Ladd, *Theology of the New Testament*, 70.
68. Deere, *Surprised by the Power of the Spirit*, 225.
69. Ladd, *Gospel of the Kingdom*, 21.
70. http://www.fuller.edu/academics/faculty/charles-kraft.aspx.
71. Kraft, *Christianity with Power*, 3. The Church of the United Brethren in Christ defines itself as a Protestant, evangelical, orthodox and Arminian denomination. They are from a German background, which developed as a result of the eighteenth-century awakenings in Europe, through Wesley, and in the USA, through Whitefield and Edwards. http:// ub.org/about.
72. Kraft, *Defeating Dark Angels*, 14–15.
73. Kraft, *Christianity with Power*, 3–4.

to work. He deduced that the solution was to combine both approaches.[74] His conclusion was that as an evangelical missionary, his theology was "more like deism than like biblical Christianity."[75] This was the challenge for Kraft: Christianity was to attempt to be biblical in its expectation, and powerful in its practice. Kraft believed there had to be more to offer people than just correct belief, there must be correct experience also, which is similar to the desire of Wimber for people to engage with the reality of God's kingdom coming in power to meet their deepest needs.

While an academic teacher, he defined himself as a missionary and trainer of missionaries, from an evangelical perspective that was committed to the authority of the Bible.[76] His interest lay in the way Christians communicate their message. He looked at how the biblical text was understood and taken from its original context into new contexts. He raised the issue of "monocultural" interpretation, which believed that moving from the biblical languages and culture to "Euro-American" language and culture was a movement from a less adequate to a more adequate context.[77] This led to a range of interpretation, within an accepted spectrum, on certain spiritual issues.[78] Yet what Kraft does not appear to allow interpretation on is the issue of the power of the kingdom of God. He states that healings result when the kingdom comes near, leading him to ask if there are no healings does that mean that the kingdom is not near to many churches?[79] This statement explicitly connects the kingdom of God with manifestations of power. It also roots that theology within the context of the local Church. Kraft is not saying that an absence of powerful experience necessarily infers an absence of the kingdom of God. What he does appear to be challenging is the notion that the way things are is the best scenario. This we will consider in the kingdom of God's critique of the Western Church. Kraft rejected the primacy of systematic theology, believing it was culturally influenced by Greek thought. Instead, he argued for a more experiential than cerebral evangelicalism.[80] This influence on Wimber seems to have led him to consider the issue of power encounters, healings, and demonic deliverance within a Euro-American context. It could be argued that Wimber aims to demythologize the Western culture and re-establish the biblical culture

---

74. Kraft, *Christianity in Culture*, 7.
75. Kraft, *Christianity with Power*, 39.
76. Kraft, "Interpreting in Cultural Context," 357.
77. Ibid., 358.
78. Ibid., 360.
79. Kraft, *Two Hours to Freedom*, 14.
80. Marsden, *Reforming Fundamentalism*, 288.

as the norm for evangelism and Church life. The influence also passed from Wimber to Kraft.[81] He already notes that he had a desire to learn about spiritual power, so he began to attend the Wimber lectures.[82] Kraft notes that in 1982, while in Wimber's class at Fuller, he was encouraged to "try it and see what happens." The result was that when he began to act on what he believed Jesus was telling him, "amazing things happened."[83] This was part of the Third Wave movement, discussed earlier, which saw evangelicals move from an intellectual assertion in the power of Jesus, to an experiential participation in "the continuance of those mighty works in the present."[84] While it may be possible to see the influence that Kraft was on Wimber's theology, it is also interesting to see that Kraft learned from Wimber. This symbiotic relationship crossed educational bounds, so that an academic scholar learned from a ministry practitioner, without allowing his popular credentials to negate his academic worth.

C. Peter Wagner

Wimber credits Wagner with dramatically changing his theology of evangelism to include signs and wonders. This came from Wagner's own experience as a missionary in South America.[85] An ordained Congregational minister, he served in Bolivia, under the South American Mission and Andes Evangelical Mission. He worked as a professor in the George Allan Theological Seminary, Cochabamba (1962–71).[86] It was while a missionary that Wagner's view changed from being dispensational and cessationist, to being open to the supernatural.[87] This happened through a personal experience of healing,[88] through E. Stanley Jones, a Methodist Missionary to

---

81. Kraft stresses their similar background as Conservative Evangelicals who were critical of many of the excesses of the Pentecostal and Charismatic Movements. Kraft, *Christianity with Power*, 7–8.

82. Kraft, *Christianity with Power*, 1–2.

83. Kraft, *Defeating Dark Angels*, 87.

84. Kraft, *Christianity with Power*, xi.

85. Wimber, *Power Evangelism*, 11.

86. McGee, "Wagner, Charles Peter (1930–)," 875.

87. Wagner notes four roadblocks in his own theology to experiencing the power of the Holy Spirit: Dispensationalism, Anti-Pentecostalism, a limited view of power, and a secular humanist worldview. Wagner, "God Wasn't Pulling my Leg," 51–52.

88. Jackson, *Quest for the Radical Middle*, 55. He cites this as the first stage in his journey toward openness, the second being a study in Latin American Pentecostal Church Growth, and the third a period of ministry in the late 1970s with the Church of God, Cleveland, TN, teaching on Church Growth. Wagner, "God Wasn't Pulling my

India.[89] This led to an openness to charismatic theology and phenomena, which would have dovetailed with Wimber's own journey. While I have attempted to note the influence that Fuller had on Wimber, Wagner cites Wimber as being used to make him a "participant" in signs and wonders.[90] Wagner's theological convictions also changed from a pessimistic premillennialism, shaped by dispensationalism, to understanding that the kingdom ought to effect social transformation.[91] This may suggest the journey that evangelicals, and Fuller Seminary, were making toward an engagement with the needs confronting Christians in society and through personal interaction with others, rather than a passive observation and declaration that the kingdom is coming. It also reminds one of the personal application of the kingdom of God, as Wagner notes the end is not the miracles themselves. Rather, the end is reconciling people to God.[92] This is why power evangelism is a very practical theology, as it engages with the deepest and most pressing needs of people, their spiritual condition. It does more than inform of a new theological doctrine, but is a theological method of praxis. It is interesting to see that later reflection on this subject has led Wagner to espouse a kingdom-based social philosophy that effects governmental politics and social policy.[93] This may be a narrowing of the wider principles of Ladd and Wimber, focusing the work of the kingdom through political means and establishment. It may also be interpreted as defining one political opinion rather than a trans-political ideal that connects spiritually with individuals and societies.

In 1983 Wagner proposed a "third wave of the Holy Spirit," the first being Pentecostalism, the second the Charismatic Renewal, and this third amongst evangelicals in the mainstream churches.[94] This movement of the Holy Spirit is believed to have begun in the 1980s amongst evangelicals who would be unhappy being defined as either Pentecostals or Charismatics.[95] He chose this label because of the feeling that the label "charismatic" did

---

Leg," 53–54.

89. Wagner, *Third Wave of the Holy Spirit*, 22.

90. Ibid., 23.

91. Wagner, *Dominion*, 61.

92. Wagner, *Third Wave of the Holy Spirit*, 87.

93. Wagner, *Dominion*, 16.

94. Synan, *Century of the Holy Spirit*, 359.

95. Wagner, *Third Wave of the Holy Spirit*, 18. Wright, "Profiles of Divine Healing," 271. Wagner notes that the main difference was the understanding of the Baptism in the Holy Spirit, while the outworking of the Holy Spirit's presence, in healing and exorcism, remain the same.

not fit, and that there was no desire to become Pentecostals.[96] This Third Wave became associated with people like Wimber and movements like the Vineyard.[97] It could be argued that Wagner gave the theology of Wimber the designation that separated him from other Holy Spirit focused movements. He gave him a theological identity, and a sense of unity with others of a like mind.[98] This designation would cover a number of new denominations as well as those that remained with the traditional denominations. It could also be argued that the ethos of the Third Wave further separated Fuller Seminary from dispensationalism, which was singled out for disagreement.[99] Wagner's influence on Wimber, and vice versa, marked the path of the Third Wave.[100] Evangelicals who would naturally be disinclined away from Pentecostal and charismatic practice, came to engage with the work of the Holy Spirit. This is connected with the evangelism and mission.

The Missionary Context

With the missionary influences in Fuller Seminary, it could be argued that Wimber's theology was an attempt to apply missionary principles to Western culture. This is seen through Kraft's championing of Wimber's course at Fuller, although personally not charismatic. He saw it as being of a non-Western emphasis.[101] Michael Reid comments on the North African context of Kraft, which emphasized pragmatism and saw strategic level spiritual warfare as an effective means of evangelism.[102] It may be that what Wimber is trying to do is to apply missionary principles to his own Western setting. He is drawing on the experiences of his ex-missionary colleagues and implementing their consequences in the Western world. This would specifically happen as the kingdom of God challenged the spiritual forces in the world. Wimber sought to understand the power of God, as a manifestation of his kingdom, confronting the kingdom of darkness. He calls

---

96. Wagner, "God Wasn't Pulling my Leg," 59–60.

97. Wright, "Profiles of Divine Healing," 271.

98. Wimber, "Introduction," 31. He notes "the absence of divisiveness" as an encouraging, and key point, to his theology.

99. Hacking, *Sign and Wonders*, 29.

100. Wagner, "God Wasn't Pulling my Leg," 50.

101. Marsden, *Reforming Fundamentalism*, 293. Kraft sees missions as being more than a series of theoretical principles furthering knowledge and technique. He notes that this emphasis on the technique is essentially secular rather than emphasizing the spiritual aspect. Kraft, *Christianity with Power*, 45. It may be that Wimber is offering this spiritual mandate for mission much clearer than traditional missiology.

102. Reid, *Strategic Level Spiritual Warfare*, 13–14.

them "power encounters," when demonic power is expelled. For Wimber this is not just within individual lives, but also when any system or force that encourages unbelief is confronted. This happens as God's kingdom works through individual believers and the Church, especially in missions.[103] It seems that Wimber's theology has been affected by the missionary culture of some of the Fuller faculty, and he is now seeking a new application for these principles.

Wimber notes that often the power of God is needed to be seen amongst "primitive peoples" so that they will believe.[104] Rather than placing all the emphasis on other cultures, other than the Western context in which Wimber ministered, he applies power evangelism to his own situation. He suggests that it can have the same effect as in other contexts.[105] Wimber is seeking to connect his theology with a missionary context, something which E. E. Wright believes is an essential part of missions.[106] Mission, then, according to Wimber is a theological praxis of certain central truths about God's power confronting demonic power. C. J. H. Wright sees the theological basis for missions as essential to a proper hermeneutic, indeed the central message of theology.[107] While Wimber appears to be a pragmatist, it is his theology that underpins his praxis. His understanding was to release people, through training them in his understanding of power evangelism, to do the work of missions in their own context.[108] His theology was to serve the missionary purpose of the Church as it ministers to the Western world.

Wimber roots his theology in the Western Church and seeks to carry over missionary principles from other contexts.[109] D. J. Bosch notes that the traditional view of mission had little doubt about the apparent depravity in many non-Western cultures.[110] The view that the culture from which one is reflecting is superior to other cultures appears to be something that Wimber

---

103. Wimber and Springer, *Power Evangelism*, 52.

104. Ibid., 54.

105. Ibid., 93. He notes: "We have seen that it can flourish in Western societies with the same results that occurred in the first century or that are reported from Africa, South and Central America, and Asia today."

106. Wright, *Practical Theology of Missions*, 27.

107. Wright, *Mission of God*, 36. He raises a concern that some biblical, historical, systematic and practical theology is presented with an absence of mission.

108. Wimber, *Everyone Gets to Play*, 7. "I can either get a tent and have a huge revival where I can do this by myself, or I can release it to the people, and equip them to play."

109. The application of missionary theology to the Church is also dealt with by: Blauw, *Missionary Nature of the Church*; Hedlund, *Mission of the Church in the World*.

110. Bosch, *Transforming Mission*, 293.

challenges. He argues for the missionary spotlight to be shone upon the Western Church itself. This is an understanding that the Western position is one of the many "multidirectional" perspectives of mission, which Wright suggests influences how people understand God.[111] Wimber notes that Western culture has been influenced by other cultures through the influx of Eastern religions.[112] While the influences may have come from foreign missions, Wimber sees the context of foreign missions as now being established in Western culture. David Smith sees this pluralism as a key challenge to the Western world. Once Christendom claimed ownership of all truth; however, now there are other voices raised within Western culture.[113] In this context, Wimber's theology suggests that the power of God can confront the demonic kingdom, and establish the kingdom of God. This influence appears to come through the missionary context that had an impact on his own theology.

Wimber's theology seems to have been molded by a missionary emphasis, as I have noted. This places the spreading of the kingdom of God central to the activity of the Church, and of primary focus for Christians in the world. Ladd picks up on the connection between evangelism and the mission of the kingdom, stating that there is no room for "rosy optimists" who expect the kingdom of God to conquer the world, nor for "despairing pessimists" who feel the task is hopeless. Rather, he argues for a realism that accepts the opposition to the coming kingdom of God, but also understands the kingdom's power.[114] There may be an issue with the context here, in that the missionary context of Kraft in North Africa and Wagner in South America, could be said to be somewhat different from Wimber's in Southern California. What underpins this theology is the notion that wherever the context may be, the reality of spiritual evil remains constant, but God's power is the greater.[115] It could be argued that while the individual contexts are markedly different in terms of development, socio-economic status, and even academic attainment, the core issues that lie at the root of society remain the same. Rather than placing the blame on humanity itself, this missionary emphasis shifts the focus to perceived evil spirits that affect the actions and attitudes of humanity. Ladd believes that the missionary influence comes directly from Jesus, rather than any specific missionary

111. Wright, *Mission of God*, 38–39. He further states that the Western position itself is contextual.

112. Wimber and Springer, *Power Healing*, 26; Wimber and Springer, *Dynamics of Spiritual Growth*, 9.

113. Smith, *Mission After Christendom*, 60.

114. Ladd, *Gospel of the Kingdom*, 139.

115. Wagner, *Third Wave of the Holy Spirit*, 45.

context in the world. He notes that Jesus' mission was to bind and destroy Satan.[116] This struggle with Satan he places at the heart of Jesus' mission, and that through Jesus the kingdom of God would conquer the kingdom of Satan.[117] This emphasis represents the theological background of Ladd, rather than the missionary background of Kraft and Wagner. He interprets what they experienced in the context of theology, giving a biblical rationale for that with which they interacted. The themes of spiritual warfare is a key thought in Wimber's own theology of the kingdom, and the influences here appear to shine through.

Reflecting on the incarnation and Christ in relation to the kingdom of God, the focus shifts to those who practice the missionary work. Ladd connects the coming of the kingdom not with its reception by people, but clearly with the incarnation.[118] In this sense the kingdom of God is a greater application than just the Church; it speaks of the wider salvific theology of the incarnation. It must be, however, rooted in the human as the Church receives and witnesses to the kingdom. Whether the division can be maintained is unclear, as to remove the human aspect of the kingdom may make it nothing more than esoteric ideal. The theory may be greater than the individual reception of it; however, it seems to require a rooting in personal experience. As Ladd notes, the Church's role is to witness to the kingdom.[119] This is why Wright sees the Church as a counterculutral group that changes its culture, becoming itself a center of cultural change.[120] As shall be considered, this appears to be similar to Wimber's emphasis that the Church acts as an agent of the kingdom of God, and brings that kingdom's power into situations to effect change. It also has cross-currents with the challenge that the doctrine of the kingdom of God has upon Western culture, in particular. James Kallas seems to disagree with the division between the members of the kingdom and the theology of the kingdom itself. It is the members of the Kingdom that are to do the works of the kingdom, "to bring it in." Their role is to announce the demise of Satan's kingdom and the triumph of Christ's. They bring in the kingdom through healing the sick, raising the dead, and casting out demons.[121] This seems to be a much closer connection between the kingdom of God and the members of that kingdom, who appear to have a fundamental role in the work of the kingdom. This also appears to side

---

116. Ladd, *Theology of the New Testament*, 64.
117. Ibid., 192.
118. Ibid., 102.
119. Ibid., 111.
120. Wright, *Practical Theology of Missions*, 247.
121. Kallas, *Real Satan*, 90.

more closely with Wimber's own view of participation in the kingdom of God. Practically, it would also offer a sense of belonging to and ownership of what is being done, that it is not some abstract idea that defines Christianity, but the members of the kingdom effecting the rule of the kingdom.

Wimber's View of the Kingdom

The theology of the kingdom underpins Wimber's theology of power evangelism. Nigel Scotland suggests that while Charismatic Christians have addressed a great degree of theological issues, the concept of the kingdom of God has been central.[122] Relating this to Wimber, Mark Stibbe suggests that the kingdom of God is the central theme of Wimber's theology.[123] Wright suggests that Wimber's understanding of the kingdom comes from two sources: George Eldon Ladd, whose influence has already been noted, and James Kallas.[124] We have seen that there was a degree of cross-pollination through the Fuller faculty, the missionary experiences that some of the faculty had, alongside a desire to move away from the dispensationalism and fundamentalism of the early twentieth century. For Wimber these two authors provided a new application for some of these missionary experiences to be applied within the context of the Western world.

For Wimber the kingdom of God was the means by which Jesus ruled over his willing subjects and the forces of evil in the world, reflecting the absolute rule that he exercised in heaven. In this sense Wimber sees Jesus as coming to earth to reclaim the earth for God.[125] Here we see the beginning of the already/not yet tension in Wimber's theology, where the spiritual forces that controlled the world were being routed by the authority of the Son of God. We also see the beginning of the connection between the kingdom of God and spiritual warfare. Jesus exercised this authority by power manifestations of his authority in healing the sick, casting out demons and raising the dead, to demonstrate that the kingdom had come.[126] There seems to be a disparity in Wimber's own thinking on this matter. While he explicitly states that the kingdom had come through the work and ministry of Jesus, he states elsewhere that the purpose of the miracles was not to show that

---

122. Scotland, "From the 'not yet,'" 275.
123. Gunstone, *Meeting John Wimber*, 91.
124. Wright, "Profiles of Divine Healing," 273.
125. Wimber, *Kingdom Come*, 13.
126. Wimber and Springer, *Power Evangelism*, 30; Wimber and Springer, *Dynamics of Spiritual Growth*, 171.

the kingdom had come, but to point to the fact that the King had come.[127] Whether this is simply semantics, or whether there is a division in Wimber's thinking between King and kingdom, is unclear. Although it seems that the King and kingdom are closely tied to each other; nevertheless, he wants to distinguish between them. The question "Why?" needs to be asked. It could be that he wants to clearly divide the rule of Christ with any institution that may claim to be the vehicle of that rule, as we shall see in the debate concerning the connection of the Church and the kingdom. It may be that he sees a distinction between the rule of Christ and the actions of Christ, suggesting that the purpose of the actions of Christ are to integrate converts into the rule of Christ. It does, however, seem a strange distinction as without the King there would not be a kingdom; therefore, the action of the King demonstrates that the kingdom has come. Where he may be going is toward the time when the King would leave but the kingdom would continue, and it would be served by the Church. Yet, this may mitigate any continuance of miracles, as the King was no longer present.

The theology of the kingdom became one of the key defining characteristics of the new Vineyard movement. Berton Waggoner notes that the theology and practice of the kingdom is the main characteristic of the Vineyard.[128] The kingdom is the tension between that which is already present in the world, and what is yet to come when Christ returns.[129] The theology of the kingdom is intimately connected to the practice of miracles, healing, exorcism as well as social justice, through the presence of the Holy Spirit.[130] J. D. G. Dunn agrees with this assessment, and suggests that even during the earthly ministry of Christ the manifestation of the kingdom only happened because "the eschatological Spirit was present in and through him."[131] These statements seem to answer the division in Wimber's own writings about the King and the kingdom. The fact that the King is no longer physically present could tend toward a cessationist understanding of miracles. Yet, Waggoner draws the line between the presence of the Spirit and the practice of miracles. What seems to be becoming evident is the issue of praxis—that Wimber's theology of the kingdom is something that is to be done, not just believed. Morphew calls this "inaugurated eschatology" in which the coming kingdom is received and begins to affect the present world.[132]

127. Wimber, *Way In is the Way On*, 190.
128. Waggoner, "Theology & Practice."
129. Ibid.
130. Ibid.
131. Dunn, *Jesus and the Spirit*, 48–49.
132. Morphew, "Why is the Kingdom of God so Important?"

This would manifest in opposition to perceived spiritual forces that control the world, through the Church acting in spiritual warfare. While Wimber anticipated the return of the King, he did not postpone the coming of the kingdom until that event.

Wimber's inaugurated eschatology was not something that would have been shared with other Charismatics of the time. Nigel Scotland suggests that much of Charismatic-kingdom teaching was futuristic, when Christ would return for his Church at the end of the age. He suggests that Wimber's position came to the fore because the Church did not seem to be responding to the Charismatic Movement as much as had been anticipated.[133] Whether this is a correct assessment will be determined by one's pre-convictions on the issue of renewal. If it is a critical position, then certainly Scotland may have a point. If, however, it is a positive assessment of Charismatic Renewal then any hint at a possible experience could be deemed to be positive. Scotland further explains this in terms of a distancing from the Pentecostal Pioneers who reflected on the work of the Spirit. He states that what fuelled Wimber's theology was a desire to see how the power of Christ would move in people's lives in the present age. Such signs and wonders demonstrated that rule of Christ.[134] Whether Wimber's theological reflection can be traced to a disappointment amongst Charismatics, and perhaps even Pentecostals, to the extent of their theological impact cannot be absolutely confirmed. There may be some warrant in seeing the missionary influence on Wimber, through the faculty in Fuller, manifesting itself in dissatisfaction with the current state of the Western Church. What is worth noting, however, is that the Fuller faculty did not seem to entirely endorse the connection between the kingdom of God and miracles, signs, and wonders. Kraft believes that the normal principles of the kingdom are wider reaching than simply the area of spiritual power.[135] More explicitly, Ladd sees the coming of the kingdom coming quietly, unobtrusively and even secretly. He states:

> It can work among men and never be recognised by the crowds. In the spiritual realm, the Kingdom now offers to men the blessings of God's rule, delivering them from the power of Satan and sin. The Kingdom of God is an offer, a gift which may be

---

133. Scotland, "From the 'not yet,'" 275.

134. Scotland, "From the 'not yet,'" 283. Scotland further suggests that Wimber believed Church had disregarded the power of God because it could not handle it. Jack Deere agrees with the assessment, but adds that the absence is because the Church is not praying for miracles out of unbelief, which leads to a powerlessness. Deere, "Vineyard's Response to the Briefing," 8.

135. Kraft, *Christianity with Power*, 114.

accepted or rejected. The Kingdom is now here with persuasion rather than with power.[136]

This specific connection between a quiet coming of the kingdom and the power emphasized by Wimber is an issue. Those on whom he has drawn seem to point away from the very emphasis that Wimber espouses. This understanding of the kingdom may sit better with Eugene H. Peterson's view of subversive spirituality. It claims that success in ministry only comes because the people being ministered to do not grasp that Christ is working through the Church to transform their world through subverting its principles.[137] Whatever the reason for Ladd's caveat, the work of the kingdom seems constant between him and Wimber. They both look for the evidence of the kingdom coming in a significant way in the world. One looks for quiet ways, the other for dramatic evidences.

The Kingdom is Living between the Ages

Kingdom theology places Christian living and Church ministry between two events: the incarnation of Christ which inaugurated the King, and the return of Christ which consummates the kingdom. Kraft suggests that there is paradox in this theology.[138] It suggests that the coming age is already here, in some sense, because of Christ.[139] Wimber suggests that the Church exists between the inauguration and consummation of the kingdom of God.[140] This time Wimber calls an "interim period" in which the victory over Satan needs to be applied in people's lives, as Christ's authority is applied against the ongoing work of Satan.[141] Kallas suggests that this world was "seized by Satan" and God took action by sending Christ to take on this enemy. Throughout this time of warfare, between the incarnation and the coming again of Christ, humanity is caught in the middle.[142] It is this time of being caught in the middle, between the beginning of God's kingdom taking root in the world and the ending of all hostilities finally, that is living between the ages. It reflects on the fact that there may be certain promises for humanity and opportunities to experience God's power, but there may also be

---

136. Ladd, *Gospel of the Kingdom*, 55.
137. Peterson, *Contemplative Pastor*, 27–28.
138. Kraft, *Defeating Dark Angels*, 22.
139. Dunn, *Jesus and the Spirit*, 42.
140. Wimber, *Kingdom Come*, 14, 20.
141. Wimber and Springer, *Power Evangelism*, 57–58.
142. Kallas, *Real Satan*, 50.

times of disappointment because the power of God is not experienced as has been anticipated. Ladd sees that the kingdom of God is revealed in the world in different stages where individuals experience different degrees of its power.[143] This seems to suggest a dispensational understanding of God's relationship with humanity. In certain stages there are different levels of experiencing the reality of God's kingdom. Ladd points toward a present experience, but one that is filtered through the promise of the coming kingdom and the reality of the kingdom of Satan as being present in this age.

Dunn offers a distinctly charismatic understanding of living between the times. He suggests that Jesus' consciousness of the Holy Spirit because Christ's proclamation was more than simply the immanence of the future kingdom; it was the presence of the kingdom that was unique.[144] This connects the kingdom of God with the presence of the Spirit to perform works of power. It could also provide a theological rationale for associating the kingdom with power evangelism. Dunn's view appears to dovetail with that of Wimber in emphasizing the presence of the kingdom as a practical reality rather than an abstract theory. For the kingdom to be practiced in any of the practical applications there is a need to demonstrate its effect in praxis. This is what a Charismatic and Reformed ministry model attempts to accomplish. G. R. Beasley-Murray also draws the association between the kingdom and experiencing elements of its power. He roots the experience in the present experience of those who heard Christ as "the emancipating power of God" was at work amongst them. This also pointed toward the complete implementation of the kingdom in the future.[145] This comment could suggest that experiencing the future realty of the kingdom, in the present, was linked to Christ as the King being personally present. Craig L. Blomberg believes that this connection between kingdom and reign, between power not place, is correct.[146] It does not necessarily draw a line of connection between what Christ was said to have accomplished and a current experience of kingdom power. It would have to be further proved whether the current expression of kingdom power is to be expected without the physical presence of Christ. If Dunn's point is taken, then that problem may be resolved as the presence of the Spirit could be said to be present in the Church today. Blomberg suggests that any current experience of signs and wonders ought to be assessed through this concept of the kingdom.[147] He does not further

---

143. Ladd, *Gospel of the Kingdom*, 22–23.
144. Dunn, *Jesus and the Spirit*, 89.
145. Beasley-Murray, *Jesus and the Kingdom of God*, 80.
146. Blomberg, "Response to G. R. Beasley-Murray on the Kingdom," 31.
147. Ibid., 32.

elaborate on how that could be practiced. It could be done positively, where any manifestation of power is associated with the kingdom's presence. It could also be more critically applied, where any claim of kingdom power is judged according to theological criteria of what it may point toward. If this is the case, then an agreed theological statement on what constitutes a proper manifestation of the kingdom would have to be agreed.

Wimber's view emphasizes the victory of Christ on the cross, but it also recognizes that there are ongoing issues that people have to deal with which may cause them to question Christ's victory.[148] Reflecting on the fact that sometimes the victory is more evident than other times, Wimber notes the intermittent nature of the kingdom of God. The key for the Church is to find out the will of God in a given situation and to co-operate with it. This means that even if we die believing but not receiving, it contributes to God's purposes.[149] It seems that what Wimber is getting at here is that not everyone experiences the evidence of the power of the kingdom. This may lead to a rejection that the kingdom is present at all, or a view that the kingdom has not overturned the kingdom of Satan. This is why Wimber emphasizes that there are two kingdoms that everyone lives under—the kingdom of Satan and the kingdom of God.[150] The interplay between these two kingdoms seems to be one of battle, where the kingdom of God fights against the kingdom of Satan. The battle lines are drawn by followers of both kingdoms who fight over humanity in spiritual warfare. This balance of living between what Wimber calls this "present evil age," with the experience of the life of the age to come, appears to be contradictory. How he gets around that contradiction is to say that the age to come is present, only partially, and will be completed only when Christ returns.[151] He attributes this understanding to Ladd, and argues that it gives a rationale why physical healing is not always experienced immediately.[152] Ladd comments that the age to come is a distinct contrast to the present age because, in the age to come, sin and wickedness will be destroyed.[153] This tension reminds people that there may be difficulties living in this present age. However, there is a hope for complete deliverance for the age to come. The issue remains over

---

148. Kraft, *Christianity with Power*, 109: "Jesus believed in two kingdoms, the kingdom of God and the kingdom of Satan. As he makes plain in Matthew 12:22-29, these kingdoms are at war with each other. Further, the Kingdom of God is now assured of victory because of Jesus' death and resurrection."

149. Wimber, *Way In is the Way On*, 153.

150. Wimber, *Kingdom Come*, 19.

151. Wimber, *Kingdom of God*, 33.

152. Wimber, *Kingdom Suffering*, 19-20.

153. Ladd, *Gospel of the Kingdom*, 34.

the extent to which the experiences of the age to come can be expected to be lived in the present age.

Although he argues for a partiality in the experience of the age to come, Wimber does not allow for that partiality regarding our own identities. He argues against "two mes," one that is of the present age and one that is of the age to come. Christians are entirely of the age to come, and the present age only takes root when there is neglect of their spiritual identity.[154] This could place the emphasis for illness, psychological problems and lack of spiritual power directly into the hands of the Church. While this may offer a solution for the present discouraging situation, which Scotland mentioned previously, it could be said to underestimate the sovereignty of the kingdom of God and the King. If, as Wimber has argued, the kingdom is primarily about the King, then the question over the power of the King is raised. Wimber seems to place this responsibility in the hands of the Church, whose role it is to demonstrate and display the kingdom of God.[155] This raises the same issue as the extent to which the kingdom comes in this present age. It seems to place a significant pressure on the Church to perform the works of the kingdom. Yet, if the kingdom is coming only partially, as Wimber suggests, is it wrong to judge the Church for not experiencing the manifestations of the kingdom in a dynamic manner? D. A. Carson suggests that these debates can lead to errors in understanding the kingdom, when the emphasis on present or future is unclear.[156] Whether there are errors will be determined by the theological criteria used to judge the kingdom's claims in the present, as noted previously. It may be better to call them distinctions in emphasis, some centering on the present experience of the kingdom, others on the future. This would mean that an emphasis on the present may have to engage with why certain power claims are not experienced, and an emphasis on the future may have to engage pastorally with those who have been disappointed in their kingdom expectation.

Wimber states that if we do not experience kingdom power in every situation, it is not because there is something wrong with our faith.[157] Whether that can be justified or not, the issue remains that if there is a promise of kingdom power, but it does not materialize, who should bear the burden of that question? Ladd states that there is a requirement for "perfect trust" in the present to experience the future realm of the kingdom.[158] He also states

154. Wimber and Springer, *Power Healing*, 87.
155. Wimber, *Kingdom of God*, 15.
156. Carson, "Common Errors."
157. Wimber, *Kingdom Suffering*, 19–20.
158. Ladd, *Gospel of the Kingdom*, 21.

that the blessings of the kingdom "are now available to those who embrace the Kingdom of God."[159] It seems that this issue remains unresolved within Wimber. Ladd could be taken to mean that the emphasis is placed upon the degree to which individuals interact with the kingdom. Whether, in the heat of practical need, individuals will perform a theological juggling act to try to understand why they are not experiencing the power of the kingdom, remains to be seen. Ladd seems to suggest that a focus on the coming of Christ to inaugurate the age to come may be a possible focus for individuals to reflect upon, anticipating a time when God's rule is unchallenged.[160] Until that time there would be a backlash from Satan's kingdom aimed at the people of God; however, God would protect from the coming judgment on the kingdom of Satan.[161] This may provide a possible source of comfort at a time of difficulty. However, it does not resolve the issue that people may be expecting a powerful manifestation that does not arrive. Wimber's motives may have been pure in his desire to encourage the Church in the praxis of kingdom life, rather than offering a rationale why the manifestations of kingdom life may not be seen. Yet, the issue of blame for continuing need does not appear to be categorically resolved.

The Relationship between the Kingdom and the Church

The next area to consider is how the Church, made up of the members of the kingdom, relates to the kingdom of God itself. Some consider the relationship to be closer than others. Augustine of Hippo offers the classic relationship between the Church and the kingdom, stating that the Church currently is the kingdom of Christ and the kingdom of heaven.[162] Recent thinking seems to be moving away from this axiom, even within the Catholic tradition. *The Catechism of the Catholic Church* suggests a close relationship, that when Christ's word is welcomed the "seed" of the kingdom begins in people's lives.[163] This does not make a clear connection between Church and kingdom, but does seem to suggest that there is a tentative connection. It is this tentative connection that requires consideration as it deals with how the Church is to represent the kingdom in the world, and

---

159. Ibid., 50. He goes on to say that the primary experience of the life to come is eternal life, in which people belong to God and he to people, and fellowship is shared between them. Ladd, *Gospel of the Kingdom*, 72.

160. Ladd, *Theology of the New Testament*, 61–62.

161. Kallas, *Real Satan*, 51.

162. Augustine, *City of God*, 365.

163. *Catechism of the Catholic Church*, Part 1, para. 764, 219.

the connection between membership of the kingdom and ministry in the Church. Harper and Metzger note that the separation of any substantive connection between the kingdom of God and the Church was championed by dispensationalism, in protest at a liberal postmillennialism that sought to improve the world through social means.[164] It may be that what Wimber is working through, in the theological connection between the kingdom and the Church, is the dispensational history of American evangelicalism. He emphasizes the role that the Church is to play in witnessing to the kingdom, as we shall see, through proclamation and practice. It could perhaps be suggested that Wimber's theology represents a reformed (in the sense of changed, not the theological designation) dispensationalism that is characterized by an openness to the spiritual gifts.

Ladd reflects on this further, and explicitly states that the kingdom and the Church are not to be confused. The kingdom creates the Church and the Church participates in the proclamation of the kingdom, but it is not the kingdom.[165] Ladd even goes as far as saying that it is not helpful to categorize the Church as part of the kingdom, or that in the coming age the two will be synonymous.[166] It may be that what was being feared here was a connection between one specific denomination or expression of Church and the kingdom of God.[167] This could have meant that unless one is a member of that specific expression of Church, one is not a member of the kingdom either. It may also suggest that the distinctive of that expression of Church ought to be understood as the distinctive of the kingdom also, and that there may be no room for maneuvering. In reflecting upon the relationship between the kingdom and the Church in Wimber, we touch on what has been deemed to be a key area in the theological development of the Vineyard. John P. Schmidt argues that Wimber's close relationship between the two in praxis represented a shift in evangelical thinking. An emphasis on doing the works of Jesus today, because the kingdom was present, was a revolutionary message.[168] He further suggests that Wimber and Ladd agree in not connecting the Church with the kingdom, but that the kingdom gave birth to the Church; and the Church witnesses to and is an instrument of, and acts

---

164. Harper and Metzger, *Exploring Ecclesiology*, 55.

165. Ladd, *Gospel of the Kingdom*, 117.

166. Ladd, *Theology of the New Testament*, 110–11.

167. Wagner sees a necessity for a division between Church and kingdom because of the faults of genuine believers who battle their own sin nature, which may put people off the kingdom; and the inclusion of nominal members on Church rolls, which may make them think Church membership is related to kingdom membership. Wagner, *Church Growth and the Whole Gospel*, 9.

168. Schmidt, "New Wine from the Vineyard."

under the authority of the kingdom.[169] This connection between the Church and the kingdom appears to be one of action, in which the Church demonstrates the power of the kingdom, as Christ had done on earth.

Wimber makes the point that the Church is not the kingdom of God. He states that the Church is the community of the kingdom, and belongs to the kingdom; but, it is not the kingdom, it is a fellowship of people.[170] It is in this context that, Wimber argues, God exercises authority.[171] The reason for Wimber's concern about misunderstanding the relationship between the kingdom and the church are the practical implications. Wimber notes that if the kingdom and Church are seen to be the same, then it might make people assume that membership of the Church is also final salvation. It could also lead to an authoritarian leadership style, where leaders assume that they are speaking and acting with the authority of God.[172] These implications may be particularly relevant to a culture such as that of Northern Ireland, where there is a large Church-going percentage. Tearfund suggests that 45 percent of the population in Northern Ireland attend Church regularly, Scotland has 18 percent, England 14 percent and Wales 12 percent.[173] These statistics do not refer to how many people profess a personal faith, or those who have entered the kingdom of God. It tells of a general social trend amongst British people. When applying these principles to Northern Ireland, a clearer line of demarcation may be needed, regarding the kingdom of God, than those who attend a local congregation. This may be why Wimber suggests that the kingdom creates the Church. It is through the witness of the kingdom that individuals come into fellowship with the Church.[174] This may also be why Harper and Metzger refer to the Church as "the doorway to the kingdom."[175] In this sense, Wimber could be seen to be arguing for a causal relationship between the kingdom and the Church. It is through kingdom witness that people enter the kingdom, and having entered the kingdom they are committed to Church. Ladd also wants to emphasize the spiritual aspect of the Church. He argues that the kingdom of God works through the Church, which is itself a fellowship of those who have received kingdom life.[176] Kraft highlights the term "adoption" that through entering the

---

169. Ibid.
170. Wimber, *Kingdom of God*, 14.
171. Wimber, *Kingdom Fellowship*, 10.
172. Wimber and Springer, *Power Evangelism*, 34.
173. *Church Going in the UK*, vii.
174. Wimber, *Kingdom Fellowship*, 13; Wimber, *Kingdom of God*, 16.
175. Harper and Metzger, *Exploring Ecclesiology*, 60.
176. Ladd, *Gospel of the Kingdom*, 115–16.

kingdom individuals become adopted children of God.[177] There may be a critique here of Churches where there is a mixed membership, and because of that membership there is an assumption of spiritual membership also. This is an issue that Wimber takes up concerning Church fellowship and the kingdom, as shall be noted. To argue for a strong divergence between the kingdom and the Church may remind the Church of its own imperfection. E. Stanley Jones defines the Church not as imperfect but as relative to the kingdom, so it points people away from itself and to Christ.[178] This may also give an expectation of perfection yet to come when the kingdom comes in its entirety, when the kingdom is completely revealed without being blurred by any perceived human faults, and not using the Church to exercise spiritual warfare on the kingdom of Satan. That hope may sustain and strengthen the Church through opposition and even persecution.

The connection between the kingdom and the Church does manifest itself, however, in the witness of the Church. Wimber states that the Church witnesses to the kingdom through demonstrating and telling of God's actions.[179] This happens not only as the Church proclaims the message of the kingdom, but as it heals the sick, casts out demons and wages war on satanic strongholds.[180] The connection Wimber suggests between the kingdom and the Church is in how the Church displays the kingdom. The Church seeks to manifest the power of God as it witnesses to God. Ladd also highlights this connection to the actions of people, while maintaining that the kingdom is never subject to individuals, always remaining God's kingdom.[181] Yet, Ladd also connects this action with the keys of the future kingdom of heaven, which were said to be entrusted to Peter (Matt 16:19). This is the power to open or close access to the blessings of the kingdom.[182] There may appear to be some issue of discontinuity here. While the kingdom is said to be greater than one specific denomination or individual leader, the question of how individuals can close entrance to that kingdom is not explained further. Perhaps Ladd is alluding to spiritual warfare, in which the kingdom of God confronts the kingdom of Satan. This happens when the Church moves beyond exclusive proclamation to practicing the kingdom's power.[183] Perhaps Ladd and Wimber are both wanting to emphasize the role for the Church

---

177. Kraft, *Defeating Dark Angels*, 81.
178. Jones, *Unshakable Kingdom*, 35.
179. Wimber, *Kingdom Fellowship*, 16 and 20; Wimber, *Kingdom of God*, 14.
180. Wimber, *Kingdom Come*, 23.
181. Ladd, *Theology of the New Testament*, 102.
182. Ladd, *Gospel of the Kingdom*, 113.
183. Kallas, *Real Satan*, 90.

to play in this age. Perhaps they may also be reminding the Church of its necessity to participate in the role, ministering to individuals and confronting spiritual evil powers.

A further area in which Wimber sees a connection between the kingdom and Church is regarding fellowship. He suggests that individual congregations can be understood as "outposts of the kingdom," places where spiritual training, through prayer, Bible study, and spiritual disciplines prepare Christians for active service.[184] Underpinning this notion is an understanding of conversion that connects personal faith to a committed member of the Church, generally and locally.[185] It seems that for Wimber commitment to the kingdom was manifested in commitment to the Church. This seems also to portray Wimber's heart for the Church, something that he appears to have loved deeply. Don Williams writes that Wimber was not a loner; he was committed to community and a passionate Churchman.[186] Wimber is emphasizing the importance of local and personal fellowship in the Church. Ladd calls this fellowship "a bit of heaven on earth."[187] The fellowship of the Church reflects the belonging to the kingdom, and ultimately the fellowship that there will be when the kingdom comes in all of its fullness.

The Relationship between the Kingdom and Spiritual Warfare

The notion of direct confrontation with evil, demons, and Satan is implied by Wimber's theology. Such confrontation appears to have its foundation in the clashing of the kingdom of God and the kingdom of Satan.[188] In this, Wimber takes a literal view of the devil and evil spirits.[189] Wimber, rather than seeking to reinterpret the devil and evil spirits, applies the missionary theology of the kingdom of God for a praxis of confrontation. He seems to

184. Wimber and Springer, *Power Evangelism*, 40.
185. Wimber and Springer, *Dynamics of Spiritual Growth*, 182.
186. Williams, "Theological Perspective and Reflection," 183.
187. Ladd, *Gospel of the Kingdom*, p.23.
188. Wagner, *Church Growth*, 6.

189. This was not a uniformly accepted principle. Bultmann suggests that the knowledge of the universe that humanity currently has means: "we can no longer believe in spirits, whether good or evil." Bultmann, *Kerygma and Myth*, 4–5. Glenn sees Bultmann's view as having good intentions, to free Christianity from the «offensive mythical thought forms of the ancient world» to enable contemporary belief. Glenn suggests that this is a good intention. However, he argues that it confuses genuine offence and false offence, concluding that the Christian gospel carries a degree of offence implicitly. Glenn, «Rudolf Bultmann," 74, 81.

understand that the kingdom of God comes into conflict with the kingdom of Satan through the practice of deliverance ministry, miracles, signs, and wonders.

Wimber sought to build on his theology of the relationship between the Church and the kingdom regarding spiritual warfare. Scotland suggests a change in Wimber's theology of spiritual warfare, from an overemphasis in the early years, to a "more circumspect" theology.[190] The Church was the community of people that God sent to take the struggle of the kingdom against the evil in the kingdom of Satan.[191] As such, the Church becomes the instrument of the kingdom and an emphasis of discipleship comes to the fore. So, Wimber believes that to be used to confront spiritual evil requires a deep commitment to both the kingdom and the Church.[192] Wimber appears to be seeking to demonstrate the role that the Church has to play in relation to the kingdom of God. We have noted that he did not understand the Church and the kingdom to be interchangeable concepts, but he did suggest a causal relationship. The kingdom birthed the Church, and the Church initiates people into the kingdom. He now turns to consider spiritual warfare.

Wimber set the relationship between the kingdom of God and spiritual warfare within the context of the cross. He notes that at the moment of Christ's death the sun stopped shining and the Temple curtain was torn in two. This signaled that two kingdoms were in conflict, so that with the resurrection the victory of the kingdom of God was sealed.[193] Beasley-Murray describes the events of the cross as an opponent besting his adversary and exploiting the resultant victory.[194] Ladd agrees with this assessment, that the death of Christ destroyed the power of Satan. He concludes that while complete defeat is anticipated at the end of the age, the cross marked the initial defeat.[195] This would appear to place spiritual warfare in the context of the already/not yet tension that was considered earlier. The cross marked the beginning of the end, yet there was complete destruction of the enemies

---

190. Scotland, "From the 'not yet' to the 'now and not yet,'" 284.

191. Ladd, *Gospel of the Kingdom*, 121.

192. Wimber, *Kingdom of God*, 15.

193. Wimber and Springer, *Power Evangelism*, 57. The connection between the cross and eschatology is a difficult issue to resolve. Geerhardus Vos suggests that it cannot be seen entirely as eschatological, something to be anticipated, it must have a present application for Christian living. Vos, *Pauline Eschatology*, 58.

194. Beasley-Murray, *Jesus and the Kingdom of God*, 109.

195. Ladd, *Gospel of the Kingdom*, 46, 50. Ladd sees the conquest of God's kingdom over the kingdom of Satan as happening in three stages: First, the victory of the cross; second, the power to deliver people from demonic captivity; and, last, the final destruction of Satan's power.

of God yet to come. It is within that context that the Church acts as soldiers and agents of spiritual warfare. One issue that may be relevant here is the degree to which the cross affected the spiritual world. Keith A. Mathison states that in exorcism, Jesus destroys the kingdom of Satan.[196] This appears to be a very strong statement in which a greater power is released upon a lesser kingdom. Wimber and Ladd, however, seem to suggest that it is a partial effect. The work of implementing the kingdom, therefore, comes through the Church which wages spiritual warfare. Reid notes that this places a significant pressure on individual Christians to either succeed or fail in evangelism, which he suggests, is a works-based gospel.[197] This may be a valid comment, as the emphasis shifts from what Christ is said to have accomplished on the cross, to how the Church implements that victory. There may also be a degree of post- millennialism within this emphasis, where a gradual improvement of world conditions increase as Satan is bound.[198] There may also be an element of amillennialism in Wimber's theology. Kim Riddlebarger notes the amillennial expectation that forces of evil will continue to persecute the Church.[199] It may be that Wimber is attempting to distance himself from the premillennial emphasis of dispensationalism, and entering into a newly realized eschatology. This could be deemed to be a mix of different eschatological elements, the optimism of postmillennialism in expecting the kingdom of God to change things, and the realism of amillennialism in expecting opposition to the Church.

Spiritual warfare and the kingdom of God reflects upon the cross and the actions of Jesus. Wimber suggests that Jesus' ministry demonstrated the immanency of the kingdom, that it was not consigned to a future age. The physical demonstration took place when he confronted evil spirits, demons, healed the sick and raised the dead.[200] Jesus was seen as the invader, who came to consign Satan to the offensive, and then pass the baton on to the Church.[201] Mathison agrees, since the exorcisms performed by Jesus demonstrate that the kingdom of God is already present.[202] Dunn also agrees with this assessment—the exorcisms of Christ suggest that the

---

196. Mathison, *From Age to Age*, 391.
197. Reid, *Strategic Level Spiritual Warfare*, 23.
198. Mathison, *When Shall These Things Be?* 215–16.
199. Riddlebarger, *Case for Amillennialism*, 124.
200. Wimber and Springer, *Power Evangelism*, 32.
201. Ibid., 43; Kallas, *Real Satan*, 60.
202. Mathison, *From Age to Age*, 360, 386. He further states that exorcisms indicate the defeat of Satan and healings the reversal of his power.

kingdom of God has already come.[203] For Wimber, all the contemporary manifestations of spiritual warfare reflect upon the example that Jesus left. Yet, rather than one individual doing battle, the role has passed on to the Church (John 14:12). It is this direct confrontation and continual interaction between the kingdom of God and the kingdom of Satan that sums up Wimber's understanding of spiritual warfare.[204] Wimber's view appears to move the Church toward active participation in the kingdom of God. This is seen specifically in a spiritual manner, through confronting the evil in the world that manifests itself in many different ways. While he does not exclude social battles, Wimber interprets them in a spiritual manner. He argues that to counteract the social evils in the world, the Church must target those who are the perpetrators of those evils, turning them around into servants of the kingdom of God in their various positions.[205] This seems to be different from later reflections on spiritual warfare in which individuals were encouraged to "actively confront" the greater principalities and powers that control the world.[206] Scotland suggests that this was not Wimber's theology, and in it he rejected any sort of dualistic theology.[207] There may be a difference here between the theology of Wimber, which Wagner defines as ground level spiritual warfare, and the strategic level spiritual warfare that other authors suggest. Wagner comments that some critics believe that in engaging in strategic level spiritual warfare people are overstepping their authority.[208] Wimber may well have been one such critic. His emphasis highlights that the spiritual battle is fought in individual lives, as people are won to the kingdom. It also highlights that the means to effecting global change is through individuals. This appears to be different from the model suggested by Kraft, who seems to propose a wider warfare model. What appears to be significant is that he does not encourage individual Christians to take on the spiritual forces that control or inspire the individual acts of the kingdom of Satan. It could be argued that he considers this to have already

---

203. Dunn, *Jesus and the Spirit*, 47.

204. Wimber, *Kingdom of God*, 17.

205. Wimber and Springer, *Dynamics of Spiritual Growth*, 196.

206. Wagner, *Dominion*, 126; Kraft, *Defeating Dark Angels*, 19. Along with territorial spirits, Kraft sites a number of personal issues which he believes are caused by the demonic: social organizations and groups, homosexuality, drug addiction, lust, incest, rape, and murder.

207. Scotland, "From the 'not yet' to the 'now and not yet,'" 284.

208. Wagner, *Spiritual Warfare Strategy*, 22–23. Ground level spiritual warfare includes "casting demons out of people . . . Occult-level spiritual warfare deals with demonic forces released through activities related to satanism, witchcraft, Freemasonry, Eastern religions, New Age, shamanism, astrology, and many other forms of structured occultism."

been accomplished by the cross. The work is now a struggle to implement that victory personally.

In spiritual warfare the kingdom of God confronts the kingdom of Satan. Wimber believes that it is important to understand who we are fighting. Wimber outlines the various designations that Satan has, underlining the fact that the kingdom of Satan was Christ's real enemy, and the final victory is assured.[209] The role of this enemy is seen in the actions which he takes; Kallas suggests calling him "the prosecuting attorney," arguing that Satan's role is also to serve God by seeking out the guilty and trying them.[210] This does not seem to sit with Wimber's teaching on spiritual warfare because why would Jesus and the Church, in fighting for the kingdom of God, take on a fellow servant of God? It also seems to contradict what Wimber understands to be the primary goal of the enemy, which is the denial of final salvation.[211] It may be that Kallas is influenced by his own understanding of monotheism, which he takes to mean one supreme God, reigning over all other lesser gods and spiritual beings, such as angels and even demons. In ruling over these spiritual powers, God exercises indirect authority by delegating to them certain functions.[212] Whether this is the incipient monolatry that Michael S. Heiser speaks of as being present in the Old Testament is unclear.[213] Kallas is not specifically calling demons and evil spirits gods, but he is suggesting that their authority may be a delegated from one God. Kallas further notes that Jesus came to bind the strongman because he is stronger than Satan.[214] Again, this seems hard to reconcile with the thought that Satan carries out God's will. May it not fall into the category of a house divided against itself (Matt 12:25–28; Mark 3:23–25)? It may be that what Kallas is attempting to do is demonstrate the spiritual power and authority of these evil spirits, and the real work of spiritual warfare. Suggesting a divine purpose for their actions could call into question the legitimacy of spiritual warfare.

Wimber anchors spiritual warfare in the actions of the Church performing signs and wonders. He states that the number of Christians

---

209. Wimber and Springer, *Power Evangelism*, 39. He notes: Destroyed, Deceiver, Liar—the Butcher of the World.

210. Kallas, *Real Satan*, 23.

211. Wimber and Springer, *Power Evangelism*, 44.

212. Kallas, *The Real Satan*, 17. "Counterpoised to this group of angels whose task it was to express the love or protection of God, there was another group whose task it was to express the wrath or displeasure of God. These were the once charged with raining disaster on the face of the earth, causing woe and havoc." Kallas, *Real Satan*, 21.

213. Heiser, "Monotheism, Polytheism, Monolatry, or Henotheism?" 28.

214. Kallas, *Real Satan*, 13.

practicing power evangelism determines the extension of the kingdom of God.[215] Wimber describes practitioners of power evangelism as "self-conscious members of God's army."[216] This army encompasses an all-of-life theology in which, Wimber notes, there are no "demilitarized" zones.[217] He likens this experience to the difference between a navy vessel and a cruise liner, the former is for active service, the latter is for enjoyment and recreation.[218] There seems to be an emphasis away from observation, toward participation in kingdom life through the Church. This is an area that will be considered in chapter 6. Wimber wants every member to be active and participating in spiritual warfare to some degree or another. This may be because, as Kraft states, engagement with the kingdom of Satan happens so often that it cannot be ignored.[219] Wimber's emphasis on praxis seems to come through here again, so that no Christian will be caught unaware of the battle in which they are involved or by the attacks of the kingdom of Satan. Wimber wants Christians to be aware of the counter-attack of the enemy, and the fact that the Church can attack back.[220] Wimber connects this counter-attack specifically with power evangelism, where the greater power of the kingdom of God is demonstrated against the lesser power of the kingdom of Satan. Erwin van der Meer sees the issue of spiritual warfare as the key concept in power evangelism.[221] Wimber's understanding that God confirms the gospel with miracles could be said, therefore, to equip the Church to serve the kingdom of God. It does raise the question of those who do not practice power evangelism, whether they will be effective in spiritual warfare at all? It may be that Wimber is emphasising this point to support the significance of his own theological position and, perhaps, even the superiority of his own theological position. If, however, there are some genuine concerns and disagreements with power evangelism, Wimber's view could be taken to imply either a disinterest in spiritual warfare, a lack of commitment to the kingdom of God, or a desire to have an easier life than fighting in God's army.

How the kingdom of God is to exercise spiritual warfare through the Church is also covered by Wimber. He argues for a need to be prepared and equipped to fight because there is no place for the assumption that the

---

215. Wimber and Springer, *Power Evangelism*, 201.
216. Wimber, *Kingdom of God*, 23. Wimber and Springer, *Power Evangelism*, 144.
217. Wimber, *Kingdom of God*, 23.
218. Wimber and Springer, *Power Evangelism*, 38.
219. Kraft, *Defeating Dark Angels*, 18.
220. Wimber, *Kingdom of God*, 20.
221. van der Meer, "Strategic Level Spiritual Warfare," 79–80.

enemy's power is broken.[222] He suggests a twofold approach to preaching the gospel and then demonstrating the power of the kingdom through signs and wonders.[223] It is this two-pronged approach that is definitive of Wimber's theology, and something that shall be considered further in chapter 4. The association of proclamation and presence may also fit well with the proclamation model of discipleship as outlined in chapter 5. Ladd believes that the importance of proclamation is because the primary manifestation of the kingdom of Satan is seen in a religious context, as blindness to the gospel. This is because Satan's main aim is to keep people away from the gospel.[224] For this reason, Ladd argues that the gospel that is to be preached is the gospel of the kingdom of God, announcing the fact that the kingdom has come near, and that God has taken action in Jesus to bring deliverance.[225] It is not, however, proclamation alone that is spiritual warfare; it is proclamation accompanied by demonstration of the kingdom of God's power.[226] Wimber can appear to be quite critical of the Western, materialistic and scientific mindset, as shall be considered, and this may be a manifestation of the criticism. The argument seems to be that something more than intellectual assent is needed in presenting the gospel of the kingdom, so something more than simply telling the story is required. What is needed appears to be a demonstration that the power of the kingdom is superior to all other powers. This builds on the ideas discussed previously that there is the already/not yet tension in the kingdom of God, and that there is ongoing work to implement the victory Christ wrought on the cross. Yet, it raises the question of whether the message of the cross is enough to deliver people from Satan's kingdom? It may also be considered to be unnecessarily loaded toward the power of Satan's kingdom and the manner in which human beings are enslaved by that kingdom. Gustaf Aulén notes that Satan has no rights to humanity, but that because of justice there is a need for him to be driven out and defeated.[227] Whatever the position held on this matter, the view of Wimber suggests that there is a power in the kingdom of God.

One aspect of spiritual warfare highlighted by Wimber is the issue of a healing ministry. He argues that Jesus understood the source of sickness as being evil, coming from the kingdom of Satan, and that it manifests itself

222. Wimber and Springer, *Power Evangelism*, 58; Kraft, *Defeating Dark Angels*, 22.
223. Wimber, *Way In is the Way On*, 76.
224. Ladd, *Gospel of the Kingdom*, 31.
225. Ibid., 47.
226. Ladd, *Theology of the New Testament*, 114.
227. Aulén, *Christus Victor*, 27–28, 56. He further defines the death of Christ as have a "double-sidedness," being offered to God but also liberating humanity from Satan.

through the deepest sickness of sin, physical sickness and poverty. There is, however, no guarantee of immediate healing in the moment, but there is a hope of complete healing when Christ returns, along with all aspects of suffering.[228] This association of sickness with evil could make some sick people feel as if the cause of their illness is sin. Yet, Wimber is careful to point out that although no one prays for sickness, there is an understanding that God works through sicknesses to accomplish a kingdom purpose. There is, however, no need to passively accept sickness; rather, there is a promise of kingdom power for healing.[229] An apparent difficulty with this is discerning when sickness is a clear manifestation of the kingdom of Satan, and requires spiritual warfare to be exercised upon it, or when God is using it for some purpose. There appears to be no solution to this conundrum. Instead, there is an emphasis on the sickness of the soul, which is understood to be a manifestation of Satan's power, for Wimber claims every aspect of human life is under that power.[230] Wimber's view of healing has been criticized by some. Philip Selden has considered healing in the light of spiritual warfare. He argues that a focus upon healing is a misdirection away from the real focus which ought to be on salvation, and in doing this there will not be any disappointments for those who expected healing but were not healed.[231] Robert Dickinson cites the example of Wimber's friend David Watson who, although prayed for, was not healed.[232] There could be many reasons why Wimber seems to be so positive about healing, ranging from personal enthusiasm to a deep pastoral concern for those in need. His view may be the "unqualified optimism" that Ladd believes is dangerous to have.[233] It may also be a question of emphasis, and sickness seemed to be the most evident manifestation of the kingdom of Satan with which Wimber was confronted. It may also be an issue of perspective: those who emphasize the salvation of individual converts against those who emphasize the demonstration of miracles as signs of the kingdom.

One area in which Wimber emphasizes spiritual warfare is personally, where Christians fight against their own fallen, sinful nature. He attributes this to the enemy exciting our "fifth column," in opposition to the life of faith that God has given us, the power to work through and resist temptation.[234]

228. Wimber and Springer, *Power Healing*, 35.
229. Ibid., 36–37.
230. Ibid., 56.
231. Selden, "Spiritual Warfare V," 34.
232. Dickinson, *God Does Heal Today*, 130.
233. Ladd, *Gospel of the Kingdom*, 137.
234. Wimber and Springer, *Power Evangelism*, 39.

While not absolving human responsibility in giving into temptation, Wimber does allow for a more direct category in which demonic and satanic influence leads Christians into sin.[235] Wagner suggests that the reason for these personal attacks is because of the rapidly advancing kingdom of God in the world.[236] While this may dovetail with previous discussion concerning spiritual warfare, it is also dependent upon perspective. We have already noted that Scotland sensed a degree of disappointment, amongst Charismatics, at the perceived impact the kingdom of God appeared to be having.[237] It may be that Wagner is being unnecessarily triumphalist in his understanding of spiritual warfare, for many of the possible reasons Wimber may have had about healing. There may also be an issue of how the success of the kingdom of God could be interpreted. Would it be how many healings have taken place, how many new converts, how many new churches started, or even how many Christians have been elected to political office? This is one of the reasons why I have chosen to limit my research to theological reflection, precisely because these criteria are incredibly difficult to discern, and disproving them may have an effect on people's faith. As an insider in this research, this is a serious issue because my own pastoral heart and responsibilities to my local congregation are paramount to a successful application of the principles contained in this research. Wimber's position may raise the issue of the demonization of Christians. He writes that Christians can be affected and controlled by evil spirits, especially if they live in unconfessed and serious sin. Christians have been delivered from the power of demons but can still be affected by them.[238] Wayne Grudem suggests that the problem may have to do with the terminology, "possession" speaking of an overwhelming of an individual; therefore, any discussion of demonization carries with it that same status. He argues for degrees of demonization, ranging from opposition to almost complete control; therefore, the question is one of the degree to which a Christian can be controlled by a demon?[239] The issue then becomes one of where the line is set. If it is too high it could make a Christian who is coming under a severe spiritual threat feel that the cause is demonic, or that every source of opposition is

---

235. Wimber and Springer, *Power Healing*, 120; Wimber and Springer, *Power Evangelism*, 167: "Satan's methods of attack vary: people are tempted or inflicted with physical and emotional hurt, their lives are threatened or they are possessed by demons. Demons exert various degrees of influence over people. In some cases, such as demonic possession, they gain a high degree of control over the human will."

236. Wagner, *Spiritual Warfare Strategy*, 45.

237. Scotland, "From the 'not yet' to the 'now and not yet,'" 275.

238. Wimber and Springer, *Power Healing*, 120.

239. Grudem, *Systematic Theology*, 423–25.

demonic. This could lead to Christians being too focused on the demonic. Perhaps this is why Stephen Hunt notes that many Churches are warning caution on such issues.[240] This again brings to mind the missionary context of the Fuller faculty to which Wimber was exposed. It also raises an issue of a too-focused concern with things evil and demonic. This may be why Dickinson believes Christians are not called upon to exorcise demons, but to stand against them in God's armor.[241] There is an emphasis on spiritual warfare within Wimber's theology of the kingdom, and it may be that the concern expressed in some circles at this emphasis is because it has not been emphasized before.

The Future Coming of the Kingdom

The last aspect of Wimber's theology of the kingdom I want to consider is the expectation that the kingdom will come, in all of its fullness, at a future time. Wimber roots this expectation in the manifestation of the Kingdom's power, as miracles, deliverance, exorcism and healing all point to the coming of the kingdom of God and an end for ever to the kingdom of Satan.[242] Wimber seems to consistently point to the fact that what is experienced now in the kingdom of God is only a shadow of what will come, but it does not undermine the fact that the kingdom of God is currently present.[243] This theme of expectation is also evident in Ladd's writings. He agrees with Wimber that the kingdom is already present and, as we have seen, he also anticipates the coming return of Christ. This event, of the "personal, glorious, victorious Coming of Christ," will fully realize the kingdom of God.[244] Then there will be no more causes of sickness or illness, because human bodies will be transformed.[245] Despite these promises, Ladd argues that considering the current spiritual battle that the kingdom of God is involved in with the kingdom of darkness, there is an eschatological hope of Christ's return.[246] Neither Wimber nor Ladd describe in any detail the specific events that will lead to the return of Christ. Instead they frame it in a general

---

240. Hunt, "Managing the Demonic," 215.

241. Dickinson, *God Does Heal Today*, 265–66. He notes that there is only reference to the apostles driving out a demon (Acts 16:18), and other New Testament references do not refer to demonic possession (1 Cor 10:20; Jas 2:19; Rev 9:20).

242. Wimber and Springer, *Power Evangelism*, 162–63.

243. Wimber, *Kingdom of God*, 29.

244. Ladd, *Gospel of the Kingdom*, 39.

245. Ibid., 69.

246. Ladd, *Theology of the New Testament*, 407.

picture of ongoing spiritual battle, as the Church fights for the kingdom of God and the kingdom of Satan reacts.

It has been noted before that there may be elements of both amillennialism and postmillennialism in Wimber, which may suggest he is continuing to drift from the fundamentalist dispensationalism of the early twentieth century. It could be argued that the implications of Wimber's theology of the kingdom of God leads to a postmillennialism, in which the Church goes through tribulation, is battered and attacked by the kingdom of Satan, but eventually triumphs.[247] Whether he specifically intended this, or whether he came to it by the logical outworking of his theology, is unclear. There appear to be points of commonality between Wimber's view and postmillennialism regarding the inauguration of Christ's kingdom already having happened, and that the kingdom is not just limited to people's hearts but has a global application.[248] These principles seem to sum up Wimber's understanding of the kingdom of God and the expectation of what will happen as that kingdom grows and battles the kingdom of Satan. The expectation of Wimber in the coming of Christ also appears to dovetail with postmillennialism. Loraine Boettner notes that the postmillennial expectation was that the present kingdom would be surrendered to the Trinity, and a perfected kingdom instituted.[249] It is asserted by Christopher Catherwood that Wimber moved his theological position on eschatology from premillennialism to postmillennialism.[250] Nigel Wright also tried to trace the influence of postmillennialism in the Restorationist Church in the UK, of which Wimber was one of its influences. While he does not specifically state that Wimber was a postmillennialist, he contends that Wimber's theology sat well with those who were.[251] J. Battle also draws the connection between the spiritual warfare practitioners and postmillennialism.[252] Wimber's expectation of the coming kingdom was that the kingdom, which was already here, would continue to effect change in the world, through spiritual warfare waged by the Church, and would end in fulfillment at Christ's return. This may be said to give an excuse why the promise of miracles is not uniformly experienced today, pointing people to a fuller experience when the kingdom comes entirely. This may be seen as both positive and negative: positive by encouraging hope, but negative in not practically alleviating present suffering. It could

---

247. Hosier, *End Times*, 33.
248. Mathison, *Postmillennialism*, 178–80.
249. Boettner, *Millennium*, 286.
250. Catherwood, *Evangelicals*, 110.
251. Wright, "Restorationism," 7.
252. Battle, "Spiritual Warfare in Revelation," 14.

also positively and negatively affect the work of the Church: positively, in pointing to a moment when things will improve so their work will be complete; negatively, in reminding them that there may be things which cannot be overcome until the kingdom comes completely.

A Critique of Western Culture and the Western Church

We noted previously that Kraft was a supporter of Wimber's course at Fuller because he understood it to be non-western.[253] Kraft dealt with the issue of cultural superiority, which he believed began from the Jewish belief that their culture is right and continues through the imposition of one culture upon another.[254] This theme of questioning the Western interpretation of Christianity appears to have fuelled Wimber in his thinking of the coming of the kingdom. Wagner points out that both he and Kraft understand the issues that preoccupy Western Christians as being, essentially, irrelevant to a missionary context. It is for this reason that their views on culture, demonology, and healing are critiqued less by third-world Christians than those in the West.[255] This is a serious challenge to the Western Church concerning how we filter new theological ideas into our ecclesiastical praxis. There has been a tendency amongst some Reformed writers to view new ideas with a degree of suspicion. Charles Hodge, commenting on theological method, notes that all doctrine must be consistent with the truth, and the truth must be authenticated by Scripture. He concludes that theology is not a revelation of new truth.[256] This has led to a suspicion of any new theological ideal that does not agree with what has already been believed. Kraft suggests that a cross-cultural witness leads to new theological invention.[257] He further explains that as the Church contextualizes the gospel, a new event happens in the history of the people.[258] While this does not suggest that new theological axioms may be discovered, it does suggest that as theology is applied to different contexts, new models of praxis may result. T. E. Jenkins suggests that Hodge was motivated by a disagreement with the modernists and liberals of his time, so he concluded that new beliefs are simply old

---

253. Marsden, *Reforming Fundamentalism*, 293.

254. Kraft, "Culture, Worldview and Contextualisation," 384. Kraft also writes of the myth of cultural superiority, in which one culture assumes its superiority over what is seen as a lesser culture. Kraft, *Christianity in Culture*, 51.

255. Wagner, *Spiritual Warfare Strategy*, 75.

256. Hodge, *Systematic Theology*, 1:15.

257. Kraft, *Christianity in Culture*, 16.

258. Ibid., 178.

heresies repackaged.[259] The position has also been challenged by Nancey Murphy, Stanley J. Grenz, John R. Franke, and Kevin J. Vanhoozer.[260] This may explain the reluctance to embrace new theological emphasizes within the evangelical tradition. Whether the views of Wimber would fall into the category of modernism and liberalism would depend upon one's own theological convictions. Whether Hodge would have considered Wimber's position as corresponding to the same challenges he faced in his day cannot be categorically defined either. I would suggest that Hodge represents the heart of one who, while not closed to new ideas per se, is concerned when new theologies are suggested that undermine his existing theological axioms. Rather than a cold criticism, it could be understood as a heartfelt response to maintain his view of the purity of the Christian faith.

Tom Wright identifies the remit of this designation as "the West," including North America, Europe and their colonial settlements. It also includes Australia and New Zealand, which are Eastern, but he identifies them as Western in culture. Wright juxtaposes this against the majority of the world's Christians, who live in Africa and South East Asia. Wright comments on this from a political basis—many Western governments do not try to implement Jesus' teaching, yet the rest of the world associates "the West" with Christianity.[261] Kraft suggests that there has been a syncretism within the Western Church that associates their way of life with the biblical way of life. This, he argues, is similar to the more overt syncretism in non-Western cultures that bring aspects of tribal religion into Christianity.[262] Wimber appears to have been influenced by this idea. This led him to suggest that the West has influenced the expectation of theological praxis within the Church. Wimber suggests that the Western Church has become a secular institution to such an extent that it is viewed as another social society seeking support.[263] This may be to do with the Western Church's worldview. Before Wimber's critique of the Western Church is considered, I want to look at his wider critique of Western society and culture.

Wimber suggests that the Western world is built upon a high view of the individual, but a correspondingly low view of community. While there is an understanding of corporate entities, it is not the notion of community that Wimber sees suggested in the Bible, where individual converts are

---

259. Jenkins, *Character of God*, 51.

260. Murphy, *Beyond Liberalism and Fundamentalism*, 42–43; Grenz, *Renewing the Center*, 71–73; Franke, *Character of Theology*, 88–89; Vanhoozer, "On the Very Idea."

261. Wright, *Simply Christian*, 12.

262. Kraft, "Culture, Worldview and Contextualisation," 390.

263. Wimber and Springer, *Power Evangelism*, 65.

joined together in Church, sharing their gifts for the common benefit.[264] This will be considered further when the contextual application of discipleship is discussed. Accompanying this individualism is a general skepticism about spiritual things. Wimber argues that this is in part due to the educational philosophy of the Western world, where everything is questioned and categorical answers are sought to spiritual claims.[265] Grudem suggests that Wimber teaches a shift from the Western worldview to a biblical worldview, which is open to the possibility of supernaturalism.[266][267] This position is supported by Kraft, who suggests that a scientific philosophy defines Western epistemology, believing it leads into absolute truth. This manifests itself in a cultural imperialism, assuming that God has placed the Western world in charge of the globe.[268][269] If this is the case, then it would assume that the cultures and educational criteria of the rest of the world is inferior to the way Western people view the world. Kraft believes that this worldview, of secular materialism and naturalism, has so penetrated even Christian institutions that it has made the supernatural even further away from the Western experience. He further argues that this does not take into account that over two-thirds of humanity have a different worldview.[270] Kraft lays the blame at Enlightenment thinking.[271][272] Any attempt, therefore, to institute a means of understanding the world spiritually, from a perspective which may be accepted in another culture, would need to change for what is perceived to be the more advanced culture. It would also challenge the

264. Wimber and Springer, *Dynamics of Spiritual Growth*, 163.

265. Ibid., 181.

266. Grudem, "Power Religion," 51: "But he has never taught that we should shift to an Eastern world view with its 'religious mysticism,' its 'anti-rationalism,' and its 'syncretism.'"

267. Rosemary Radford Ruether suggests that even biblical Christianity was affected by its culture, assimilating elements of it into early theology: the notion of community from Judaism, apocalyptic ideas from sectarian Judaism, mystical ideas from sectarian Judaism and the Greek religions, civil and imperial religion from Rome and nature religion from European paganism. Ruether, "Redemptive Community," 217.

268. Kraft, *Christianity with Power*, 13.

269. There may be some debate concerning whether Western culture is as influential as it is perceived to be, or that there is one, homogeneous Western culture at all. Huntington, "West, Not Universal," 28.

270. Wagner, *Third Wave of the Holy Spirit*, 76.

271. Kraft, *Christianity with Power*, 25.

272. Francis Schaeffer defines the enlightenment as a utopian dream about the primacy of reason, nature, happiness, progress and liberty. It was humanistic: "Here was man starting from himself absolutely." Any notion of God was deistic, asserting that while he may have created the universe, he had no contact with it. Schaeffer, *How Then Should we Live?* 148.

perception of advancement, as it represents the minority position. Warner draws a line of connection between the rationalists and fundamentalists regarding religious experience. Both are skeptical of spiritual experience, although allowing for them in biblical times, but wary of claiming them today. Accordingly, liberalism and fundamentalism dogmatically: "are equally indisposed to the possibility of contemporary divine self-revelation and miraculous intervention."[273] Again, we see a possible anti-fundamentalist dynamic at work within Wimber that argues for an experienced religion as well as a cerebral and historical religion. It is also interesting how two different views, with two different spiritual agendas, end up practically at the same conclusions. This may challenge cessationism with where it leads; namely, a secular, non-supernatural Christianity.

The question arises over whether Wimber's theology is seeking to simplify Western understanding and encourage a less developed worldview? There may be a sense in which the Western worldview does not believe it has been influenced by any other worldview, but has developed independently. Yet, one of the key characteristics of the Western worldview, according to Kraft, is the openness to change.[274] The issue of which perceived direction that change ought to lead determines whether that which is believed to be primitive will be accepted. Schaeffer notes that while the evidences of this world-view shift are manifest, it is the philosophy that undergirds the worldview that needs a Christian comment. The main challenge is the belief that humanity has only knowledge from itself.[275] Ironically, Schaeffer's view is believed to have given birth to the religious right in America and, while challenging a world-view, produced a new worldview in the process.[276] What this does show is that there was a degree of debate concerning the Western worldview: Wimber's from the position of spiritual experience, and Schaeffer's from the perspective of religious freedom and truth. Wimber's suggestion is that the Western world can learn from other cultures that may not have achieved the same level of educational, scientific or social attainment.

Wimber's critique of the Western Church is built upon this issue of world-view. He defines a worldview as the psychological reinforcement of how society functions in human terms. This manifests itself by one society assuming that their way of life, values and cultural norms are superior to all other cultures. Through this worldview a sense of safety is engendered whereby people feel that their principles fend off foreign principles that

273. Warner, *21st Century Church*, 247.
274. Kraft, *Christianity with Power*, 27–34.
275. Schaeffer, *Christian Manifesto*, 423.
276. Duriez, *Francis Schaeffer*, 191.

challenge their cultural norms, and bring a strong sense of belonging to that one community. Accordingly, a worldview interprets all new information and rejects any which may be contrary to the accepted worldview. There is, therefore, an opposition to and rejection of any new worldviews.[277] Wimber does concede that world-views are necessary for societies, and so the goal of the Church is to isolate those aspects of worldview that oppose and limit the effectiveness of the gospel, and exclude them from the Church's worldview.[278] Worldviews cannot be uniformly removed from every context because they undergird the culture, giving society a sense of legitimacy and providing them with a means of evaluating things within society.[279] When applied to the Church, it could be argued that there are denominational, theological, and even congregational worldviews.[280] What Wimber appears to be arguing against is a wider world-view than that of a given congregation, or even denomination. He is addressing the worldview of Western Christianity in general. This worldview is deemed to have influenced and shaped the theological principles and spiritual expectations of the Christian Church. Wimber appears to be arguing that the influences on the Western Church are contrary to biblical Christianity, and are from an alternative source. In this sense Wimber may be adopting a position of being a missionary to his own culture, which now appears to be at odds with his own religious assumptions.[281] It could be argued that Wimber's critique of the Western Church is an indirect form of reverse missions. Indirect, because it does not include missionaries from another culture coming to the West, but those who have gone from the West to other cultures and who have applied the principles they have learned.

Wimber suggests that there is a reluctance amongst Western Christians to practicing power evangelism, which leads to an ineffective ministry dealing with demonic oppression, illness and serious sins.[282] What appears

277. Wimber and Springer, *Power Evangelism*, 131–32.

278. Ibid., 131.

279. Ibid.

280. Douglass, *What is Your Church's Personality*, 4–8. He cites the philosophy of ministry as defining the congregation, influenced by the Church's personality, the community context and the theological convictions of the people. It is akin to a computer operating system, each different, but all useful.

281. British Missionary work is defined by Brian Stanley as propagating "the imagined benefits of Western society alongside the Christian message." Stanley, *Bible and the Flag*, 157. It may also be worth noting that, while Kraft in particular emphasizes the African culture as an alternative to the Western, there is debate surrounding the Africanizing of Christian music in Africa. Nketia, "Contribution of African Culture," 265–78.

282. Wimber and Springer, *Power Evangelism*, 82.

to underpin this reluctance is a mindset that omits the supernatural from evangelism and has no expectancy of God's power being seen.[283] Wimber suggests that it is not just a passive omission of the supernatural, but "a powerful bias against accepting supernatural phenomena as valid." For this reason the Western Church is not experiencing the revival of other parts of the world.[284] Again, the issue of perspective is significant here. How revival can be quantified will be different according to the different criteria laid down by each commentator. If the criterion is Church attendance, then Wimber may have a point. If the whole culture of the Church is opposed to power evangelism, then those who adhere to the minority position may feel marginalized. It may also be an issue to claim that only those who are open to the theological position are able to interpret and critique it properly.[285] This may lead to questioning of Wimber's view of the Western Church, for he represents a minority position within it, yet he claims that to reject his position is not to prioritize the best interests of the Church.

Wimber suggests that worldview determines theology. While some evangelicals claim their theology is based upon biblical exegesis, it is actually the Western worldview that formulates their doctrine. Wimber, therefore, argues that to become involved in signs and wonders a shift of worldview is needed, not just a theological shift.[286] The materialistic position, which denies contemporary signs and wonders, rules out anything supernatural, or seeing them as a thrilling experience and the end in themselves. This does not see the purpose of signs and wonders as demonstrating the kingdom of God.[287] Wimber suggests that this leads to a division of Christian living, some things being defined as natural and others as supernatural, and hence unrelated to everyday life. He contends that this contradicts the Bible's view of supernatural intervention in natural life.[288] While Wimber may have a point in worldview molding theology, there may still be a need for a theological conversion before adopting power evangelism. It could also be claimed that this view downgrades the genuine theological issues that cessationists have with Wimber's theology and practice. It may also assume that if cessationists were from an alternative culture, then they would not hold their view.

283. Ibid., 103–04.
284. Wimber and Springer, *Dynamics of Spiritual Growth*, 181
285. Lyons, "Fourth Wave," 175.
286. Wimber and Springer, *Power Evangelism*, 147.
287. Ibid., 151–52.
288. Ibid., 143.

Kraft agrees and argues that the Western Church's worldview is based upon a number of assumptions. First, that Christian influence is sufficient to thwart demonic influence; second, that demonization is obvious; and, third, because demonization is obvious it could only happen in other cultures.[289] This has led to what Kraft calls a spiritual blindness in which many Christians do not see their need for deliverance; instead, they lean upon counselors who aid them to live with their problems.[290] In the context of worship, Western Christians are asserted to listen to sermons to attain new knowledge, but experiencing a relationship with God is secondary.[291] This leads to what Wimber defines as an irrationality regarding healing. This is based upon a lack of positive models and experiences in the Western Church.[292] Warner suggests that, to counteract this, there is a need for distance between evangelicals and the Western worldview, begging the question of whether it is even possible.[293] To do this one suggestion may be that of Wimber—to associate the Western worldview as being under the dominion of Satan, and that Jesus came to change that.[294] This will lead the Western Church to re-evaluate the connection between the kingdom of God and the kingdom of Satan, along with their ongoing spiritual warfare. It is a restatement that the spiritual world is as real as the natural.[295] Wagner believes that this will be the hardest issue for the Western Church to comprehend.[296] Kraft sees it as addressing the issue of the disappointment of the non-Western Church with the theology that disconnects the power of God with the current Church. In this sense, he suggests that the Western worldview hinders Christianity in general.[297] There seem to be elements of a persecution feeling here, where those advocating a change of the Western worldview are reacting against the worldview. It seems as if the Western Church reflects the Western worldview as the context in which it ministers. It may, therefore, be easier to attribute the issues facing the Western Church to demons than to the people's inhumanity to one another. Wimber's view may also excessively emphasize the spiritual causes of problems, which could abdicate the responsibility of human beings.

289. Kraft, *Defeating Dark Angels*, 44.
290. Kraft, *Two Hours to Freedom*, 26.
291. Kraft, *Christianity with Power*, 43.
292. Wimber and Springer, *Power Healing*, 141.
293. Warner, *21st Century Church*, 245–46.
294. Wimber, *Way In is the Way On*, 151.
295. Wimber, *Kingdom of God*, 23.
296. Wagner, *Third Wave of the Holy Spirit*, 57.
297. Kraft and Kraft, "Communicating and Ministering," 346.

Partial Theological Conclusion

In addressing the influences on Wimber and his own doctrinal contribution, I have endeavored to highlight his standing as a theologian. It has been concluded that Wimber may well fit the definition of what a theologian is. This seems to be particularly true of an "ecclesiodemic" such as Wimber.[298] The theological context of dispensationalism and fundamentalism has also been discussed with relation to Wimber. Fuller Seminary's own position as a voice for new evangelicalism also appears to have contributed to Wimber's developing theology.[299] It also seems that while Wimber was not associated with fundamentalism, he had to cope with the same statements of judgement that fundamentalists issued against each other.[300] Wimber is careful to point out the evangelical nature of his theology.[301] Yet he seems to want to move people from knowledge to participation in theology.[302] This may suggest the theological worth of Wimber, and the influences that may have helped to shape his theological views.

The influence of Fuller Seminary on Wimber (where he taught from 1982–87) has also been discussed. It has been noted that the influence of Fuller led Wimber to reassess his views on the gifts of the Holy Spirit, and adopt a continualist position.[303] This influence appears to have come through George Eldon Ladd, Charles Kraft and C. Peter Wagner. In particular, it seems that Ladd's theology of the kingdom of God gave Wimber a framework for his own theology.[304] Regarding Kraft, there appears to have been a cross-pollination of theological influence. Wagner is specifically stated by Wimber as effecting a significant change in his theology of evangelism.[305] It was also Wagner who designated Wimber's theology as "third wave."[306] Fuller Seminary seems to be both the provider of theological influence on Wimber, as well as the receiver of his own theological influence.

---

298. Fabricius, "Ten Propositions on being a Theologian."

299. It is interesting that E.J. Carnell, President of Fuller Seminary, encouraged the faculty to drop the term because it had become misunderstood. Murray, *Evangelicalism Divided*, 20.

300. Jensen, "John Wimber Changes His Mind," 11.

301. Wimber, *Kingdom of God*, 27; Wimber and Springer, *Dynamics of Spiritual Growth*, 29.

302. Wimber and Springer, *Power Evangelism*, 108.

303. Jackson, *Quest for the Radical Middle*, 51 and 54.

304. Ibid., 55.

305. Wimber and Springer, *Power Evangelism*, 11.

306. Synan, *Century of the Holy Spirit*, 359.

One specific element of Fuller's influence on Wimber was the missionary context of some of the faculty. This influence is seen by Kraft's identification of Wimber's theology as non-Western.[307] It could be argued that Wimber was attempting to apply missionary innovations to his own Western context. This seems to have happened specifically through Wimber's theology of the kingdom, which appears to be the building block for his power evangelism.[308] It appears that Wimber takes the theology of kingdom power from a missionary context, and then applies it to his own context through power evangelism. While the influences of the Fuller faculty have been noted, on this one issue Wimber and Ladd diverge, as Ladd does not associate the kingdom of God with power.[309] It may, therefore, be that Wimber took elements of Fuller theology, the parts that supported his own presuppositions, and applied them to his own theology.

There were a number of aspects that Wimber's theology of the kingdom addressed as connected. One issue was that of living between the ages, which Wimber call the "interim period," where the authority and victory of Christ needs to be applied.[310] It was noted that Wimber's view reflected on the victory of the cross, but also the need for ongoing spiritual battle to deal with the enemies of God.[311] This appears to offer a rationale as to why people do not experience the power of God on every occasion, without laying the source of the blame at the feet of believers' faith. The issue of participation in the kingdom is also addressed in Wimber's understanding of the relationship between the Church and the kingdom. Wimber appears to be very clear in not connecting the Church with the kingdom for a number of practical reasons.[312] This is not to say that there is no connection, but that the Church is not the kingdom of God in the world today. Wimber sees a connection between the Church and the kingdom through fellowship, where believers grow in their faith.[313] For Wimber it seems that the Church is important to the kingdom, but that the kingdom has a greater influence and application than the Church.

Wimber sees the kingdom of God as acting through spiritual warfare. This was built upon the relationship he understood between the Church

---

307. Marsden, *Reforming Fundamentalism*, 293.

308. Scotland, "From the 'not yet,'" 275.

309. Ladd, *Gospel of the Kingdom*, 55.

310. Wimber and Springer, *Power Evangelism*, 57–58.

311. Kraft, *Christianity with Power*, 109.

312. Wimber, *Kingdom of God*, 14; Wimber and Springer, *Power Evangelism*, 34.

313. Wimber and Springer, *Power Evangelism*, 40.

and the kingdom.[314] Wimber emphasizes the role that the Church is to have in serving the kingdom, and the importance for Christians to play a role in that service. Wimber connected spiritual warfare to the victory that Christ won when he died on the cross and rose again.[315] In this context Jesus is seen as coming on the offensive, to do battle for the kingdom of God with the kingdom of Satan.[316] His view seems to be that the battle was waged in the individual, not with the higher spiritual forces.[317] Wimber seems to argue that spiritual warfare is exercised through believers performing signs and wonders.[318] This happens specifically through healing.[319] This has attempted to demonstrate that the kingdom of God is the underlying principle that defines the rest of Wimber's theology and praxis. Wimber also points to a coming time when the kingdom of God will come in all fullness, which appears to be a mix of amillennialism and postmillennialism.[320] There is an optimism in Wimber's theology of the coming kingdom that seems to dovetail with elements of each eschatological position.

Wimber also seeks to challenge the Western Church with his theology, particularly on its apparent widespread theology of cessationism. Wimber sees the Western world as built on a strong individualism, but a weak sense of community.[321] He argues that part of this comes from the educational philosophy that rules out supernaturalism.[322] This may again support the missionary influence on Wimber's theological development, and his seeking to apply missionary principles to the Western Church's context.

The Literature Review

I now want to consider the salient literature concerning the presence and work of the Holy Spirit within the Church. This forms, according to Swinton and Mowat, an important part of qualitative research.[323] The outline for the Literature Research follows a dedicated method in which, as Diana Ridley describes, the background of the academic debate is considered

314. Wimber, *Kingdom of God*, 15.
315. Wimber and Springer, *Power Evangelism*, 57.
316. Ibid., 43; Kallas, *Real Satan*, 60.
317. Wagner, *Spiritual Warfare Strategy*, 22–23.
318. Wimber, *Kingdom of God*, 23. Wimber and Springer, *Power Evangelism*, 144.
319. Wimber and Springer, *Power Healing*, 35.
320. Hosier, *End Times*, 33.
321. Wimber and Springer, *Dynamics of Spiritual Growth*, 163.
322. Ibid., 181.
323. Swinton and Mowatt, *Practical Theology*, 38.

in this chapter before any further discussion.[324] In this chapter I aim to consider the main texts of John Wimber, Charismatic pneumatology, Reformed pnuematology, confessional literature, Reformed and Charismatic Literature, and contemporary ecclesiology. This chapter further proposes to outline a field of study that considers the interaction between Reformed and Charismatic theology, and intends to highlight the feasibility of continued research into this area, specifically from the view of John Wimber.

The Main Texts: The Writings of John Wimber

John Wimber wrote widely, for a popular audience, on the connection between the kingdom of God and the manifestation of the power of the Spirit in authenticating the gospel preached. *Power Evangelism* is Wimber's book on the work and witness of the Church to the kingdom of God.[325] Wimber does not come across as being judgmental of those who are not practicing power evangelism. While the argument of the book may be ecumenical in spirit, in acknowledging the validity of other positions, it is not a theological treatise. This is a general issue with his writings; namely, their narrative nature. There is a tendency to develop theological points on the basis of experiences. The chapters often begin with an example and lead to theological reflection.[326] This could question the legitimacy of his reflection as it may appear he is molding his argument on these experiences, rather than judging them in reflection upon them. Wimber challenges the cessationist approach to the Bible, which rejects supernaturalism as being influenced more by Western culture than exegesis.[327] He issues a wider critique of the doctrine of *sola scriptura*.[328] There may also be a question over whether his

---

324. Ridley, *Literature Review*, 7.

325. Wimber and Springer, *Power Evangelism*, 33–34. The first section considers the roots of power evangelism that lives between the ascension and return of Jesus and offering foretastes of that coming kingdom. This flows into a second section on spiritual warfare, a third on active participation with the Holy Spirit, a fourth on divine appointments, a fifth on contemporary worldviews, and lastly on how Jesus operated in miracles.

326. Wimber begins the book with a reflection upon "Scott" who received the Spirit in 1967 (25), and Melinda who needed deliverance (51). Chapter 8 is also significant as he outlines the events that led to the first outpouring of the Holy Spirit in his Vineyard Fellowship, through a "young man," later known to be Lonnie Frisbee (61ff). His own ministry on a plane from Chicago (75); "Kerry James' divine appointment at a restaurant" (101); and why Asians view the West in a given way (129). It is only in sections 6 and 7 that there is a reflection on theological premise.

327. Wimber and Springer, *Power Evangelism*, 147, 151–52.

328. Nathan and Wilson, *Empowered Evangelicals*, 259. This view was taken by the

writings fulfill the criteria for theology.[329] This underlines Wimber's practical emphasis on theology, that he is looking to understand how things are actually done. The issue is whether it is better to define the principle and then apply to praxis, or examine the praxis and critique the principle. In one sense this book considers the praxis first, examining it in the light of theological rationale, and then bringing it to Wimber.

Power Healing is Wimber's understanding of the nature of healing and the causes of ill health, coming from his own experiences from personal reflection upon his family's health problems. *Practical Healing* is a workbook published on the areas outlined in *Power Healing*.[330] His argument is that Jesus healed because of compassion and mercy, but his emphasis was on healing the whole person, bodily and spiritually.[331] Wimber also considers the issue of Christians being possessed by demons.[332] This would be an area of concern for Reformed Christians, depending on the understanding of the term "possessed."[333] The anecdotal nature of this book challenges Reformed readers on the issue of the primacy of the Bible in theological formation, as Dickinson points out.[334] Wimber suggests that healing may be rejected because of the error of the practitioner, or apparent new age or occult associations.[335] What Wimber fails to do is to distinguish between cessation-

---

Reformers to challenge the Roman Catholic Church of their time concerning the basis for their authority. Rather than accepting the primacy of the bishops and Pope, the Reformers argued for a "return to the teaching of the early church. They insisted that Scripture was the sole source of revelation, that it was the final authoritative norm for doctrine and practice, that it was to be interpreted in and by the church, and that it was to be interpreted within the context of the rule of faith." Mathison, "Sola Scriptura," 41. He further suggests that this is built upon the ideas that the Bible is perfect, sufficient, inspired, infallible, authoritative and supremely normative. Gaffin and White suggest that this doctrine means also a rejection of "new revelations." Gaffin and White, "Eclipsing the Canon?" 133. This leads to a conviction that "God has spoken" suggesting that the Bible is all that is needed. See Johnson, *Case for Traditional Protestantism*, 20.

329. Charles Hodge notes that the Bible contains the truths which the theologians collect, interpret and systematize in relation to each other. It is unclear if Wimber fulfills these criteria. Hodge, *Systematic Theology*, 1:1–2.

330. Wimber and Springer, *Practical Healing*.

331. Wimber and Springer, *Power Healing*, 76.

332. Ibid., 129.

333. Grudem addresses this issue by questioning the meaning of the term "possessed." He argues that there is a wide variety of demonic attack that Christians can experience, even to the point of apparent control. Grudem, *Systematic Theology*, 423–25.

334. Robert Dickinson reiterates that the position of the Reformed Churches, and particularly PCI, is to reflect upon the teaching of the Bible as the "only infallible rule and faith and practice"; therefore, a biblical theology of healing would be essential. Dickinson, *God Does Heal Today*, 5.

335. Wimber and Springer, *Power Healing*, 26.

ism and opposition to healing ministry. He assumes that because certain streams are cessationist this is why they are opposed to healing ministry.[336] Dickinson believes that prayer for healing ought to be practiced, but not publicly.[337] In this sense Wimber's theology of healing is a broad approach and does not consider the varieties of opinion on the issue. It may be that he cannot understand the opposition to his practice, so he assumes that criticism is of his doctrine rather than his praxis.

The Kingdom of God is a book circulated by Vineyard on Wimber's understanding of the nature and work of the kingdom and how that manifests itself in miracles, signs, and wonders.[338] In this, he identifies power evangelism as "distinctly evangelical, unlike many of the renewal movement practices."[339] This book was not widely published outside of the Vineyard. While there are many similarities with the issues raised in *Power Evangelism* and *Power Healing*, it does not have the same narrative basis for the arguments. It has the feel of something published as sermon notes. There are few references and it appears to be primarily focused on biblical exegesis.

The purpose of *The Dynamics of Spiritual Growth* is twofold: to encourage believers in their discipleship, and to root them in the doctrines of historical, orthodox Christianity. This is a practical book that aims to aid people who want to become more Christlike in their daily lives.[340] He maintains that baptism in the Holy Spirit takes place at conversion, which would dovetail with the accepted Reformed teaching on the matter.[341] This book follows the same pattern as *Power Evangelism* in beginning with an experiential reflection and then extrapolating theological principles.[342] While this is a basic book of Christian belief, it seeks to deal with the main issues of the Christian faith, applying them to the daily Christian life. There is much that a Reformed believer could agree with in this work; however, it is built on the

---

336. Ibid., 31.

337. Dickinson, *Does God Heal Today?* 92.

338. Wimber, *Kingdom of God*.

339. Ibid., 27.

340. Wimber and Springer, *Dynamics of Spiritual Growth*. The same book was published in America as *Power Points*. Wimber also produced a study book along the same lines, Wimber and Springer, *Way to Maturity*, 55. The book is arranged into eight sections, each of which deals with an aspect of spiritual growth. While maintaining a high view of the Bible Wimber maintains that God communicates through dreams, visions and even prophetic utterances.

341. Wimber and Springer, *Dynamics of Spiritual Growth*, 139–40.

342. This is particularly evident in the section on hearing God's voice, where Wimber reflects on an experience in the Las Vegas desert and then looking for a rationale to understand that experience. Wimber and Springer, *Dynamics of Spiritual Growth*, 17–19.

assumption that there is a contemporary charismatic experience of the Holy Spirit. If this is questioned then the whole ethos of the book may be rejected.

Two books were completes as compendiums after his death: *The Way In is the Way On* and *Everyone Gets to Play*.[343] Many of the areas covered in these books are also covered in his other writings and, specifically, his series of booklets on the nature of the kingdom of God.[344] The first book covers areas of Christian living and ministry, but not the issues of miracles, signs and wonders. He challenges the notions of superiority in leadership, arguing for servanthood.[345] His exposition on the nature of grace would be concurrent with that of Reformed theology also.[346] Like much of Wimber's writings he begins with a recollection or story, moves to discuss the theology, and then to a conclusion.[347] In the second compilation, he deals with the lack of love in much contemporary Evangelicalism, a "show-it-to-me-in-the-Word" philosophy that he defines as Pharisaism.[348] There seems to be an anti-intellectual polemic in some of his statements, about training specifically, that seems contradictory to the position he once held as a seminary teacher.[349] He seems to be making the point that all Christians ought to have the opportunity to participate in the ecclesiastical function. Wimber's last three books outline the role of the Church in the world today and how the Church is to communicate with God through prayer, witness for Christ which will strengthen the work of the Holy Spirit, and to love and accept all

---

343. Wimber, *Way In is the Way On*; Wimber, *Everyone Gets to Play*.

344. Wimber, *Kingdom Mercy*; *Kingdom Ministry*; *Kingdom Living*; *Kingdom Suffering*; *Kingdom Come*; *Kingdom Fellowship*.

345. Wimber, *Way In is the Way On*, 32–34.

346. Ibid., 85.

347. This may cause difficulties for a Reformed Christian as Wimber appears to begin from experience and extrapolate theology to explain the experience. Boice writes: "True knowledge of God is also more than knowledge by experience." Boice, *Foundations of the Christian Faith*, 22. This is further explained by Packer who links knowing God to the Bible as the Holy Spirit applies it to human life. Packer, *Knowing God*, 32. This is a wider hermeneutical principle of how believers extrapolate knowledge. Frame notes that using the Bible is "the normative perspective" that enables an understanding to come from perspectives gained by experiences, which lead to a truth. Frame, *Doctrine of the Knowledge of God*, 192–93. Johnson believes that Reformed theology is essentially practical and not "irrelevant theological abstractions." It is his conviction that Reformed doctrine has practically affected his experience. Johnson, *When Grace Comes Home*, 16. The effects of that change provide the substance for the rest of the book. In this sense Wimber may be following a Reformed exegetical principle, perspectively considering doctrine in the light of experience.

348. Wimber, *Everyone Gets to Play*, 32.

349. Ibid., 47–48.

peoples.³⁵⁰ Although small books, they contain a challenge to the manner in which the Church practices discipleship and ministry today, which will aid our discussion in applying Wimber's principles contextually.

There have been some works written about John Wimber and the Vineyard. Jackson's *The Quest for the Radical Middle* details the history and development of Vineyard from the beginning to the early twentieth century.³⁵¹ While written by someone involved in the institution, the book is not a hagiography, as it was written without any approval from the Vineyard. This book aids research by giving a survey of the Vineyard Movement and Wimber's influence on it, demonstrating that Vineyard stands in the Evangelical tradition more than the Charismatic.

There are also a number of popular books reflecting on certain individuals' interaction with Wimber.³⁵² These publications appear to be anecdotal and, therefore, have a limited academic use, apart from giving a context to the ministry of Wimber. David Pytches has edited, what could be described as a *festschrift* to Wimber, in which various aspects of his theology and practice are evaluated by thinkers who knew him.³⁵³ These may be of a greater value in that there is a theological review of Wimber as well as reminiscences of interactions with him. John Goodwin has written on Wimber and classifies him and the Vineyard as stemming from the new age and occult traditions.³⁵⁴ These connections are tenuous at most and would need to be documented with more evidence than Goodwin supplies. *John Wimber: Friend or Foe?* gives a brief summary of the key doctrines of Wimber from an Australian Anglican Evangelical perspective. The context is an interview between Philip Jensen and representatives from Vineyard—John Wimber, Jack Deere, and Paul Cain—concerning the main axioms of their theology along with reports from the 1990 Spiritual Warfare conference in Sydney. The key issue is the validity of the reports of healing made by Wimber. Mention is made of significant medical complaints right down to normal, everyday issues.³⁵⁵ The challenges are medical, psychological, and theological. While the former two are beyond the bounds of this research, the theological critique is exceptionally helpful.

---

350. Wimber, *Prayer; Witnesses for a Powerful Christ.*

351. Jackson, *Quest for the Radical Middle*. For as history of the Vineyard after Wimber's death see Miller, "Routinizing Charisma."

352. Gunstone, *Meeting John Wimber.*

353. Pytches, *John Wimber*. Such personal reminiscences may enable an understanding of the experiences that molded Wimber as a theologian, his *sitz im liben*.

354. Goodwin, *Wimber the Gnostic.*

355. *John Wimber: Friend or Foe?*

Although Jensen's response to Wimber appears critical, Stephen Hunt believes the Anglican Church was reaching out to Wimber for renewal.[356] Hunt's emphasis is on English Anglicanism and does not consider the Reformed Churches in his critique, to its loss. David Gibb considers power evangelism regarding demonic deliverance and whether this ministry can be expected today. His conclusion is that Wimber represents something different from traditional Evangelicalism by not emphasizing the sovereignty of God.[357]

Wallace Benn and Mark Burkill, who believe that Wimber teaches a dualism of equality between God and the devil, highlight this theme.[358] If this is a valid comment, then there are significant areas that need to be resolved in order to marry Wimber with Reformed doctrine, not least the sovereignty of God.[359] *Signs, Wonders and Evangelicals* considers the impact of John Wimber and concludes that his ethos can revitalize the contemporary Church.[360] *Wonders and the Word* is a theological critique of Wimber that considers not only signs and wonders, but also the wider issue of emotions in religious experience.[361] Their conclusion is that while they have some theological questions about his beliefs and methods, he remains a Christian brother who is doing good deeds.[362] This demonstrates that there does not have to be agreement on every area of doctrine and practice, to appreciate the effect that people are having in gospel ministry.

There have also been a number of academic works concerning the theology and practice of John Wimber and the Vineyard, specifically regarding healing and power evangelism.[363] While both of these works deal particularly with Wimber's view of healing, they provide a wider function of grounding his work within an academic context, and they show the areas of divergence with other healing methodologies in the Charismatic tradition. With the focus of this book being on congregational praxis, and following a constructivist method, these works are cited to support Wimber as a theologian rather than their comment on his theological positions.

356. Hunt, " Anglican Wimberites," 110.

357. Gibb, "Look Back in Wonder?" 42.

358. Benn and Burkill, "Theological and Pastoral Critique," 102.

359. Pink defines the sovereignty of God as his ability to do whatever he desires, both in heaven and on the earth, that he possesses all power so that no one can defeat or subvert his authority in his work. Dualism would radically undermine this position. Pink, *Sovereignty of God*, 20–21.

360. *Signs and Wonders and Evangelicals*.

361. *Wonders and the Word*.

362. Ibid., 155.

363. Hunt, "At the Cutting Edge"; Warrington, "Teaching and Praxis"; Gibb, "Look Back in Wonder?"

Charismatic Pneumatology

Charismatic authors have considered a wide range of subjects beyond pneumatology, but it is their treatment of the doctrine of the Holy Spirit that is now being considered. I begin with David Petts' work on the Holy Spirit, simply because, as an undergraduate theology student, I was lectured by Petts on this book.[364] The difficulty with this book is that the author seems preoccupied with proving the validity of his denominational understanding of baptism in the Holy Spirit, initial evidence and healing, and so it stands as a Pentecostal version of some of the Reformed works that shall be considered.

Keith Warrington has produced two works dealing with pneumatology; one is a general piece and the other a consideration of healing and suffering in the Christian life.[365] Warrington affirms the role of the Spirit in evangelism, stating that the Spirit was given for this express purpose and that every Christian can be used by the Spirit.[366] While affirming healing, he does not underestimate the role of suffering in spiritual formation.[367] Warrington's Pentecostal Pneumatology has much in common with Wimber, and Evangelicalism at large, especially on reception of the Holy Spirit at salvation.[368] Warrington also edited a compendium, entitled *Pentecostal Perspectives*, in which a series of Pentecostal authors consider some of the main points of their theology and further expounded in *Pentecostal Theology*.[369] This demonstrates that the Pentecostal and Charismatic Movements have theological opinions beyond that of pneumatology. It also gives a firm foundation against which to judge other positions.

Regarding spiritual gifts there are three older works of Donald Gee,[370] Harold Horton[371] and Lester Sumrall[372] that demonstrate the traditional Pentecostal view. This view is further expounded in David Lim's book[373]

---

364. Petts, *Holy Spirit*.
365. Warrington, *Healing and Suffering*, and *Message of the Holy Spirit*.
366. Warrington, *Message of the Holy Spirit*, 127, 187.
367. Warrington, *Healing and Suffering*, 196.
368. Warrington, *Message of the Holy Spirit*, 88.

369. Warrington, *Pentecostal Perspectives*. Areas covered are historical, doctrine of inspiration, pneumatology with reference to the spiritual gifts and the baptism in the Holy Spirit, eschatological, exorcism, worship and sacraments. Warrington, *Pentecostal Theology*.

370. Gee, *Concerning Spiritual Gifts*.
371. Horton, *Gifts of the Spirit*.
372. Sumrall, *Gifts and Ministries of the Holy Spirit*.
373. Lim, *Spiritual Gifts*.

and Warren D. Bullock considers the issue of prophecy, tongues and interpretation from a Pentecostal perspective.[374] Michael Green's book considers the Holy Spirit from an Anglican Charismatic tradition and gives a useful insight into how these two traditions mix.[375] These works demonstrate the wide spectrum of reflection not only on pneumatology generally, but also the issues of spiritual gifts specifically. They complement the work of Petts and Warrington. However, there appears to be the same focus of proving the necessity of second blessing and initial evidence.

There are also a number of books on the history of Charismatic manifestation. Keith J. Hacking considers the evidences of spiritual gifts throughout the New Testament[376] and Max Turner considers New Testament texts and church history.[377] While both of these books exegete the relevant biblical texts, Turner, in particular, wants to draw a line of connection through history and into the present. Dealing with the historical evidence for spiritual gifts, Donald W. Dayton considers the groundwork laid down by the nineteenth-century Holiness Movement and its emphasis on Spirit baptism.[378] Peter Hocken traces the development of the Charismatic Movement throughout Great Britain but, as shall be seen, makes no reference to Reformed involvement.[379] Hocken offers a narrative account of the historical development of the Charismatic Movement, giving comparisons with what was happening in North America also and is an interesting companion to this book.

Tom Smail, Andrew Walker and Nigel Wright consider the Charismatic Movement from three perspectives, beginning with their own testimonies, through theological reflection to contemporary considerations. Included are chapters on the Faith Movement and Toronto Blessing.[380] There are some larger issues that are considered in this work and it is a helpful critique from those personally involved in the Renewal movement. Mark Cartledge also offers a survey of the Charismatic movement, considering the areas of worship, spirituality and history.[381] This again demonstrates that Charismatic Renewal has more to offer than a theology of signs and wonders, but is a deep spiritually reflective movement.

374. Bullock, *When the Spirit Speaks*.
375. Green, *I Believe in the Holy Spirit*.
376. Hacking, *Signs and Wonders*.
377. Turner, *Holy Spirit and Spiritual Gifts*.
378. Dayton, *Theological Roots of Pentecostalism*.
379. Hocken, *Streams of Renewal*.
380. Smail et al., *Charismatic Renewal*.
381. Cartledge, *Encountering the Spirit*.

Reformed Pneumatology

I want to begin by considering some Reformed comments on the person and work of the Holy Spirit. Sinclair Ferguson,[382] Donald G. Bloesch[383] and Edwin H. Palmer[384] and, in Britain, J. McIntyre, cover the main areas of pneumatology from a Reformed perspective.[385] Bloesch gives one chapter specifically to Pentecostalism, considering its historical and theological development. Bloesch, while not uncritical of Pentecostalism, sees a number of benefits it has had on the Church.[386] As this book is concerned with Reformed and Charismatic theology, a positive estimation from a Reformed perspective is helpful. This openness to the Charismatic tradition continues in Brown's book.[387] Brown does not deviate from the traditional Reformed position but neither does he demonize those who hold a Charismatic position. In a sense these are ecumenical works that allow for a differing perspective on spiritual gifts without questioning the authenticity of those who follow a charismatic line.

There is a tendency amongst Reformed writers to approach Charismatic issues in a "negative" manner, as E. H. Andrews points out, beginning with the premise that the gifts cannot continue today because some of them have fulfilled their purpose of maturing the Church.[388] This argument assumes that the Church today has reached a certain level of maturity, and assumes that gifts such as tongues and prophecy cannot aid the Church today. Palmer considers spiritual gifts, specifically glossolalia, in the context of the baptism in the Holy Spirit, which he asserts happens at conversion.[389]

---

382. Ferguson, *Holy Spirit*.

383. Bloesch, *Holy Spirit*.

384. Palmer, *Holy Spirit*.

385. McIntyre, *Shape of Pneumatology*, 217, 224. He states that the indwelling of the Holy Spirit has produced the Protestant Ethic. Further on, he restates the rejection of speaking in tongues as an evidence of Baptism in the Holy Spirit and the ideal of a two-stage Christian experience.

386. Bloesch, *Holy Spirit*, 197–204. He considers eight areas of concern: legalism, illuminism (prophecy of a level with Scripture), anti-intellectualism, spiritual sensualism (search for higher divine experiences), a theology of glory but not the cross, sectarianism, faulty Trinitarian doctrine, and a tendency toward secularism. In 204–07, he considers eight areas of benefit: spiritual experiences after conversion, gifts of the Spirit, energizing work of the Spirit, evangelism and fellowship central to ecclesiology, priesthood of all believers, reality of the devil, signs and wonders in evangelism, and the importance of conversion.

387. Brown, *Follow the Wind*.

388. Andrews, *Spirit has Come*, 247–49.

389. Palmer, *Holy Spirit*, 110.

This is the main thrust of his argument, one that is held across Reformed theology and by Wimber. John D. Harvey also considers the presence of the Holy Spirit in the contemporary church and, while not completely ruling out the possibility of spiritual gifts, his emphasis is on the Spirit at work in sanctification.[390] This seems to be a common thread in Reformed pneumatology; that one of the contemporary works of the Spirit is to further sanctify believers. This work builds upon the argument that the presence of the Spirit, confirming the gospel with signs following, needs to be considered in a Reformed context.

The second genre of Reformed pneumatology that I want to consider is those works that deal specifically with the Pentecostal and Charismatic Movements and theology. Warfield's *Counterfeit Miracles* is a seminal work in this area. His argument is the gifts of the Spirit "belonged . . . exclusively to the apostolic age."[391] His focus was more on Catholic mysticism, as the time of writing predated both Azusa and Sunderland. Yet the themes identified, shaped and continue to influence the dominant position amongst conservative Reformed theologians.[392] Walter J. Chantry adopts the same overall position as Warfield, but he puts forward the notion that miracles have ceased because the apostles performed them and there are not any contemporary apostles.[393] Richard B. Gaffin Jr. also approaches cessation through the view of the temporary nature of the apostolate and the foundational role they were to play in the Church (Eph 2:20).[394] David J. Engelsma specifically refers to apostles as a temporary office.[395] The difficulty with this argument is that it is built upon a presupposition that only apostles performed miracles and that, if disproved, would undermine the argument. There may also be merit in considering different types of miracles, some of which may not have been performed by apostles and so may be able to be performed today.

O. Palmer Robertson argues for the cessation of the charismata through the supremacy of Scripture and gives a number of reasons why continuing revelation cannot continue.[396] Kenneth L. Gentry agrees with

390. Harvey, *Anointed with the Spirit and Power*, 168.

391. Warfield, *Counterfeit Miracles*, 6.

392. For a specific challenge to Warfield see Ruthven, "On the Cessation of the Charismata." Ruthven believes that Warfield works back from his conclusions to prove them and offers an essentially deistic view of miracles.

393. Chantry, *Signs of the Apostles*.

394. Gaffin Jr., *Perspectives on Pentecost*, 89–102.

395. Engelsma, *Try the Spirit*. He believes that the Pentecostal position insults Christ because of the second blessing doctrine.

396. Robertson, *Final Word*, 87–126.

Robertson that once the canon was set, prophecy in particular ceased.[397] R. Fowler White suggests that contemporary revelation comes only from the Bible.[398] There is a consistent challenge to understanding contemporary revelation on the same level as Scripture. This may be hyperbole, as few Charismatics may suggest this. Kenneth Berding argues that there has been a misunderstanding of what spiritual gifts are; they ought to be seen as special ministries, where the Holy Spirit guides believers into what best satisfies in a given context.[399] This is also taken up by Vern. S. Poythress, who places both spiritual gifts and ministry gifts as blessings to the Church.[400] As shall be seen, this view is remarkably similar to the position put forward by Wimber on spiritual gifts.

The third genre of Reformed pneumatology is the polemical works that seek to criticize the Charismatic tradition. Calvin H. Chambers makes comment regarding worship reflecting upon the centrality of preaching and the sacraments within the Reformed tradition.[401] This is an issue of contention from both sides of the debate, and comment upon this theme created the questions of this book. Two popular polemical works are those of John MacArthur[402] and Peter Masters with John C. Whitcomb.[403] Both of these books start with the premise of disproving the validity of charismatic claims regarding healing and continuing revelation. Masters and Whitcomb believe that, while the source of charismatic phenomena is not demonic, it can become an opening for the demonic.[404] Equally, Victor Budgen proposes cessationism and argues that, if anyone asserts a Charismatic position, the door is opened for demonic deception.[405] This becomes a self-fulfilling argument so that, if a contrary position is offered, the root can be claimed to be demonic and thus limit debate. MacArthur believes that there is not one element of truth within the Charismatic position.[406] Reading both these books, there is little evidence of grace when it comes to the opposing opinion, or appreciation of any benefits it may bring to the Church. Donald

---

397. Gentry, *Charismatic Gift of Prophecy*.
398. White, "Contrary to What You May Have Heard."
399. Berding, *What are Spiritual Gifts*, 35.
400. Poythress, *What are Spiritual Gifts*, 30–33. He even goes as far as allowing the possibility of tongue speaking in the Church, 37.
401. Chambers, *In Spirit and in Truth*.
402. MacArthur, *Charismatic Chaos*.
403. Masters and Whitcomb, *Charismatic Phenomena*.
404. Ibid., 110.
405. Budgen, *Charismatics and the Word of God*, 242.
406. MacArthur, *Charismatic Chaos*, 355.

Bridge has tried to give a critique, without demonizing disagreement, by presenting both sides of the opinion in an attempt to form an ecumenical synthesis.[407] This is an attempt to understand that agreement on all issues is not necessary and that strength can be achieved through co-operation.

Gaffin sums up the Reformed position by highlighting the place of the Pentecostal experience in the Bible. He comments on the Charismatic Movement regarding the order of salvation (ordo *salutis*) and he puts Pentecost in the history of salvation (historia *salutis*), not the order of salvation. He believes that these are misunderstood in Charismatic theology so that the outline in Acts becomes normative for contemporary Christian experience, while Pentecost was a once only event.[408] Essentially, this states that Acts is a narrative book and cannot be used to assert Christian doctrine. This means that experiences in Acts cannot be considered to provide a model for ongoing Christian experience.

David S. Lim suggests that the doctrine of continual fillings of the Holy Spirit is specifically applicable to a Reformed setting because of the lack of dramatic conversion experiences amongst its members.[409] Lim highlights one of the significant differences between the Pentecostal/Charismatic streams and the Reformed; namely, the nature of their faith. Reformed theology emphasizes the notion of covenant and the inclusion of the believer's children within the parent's covenant. This could lead to the children becoming disciples without ever having a dramatic conversion experience.

Confessional Literature

As the background of this book is the PCI, it is necessary to consider how commentators understand what the WCF states concerning the Holy Spirit, as every Presbyterian minister must subscribe to that confession. While the text of the Confession does not directly consider the issue of the work of the Holy Spirit, it makes mention in connection with the Holy Scriptures which made "those former ways" cease.[410] This is a general statement on the work of the Holy Spirit and, as O. Palmer Robertson states, the WC is

---

407. Bridge, *Power Evangelism*; Bridge and Phypers, *Spiritual Gifts and the Church*.
408. Gaffin Jr., "Challenges of the Charismatic Movement," 48–57.
409. Lim, "Evangelical Critique," 219–29.

410. WCF 1:1. Reference is also made to the ceasing of new revelations (1:6), that the Holy Spirit governs the elect (8:8); as well as effectually calling (10:1); quickening (10:2); saving (10:3, 14:1); justifying (11:4); indwelling (13:1); sanctifying (13:3, 19:7); enabling to do good works (16:3); keeping secure (17:1); assuring of salvation (18:2); produce faith (18:3); enable worship (21:3).

deficient for not devoting a chapter to this issue.[411] Charismatic issues were not as relevant at the time of the Westminster Assembly as they might be today, which may explain the reason for the omission.[412] In considering the teaching of the WCF, I want to look at the Holy Spirit and the Bible and the Holy Spirit and sanctification. Essentially, the work of the Holy Spirit can be seen in three ways, according to Wayne R. Spear: inspiring the Scriptures, persuading people to accept the Scriptures as inspired, and guiding believers and the Church to interpret the Scriptures.[413] It is in the last area that any debate concerning contemporary Charismatic practice within the Reformed tradition rests, and it may leave open a possibility for contemporary revelation and direction.

Underpinning the WCF's pneumatology is a conservative view of the Bible.[414] The key paragraph to consider in this regard is WCF 1:6, and this may lead to ruling out any possibility of further or subsequent revelation. In commenting on this, PCI states that this rules out any prophetic utterance, and Erik Wait believes that it also rules out tongues.[415][416] The contextual reason, according to Rowland S. Ward, is the placing of the Apocrypha in the Canon and Anabaptists claim of ongoing revelation.[417] There may be some argument in saying that the Charismatic Movement is the twentieth century's manifestation of the Anabaptist tradition.

Robert Shaw also sees an anti-Catholic polemic in this statement, not of additions to the Canon of Scripture, but of the purity of the Church and her worship. He believes that because there are no definite statements concerning how the Church ought to be administered and worship conducted, to counteract the aesthetic elements of Catholic worship, a statement on the sufficiency of Scripture is needed.[418] Robert Letham defines this as "a mystical view of the Christian faith" rather than sacrament, although, the focus appears to be medieval Catholicism.[419] A. A. Hodge refers to

---

411. Robertson, "Holy Spirit in the Westminster Confession," 57.

412. Palmer Robertson states that if the Divines were to deal with prophecy and tongues in the Confession they would need to have exercised the gift of prophecy themselves. Robertson, "Holy Spirit in the Westminster Confession," 96.

413. Spear, "Word and Spirit," 41–42.

414. This view understands the Bible as inspired by God, without error and without fault, clearly declaring God's Word. See Thompson, *A Clear and Present Word*.

415. *Firm Foundations*, 17.

416. Wait, "Tongues and the Westminster Confession."

417. Ward, *Westminster Confession of Faith*, 35.

418. Shaw, *Exposition of the Westminster Confession*, 49.

419. Letham, *Westminster Confession of Faith*, 140.

these developments as "traditions of men" that are implemented in Catholicism.[420] B. B. Warfield sees the anti-Catholic polemic focused on the Protestant Church of England and Archbishop Laud, whom he defines as "Anglo-Catholic and Arminian," rather than Roman Catholicism.[421] This highlights one of the distinctives of Reformed theology that is the regulative principle, which shall be considered further in chapter 3.

G. I. Williamson highlights the relationship between the knowledge of God's will and the Bible and, so, concludes that humanity needs no knowledge beyond that which is expressly taught in or "deducible from Scripture."[422] R. C. Sproul calls this guidance "inscripturated divine revelation," which means that God speaks through the Bible as it is engrafted within a believer.[423] This emphasizes the sufficiency of Scripture for all personal spiritual development and theological reflection on the nature and worship of the Church, which was a theological axiom for the Reformers.

Commentators on the Confession have traditionally emphasized the work of the Holy Spirit in adoption and sanctification, but not empowerment.[424] Smith highlights the exclusive aspect of the Spirit's work in sanctification and states that believers work with the Spirit in effecting this change.[425] This emphasis could be because of the apparent "worldliness" of the Church in the seventeenth century, and so an emphasis on the Holy Spirit transforming believers is promised. Williamson believes the WCF teaches that sanctification is effected by the Bible, sacraments, prayer and discipline, by which the Holy Spirit is made effectual to believers.[426][427] Shaw further expands this notion by saying that the Holy Spirit aids the believer and that, without this aid, sanctification would not be possible.[428] Sproul believes that, because the Spirit provides the necessary tools for spiritual development, success will be inevitable.[429] This would link the work of the Spirit with the ministry of the Church, something that is an argument of this book. It could, however, be interpreted as exclusively the effort of the

---

420. Hodge, *Confession of Faith*, 38–39.

421. Warfield, *Westminster Assembly*, 159.

422. Williamson, *Westminster Confession of Faith*, 15.

423. Sproul, *Truths we Confess*, 1:20.

424. WCF 13:3.

425. Smith, *Foundations of the Faith*, 130, 135–36.

426. Williamson, *Westminster Confession of Faith*, 152.

427. Hodge, *Confession of Faith*, 240. Hodge also believes that the sacraments play a sanctifying function in the spiritual development of the believer.

428. Shaw, *Exposition of the Westminster Confession*, 187.

429. Sproul, *Truths we Confess*, 2:109.

believer, not the dependence on the Spirit, to make spiritual progress. This connects with Wimber's theology of spiritual development.

Garnet Howard Milne has challenged the traditional interpretation that the WCF teaches cessationism. He agrees with the other commentators that the context is the sufficiency of Scripture but argues that some of the Westminster Divines were "continuationists."[430] He contends that the WCF does not provide a definite answer on the question of whether the "former ways" have ceased forever.[431] He proposes two contextual areas: first, "divinely inspired dreams";[432] and, second, prophecy, which he situates within the context of the Bible. Through preaching, "genuine divine prophecy" can be exercised and "insight into the future" may be discerned for those who live by the Bible.[433] His conclusion is that the framers of the WCF composed it so that it would not restrict believers to one view, but different viewpoints could coexist with toleration for each other.[434] He is not alone in this assertion, as Dean R. Smith highlights how some Scottish Presbyterians and Covenanters exercised the gift of prophecy and healing.[435] Willem Berends surveys key Reformation and Puritan figures and concludes that, while they believed in the sufficiency of Scripture, they would not rule out the possibility of prophetic revelation.[436] Milne does allow for some extra-biblical revelation but it is tied to the Bible; namely, knowing what verse to read in a specific situation without preparation, and may not necessarily reflect contemporary Charismatic practice. It does, however, allow a confessional church to remain open to further spiritual experience.

Reformed and Charismatic Literature

Cornelius van der Kooi notes that there appears to be a "rapprochement" in relationships between the Reformed, Charismatic, and Pentecostal

---

430. Milne, *Westminster Confession of Faith*, 6–7.

431. Ibid., 109.

432. Milne, *Westminster Confession of Faith*, 147–53, 159–65: He cites Archibald Johnston, Lord Warriston, 1611–63), Richard Baxter (1615–91), and William Bridge (1600–71) as examples.

433. Milne, *Westminster Confession of Faith*, 206–18; He cites George Keith (1638–1716), James Usher (1581–1656), John Selden (1584–1654). Milne, 221–53: He cites as Scottish examples Archibald Johnston (1611–63), Samuel Rutherford (1600–61), Alexander Henderson (1583–1646), Robert Blair (1593–1666—Moderator of the first Irish Presbytery), George Gillespie (1613–48) and James Durham (1622–58).

434. Milne, *Westminster Confession of Faith*, 258.

435. Smith, "'Charismatic' Scottish Presbyterians."

436. Berends, "Prophecy in the Reformed Tradition," 43.

traditions regarding the teaching of the doctrine of the Holy Spirit.[437] This begins to paint the picture of what began, historically, with Edward Irving, who bridges the divide between Reformed theology and charismatic experience, although it predates both the Pentecostal and Charismatic Movements.[438] Irving experienced charismatic phenomena in his London congregation, the Caledonian Chapel, Hatton Garden. He has been claimed as a reformer who focused the Church upon the person of the Holy Spirit.[439] While his influence is not as commonly known as the Pentecostal Pioneers, or those involved in Charismatic Renewal, he represents the fountainhead of Charismatic and Reformed theology.

Under the ministry of the Presbyterian Charismatic Communion, Brick Bradford wrote on the area of the power of the Holy Spirit.[440] Bradford suggests a synthesis of the Reformed tradition, emphasizing the presence of the Spirit; and the Pentecostal tradition, emphasizing the power of the Spirit. This, he suggests, is a balanced view.[441] He suggests ten areas in which Charismatic Renewal has affected believers for the better.[442] Bradford represents the melding of the Reformed and the Charismatic, yet retains the specific denominational distinctives that make the Reformed faith what it is.

"Empowered Evangelicals" is a designation used for Evangelicals who are open to the Holy Spirit but who fall short of being defined as Charismatic. The title comes from Nathan and Wilson's book, which seeks to bring together the worlds of Charismatic and Evangelical.[443] They comment there are many non-Charismatic, Conservative Evangelicals, who are adopting Pentecostal practices such as healing, deliverance and receiving prophetic words, yet maintain that the Baptism in the Holy Spirit happens at conversion.[444] Banister tells the story of how his Evangelical Free Church began to open itself to Charismatic Renewal through a slow personal renewal of the

---

437. van der Kooi, "Wonders of God," 34.

438. Irving, *Day of Pentecost*. See also: Strachan, *Pentecostal Theology of Edward Irving*; Dallimore, *Life of Edward Irving*; McFarlane, *Edward Irving*; G.W.P. McFarlane, *Christ and the Spirit*; Warfield, "Irvingite Gifts."

439. Vreeland, "Edward Irving," 1.

440. Bradford, *Releasing the Power of the Holy Spirit*. This is now known as Presbyterian Reformed Ministries International.

441. Ibid., 14.

442. Life of God in the congregation, increased prayerfulness, love for the Bible, production of spiritual fruit, emphasis on the usefulness of every believer, heightened worship, consciousness of the body of Christ, evangelistic boldness, social consciousness and wide spread ecumenism. Bradford, *Releasing the Power of the Holy Spirit*, 19–21.

443. Nathan and Wilson, *Empowered Evangelicals*.

444. Ibid., 11.

minister.[445] The book argues that there is openness to charismatic manifestation from Puritanism right through the Great Awakenings of Wesley, Whitefield and Edwards to Lloyd-Jones. This dovetails with the work of Milne on the WCF and charismatic phenomena. It is possible to look at history and read our own beliefs into the theology, so care is needed not to look for justification for our positions at the expense of what is said.

There are two books that specifically deal with the integration of Charismatic and Reformed theology. The first is by Storms, who draws on the theology of Ligioner Ministries (Orlando) and Vineyard Ministries (Anaheim) and synthesizes them in a Reformed and Charismatic methodology.[446] Storms claims that his theological change did not happen because of experience, but by a reflection upon the teaching of the Bible, which led to a connection with the Vineyard through his seminary friend, Jack Deere. This book provides a specifically Reformed outlook on charismatic phenomena and is a tightly argued thesis for the integration of the two. What is significant about Storm's theory is that he emphasizes the need for each, stressing how they complement each other.

The other book is written by Robert Fyall, who argues that a charismatic heart heightens the expectation from preaching and anticipates hearing God speak through expository ministry.[447] Fyall considers the issue of spiritual gifts in evangelism, which provides an expectation that God will meet the needs with which the Church is confronted, while never being dominated by a search for miracles. Perhaps most noticeable are Fyall's comments on how numerous Reformed leaders have spoken positively of charismatic issues, but he does not cite any examples of Charismatics extolling the Reformed tradition.

Henry Lunshof's dissertation argues that there are certain Charismatic elements that Reformed Churches need to adopt and that Charismatic churches would benefit from a Reformed influence.[448] Lunshof sees the Charismatic emphasis bringing new life to traditional churches by evoking growth and relevancy. Whether it will accomplish this is unclear, but Lunshof understands that the two streams complement each other.

---

445. Banister, *Word and Power Church*.

446. Storms, *Convergence*.

447. Fyall, *Charismatic and Reformed*. His suggestions are for Charismatic and Reformed believers to pray together. This will lead to a greater degree of freedom in Reformed worship that draws upon the Charismatic emphasis of transformed living being married with the Reformed emphasis of sound doctrine.

448. Lunshof, *Reformed and Charismatic*.

Brad Long, Paul Stokes, and Cindy Strickler have published a contextual book on how the Church can grow with the aid of the Spirit.[449] This book considers examples of how churches have adopted a synergistic approach to Charismatic theology. What is of significance to this book is its Reformed denominational background; that they represent various streams of Presbyterianism. It shows that there are elements of Charismatic practice that can be implemented in the praxis of a Reformed congregation. The emphasis on humanity's response to the work of the Holy Spirit is significant. They suggest that this is the only way in which charismatic principles can be introduced.[450] This represents that important theme that what we do is as important as what we believe, something we considered earlier. It also reminds Reformed Christians that there is a part to play, which may challenge Gaffin's *ordo salutis*.

John Piper has written and preached on this subject with the aim of demonstrating that miracles, signs, and wonders are for the Church today. He aims to prove that cessationism is not in sympathy with the teaching of the New Testament, out of his: "God-centered, Bible-based, Calvinistic commitment to the sovereignty of God and the supremacy of his revealed Word."[451] Piper's theology is practical, as it is worked out in the context of his local congregation. He represents the marriage between Reformed theology and Charismatic openness for which this book argues. If the criticism of Wimber's writings stand, that it is molded by experience, then Piper presents a Bible to experience argument.

While not directly concerned about the connection between Reformed and Charismatic theology, Martyn Lloyd-Jones' treatment of the Baptism and Gifts of the Holy Spirit has a significant influence on the discussion.[452] Lloyd-Jones argued that the "sealing of the Spirit" was an experience after salvation, whether separable or subsequent is unclear.[453] Lloyd-Jones' influence on Reformed theology and Churches is significant, but his theology is a homiletical one; therefore, his references are not cited to follow up. He does, however, remind us that a Reformed congregation and pastor were considering these issues during the Charismatic Renewal.[454]

449. Long et al., *Growing the Church*.
450. Ibid., 15.
451. Piper, "Signs and Wonders."
452. Lloyd-Jones, *Joy Unspeakable*. Lloyd-Jones' influence was over many young men from Church of England backgrounds, like David Watson and Michael Harper, who came to him in order to theologically understand their charismatic experience. Atherstone et al., «Lloyd-Jones and the Charismatic Controversy," 115–16.
453. Lloyd-Jones, *Joy Unspeakable*, 317.
454. These sermons were preached in Westminster Chapel, Buckingham Gate,

Coming out of these discussions are two spiritual autobiographical works from Jack Deere concerning his change from Cessationist to Charismatic.[455] Much of the argument is based on exegesis of key biblical texts from Deere's background as an Old Testament seminary professor.[456] Deere could be understood as the Vineyard theologian and he restates much of Wimber's teaching. Yet, his books elevate experience to a point where the theology appears to be used to support it. This means that a critical evaluation of the experience is needed also.

Wayne Grudem has done research in drawing together Reformed, Evangelical and Charismatic theologies on the Holy Spirit. His first work on the gift of prophecy outlines the difference between prophecy and preaching.[457] He understands that prophecy was to give specific, localized information, not general guidance.[458] This would mean that such charismatic manifestations would not guide denominations or interpret prophecy, but direct a local congregation. In his mind there would be no conflict with Reformed theology as the great theological axioms would not be challenged. Grudem also brought together a symposium to consider the issue of miraculous gifts.[459] While none of the participants are recorded as having changed their theological positions because of the authenticity of the other arguments, it helped to dispel some of the myths concerning the positions of those holding an alternative view.

There has also developed a greater willingness, amongst writers from different traditions, to engage with the subject of Pneumatology, examples of which are Daniel B. Wallace and M. James Sawyer.[460] While definitely Cessationist, this work tries to examine the reaction which has taken place in Cessationist theology to things Charismatic. Essays, from writers such as J. I. Packer, on how the Holy Spirit leads believers and to what end, namely, character transformation;[461] Jeff Louie on how the Spirit controls the local Church, which is seen through the power of prayer;[462] and Donald K. Smith on the Holy Spirit and missions that work to bring people to an understand-

---

London, in 1964–65.

455. Deere, *Surprised by the Power*; Deere, *Surprised by the Voice*.

456. Deere, *Surprised by the Power*, 219–27.

457. Grudem, *Gift of Prophecy*.

458. Ibid., 245.

459. Grudem, *Are Miraculous Gifts for Today?* The four positions are: cessationist, R. B. Gaffin Jr; open but cautious, R. L. Saucy; third wave, S. Storms; and Pentecostal/Charismatic, D. A. Oss.

460. Wallace and Swayer, *Who's Afraid of the Holy Spirit*.

461. Packer, "Ministry of the Holy Spirit," 109.

462. Louie, "Holy Spirit and the Local Church," 236–37.

ing of the truth, are included.[463] This speaks of the fact that pneumatology is not the exclusive domain of Charismatics, nor does having reservations about certain Charismatic practice mean a dismissal of any notion of the Spirit's power. Also in the genre of offering a middle way between Charismatic and Reformed, are David Pawson[464] and Don Williams.[465] Both writers come from an Evangelical background and have come to espouse a Charismatic theology. Pawson considers the points of commonality and Williams considers the outworking of kingdom theology from a Presbyterian viewpoint.

Contemporary Ecclesiology

There has been considerable interest in ecclesiology in recent years. David Clark has considered the role of Church in a culture that can no longer be defined as Christendom. His argument is that community exists at the heart of Church and is expressed through a diaconal or servant ministry that is released, as leadership equips the laity to perform it.[466] Part of this book considers the role every member has to play in a ministry model, so this book will further aid the discussion. Steve Chalke and Anthony Watkins, who consider how the Church can incarnate the love of God in today's culture, further explore the issue of community. They suggest eleven models communicating to different groups.[467] The issue of community is also considered by Steve Taylor who suggests a model of Church that reaches out beyond a simple message of loving God to loving God's people also.[468] In considering the place of community in a Reformed and Charismatic model, Taylor's emphasis on relationships is of value. Tim Chester and Steve Timmis also consider similar themes. Their argument is that the Church needs to center around the twin themes of gospel and community because once a response to the gospel has been elicited, then commitment to the community is implied.[469] The argument of this book is that the local Church is central to the gospel ministry of proclamation, discipling, and releasing into ministry, which is a similar theme to *Total Church*.

463. Smith, "Holy Spirit in Missions," 251.
464. Pawson, *Word and Spirit Together*.
465. Williams, *Signs, Wonders*.
466. Clark, *Breaking the Mould of Christendom*.
467. Chalke and Watkins, *Intelligent Church*.
468. Taylor, *Out of Bounds Church*.
469. Chester and Timmis, *Total Church*.

Some works specifically consider charismatic issues regarding the Church. Percy has considered the issue of power in the Charismatic churches. His emphasis appears to be how Churches, which express a strong commitment to verbal inspiration, form their ministry and theological ethos. His conclusion is that there is not one form of Charismatic church but many different expressions of that spirituality.[470] This will help my research as it challenges whether charismatic experience is dependent upon Arminian theology, so perhaps Reformed theology can coexist with it. Stephen Hunt has written on Charismatic evangelism from a sociological perspective and, specifically, the Alpha course.[471] While not directly related to the theological issue in the Charismatic Movement, Hunt considers how Alpha has repackaged Evangelical Christianity in a time when its popularity appears to be waning. This work gives an interesting position regarding Charismatic theology and how it continues to evangelize contemporary Britain.

There have also been a number of popular books written on the issues of how the Church has exercised its ministry, biblically and effectively. Rick Warren's *Purpose Driven Church* has received wide attention and this book builds upon the life development process for its outline.[472] Mark Dever, writing from a reformed Baptist position, has responded to the Warren type of "how to" literature by highlighting nine marks of what he considers to be a healthy Church.[473] In many of these marks he is arguing for a historical methodology and these proven methods for contemporary effectiveness. This is further expanded in his book with Paul Alexander, which considers how the church reaches out, worships God and disciples believers, and then releases members into leadership.[474] I have also relied on this book to help with the outline of the chapters of this book. These provide insights into the working of large, North American churches, which may not have the same application to a British setting. Their denominational pedigree is different; however, the impact, particularly of Warren's work has been wide.

Two books written by Michael Horton, from a specifically Reformed position, are *Where in the World is the Church?* and *People and Place*.[475] The first argues for an integration of Christians into every area of society, and the second considers the issue of belonging to the Church on the basis of the

---

470. Percy, *Power and the Church*, 184.

471. Hunt, *Alpha Enterprise*.

472. Warren, *Purpose Driven Church*.

473. Dever, *Nine Marks of a Healthy Church*. He highlights expository preaching, theology, gospel, conversion, evangelism, membership, church discipline, discipleship and growth, and leadership. Similar themes are considered in Stott, *Living Church*.

474. Dever and Alexander, *Deliberate Church*.

475. Horton, *Where in the Word is the Church?*

covenant signs of baptism and Eucharist. Graham Tomlin also argues for an integration of every member's gifts into the work of the Church, which moves conversion beyond the initial experience and into discipleship.[476] These themes are significant to the argument of this book as they are foundational elements in the Reformed understanding of Church.

One emphasis, which has had significant influence on the thinking of this book, is the "Deep Church" theology.[477] This series of essays, edited by Andrew Walker and Luke Bretherton, give an insight into the contemporary movement.[478] Deep Church has a bearing on this book because, as Walker comments, the Charismatic Renewal of the 1960s and 1970s "captured something of the character of deep church."[479] These works challenge the culture of Evangelicalism today, which emphasizes numerical growth at the expense of spiritual growth, and offer an alternative to narrow reformed orthodoxy and emotional charismatic experience. Stackhouse seeks to challenge what he calls the "faddism" of the Charismatic culture in Britain, which always looks for the "next big thing" to answer all the needs of the Church, without considering historical models of spirituality. He also challenges the Church Growth Movement, which understands ecclesiastical health as quantity not quality, and worship that is anthropocentric rather than divine focused.[480] Stackhouse challenges the Charismatic Renewal from the inside and raises issues of concern over the quality of preaching, sacramental reductionism, the morality of those who profess to be Spirit filled, the daily routine of prayerfulness, and the importance of valuing the story and needs of individual Christians. This understands the Church itself as a sacrament and the centrality of the Church for the Christian life. This book does for the Charismatic Movement what Banister and Storms seek to do for the Evangelical and Reformed Movements. Jim Belcher also writes on Deep Church issues; his aim is to provide a middle way between the Emergent Churches and the traditional expressions of Church that connect with a spiritual tradition.[481] This emphasis of taking a middle line has affected the argument of this book because it suggests a middle line between Char-

---

476. Tomlin, *Provocative Church*.

477. This phrase was coined by C.S. Lewis in a 1952 letter to *The Times* which urged the Catholic and Evangelical wings of the Church of England to unite in order to stand against modernity and to rediscover the historical roots of the Church. Schneider, "C.S. Lewis, Church Unity, and the Dynamics of the Hallway."

478. Walker and Bretherton, *Remembering Our Future*. Areas considered are Scripture and tradition, multi-faith society, community, worship and the sacraments.

479. Walker, "Recovering Deep Church," 1.

480. Stackhouse, *Gospel Driven Church*.

481. Belcher, *Deep Church*.

ismatic and Reformed, which stresses historical spirituality and challenges the excesses of the contemporary Charismatic Movement.

Partial Literary Conclusion

This review of the salient literature reveals that there is academic interest in the connection between Reformed and Charismatic theology, specifically dealing with Churches that emphasize adherence to the Westminster Confession of Faith, through Milne, Berends, and Smith. There does not appear to have been any connection suggested between Wimber and Reformed theology, although he has been critiqued from a Reformed perspective. It has also revealed that the dominant position of cessationism within Reformed theology appears to have a significant confessional and contemporary challenge. This chapter has raised the question of the interaction between Reformed and Charismatic belief and offers hope that there may be merit in a potential harmonization of the two streams. Specifically, it has proposed a consideration of Wimber's contribution to the debate and a possible synthesis between his theology and Confessional Presbyterianism.

3

How the Study will Work

Introduction

IN THIS CHAPTER I want to explain the source and diversity of my data, discuss the methodology I have chosen, and clarify the type of questions this book can and cannot address. This work will, primarily, be a study in practical theology, relating to the mission of the local Church, within the context of a Reformed denomination in the British Isles. This research fits into the discipline of practical theology because, according to Paul Ballard and John Pritchard, it deals with the life and practice within the Church, which takes the living context seriously as the foundation for the issues this book hopes to discuss. It also has the practical goal of addressing the "witness and struggle for the Kingdom of justice and peace."[1] John Swinton and Harriet Mowat also highlight the practical element of such research by defining practical theology as that which seeks to encourage the Christian community to remain faithful to the "performed gospel."[2] This lies at the heart of this research because the subject deals with how a Reformed congregation can practice their gospel ministry in the world.

This book may not have as wide a context as an abstract piece of writing; however, part of practical theology is "faithful accurate description of the way things are."[3] Robert J. Schrieter brings out the idea that theology is not abstract, but rooted in its context, so that "knowledge of the context

1. Ballard and Pritchard, *Practical Theology in Action*, 5–6.
2. Swinton and Mowatt, *Practical Theology and Qualitative Research*, 5.
3. Anderson et al., *Studying Congregations*, 16.

is part of the theology itself."[4] While the way things are, or the context, cannot necessarily be defined as the way they ought to be, they are, nonetheless, what forms the background of the topic under consideration. For these reasons, this book can be placed within the theological discipline of practical theology.

I have chosen to follow the principles of the Qualitative Constructivist/Interpretivist Format as outlined by John W. Creswell.[5] This format asserts that human communities construct how they understand truth.[6] This fits well with the research as I am looking at what happens in the practice of Reformed congregational life. I am considering the definition of Eduard Schweizer that the Church is something which really "takes place" when people come together for worship.[7] I am going to consider some practical issues and how they relate to the practice of the Confessional Reformed Churches and, specifically, the Presbyterian tradition. Dealing with any congregation or denomination means considering the beliefs and practices of a great number of individuals formed by many experiences; and, as such, practical theology aids this book by considering human experience and challenging these experiences to enable a better practice of gospel ministry.[8] Richard Osmer notes two tasks of practical theology that could have a bearing on this research. One of these is the Normative Task, which seeks to "open out to forms of theological and ethical reflection." This book seeks to do this regarding Charismatic and Reformed theology. The other is the Pragmatic Task, which seeks to formulate strategies of action to influence events in a desirable manner.[9] I seek to do this by offering a mode of implementing Charismatic practice in a Reformed context. In this context of the gathered Church, I propose to introduce a conversation between the teachings of John Wimber and the theology of the Reformed faith on the practical areas of evangelism, discipleship, and ministry operation.

---

4. Schreiter, "Theology in the Congregation," 26.

5. Creswell, *Research Design*, 74–75. Accordingly, I include an introduction to the theme—setting the scene, review of the literature and method—then the procedural elements of the contextual applications.

6. Swinton and Mowat, *Practical Theology and Qualitative Research*, 35.

7. Schweizer, *Church Order in the New Testament*, 189.

8. Swinton and Mowat, *Practical Theology and Qualitative Research*, 5–6. Savage and Presnell note that we are a product of our stories affecting our self-understanding of who we are, what we think and how we act. Savage and Presnell, *Narrative Research in Ministry*, 25.

9. Osmer, *Practical Theology*, 139 and 175–76. He states that this has specific application for mainline churches that seek to rework their identity and mission beyond their time of influence and power, culturally.

This subject was raised in my mind when I read a statement by William W. Kay:

> ... it was clear that Presbyterian institutions in Northern Ireland and Scotland and high Anglicans have been least receptive to Pentecostal and Charismatic trends. [10]

Kay makes the statement within the context of worship styles, and the compassion between Anglicanism and Presbyterianism raises a number of concerns. First, rationale for the worship styles of high Anglicanism and Presbyterianism are radically different. Second, I knew from personal experience the widespread practice within Irish Presbyterianism of worship bands, ranging from those congregations who would have a Charismatic leaning to those who were cessationist.[11] No reference was given to the *Irish Presbyterian Hymnbook*, published in 2004, which included a wide variety of praise including some from the Charismatic perspective.[12] The fact is that there is a wide spectrum of worship styles within congregations and the singing of historical Protestant hymns, metrical versions of the Psalms, paraphrases of the Bible and modern praise will often be experienced within congregational worship. McIntyre notes there has been a degree of "success" in this area within the Church of Scotland.[13] Third, Kay gives no discussion why Presbyterianism, in particular, has a strong rationale for their worship style; namely, the regulative principle. Expediency or pragmatism or even relevancy, are not issues that formulate Presbyterian worship, but how the Bible directs us to worship.[14] Fourth, would a discussion regarding the im-

---

10. Kay, *Apostolic Networks in Britain*, 228. It is noteworthy that Kay cites a friendship between Martyn Lloyd-Jones and Billy Richards. Atherstone at al., "Lloyd-Jones and the Charismatic Controversy," 121. Kay makes no mention of this friendship in a previous work. See Kay, *Inside Story*, 209–12. Perhaps Kay's thinking is unclear on this matter.

11. From the Charismatic side there is West Church, Bangor and Orangefield Presbyterian Church, from the cessationist side there is Waringstown Presbyterian Church and First Portadown Presbyterian Church. David Bailie, Minister of West Church, writes of their experience: "And a later experience of the Holy Spirit in West Church underlined the dynamic given to people through an infilling with the Spirit, different people receiving different gifts according to the Spirit's anointing and empowering.» Baillie, «50 Years of Ministry."

12. *The Irish Presbyterian Hymnbook*.

13. McIntyre, *Shape of Pneumatology*, vii.

14. For a contemporary discussion of the Regulative Principle see: Muller, *Scripture and Worship*; Hart and Muether, *With Reverence and Awe*; Gore Jr, *Covenantal Worship*; Dawn, *Reaching Out Without Dumbing Down*; Hart, *Recovering Mother Kirk*; Old, *Worship Reformed According to Scripture*; Keller, "Reformed Worship in the Global City."

pact of Pentecostal/Charismatic worship styles, which takes no account of spiritual gifts or signs and wonders, limit any discussion of their merit about Irish Presbyterianism and reduce Pentecostal and Charismatic influence to a musical preference and style? Fifth, there is no reference to the historical practice in early Irish Pentecostalism of Psalm singing.[15] Cartledge believes that Charismatic influence does travel amongst denominations and, while the contextual form is different, it is, nonetheless, there.[16] Sixth, there is historical evidence that the Charismatic Renewal in Ireland began within Presbyterianism when, in 1967, Rev. Tom Smail was invited to Ballysillan congregation by the minister, Rev. John Wynne, who had become aware of the developing Charismatic Renewal worldwide.[17] Smail spoke in both Ballysillan and West Church, Bangor, laying hands on Rev. David Baillie, who would become a key voice in the Irish Renewal Movement. This gave birth to the Charismatic Fellowship including some 100 ministers.[18] This being said, I wanted to ask whether Irish Presbyterianism is as unreceptive to Pentecostal and Charismatic practice as Kay believes, and to address whether Charismatic principles are generally incompatible with Presbyterianism, specifically through a conversation with John Wimber.

The Research Questions

The object of this study will be to assess whether the theology and practice of John Wimber can be applied to a Reformed context, specifically Presbyterianism, allowing respect for its traditions while it challenges its present mission. Studying the theology of John Wimber is itself practical theology because, as Eddie Gibbs points out, his theology did not come out of detached study but out of "the challenges of local Church ministry."[19] This

15. Robinson, *Pentecostal Origins*, 163. George Jeffreys led a Ballymena Convention in 1916 by singing the Old Hundredth Psalm.

16. Cartledge, *Encountering the Spirit*, 56.

17. Smail writes that he appeared to be an unlikely candidate for Charismatic Renewal, in both ecclesiastical tradition and temperament. His emphasis was preaching and correct theology, rather than exuberant praise of renewal. This resulted in, what he calls, a "gentle but persistent wooing" over a ten-year period. Smail, "Renewal Recalled," 8.

18. Gibson, *Charismatic Movement in Northern Ireland*, 67–68. The group disbanded in 1969 with the advent of the Troubles and the increased difficulty in travel. The meetings were often interrupted by terrorist activity. See also Flynn, *Charismatic Renewal and the Irish Experience*. This mainly covers the Catholic Renewal.

19. Gibbs, "John Wimber," 137. This has been considered when I discussed the literature of Wimber in Chapter 2. It may be a misnomer to assume that theology is in any way detached from context. The discussion on the Confessional Literature in Chapter 2 defines the context that influenced the theological foci of the WCF.

question, therefore, reaffirms this book's place within practical theology, as it is addressing the practice of Reformed Churches and raises some challenges to this practice and how it may be improved.[20] This harmonizes with the central discussion of practical theology, according to Ray Anderson, which is the relation of theory to practice.[21] This is something which missional thinking has been considering. It is also built upon a principle birthed from the evangelical revivals of the eighteenth century, and the missionary movements of the nineteenth century, in which Protestant missions operated in networks that crossed denominational lines.[22] Susan Hope notes that every Christian stream takes a degree of their history and tradition with them. What is being challenged is whether the pre-packaged form of our religious traditions are what is needed for missionary activity today. Instead, she suggests there needs to be a "listening" to the Holy Spirit so what is really needed is revealed.[23] These notions underpin the scope of this book, which seeks to look beyond the theological package of Reformed teaching, to consider Wimber's suggestions.

Practical theology is being used in this book to perform a hermeneutical task in reflecting on how the Reformed Church performs its witness and worship; considering the relationship between what it believes and what it does in a number of contextual applications, to suggest an improved future practice.[24] The book has a practical focus on "the cultivation of ecclesiastical religious life" as described by Gerald Birney Smith.[25] This means that I am asking questions about how theology is put into practice within a local congregation. This is significant as Wimber himself notes that the Church often "seems to soak up the spirit of the culture."[26] Essentially, in dealing with ecclesiology it is dealing with practice. This is a form of qualitative research that seeks to understand "the knowledge of the other" through studying how Reformed theology and a Presbyterian congregation relates to the world.[27] This is followed up by practical applications regarding evangelism, discipleship and ministry, and asking five further questions.

1. Can I as a Presbyterian minister honor my theology and traditions while developing a Charismatic ministry model?

20. Ballard and Pritchard, *Practical Theology in Action*, 18–19.
21. Anderson, *Shape of Practical Theology*, 14.
22. Stanley, "Christian Missions," 444.
23. Hope, *Mission Shaped Spirituality*, 47.
24. Swinton and Mowat, *Practical Theology*, 11–12.
25. Smith, *Practical Theology*, 84.
26. Wimber, *Beyond Intolerance*, 8–9.
27. Swinton and Mowat, *Practical Theology*, 33.

2. Can the congregation of a Presbyterian Church minister to the needs of human beings in the twenty-first century by implementing the ministry suggestions of John Wimber?

3. Is there a wider challenge to Irish Presbyterianism and the Reformed Churches, generally, to discover their relationship with Charismatic theology and practice?

4. Can the PCI experience some of the popularity which the Charismatic streams appear to have seen in Ireland through re-evaluating Charismatic theology and practice?

5. Will Reformed leaders, with a positive appreciation for Charismatic practice, be better equipped to lead Reformed Churches in the twenty-first century?

These questions follow the pattern suggested by Browning, which considers how our present situation is understood; what ought to be the practice in this situation; how that practice may be defended; and what ought to be used in that practice.[28] My discussion is, therefore, seeking to give a critical evaluation of the theology of John Wimber, for possible application to the life and witness of Presbyterian Congregations. The central praxis of this is "action-reflection," as Jeanne Stevenson-Moessner writes.[29] Essentially, this book is a work of critical correlation engaging in a conversation between the Reformed and Charismatic streams of the Church.[30] As such, the book follows a praxis model that not only considers the actions of Reformed Churches, but also the assumptions of these Churches that guide their practice.[31] I ask these questions, drawing on Barry W. Hamilton, about "ministry-in-its-setting," the end of which is to enable readers to experience the type of ministry that I am suggesting.[32] This is action research that seeks to promote a course of action which the research suggests those within the Reformed Churches may consider worth following. This will be a missional action, as outlined by Allan J. Roxburgh and M. Scott Boren, through experimentation and testing of the ideas of Charismatic and Reformed theology to imagine a new model of Church.[33] This aim may be

---

28. Browning, *Fundamental Practical Theology*, 55–56.

29. Stevenson-Moessner, *Prelude to Practical Theology*, 59. Stevenson-Moessner distinguishes this from praxis which she believes only relates to issues of action in regard to injustice.

30. Ballard and Pritchard, *Practical Theology in Action*, 64.

31. Ibid., 70.

32. Hamilton, "Interpretative Interactionism."

33. Roxburgh and Boren, *Introducing the Missional Church*, 22.

impossible to achieve, but the art of the conversation is an end in itself as the two streams begin to discover their collaborative journey on the spiritual path.

This book cannot answer the historical and theological differences between Charismatics and Reformed Cessationists. This book does not attempt to resolve these theological issues. Much discussion has already taken place in this area, without reaching any decisive conclusion. It is beyond the scope of a book that focuses on practical theology to engage in the biblical or systematic debate.[34] I will, therefore, suspend judgment on the biblical texts and their interpretation.[35] What underpins the limitations of this book are the same limitations that come from following only one school of theological interpretation that, according to symphonic theology, as shall be seen later, cannot ever give a complete analysis of truth.[36] It seeks, however, to adopt some of the principles of symphonic theology by looking to a different stream. Nor can this book address the miracles claimed to be experienced by those whom Wimber ministered to, as it is not in the field of either medicine or psychology. This book also seeks to make a contribution to the threefold aim of the Report on the Dialog between the WARC and Classical Pentecostals which suggested that each consider the other's theological positions, issues of commonality and disagreement, and possibilities for common witness.[37] While not offering a definitive response to these questions, it may be possible to propose a commonality between Reformed Churches and the Vineyard, as reflection happens on the contribution of Wimber.

The nature of Wimber's writings may be an issue of concern in that he was writing to a wider audience than academia, although he was a seminary academic.[38] It is also worth noting that not all accept the academic nature of Wimber and his course, MC 510 "Signs and Wonders and Church Growth," which was ultimately restructured by Fuller Theological Seminary School of World Mission in 1987, without Wimber as a teacher.[39] While this may be an issue, it underpins the essence of practical theology that is grounded in the practice of the Church and, as such, must engage beyond

---

34. Grudem, *Are Miraculous Gifts for Today?*; Bridge and Phypers, *Spiritual Gifts and the Church*; Gaffin, *Perspectives on Pentecost*; Budgen, *Charismatics and the Word of God*; Robertson, *Final Word*; Chantry, *Signs of the Apostles*; Carson, *Showing the Spirit*; Fee, *First Epistle to the Corinthians*; Fee, *God's Empowering Presence*.

35. Smith, *Practical Theology*, 71.

36. Poythress, *Symphonic Theology*, 82.

37. "Word and Spirit, Church and World."

38. Coggins and Hiebert, *Wonders and the Word*, 10.

39. Ibid., 20.

the boundaries of a purely academic audience. The research of Keith Warrington and Stephen Hunt has set the writings of John Wimber within the context of academic study and, so, this may be a moot point.[40] Packer also comments on the academic criteria of Wimber:

> He was in truth a clear headed, well focused, thrustful thinker, with his own quota of theories about evangelism, church growth and church life: so that calling him an intellectual is not really wide of the mark.[41]

This places Wimber within an academic framework and gives academic merit to any discussion of him. It is, therefore, possible to value him as a theologian, as noted in chapter 2. Having limited the book to considering how Wimber's theology may be applied to a Reformed congregation, the question will be contextual and, if proved theologically and practically, may further discussion regarding the interaction between Reformed and Charismatic theology.

Action and Qualitative Research Strategy

I have chosen to follow the principles of an "action-based" research, which, according to Louis Cohen, Lawrence Manion, and Keith Morrison, is an aid to "understand, improve, and reform practice."[42] This research aims, therefore, to aid understanding of Reformed history, theology and practice, and seeks to improve it by implementing the suggestions of John Wimber and thus further reforming Reformed practice. Anderson sees this as harmonizing with the principles of practical theology, so I am suggesting an extension of systematic theology into the life and praxis of the Church.[43] Cohen,

---

40. Warrington, "Teaching and Praxis"; Hunt, "At the Cutting Edge."
41. Packer, "Intellectual," 258.
42. Cohen et al., *Research Methods in Education*, 226.
43. Anderson, *Shape of Practical Theology*, 23. It would appear that Anderson sees systematic theology as the discipline which considers the foundation of the Church's beliefs, as outlined in the systematic theology texts, whereas practical theology looks at how these beliefs affect practice. Some believe that all theology must be practical, such as Lovin, who argues that there is a need to integrate the understanding of faith in contemporary society. He notes: "Contemporary practical theology is thus more than the "application" of theological concepts to one social situation or another. Theology is fundamentally transformed by the conditions under which the people of faith must live and by the choices through which they participate in shaping the future. We simply do not know what the doctrines of atonement, incarnation and redemption mean until we understand what they mean for persons shaped by this historical milieu. All theology must be practical theology." Lovin, "Real Task of Practical Theology." Anderson may

Manion, and Morrison further suggest a number of characteristics of action research that provide validity for my research.[44] Action research seeks improvement and learning from the results of that change. I am seeking to improve, by internal involvement as a Presbyterian cleric in a Reformed congregation, ministry and practice. Action research is "self reflective" in that those who are responsible for action seek means by which the action may be improved. In asking the research question, I am asking about the effectiveness of my own ministry. Action research has a wider application to the community on which the reflection is focused, and aims to "enlighten" that community and to free them from accepted institutional methods. Throughout this research there will be some questions asked concerning the validity of current practice within a Reformed congregation and denominationally. Action research seeks to work through small changes that can effect significant change. This is why my research concerns investigation into local parish ministry: to see if these principles may be effective in a denominational context.

As the main emphasis of the method is action research, I have also chosen to use a qualitative method because elements of this study require studying the relationship of one set of facts to another, as Judith Bell notes about qualitative research.[45] In this research I seek to place Reformed doctrine and practice alongside the theology of John Wimber to see if they are compatible. This form of approach explores, as John W. Creswell points out, a means of grasping why individuals attach meaning to a given social or human issue, building from particular to general principles.[46] This also relates to the second layer of the three layers of ecological analysis, as defined by Nancy L. Eisland and R. Stephen Warner, which studies the "meaning, value, and practices" that are shared by a given church.[47] Swinton and Mowat state that within this culture, or "social world," individuals interpret their world to seek meaning. Thus, the focus of our study is the context within which an individual, namely a Reformed congregation, seeks to understand its experiences.[48] The issue, which I am contemplating, is how ministry is currently exercised in evangelism, discipleship, and ministry training.

---

simply be arguing for good theology.

44. Cohen at al., *Research Methods in Education*, 229.
45. Bell, *Doing Your Research Project*, 7–8.
46. Creswell, *Research Design*, 4.
47. The three layers are (1) Demography, (2) Culture, (3) Organization. Island and Warner, "Ecology," 42.
48. Swinton and Mowat, *Practical Theology*, 29–30.

Role of the Researcher and Qualitative Research

I propose to compare the approach, taken by Wimber, to the prevailing practice within Presbyterianism, which may not be formulated explicitly from an abstract theology but, more often than not, is a contextual response to culture, history, Evangelical expectation, and tradition. Swinton and Mowat understand that such beliefs are part of the consideration of practical theology, as practices carry tradition and history, which has developed within communities over periods of time.[49] In this light, I want to suggest an equally valid pattern that is in sympathy with the aims and objectives of the Reformed faith and manifests the power of God in the world today.

To consider this question, I understand that I am personally involved in the area that I am to study. Yet, because I have chosen an action research model, I will seek to draw on my own experience within Christian ministry amongst the Reformed Churches to make an informed judgment applicable to a wider audience within the Reformed Churches.[50] Further, having taken a qualitative and constructivist method, the researcher is not dispassionate, but is "an active participant and co-creator of the interpretative experience."[51] This will primarily use, as source material, theological and spiritual writings from the Reformed and Charismatic communities as the basis of the discussion.[52] As a Presbyterian minister involved in parish ministry with an appreciation for Charismatic theology, there is a degree of personal involvement.

There may be an issue of objectivity, however, as the essence of action research means there is a need for personal involvement and investment in the outcome of the research. Schrieter believes that those involved in the context, leaders, congregation, and professionally and theologically trained

---

49. Ibid., 20.

50. Cohen et al., *Research Methods in Education*, 231. Savage and Presnell state that any theological statements cannot be ensured through this kind of research, but only a thorough understanding of our stories, making us a voice in a "family of intersecting stories unfolding in the narrative study of the ministry context." *Narrative Research in Ministry,* 53. I am not convinced of the validity of this assertion and hope that this research will have a wider tnheological implication than what this statement asserts.

51. Swinton and Mowat, *Practical Theology,* 35. They further comment: "What qualitative research is as a mode of knowledge formation cannot be understood apart from the person of the researcher who carries it out" (48).

52. Savage and Presnell note that studying stories intends a future recognition of what has happened and the possibility of what is to come and, as such, narrative is aimed at a tradition. *Narrative Research in Ministry,* 43. This thesis considers the past of Reformed tradition and suggests a future within a Charismatic context.

clergy, are best suited to this kind of study.[53] Hamilton comments, regarding action research for DMin projects, that the researcher is the "window" through which the research is accomplished, as reflection is made upon his "vocational" journey.[54] This is a distinction between DMin and PhD research; namely, the addressing of a practical issue and eliciting a practical conclusion within an academic context. In this sense the book sets out to solve a practical issue; its contribution to knowledge lies in assessing the value and application of praxis, and the theology that lies behind it in one practical area (namely, Wimber's approach), for a different practical ministry context.[55] This may not be exactly accurate as the discussion itself does highlight a theological issue that will enlarge knowledge. This is also why qualitative research is best suited to this study because, as Bell notes, practitioners who see the need for a change or improvement carry it out.[56] It is easy for someone outside the context to provide a polemic on the need for improvement within a structure; however, reforming practice must come from those with an investment in the change.

Creswell notes that this research falls within the definition of a "social constructivist" worldview, in which individuals seek to understand the world in which they live, with its complexity of views that are molded by their history and culture and, as such, the researchers position themselves within the research.[57] This applies to my research area in that Presbyterianism is a product of its own history and its culture defines it today, and the same forces affect my own views and ideas. The book, however, espouses more than a social constructivist worldview, it tends towards a social reconstruction position, in which theoretical/technical research is reflected against custom and tradition, to offer a shared practice enabling reconstruction of tradition.[58] This book seeks to challenge certain Presbyterian traditions and to reconstruct a new method of evangelism, discipleship and ministry models.

As the book considers a number of characteristics of a given population, there will be a descriptive element to it. However, those characteristics will be subject also to critical analysis and evaluation in the light of suggested alternatives.[59] Therefore, there is a need for wisdom, as Hamilton points out,

---

53. Schreiter, "Theology in the Congregation," 29.
54. Hamilton, "Introduction to Action Research."
55. Vyhmeister, *Your Guide to Writing*, 22.
56. Bell, *Doing Your Research Project*, 8.
57. Creswell, *Research Design*, 8.
58. Browning, *Fundamental Practical Theology*, 4.
59. Vyhmeister, "Theology in the Congregation," 151.

because, as a member of the community investigating that community, my research will inevitably become public knowledge.[60] While this may mean that confidentiality on insider information must be held back, it does not require an uncritical approach, as the focus of the research is to improve that which is significant to the researcher.

Outline for the Book

I intend to begin with the theology of John Wimber as a springboard to discuss how, as a Presbyterian minister in the Reformed and Evangelical camp, Charismatic beliefs can be understood. I will then synthesize a methodology that respects my ecclesiological traditions and distinctives, yet challenges believers and unbelievers with more than an intellectual Christianity. This will be, as Richard E. Davies comments, a decision-oriented research project that seeks to offer a practical option, which a Reformed congregation can follow, rather than a universal discussion of the relationship between Reformed and Charismatic theology.[61] The essential question is what difference harmonizing Reformed and Charismatic theology will make within a local Presbyterian context. This is a theme raised by Andrew Walker regarding the "deep church" discussion. He suggests that what is needed is not a debate on theological method, but a contribution on a catechesis for Christian discipleship.[62] This comment will influence the outline adopted by this book, the emphasis of which is on the practical application of Charismatic practice within a Reformed context.

To aid this, I propose to have a conversation with Wimber's writings, and with my own context, and see if his approach would be a possible form of Evangelicalism, in a denominational setting. I have chosen Wimber because of his own background as a Quaker minister, which is within the Reformed tradition, and because his association with the Jesus Movement, according to Stephen J. Hunt, separates him from mainstream Pentecostalism.[63] Tim Stafford and Jim Beverly believe both Wimber and the Vineyard harmonize Reformed and Charismatic theology and practice.[64] This enables a Reformed congregation to listen as to one of their own. There is also some argument that Pentecostalism does not fall into the definition

---

60. Hamilton, "Writing the 'Good' Doctor."
61. Davies, *Handbook for Doctor of Ministry*, xii.
62. Walker, "Recovering Deep Church," 14.
63. Hunt, "Were the Jesus People Pentecostals?" 4.
64. Stafford and Beverly, "Conversations."

of "conventional Protestantism," as found within the mainstream churches.[65] There may be some value in arguing that Pentecostalism represents a fourth stream of the Christian Church, namely: Roman Catholic, Orthodox, Protestant and Pentecostal.[66] Noting that the Pentecostal stream is a distinct fourth strand of Christianity means that this book will not argue for a denominational change, but will consider the application of certain Charismatic practices within a Protestant stream.

To tie together the three aspects to be considered in this book I have begun from the premise, stated by Stevenson-Moessner, that "practical theology concerns itself with movement or direction."[67] Connected to this Robert Banks writes:

> Mission generates communities of faith and obedience that are ceasely [sic] searching for understanding and influences the flow of understanding that shapes and renews the future of the Church.[68]

This flow of connection is the central outline of this book.[69] The outline, therefore, I have chosen to follow is that outlined by Wimber's own publications, beginning with *Power Evangelism* (1985), which leads to *The Dynamics of Spiritual Growth* (1990), which leads to *Everyone Gets to Play* (2008). This pattern is further outlined in the opening chapter of *Everyone Gets to Play*, called "Laying All Down for Jesus." Here, Wimber outlines the development from evangelism, which leads to an obedient lifestyle of discipleship and then is released in service or ministry.[70] A Reformed support for the outline comes from W. Tullian Tchividjian's theology of the kingdom of God,[71] and it is suggested as a model for the Reformed congregation

---

65. Hollenweger, *Pentecostals*, 507. Smail notes that he was afraid of Pentecostalism prior to experiencing Charismatic Renewal. This may define a wider attitude toward Pentecostal theology and experience in the Reformed Churches. Smail, "Renewal Recalled," 8.

66. Cox believers that Pentecostalism has not made up its mind on where it stands ecumenically at the moment with regard to its position amongst the other traditions. *Fire from Heaven*, 311.

67. Stevenson-Moessner, *Prelude to Practical Theology*, 30–31.

68. Banks, *Reenvisioning Theological Education*, 131.

69. Dodson suggests that there may be merit in understanding this outline as a discipleship model. He notes three aspects of discipleship: rational (evangelism), relational (discipleship) and missional (ministry). Dodson, *Gospel Centered Discipleship*, 41–50.

70. Wimber, *Everyone Gets to Play*, 15–22.

71. Tchividjian, *Kingdom of God*, 9–10.

of Perimeter Church, GA.[72] These are the characteristics of the missional church which attract, worship, equip and then send.[73] There are also similarities to "The Life Development Process" outlined by Rick Warren in which outsiders become committed to maturity, then membership, then mission, and lastly ministry.[74] I have modified this, by bringing together maturity and membership under the heading of discipleship and mission and ministry, as I understand a close correlation between the two purposes. There are also similarities with the process outlined by Mark Dever and Paul Alexander, although I consider the issue of leadership as being wider than eldership.[75] A similar process is the Gospel Growth Process that seeks to outreach, follow up, encourage spiritual growth, and train for ministry.[76] There is also a reliance upon the pastoral cycle within practical theology that looks at the present experience of what is happening, explores through analysis what is happening, reflects upon possibilities of suggesting change, and suggests a course of action developing from these discussions.[77] The purpose of this study is to provide tools, whereby the necessary skills are discovered, to lead a Reformed congregation forward as a missional community, empowered by the Holy Spirit.[78] This will add not only to general knowledge of the interaction between Reformed and Charismatic theology and practice, but also the practical outworking of these theologies.

Merits in the Study

I am aware that the theological reflection contained in this book is my own, and that neither my congregation nor denomination is bound to take on board any practical suggestions I may make. Yet, the aim of the book is to provide a "theoretical generalisation" that goes beyond the experiences of a local congregation, in a local area, and has an impact upon wider theological reflection.[79] This fulfills a criterion of practical theology, according to Robin

---

72. "Randy Pope is faithful and innovative. In a very quiet and systematic manner, he has led Perimeter to become a model church in evangelism, discipleship, and leadership development—all of which are very dear to my heart." J. C. Maxwell, "Introduction," in Pope, *Intentional Church*, 11.

73. Roxburgh and Boren, *Introducing the Missional Church*, 30.
74. Warren, *Purpose Driven Church*, 130.
75. Dever and Alexander, *Deliberate Church*.
76. Marshall and Payne, *Trellis and the Vine*, 85.
77. Ballard and Pritchard, *Practical Theology in Action*, 85–86.
78. Davies, *Handbook for Doctor of Ministry Projects*, 37.
79. Swinton and Mowat, *Practical Theology*, 48.

Gill who sees the result of research in this field as having "implications for theology as a whole."[80] The most basic aim is to provide a cognitive change concerning the relationship between the Reformed and Charismatic streams and, as Ballard and Pritchard point out, while this contradicts the end of the pastoral cycle, it can suggest a new basis for further research that will produce more cognitive change and may ultimately end in action.[81]

Much of the writing on Pentecostalism has emphasized the Arminian, Holiness, Methodist, Revivalistic and Premillennial influences,[82] such as Harvey Cox,[83] Donald W. Dayton[84] and Vinson Synan.[85] Regarding the Charismatic Movement, there have been some historical studies, such as that of Andrew Walker[86] or Peter Hocken.[87] As I noted earlier, Hocken does not refer to any Reformed/Presbyterian impact on the Charismatic Movement, in any direction. There has also been some consideration of Wimber's influence on Anglicanism by Stephen Hunt, but the area of the Presbyterian Churches remains open.[88] The book also draws upon Vern S. Poythress' notion of symphonic theology, as it seeks to consider a cross-pollination of the Reformed and Charismatic streams, through Wimber, to "reinforce, correct, or improve" what is learned.[89] It seeks to have each stream suggest areas that are not covered in the other stream and to fill in that gap in knowledge with their own distinctive. This is another distinctive of symphonic theology: to find some grain of truth even from those with whom there is a fundamental disagreement.[90] There is no desire that this book will proselytize either tradition to become the other, but will demonstrate that, through conversation, our knowledge and experience can be enhanced.

There have been some polemical writings concerning the inaccuracy of contemporary Charismatic phenomena from a Reformed perspective,

---

80. Gill, "Future of Practical Theology," 20–21.

81. Ballard and Pritchard, *Practical Theology in Action*, 166.

82. Premillennialism, in connection with mission, viewed the world as getting worse before the return of Jesus, therefore the Church had to rescue humanity. It was espoused by the Charismatic and Reformed Presbyterian Edward Irving first. See Stanley, *Bible and the Flag*, 76.

83. Cox, *Fire from Heaven*.

84. Dayton, *Theological Roots of Pentecostalism*.

85. Synan, *Holiness Pentecostal Tradition*.

86. Walker, *Restoring the Kingdom*.

87. Hocken, *Streams of Renewal*, 3.

88. Hunt, "Anglican Wimberites."

89. Poythress, *Symphonic Theology*, 43.

90. Ibid., 90.

and some attempts at harmonizing the differing views on the Holy Spirit.[91][92] There has been a paucity of reflection from a Reformed position positively considering Charismatic issues.[93] Considering this, I believe there is a need to re-evaluate the Pentecostal/Charismatic influence on the Reformed Churches and the Reformed influence upon the Charismatic/Pentecostal Churches. This has already been done regarding the Christian and Missionary Alliance.[94] The time is right, therefore, for a consideration of this matter. This would benefit not only Reformed scholars and congregations, but also open up a new avenue of study within the Pentecostal/Charismatic world which is, according to Vyhmeister, an aim of theological research.[95] This will improve scholarship by highlighting a gap in theological discussion by demonstrating that being Reformed does not necessarily mean cessationist, and that the Pentecostal/Charismatic Movement shares the same Reformation source as Reformed Churches. It will improve practice by allowing for a wider degree of freedom in the expression of worship in Reformed Churches, by anchoring the supernatural in Word-centered Churches and challenging the Arminian basis of much Pentecostal/Charismatic evangelism.

Regarding ecclesiastical policy, this study will increase the ecumenical reach of the Pentecostal/Charismatic Movement and theology into the Reformed tradition, and the principles of Reformed doctrine into the Charismatic tradition,[96] which is something, according to Warrington, that has been missing from Pentecostal reflection.[97] This makes a positive contribu-

91. Masters and Whitcomb, *Charismatic Phenomenon*; Robertson, *Final Word*.
92. Grudem, *Are Miraculous Gifts for Today?*
93. Fyall, *Charismatic and Reformed*, 1.
94. King, *Genuine Gold*.
95. Vyhmeister, *Your Guide to Writing*, 2.
96. There has been a tendency away from ecumenism amongst Pentecostals, which David Bunday suggests comes from "sect theory, deprivation theory and eschatological preoccupation" but contrary to the aims and objectives of Pentecostalism. Bundy, 'The Ecumenical Quest of Pentecostalism." This ecumenical reach is a reflection of "post-modern" Pentecostal scholars who take Pentecostalism as the starting point but, according to Archer, are more willing to appropriate the theological insights of other traditions. Archer, *Gospel Revisited*, 5.
97. "The question of predestination is not one that concerns many Pentecostals, most believing that although God has provided the means of salvation, he has left it to individuals to decide whether or not to take advantage of it. The notion of election is one that many are uncomfortable with, if it means that some are elected to salvation and others are not." The doctrine of eternal security is also not widely believed and so elements of guilt and fear are used to ensure the believers keep their salvation. Warrington, *Pentecostal Theology*, 38–39. There is a tendency amongst evangelical Christians to refuse any cross-pollination for other streams, specifically the non-Christian

tion to reconciliation, which is an aim of symphonic theology.[98] This is one of the aims which Wimber himself sees for his theology: emphasizing what is practical and action-based, the "controversial" elements of the Charismatic Movement will be eclipsed as the Church takes power evangelism into the "marketplace," where there will not be enough time to attack each other over differences.[99] This could be seen as avoiding confronting these differences, but it reinforces the practical nature of Wimber's theology and, as I will not be considering these differences in any great detail, it demonstrates this book falls within the remit of practical theology. This book will also aid understanding amongst both Pentecostal/Charismatic and Reformed believers about why their Churches have their unique features and will allow both streams to draw on their theological resources and traditions.

Accordingly, these aims are in sympathy with six of the eight principles of practical theology, as outlined by G. B. Smith. It emphasizes the value of theological truth for Christian life, aids theological preaching, molds the preacher's thinking, builds upon other theological disciplines, emphasizes the human element in theology, and is closely related to systematics.[100] This covers the areas of evangelism, presenting theological truth for the Christian life, preaching which aids discipleship, encompassing other theological disciplines, taking account of the role of individuals in the Church, and dealing with the theological traditions of charismatic and Reformed.

Issues of Concern

As I noted earlier, there is a need for discretion, or wisdom, because of the public nature of research and the position from which I am writing. So, when asking critical questions specifically about the theology and ministry of the PCI, there may be a need to generalize in certain areas. I am not suggesting that one model of denominational life is superior to any other. Douglass calls the local church "a mold" and denominational distinctive "the plaster." While there are many similarities, as the plaster remains a constant,

---

cultures in which the gospel is ministered. This is particularly so amongst Reformed Christians who emphasis the propensity of humanity toward sinfulness. See Stanley, "Inculturation," 22. While this may be perceived to be keeping the gospel pure, it can also alienate the gospel from relevancy to a specific context. My argument is that something can be learned from another context that may improve a theological and ecclesiastical context that appears to be fundamentally different.

98. Poythress, *Symphonic Theology,* 117–18.

99. Wimber, *Kingdom of God,* 27.

100. Smith, *Practical Theology,* 86–87.

the local mold presents the plaster in different ways in each location.[101] I want to propose a model of ministry that best touches the people for whom God has given me spiritual responsibility and which integrates evangelism, discipleship and ministry in one overarching methodology. This may be different from other contexts, but it is a local mold for Reformed theology. As Michael Horton notes, the primary calling is to Christ, and then being drawn into "the covenant community" where converts, who are also part of that spiritual community, begin to serve those around us.[102] For too long, evangelism has been separated from discipleship and spiritual development, and divorced from any concept of corporate ministry. If the Church is to adequately minister in the twenty-first century, then there is a need for something that will not only engage people but also integrate them into the local Church.

Partial Conclusion

This chapter has covered the main areas of how this book will follow its path of study. It has raised a research question of whether the theology and practice of John Wimber can be applied to ministry within a confessional Presbyterian setting. A number of additional questions, for further consideration, have also been raised, concerning the main research question. The form and nature of the research has also been set out as being action based and qualitative, as well as the role that I, as the researcher and author, will execute. the outline for the book has also been considered and why the book will follow the outline that is set, as well as the merits that exist in researching this area. Lastly, I have considered some issues of concern with this book, because of the nature of its scope and potential application to a denominational setting in which I am currently ministering. The research questions that have been raised will become the focus of the ensuing work.

---

101. Douglass, *What is Your Church's Personality*, 4.
102. Horton, *People and Place*, 90.

The Contextual Applications

4

Evangelism in a Reformed Church

Introduction

EVANGELISM LIES AT THE heart of the Christian experience and at the heart of the Church's mission on earth.[1] There are two terms that will be used in this chapter, evangelism and mission, so I want to attempt a definition.[2] Mission, first of all, I want to define as the overarching purpose of God for the world, human life, Israel and the Church, focusing on the centrality of Jesus.[3] Mission is a focus on God's purposes rather than our actions: the

---

1. Wright speaks of a missional hermeneutic, in which those who read the Bible have committed their own personal histories into the greater story of God's plan for the world. «But does so with the even stronger conviction that such commitment should be the normal stance for the whole church, for, on this reading of Scripture, a church that is governed by the Bible cannot evade the missional thrust of the God and the gospel revealed there." He also notes that the churches of the majority world are the primary missionary senders. Wright, *Mission of God*, 43–44. Reid also comments that reaching un-churched people is central to continuing the ministry of Jesus. Reid, *Radically Unchurched*, 31. He further states: "Evangelism is essential to the church because the church will cease to exist without evangelism. Further, God's plan to reach the world is through local congregations." Reid, *Introduction to Evangelism*, 93.

2. Defining mission is a controversial issue because it deals with the truth of Christianity in the face of other theologies that claim truth also. Richebacher, "Missio Dei," 588.

3. Wright, *Mission of God*, 67–68. Wright further defines this focus as meaning: "our committed participation as God's people, at God's invitation and command, in God's own mission within the history of God's world for the redemption of creation.» Wright, *Mission of God*, 23.

missio dei.[4] I, therefore, use mission as the ethos that defines praxis. This focus on the purpose or plans of God seems to harmonize with a Reformed understanding of mission.[5] Regarding evangelism, Walter Brueggemann refers to it as the "passionate preoccupation" of the Church.[6] This seems to suggest that evangelism is what the Church does in carrying out the *missio dei*. Harvie Conn, therefore, calls the Church a "news reporter for the kingdom."[7] For Evangelicals, evangelism does not just form part of their theological worldview, but is central to their practice. Pawson sees this in two forms: defensive, in which the message of the Bible is protected; and offensive, in which the message of the Bible is proclaimed.[8] These two aspects encapsulate what Evangelicalism is and what it does. This means that Evangelicalism does not just mean believing certain theological axioms, but having one's practice affected by these convictions.

If we accept the *missio dei* definition of evangelism, it is not just focused on winning individual converts to faith, but a commitment to bringing the whole world under the authority of God.[9] Evangelism, therefore,

---

4. Wright, *Mission of God*, 61–62. Bosch notes that *missio Dei* speaks of God's mission, an attribute of his character, and the Church is an instrument of that mission. *Missiones Ecclesiae*, therefore, is the service of *missio Dei*, "representing God in and over against the world." Bosch, *Transforming Mission*, 389–91. Horton also emphasizes the purpose of God in mission by underlining the purpose for which the Church exists—that is, to reflect God's glory in the world. Horton, *Putting Amazing Back into Grace*, 23. The end of this goal in history is the coming of the kingdom of God. Smith, *Mission After Christendom*, 118. This is a theme of Wimber's theology, as we have noted previously.

5. Sproul notes that the gospel is the message God gives to the Church. Sproul, *Getting the Gospel Right*, 110. Edgar comments that this sovereignty of God in all areas, especially mission in our context, is the "central concern of Reformed Theology", and it assures the Church of the ultimate triumph of God's plans. Edgar, *Truth in all its Glory*, 19–22. Wright cites the WSC, Q.1. in support of his position. Wright, *Mission of God*, 404. Again this seems to support a Reformed emphasis.

6. Brueggemann, *Biblical Perspectives on Evangelism*, 7. The difficulty comes in defining what evangelism is. W. Abraham suggests the following: conversion, faith, repentance, the kingdom of God, baptism and Christian initiation, the relationship between the intellect and the emotions, the relevancy of the ancient faith to the modern world and apologetics. Abraham, *Logic of Evangelism*, 11.

7. Conn, *Evangelism*, 18. He goes further, stating that evangelism is connected to "kingly justice" which God promised in the Messiah. Conn, *Evangelism, Doing Justice*, 43. It would seem as the Church reports the kingdom, it also works to implement kingdom principles of grace and justice in the world. We will consider this in the incarnational model of evangelism.

8. Pawson, *Word and Spirit Together*, 73.

9. Devenish, *What on Earth is the Church For?* 27–28.

"entails an invitation to come under God's rule, and learn its ways."[10] This is a holistic missional theology that not only seeks to gain proselytes, but also to make disciples and release them into ministry. This has manifested itself in a change of thinking away from considering evangelism as separate from mission, and moving toward seeing the Church as a missional community.[11] If this is accepted as the norm in our evangelistic activity, then the local Church is central to the gospel and evangelism ought not to be abdicated to external agencies.

This places evangelism within the context of the Church and within the activity center of the local congregation. Lesslie Newbigin states that it is "an integral part of the gospel" through its interpersonal relationships, not purely through theological reflection on the atonement, and it is through the community that the Holy Spirit draws us into fellowship.[12] While there may be a case for some individuals who have come to faith through theological reflection, the issue of community appears to be central. Brueggemann agrees with this, stating that evangelism encourages people to see "that an attempt to live without the Holy Character of these narratives is indeed a life of "non-sense."[13] Evangelism gives meaning to individual existence and, through placing that meaning within the context of a local congregation, a sense of belonging ensues also.

Evangelism is not purely an academic exercise, but it is an action that the Church is to do. In this light, John MacArthur defines evangelism as the personal actions of the individual believer, and mission is the corporate activity of the Church.[14] Susan Hope sees mission as both personal and corporate, through believers' witnessing and corporate evangelistic activities.[15] Whatever the validity of these distinctions, there is an individual and a corporate element that are missional in proclaiming and spreading the gospel.

While there are many different contexts in which the gospel is to be proclaimed, it is the Church whom Christ has elected to use. Through the members of the Church, the gospel is presented. Michael Frost and Alan Hirsch write that evangelism is contextual as it uses the context or culture to present Christ, which means ongoing study of how culture is developing

---

10. Tomlin, *Provocative Church*, 65.

11. This change is to see the Church as a missionary agent where the church "is to be God's hands and feet in accomplishing mission" rather than a recruitment organization for new members. Roxburgh and Boren, *Introducing the Missional Church*, 20.

12. Newbigin, *Discovering Truth in a Changing World*, 81–82.

13. Brueggemann, *Biblical Perspectives on Evangelism*, 10.

14. MacArthur, *Master's Plan for the Church*, 59–60.

15. Hope, *Mission Shaped Spirituality*, 9.

and changing.[16] Evangelism and mission, according to Timothy Chester and Steve Timmis, appear to be two elements of the same activity, and being gospel centered means two things. First, it is being Word-centered, as the gospel is a message; and, second, it is mission centered, because the gospel is a missionary message.[17] This connection between the gospel and the gospel community, rooted in a local context and presenting the gospel in a culturally sensitive manner, appears to be central to Christian ministry.

The passage of Matt 16:13–19 has provided a source for discussing the nature of the Church and even the doctrine of apostolic succession. Yet, right at the heart of what is recorded, is the simplicity of acknowledging Christ as the Messiah. It is a faith statement that the kingdom of God had invaded the kingdom of this world in the person of Jesus Christ. Wimber believes Matt 16:13–19 formed Christ's understanding of the nature of the kingdom of God, and that he has invaded the "realm of Satan" to bring the kingdom at this moment.[18] The gospel is the understanding that God's kingdom is invading a world in rebellion against him, and that the Church's role is to proclaim that kingdom message.[19] According to John M. Hull, this makes the church the agent of mission with the objective mission of not seeking to build greater churches, but to establish the kingdom of God.[20] Yet, effective mission will feed into the local Church, which is the agent for the kingdom of God, and will affect growth.

The issue of whether evangelism is sowing the message or reaping the harvest of commitment is also of significance. Kenneth Prior notes that both are equally valid.[21] It is unclear what distinction this makes practically, so whatever our understanding, a commitment to propagating the message of Christ is required. Not allowing, as David Beckett comments, the dust to grow on evangelism, is implied.[22] Evangelism is not to be left as an option for a few or for special campaigns. The mission of the gospel may be better placed at the center of the Church's activities.

Some may level the claim against the teachings of Wimber that it is a new form of evangelism, making all traditional forms of evangelism invalid.

16. Frost and Hirsch, *Shaping of Things to Come*, 88.
17. Chester and Timmins, *Total Church*, 16.
18. Wimber and Springer, *Power Evangelism*, 33.
19. Although in rebellion against God, the gospel must manifest relevance for those sinned against: "A gospel that does not address people as the sinned against poses a lot of problems for the publican, the sinned against. Either he rejects the gospel or sees it as an opiate." Conn, *Evangelism, Doing Justice*, 46.
20. Hull, *Mission-Shaped Church*, 2–5.
21. Prior, *Gospel in a Pagan Society*, 21.
22. Beckett, "Evangelism," 11.

He writes that there is no biblical evidence for evangelism being invalid if it is not accompanied by signs and wonders, but he seeks to "consciously" co-operate with the Holy Spirit in evangelism so that preaching and signs and wonders work together, "reinforcing each other."[23] This may raise concerns to a Reformed believer as WCF says that humanity is passive in conversion.[24][25] Passivity in salvation requires a response to certain stimuli, most notably preaching. Responding to the stimuli of signs and wonders may not be radically different from responding to preaching. Indeed, if we consider the Reformed view of the sacraments then there may be areas of commonality. The WCF does not appear to dismiss the need for any stimulus because if it did, then preaching itself would be problematic. Wimber is not suggesting that a rejection of the power evangelism model is a rejection of biblical theology; he has great respect for traditional evangelistic models.[26] It is for this reason that I suggest the model of power evangelism may work in a traditional setting, because it does not usurp or reject any existing models.

The evidence of power evangelism is signs and wonders and one could assume that, without this evidence, the gospel is not being fully proclaimed. Wimber does not argue this, but that signs and wonders authenticate the message of evangelism.[27] In this model, evangelism may become significantly more powerful as the message of Christ affects people's lives prac-

---

23. Wimber and Springer, *Power Evangelism*, 79.

24. WCF 10:2. WSC Q.14: sees sin as being both the nature of humanity that will not conform to God's law as well as the actions which transgress that law. Sproul defines the Reformed position as «radical corruption," that human beings are utterly depraved in God's sight, but not utterly depraved, as acts of kindness are practiced. Sproul, *Essential Truths*, 147.Wimber's thinking on the nature of sin does not appear to be fully developed. He refers to his need to be "salvaged," which may imply an acceptance of total depravity. Wimber, *Everyone Gets to Play,* 41. He is also critical of performance based Christianity, noting that his own experience was that nothing good he did would recommend him to God. He needed God's grace. Wimber, *Way In is the Way On,* 83. He affirms the human need for salvation through penal substitution; however, his emphasis is on humanity's response. Wimber, *Power Evangelism,* 36–38.

25. Wimber states that while his ministry included many who would not embrace a Charismatic position, he was not successful in every context. Yet, he notes that there are a growing number of theologians, pastors, thinkers and writers who have grasped what he has said when their theological worldview may mitigate against it. Wimber, *Everyone Gets to Play,* 166. While I have noted the teaching of the WCF earlier in this research as not necessarily being against charismatic experience, I hope this work adds to this ongoing debate. Challenging the position of the WCF may not preclude his method from being useful in a Reformed context.

26. Although Wimber does not belittle traditional evangelistic models, it could be argued that a rejection of signs and wonders accompanying the gospel is a rejection of the biblical norm (Mark 16:15–18).

27. Wimber and Springer, *Power Evangelism,* 78.

tically, as well as intellectually. It is more than believing the right things and ignoring the present situation that many people face; it is applying the gospel to human needs.

Evangelism speaks about sin and how it has affected the human race (Rom 6:23). Often, to a "traditional" Church member, sin has certain characteristics. The list in 1 Cor 6:9–10 would come to mind (i.e., sins that are obvious and visible). To define sin, I propose to use Newbigin's definition: "Sin is a corruption of the very center of human nature . . . Sin is a corruption of the nature of man due to the fact that he has become separated, alienated, turned away from God."[28] Sin is not, therefore, just the things that are done, but the source of why people do them; namely, a fallen human nature.[29] Sin is the corrupt human nature than manifests itself in the actions which display that human nature. It is a disposition toward living for one's own will rather than under a directive force of another.

It is not the recognition of sin that is the problem; rather, it is the way people judge the sinner in comparison to themselves. Keller uses the prodigal son/older brother (Luke 15:11–32) as a type of Church person. He notes that the younger brother is more obviously sinful, but the older brother is equally sinful because sin is not just law breaking, it is putting us in the place of God as Judge.[30] Such an understanding has specific application for ministry in a traditional Church. The Church interacts with the older brother, the one who has accepted the culture's standards and lived within the confines of traditional morality, often judging the prodigals. The message to such people is to "repent of the reason we ever did anything right," which was to get God under control and try to bargain with him over our own sinfulness and so become our own Savior.[31] To reach this group, the gospel must be more than simply believing the right things; it is experiencing the reality of gospel power.

How such people are reached, the model that is used needs to be chosen wisely as the methodology may obscure the message.[32] Rick Warren suggests strategically targeting those to be evangelized. Practically, this looks at the people who live close by—helping the decision of who we can

---

28. Newbigin, *Sin and Salvation*.
29. WSC Q.14, 18, 19.
30. Keller, *Prodigal God*, 43.
31. Keller, *Prodigal God*, 77–78.

32. Prior notes that the predominant method of evangelism in the British Churches has been the large-scale evangelistic meeting, pioneered by Moody and Sankey in the nineteenth Century, which are particularly effective in reaching nominal Christians. Yet, the changes in our society suggest that this may not be the most effective method any longer. Prior, *Gospel in a Pagan Society*, 11.

best evangelize, because not everyone can be reached.[33] This is helpful as, although there may be a missional heart which desires that all those within a parish area come to faith in Christ, human personalities, gifts, and talents mean there will be more success with some than others. What is important, however, is that evangelism is not just believed but practiced.

There also appears to be a trend that those most "Evangelical" in theology are sometimes least evangelistic in practice. Evangelicalism appears to mean acceptance of certain theological statements rather than what people do in sharing their faith.[34] Ryken believes this is because "Christians have lost their nerve" and have formed spiritual clubs that keep us separate from the world and make us feel safe in terms of holiness.[35] Abraham suggests another reason why interest in evangelism may be waning is its connection, almost exclusively, with fundamentalism.[36] Mark Mittelberg gives a stereotypical picture of this kind of evangelism, either "superstar Christians" or "out-of-touch individuals, who impose themselves and the gospel on everyone they meet."[37] It may be that the manifestation of this theological school has made the message confusing by the manner in which it has been proclaimed, resulting in the message of evangelism being eclipsed by the method of evangelism.

For the basis of this study, I will define evangelism in the words of Wimber himself: "Evangelism is a complex process in which the Holy Spirit works in the hearts and minds of people."[38] This is particularly poignant, when considering a context in which not every full member of a local congregation is a member of the true Church. In this instance, the message of the kingdom is of particular significance and importance. I propose to introduce a conversation between three models of evangelism from within the Reformed community, both historical and contemporary; namely, fear-based evangelism, incarnational evangelism and relational evangelism, and the theology of *Power Evangelism* specifically. This is to suggest that

33. Warren, *Purpose Driven Church*, 157.

34. Giberson and Stephens outline the perception of evangelicalism as appearing to be tied to a political or cultural position, whereas evangelicalism seeks to be biblically grounded, intellectually engaged, humble and forward thinking. Giberson and Stephens, "Evangelical Rejection of Reason." There is little reference to the action they take in the world.

35. Ryken, *City on a Hill*, 45.

36. Abraham, *Logic of Evangelism*, 8.

37. Mittelberg, *Becoming a Contagious Church*, 90.

38. Wimber and Springer, *Power Evangelism*, 105. A Reformed definition would be in sympathy with much of what Wimber states about the work of the Holy Spirit. The centrality of the Bible to the Holy Spirit's work would be central, and while other means may be used, they are subsidiary to the Bible. Kuiper, *God Centered Evangelism*, 141.

Wimber stands within the theological tradition of the Reformed Churches, and that his suggestions on power evangelism can be applied within a local Reformed context.

The Fear Model

Historically, in the Reformed Churches, the example of the fear model has been Jonathan Edwards (1703–58). Edwards was the pastor of the Congregational Church in Northampton, Massachusetts and, while no formal ties between Congregationalism and Presbyterianism existed at the time, because of the revival phenomena associated with his ministry (1734–35), he became well known amongst New School Presbyterians, who offered him President of the College of New Jersey, later to be named Princeton.[39] Edwards is particularly well known regarding his preaching.

The approach of Edwards, to preaching about hell and the coming judgment, has had a profound effect upon Reformed Evangelical preaching. The law of God, defining the standards set down for humanity, is proclaimed to condemn humanity and demonstrate the inevitability of hell, as R. Scott Clarke notes.[40] Indeed, the common terms of this style of preaching, "fire and brimstone," seems to have its genesis in Edwards: "They will find no place, where they can remain, and rest, and take breath for one minute: for they will be tormented with fire and brimstone; and will have no rest day nor night for ever and ever."[41] His sermon, "Sinners in the Hands of an Angry God," may be understood as the fountainhead of fear-based evangelism.[42] His ethos was: "There is nothing that keeps wicked men at any one moment out of hell, but the mere pleasure of God."[43] Throughout this sermon, Edwards uses graphic descriptions to elicit a response and make the individual avoid hell by paying attention to his words: words like "flames," "one holds a spider, or some loathsome insect over the fire" and "such exquisite and horrible torments."[44] Edwards uses a very descriptive style of communication

---

39. Edwards, "Jonathan Edwards," 90. Specifically the Evangelical Awakening and the 1801 Plan of Union with Congregationalists defined new School Presbyterianism. Pointer writes: "it was part of an evangelical phalanx that shared a common commitment to evangelism through revivals and to Christianising American through moral reform." Pointer, "New School Presbyterians," 174–75.

40. Clarke, "Letter and Spirit," 358.

41. Edwards, "Future Punishment of the Wicked," 80.

42. Edwards, "Sinners in the Hands."

43. Ibid.

44. Edwards, "Future Punishment of the Wicked," 79, Edwards, "Sinners in the Hands."

to demonstrate the awfulness of hell for the individual sent there, and in an age without television and the internet, such language may have been as shocking as a graphic film or novel would be today.

Some question the use of such descriptive language in the sermon, seeing it as inappropriate and the product of speculation rather than exposition. John H. Gerstner comments that all his pictures, apart from the spider over the fire, are biblical.[45] The appropriateness of such imagery may be a matter of homiletics. It may be no different from the cultural references made in sermons today that connect the text to a political issue, a moral question, or using something in the social media to illustrate the point. Peter Rollins has questioned the morality of fear- based evangelism as a "technique" which is used for the "psychological coercion" of people to become Christians.[46] Whether describing in detail something that is a deeply held belief of the Church, concerning those who are not Christians, is coercion is not clear. It may be correct, however, to challenge whether it accurately presents the Christian message or only emphasizes one aspect of it.

Che Ahn believes that fear-based evangelism does not produce the lasting results in today's Church that it may have done in the past. He does concede that fear is a motivator and may scare individuals into faith, but contends that it does not win hearts. The result is that converts will not normally have a passion for evangelism themselves.[47] Ahn draws a conclusion that may not be sustainable. While some may find themselves uncomfortable with personal evangelism, there is anonymity to mass evangelism of the congregational model practiced by Edwards. It may be better to state that fear-based evangelism encourages an abdication of responsibility to "professionals," or a "guerrilla warfare" where the gospel is thrown at unbelievers and the Church retreats back into fellowship.

The results of Edward's approach are evident. Iain Murray states, "Wheelock reported to Trumbull how the people, whom he characterized as 'thoughtless and vain,' were so changed before the sermon was ended, that they were 'bowed down with an awful conviction of their sin and danger.'"[48] There can be no doubt that the world has changed and the Church along with it, especially regarding how the gospel is presented. In Edward's time, literature would have been more widely read than today and vivid descriptions of hell would have been relevant. Josh Moody believes that the

---

45. Gerstner, *Rational Biblical Theology*, 2:494.

46. Rollins, *Insurrection*, 9–10. He writes: ". . . such examples of outward cruelty are simply the most extreme and perverse expression of techniques that we still witness in more clandestine forms today."

47. Ahn, *Spirit Led Evangelism*, 69.

48. Murray, *Jonathan Edwards*, 168.

contemporary approach to Church is influenced by business and political campaigns of which Edwards would be critical.[49] In Edward's sermons, God is seen as an angry and vengeful deity who is waiting to punish those who have not accepted his Son, because all unbelievers "are now the objects of that very same anger and wrath of God, that is expressed in the torments of hell."[50] He seems to suggest, that in hell, God is turning people over to be tormented by the devil, "the devil is waiting for them"[51]; yet, that seems to contradict the New Testament teaching on the purpose of hell (Matt 25:41) in which it was created for the devil and his angels.

It is necessary to ask whether an evangelistic model, which emphasizes fear of punishment as a motivation for conversion, is relevant for today. The response to this "hell-fire evangelism" has generally been outright acceptance or rejection. Gerstner follows the former because of the seriousness of the question of eternity. He believes there is nothing wrong with "scare preaching" in which "the divine Threatener" makes humanity afraid of hell.[52] Using such language, when referring to God, seems to contradict any notion of God's love or power (1 John 4:8). Ajith Fernando also agrees with a fear-based model, not because the fear of hell is to be used to scare people into the Church, but because, although it is unpalatable to the modern mind, the seriousness of the truth does not warrant its disuse.[53] Moody suggests the answer is both yes and no. No, because the biblical literacy of Edward's time was much higher than it is in the West today, due to the strong Puritan influences in New England. For people today the "predominant communication means is the video not the logos, sight not word."[54] Yet, Moody suggests that there may be room for an Edwardian approach in which the text is carefully examined, making it come alive with imagery in a correct understanding of our position.[55] It may be that the practice of using imagery in preaching engages an element in the human psyche that connects with the numinous rather than the logical. Particularly, when speaking about a subject such as hell, this imagery may be helpful and clarifying.

Some critics also believe that much of what is believed and preached about hell, even amongst Bible-believing Evangelicals, has its foundation more in extra-biblical sources than the text of Scripture. Brian McLaren

---

49. Moody, *God Centered Life*, 25.
50. Edwards, "Sinners in the Hands."
51. Ibid.
52. Gerstner, *Repent or Perish*, 18–19.
53. Fernando, *Crucial Questions About Hell*, 140.
54. Moody, *God Centered Life*, 23.
55. Ibid.

believes that the problem is that what is thought that the Bible says about hell is not what the Bible actually says.[56] He believes much of the theology on hell comes from Dante or Milton. There may be some merit in this argument and, in seeking to proclaim a biblical hermeneutic about hell, it is essential that these difficult questioned are answered.

The issue of what message is preached to unbelievers is one of significant debate. Donald Miller's story of the US Navy SEALs is one example of how devotion to a single method may be counterproductive.[57] This reminds us that sometimes the passion with which the Church speaks of judgment can preclude people from hearing the gospel, which brings freedom from judgment. Steve Chalke takes a similar line to this story of Miller and states that people want a positive message "that they can buy into," which appears incompatible with "pointing out that they are sinners."[58] Elsewhere, he states that when a person is lost they know it and do not need condemnation, but a way out of their lostness.[59] These challenges suggest that there may be something inappropriate about speaking of the fear of God's punishment as an evangelistic model today.

Warren believes that central to this argument is how the sin issue is dealt with in relation to loving people, unconditionally, but not accepting and approving of their behavior.[60] The problem is that when sin is denounced, it can seem as if we are attacking the person out of a sense of disgust or rejection of them. This will further place a wedge between the sinner and the gospel, which may be hard to overcome. Mark Dever highlights the importance of speaking of sin with passion and love, considering the need to make a decision for Christ. It is not "manipulative or insensitive" to be urgent about proclaiming hell; it is the truth considering the shortness of human life.[61] Yet, I wonder if an exclusive attitude to fear-based evangelism is not unfaithful to the sovereignty of God in conversion after all (1 Cor 1:21, NIV). Response to the gospel is not limited to a fear of hell.

---

56. McLaren, Interview with John Buckeridge, 25.

57. Miller, *Blue Like Jazz*, 33–34. Miller recounts a story told by a folk-singer about American hostages who had been chained to the floor and constantly shouted at by their captors. When US Navy SEALs entered the building to liberate them, they did not respond to their loud commands because they were used to being shouted at. They only responded when their liberators sat beside them on the floor, making physical contact, and spoke quietly to them. Miller reflects on a form of evangelism that only shouts commands and does not engage with people.

58. Chalke and Mann, *Lost Message of Jesus*, 117–18.

59. Chalke and Watkins, *Intelligent Church*, 97–98.

60. Warren, *Purpose Driven Church*, 216.

61. Dever, *Nine Marks of a Healthy Church*, 128.

Keller uses an innovative approach when preaching hell.[62] He believes preaching on hell is essential for two main reasons: first, that people get what they want in the afterlife, either God as Savior or themselves as their own Savior; second, hell is a natural consequence of living a "self-centered, self-absorbed, self-pitying, and self-justifying" existence, in which denial about the source of their problems—sin—continues, and yet the evidence in society mounts.[63] However, he believes that using certain symbolism about hell undermines the potency of the message and prevents people from responding to the gospel.[64] The descriptions of hell used in the New Testament have a particular relevancy for that culture as they are identified with Gehenna, the rubbish dump outside Jerusalem, where the city's refuse was incinerated.[65] That, however, may not have the same ease of understanding for people in the twenty-first century. Perhaps the same truth explained in a way that is comprehensible to our own society is needed. To emphasize judgment exclusively in terms of "God's active judgement," Keller notes, can make the truth less of a deterrent to unbelievers, and those who do respond "reform their lives only out of a self-interested fear of avoiding consequences, not out of love and loyalty to the one who embraced and experienced hell in our place." The implication, he notes, is that they become moralist, not born again believers.[66] Hell, he believes, is a person's freely chosen identity apart from God on a trajectory into infinity.[67] This is demonstrated in life, where God is rejected and addiction is followed, to give meaning to life. This "personal disintegration" continues on into eternity, where people become increasingly isolated, not only from God, but from each other. It is, therefore, essential that cultural wisdom and biblical conviction permeate our proclamation of this doctrine, giving it the intended power.

---

62. Keller believes in the need for a doctrine of hell: "The loss of the doctrine of hell and judgement and the holiness of God does irreparable damage to our deepest comforts—our understanding of God's grace and love and of our human dignity and value to him. To preach the good news, we must preach the bad." Keller, "Preaching Hell in a Tolerant Age."

63. Keller, "Importance of Hell."

64. Ibid.

65. "The interesting thing about the word *Gehenna* is that it is a reference to a ravine in the south side of Jerusalem where, about a hundred years before Jesus was born, there were these really odd kind of Blair-Witch-like murders going on. The Jews began to view this area as cursed. It basically became a trash heap or a dumping ground for Jerusalem. When the pile got too big, they just set the whole thing on fire. Can you picture this? The word *Gehenna* conjures up a very vivid image: a stinking, smoldering place of destruction and neglect." Chandler, *Explicit Gospel*, 42.

66. Keller, "Importance of Hell."

67. Keller, *Reason for God*, 78.

Wimber sees an element of the fear model as implicit within a gospel presentation. He connects the love of God with the wrath of God, propitiated by Christ on the cross (Rom 3:25; Heb 2:17; 1 John 2:2, 4:10). He writes that for us to experience salvation, Jesus had to satisfy God's justice and be punished on the cross.[68] This is different, however, from the clear and definitive descriptions of the punishments in hell used to evoke a response to the gospel out of fear. Wimber connects the wrath of God clearly with his love for humanity and, in this connection, the justice of God is proclaimed as having been fulfilled when Christ died on the cross.

The Incarnational Model

There has been historical tension between Evangelicals who see the gospel only as proclamation and those who see it as incarnational. This seeks to effect change through the presence and practice of mercy ministry. Some Evangelicals have been critical of this model, seeing it as a misleading path to take. Dever believes that some have mistaken social action and politics for evangelism and, while they may produce some change, the real difference will only be seen when Christians display character in their worship and witness.[69] The politicization of the Church in places like North America and Northern Ireland are examples of this, where spirituality is linked with a party political agenda. This can lead to sectarian attitudes, racism, even homophobia going unchallenged in the Christian community. To be true to the gospel and to the principles of power evangelism, there must be a social conscience that changes people's attitudes to others and motivates them to show mercy to their enemies.

Wimber understands this model of ministry as being in sympathy with the power evangelism model: "The manifest presence and power of the Holy Spirit in our midst is connected, inseparably, to His mercy and compassion."[70] Indeed, he sees it as a practical manifestation of signs and wonders, claiming that the one who creates miracles through our hands, also uses these hands to feed the poor and "watch over the immigrant."[71] This is not only to relieve their needs, but to aid them to become self-supporting.[72] In this light, power evangelism and incarnational evangelism may appear to be complementary. Yet, elsewhere, he appears to be somewhat critical of this

---

68. Wimber and Springer, *Power Evangelism*, 36.
69. Dever, *Nine Marks of a Healthy Church*, 133–34.
70. Wimber, *Way In is the Way On*, 63.
71. Ibid., 64.
72. Ibid., 65.

model of evangelism that connects the gospel with the meeting of specific needs. He calls it a faulty gospel that produces faulty Christians. It is a self-based gospel that is not a call to radical discipleship.[73] It could be said that the idea behind power evangelism itself is the meeting of a specific need. The power manifestation is, therefore, a complementary method of authenticating the gospel, not the end alone. This will affect our understanding of the relationship between the gospel and social justice, for social justice becomes the presence of God's kingdom invading this world."[74] This is where power evangelism could be seen as uncaring for the needs of people, because it is less concerned with their needs and more with demonstrations of power. Wimber's criticism of needs-based evangelism means that Christians are not moved by the plight of people, but merely see them as an opportunity to manifest the power of God. To separate the socio-economic or political needs of people from their medical or psychological needs seems to be a false division, as they are as much a product of the fall as separation from God (Rom 8:22–23). The ministry of social justice cannot be separated from power evangelism and from compassion for the sick, psychologically disturbed and demonized. To some degree, Wimber appears to be confused in this matter and his thinking is unclear.

There have been some who question incarnational evangelism. Keller notes that evangelism must be declaratory and cannot be substituted through "loving the poor."[75] This raised a concern that an incarnational model of evangelism alone never challenges the hearers with the call to repentance. In this instance, it may be no more than a social function that betters people's lives, without dealing with their critical need for forgiveness and reconciliation. Mercy ministry encourages people to see that they are not meant to exist alone, but that we are our brother's keepers (Gen 4:9). It is this "impulse" of mercy that, according to Keller, "makes us sensitive to hurts and lacks in others and makes us desire to alleviate them."[76] What Keller seems to be getting at is that substituting incarnational evangelism for proclamation evangelism, or vice versa, does not present the whole gospel. There is a need to combine the two so that, as the gospel is proclaimed, it is also demonstrated in ministries of mercy. Mercy ministry may, therefore, be a new designation that encompasses proclamation and presence in an evangelical ethos. It seeks to bring the proclamation into ministries of mercy and ministries of mercy into proclamation. Ryken comments that

---

73. Wimber and Springer, *Power Evangelism*, 36.
74. Ibid., 163.
75. Keller, "Gospel and the Poor."
76. Keller, *Ministries of Mercy*, 46.

whatever is being done for the needy is being done for God.[77] Brueggemann agrees with this connection and understands "social action" as springing from God's compassion for the world and must be aimed back at God if it is to be authentic.[78] It is helpful to see the ministry to the needy as being a complementary ministry to proclamation, to relational witness and to power evangelism, which opens the hearts of the needy to the reality of Christ.

There are other organizations that seek to help people, other than the Church, so it could be asked what separates the Church from them? Chester and Timmis believe the commitment to reconcile people to God through the message proclaimed separates the Church's ministry to the poor from other groups. They speak of "felt needs." It means that the deepest need in anyone is to avoid God's judgment, even if they do not recognize that need.[79] This does appear to belittle the actual pains and sorrows that people are going through, and to ignore their suffering. While it retains the appropriate focus of gospel proclamation, if it were to be followed, it would fall short in compassion. Positively, in this instance, the incarnational model is part of a wider practice within the Church, which includes both preaching the fear of God and meeting people's needs. This defines the approach as specifically Christian, rather than social or liberal, and offers an opportunity to get to the center of the Christian message, which is the heart of God in reconciliation.

There appears to be a difficulty in conducting a conversation between Wimber and Reformed theology on this matter. This may be, in part, due to Wimber's own apparent confusion on the issue. There may also be historical reasons why Reformed theology did not engage with incarnational evangelism, specifically in the twentieth century.[80] Buschart notes the Reformed emphasis on God as "the Sustainer-Ruler" of creation, in which he preserves the world.[81] This may have led to a disconnection with human needs because God was deemed to be in charge of things. It may have been assumed to be part of the sovereign will that humanity is in the condition it is in. Whatever the motivations in this theology, a re-evaluation of the connection between incarnational evangelism and power evangelism is important.

77. Ryken, *City on a Hill*, 151.
78. Brueggemann, *Biblical Perspectives on Evangelism*, 43.
79. Chester and Timmis, *Total Church*, 75–76.
80. Murray suggests that the focus of Twentieth Century Reformed Evangelicalism was preoccupied with "new evangelicalism" which emphasized a pragmatism with regard to ecumenical relations. It may be concluded that the focus was more on maintaining traditional orthodox inter-church relations and critiquing evangelistic techniques than reflecting on how to practice evangelism. Murray, *Evangelicalism Divided*, 51.
81. Buschart, *Exploring Protestant Traditions*, 105.

The practice of power evangelism seeks the change of human situations by the power of God. These situations are rooted in human suffering; therefore, the need to help practically may be a manifestation of natural power evangelism.

The Relational Model

The relational model has its history in the Reformed Churches, in Richard Baxter (1615–91), who was the pastor of the Church of England in Kidderminster, a church organized similarly to Presbyterianism. After the restoration of Charles II he was offered the Bishopric of Hereford, which he declined, and was then given a license to preach as a Non-Conformist, neither Presbyterian nor Independent.[82] Baxter emphasized pastoral ministry; not running around people's homes to keep them content as many ministers do[83], but catechism and spiritual growth: "The ultimate end of our pastoral oversight must be linked with the ultimate purpose of our whole lives. This is to please and to glorify God. It is also to see the sanctification and holy obedience of the people under our charge."[84] This would be evangelistic to unconverted members of the Church, and catechetic to spiritual members of the Church.

What underpinned Baxter's approach, "the first and most vital part of our ministry"[85], was a desire for the conversion of individuals. Robert McEvoy comments: "For Baxter, the main purpose of pastoring, as with preaching, was evangelism."[86] It is important to understand that Baxter did not pastor at the expense of preaching. Through plainness of speech, he preached for a verdict, as Edward Donnelly states, and his "preaching was characterized by a passionate evangelistic appeal"; but that longing for a decision, sent him into their homes to grasp what of the preaching they had understood, and whether they had accepted Christ.[87] It could be said, therefore, that this is a complementary method to the proclamation model. This was to be approached through visiting the family, "when they are at

---

82. Barker, *Puritan Profiles*, 293. When the Presbyterian majority in the House of Commons went to see King Charles I (1648) he agreed to a modified form of Presbyterianism that still allowed for bishops and when he recanted from this, Baxter was one who condemned him as a traitor. See Adair, *Puritans, Religion and Politics*, 209.

83. Baxter's approach of personal catechism became the envy of the Roman Catholic Counter Reformation. See Packer, *Amongst God's Giants*, 81.

84. Baxter, *Reformed Pastor*, 68.

85. Ibid., 73.

86. McEvoy, *What Can We Learn*, 37.

87. Donnelly, "Richard Baxter."

leisure," to assess the pattern of godliness in the home and, if it was absent, to "ask that they promise to reform their ways for the future."[88] This is what he calls personal ministry, working in a complementary way with preaching ministry; it reinforces the messages proclaimed on the Sunday through personal catechism.[89] Timothy K. Beougher notes that he devoted two days each week to personal catechism, when he spent one hour with them examining their grasp of WSC.[90] Seen in this light, it is comprehensible why the Westminster Assembly produced a Shorter and Larger Catechism (1647) to teach the principles of the Confession of Faith. This was also a different time, when reading was much more widespread, as noted when considering Edwards' use of imagery when preaching on hell, and this model may have been revolutionary at the time.

In the context of relationship, the work of evangelism can be advanced through telling the story of Christ. Eugene H. Peterson believes that this is an integral part of pastoral ministry as pastors listen to people tell their story of faith and life, developing "the curiosity to be attentive to the life of another." He grasps the plot of divine faithfulness throughout individuals' lives.[91] This ideal of the evangelist as a storyteller, recounting the most significant narrative that the world has ever heard, and listening to how that story is played out in individual lives, is essential to relational evangelism. This will be done without the melodramatics, which Peterson mentions, but rather through simple relational communication. While it is often not realized, conversation with people is a powerful weapon in evangelism. To be able to tell the story of Christ, in a home and in a conversational manner, may open hearts that would be hardened or closed in a mass evangelistic meeting.

Part of the incarnational model of evangelism is association and identification with the people being ministered to. This is based on the model of Paul who became relevant to his listeners (1 Cor 9:20–23). Although a Jew by birth, a Roman citizen and a Pharisee by conviction, these did not become a barrier in ministry. He identified with those to whom he was ministering. This is the twofold approach of Frost and Hirsch toward incarnational mission, where the gospel becomes part of people's culture, which challenges that culture and provides a means for identification with the culture being

---

88. Baxter, *Reformed Pastor*, 79–80.

89. Ibid., 106.

90. Beougher, *Richard Baxter and Conversion*, 136. It is noted that he even paid people out of his own allowance to permit their absence from work to attend his catechism classes. See McEvoy, *What Can We Learn*, 40.

91. Peterson, *Five Smooth Stones*, 88–89.

ministered to.[92] This begins, perhaps, by a change in thinking from attractional to missional-incarnational evangelism, and through interacting with a "noninstitutionalized set of relationships," which are "more as a web, a series of intersecting lines symbolising the networks of relationships, friendships, and acquaintances of which Church members are a part."[93] It begins in the local neighborhood, in the supermarket, the post office, and even in the pub, where religious and political identities seem less significant.

Identifying those being ministered to also means that there must be a focus upon those who are deemed to be "seekers." There may be some warrant in claiming that, generally, people are not "seekers." Steve Taylor suggests that there is a spiritual vacuum within culture that needs to be filled, a "magnetic urge toward God that is intrinsic in us all."[94] McLaren further comments that human beings are "incurably religious" and, because the Church is considered to be out of touch with reality, people opt for other religious expressions.[95] There is a need, therefore, for sensitivity to those being ministered to, and this can only be accomplished through a relationship with people, both corporately as the Church, and individually as Christians. The corporate element is significant because, unlike the anonymity of the seeker-sensitive Church of the 1980s and 1990s, it seems that "contemporary cultural observers are suggesting that . . . seekers are seeking community."[96] Mark Driscoll believes that when community is separated from evangelism an evangelistic opportunity is lost, because human relationships draw people to faith.[97] People, generally, do not want to be separated from one another, but want an intimate connection that local Church fellowship provides. This will also determine how the gospel is presented in certain contexts as specific methods of ministry may be less palatable to some than others. It may also determine the answers given in evangelism because, as the questions being asked are listened to, an understanding of how the gospel responds to them arises.[98] The essential message remains unchanged, but if people are discouraged from that message, because of the way the message is presented, it is self-defeating.

---

92. Frost and Hirsch, *Shaping of Things to Come*, 37.
93. Ibid., 43–44.
94. S. Taylor, *Out of Bounds Church?* 81–82.
95. McLaren, *Church on the Other Side*, 13–14.
96. Taylor, *Out of Bounds Church*, 101.
97. Driscoll, *Radical Reformission*, 68–69.
98. "The result of traditionalism is a Christianity that has all the right answers to all of the wrong questions, because the questions that were once pressing are no longer being asked." Driscoll, *Radical Reformission*, 51.

In challenge to the notion that the "seeker-sensitive" church provides anonymity, Bill and Lynne Hybels believe that it includes the whole congregation in personal evangelism, not just the gifted few.[99] The challenge is that it could be seen to treat people as consumers and not challenge them to be missionaries, and could avoid the preaching of "hard words of repentance."[100] In this model, it may be something more suited to the 1980s and 1990s, when consumer culture was at its peak. It seems that some seeker-sensitive Churches are now moving away from this ethos.[101] McLaren believes that what is needed is not seeker-sensitive Churches, but seeker-sensitive Christians: "In all our talk about seeker-sensitive churches and services, I fear we have neglected one small detail: seeker-sensitive Christians. Christians in the new church must really love non-Christians."[102] It can be challenging to love those who reject everything that is precious to the Church and live in a manner deemed incompatible with the teaching of the Bible. Yet, there must be a sensitivity to people. Everyone has a story to tell, a background that they have come from that has made them the people they are today.

Wimber appears to have little to comment on this matter, and that may be because the notion of home visitation was not current in North American culture. Yet, his theology of "powerpoints" may harmonize with a relational approach. He likens "powerpoints" to a climber on a mountain. The lead one plants pitons and passes the rope through them to those who come behind.[103] It is an interpretation to centralize this evangelistic ministry within the context of an individual, especially bearing in mind Wimber's suggestions on ministry, that will be considered, but the impact of an individual on another individual, evangelistically, cannot be underestimated. In this sense, relational evangelism is not opposed to power evangelism, but could be a means of presenting the gospel, incarnationally.

The Power Model

The alternative model that Wimber puts forward is evangelism as a manifestation of the power of God.[104] It is also worth noting that Wimber does

99. Hybels and Hybles, *Rediscovering Church*, 175.
100. Driscoll, *Radical Reformission*, 27.
101. Branaugh, "Willow Creek's Huge Shift."
102. McLaren, *Church on the Other Side*, 34.
103. Wimber and Springer, *Powerpoints*, 5.

104. Evangelism has always had a charismatic dimension for there is the need of the Spirit's application of the gospel. Prior, *Gospel in a Pagan Society*, 55. It also depends upon God applying the message to human hearts by the Holy Spirit. Hull, *New Century*

not see power evangelism as without faults, specifically subjectivism and enthusiasm.[105] Power evangelism does not exclude other forms of evangelism and is itself based upon a traditional call to repentance.[106] When a theological tradition has been committed to one model for a considerable time, like the Reformed Churches, anything that is claimed to make it better or more relevant may be viewed with suspicion. This may not be the result of theological incompatibility, but simply that it is different from the norm.

Yet, supernaturalism is at the core of most theologies of evangelism. Dever laments the state of "much modern evangelism," which he believes has "become emotionally manipulative, seeking simply to cause a momentary decision of the sinner's will, yet neglecting the biblical idea that conversion is the result of the supernatural, gracious act of God toward the sinner." The result is that repentance is no longer proclaimed and, in order to have a response to the gospel, an unfaithful gospel is presented that does not emphasize the truth.[107] Yet, a desire to see people affected by what the Church believes, and the conviction that God can and will demonstrate his power in the world, is not at odds with preaching repentance; this emphasis is central to power evangelism. Lord notes that Wimber stresses the work of the Spirit within the Church, whereas many other methodologies stress the work of God in history.[108] This means that power evangelism is a locally practiced practical theology of evangelism. While the great themes of eschatological hope are addressed by Wimber in his emphasis on the kingdom of God, it is the local effect of the Spirit that is central to power evangelism.

Power evangelism is a methodology that introduces people to the power of the Holy Spirit to transform human lives, not just regarding physical or emotional healing, but also attitudes. There is a need for the Church to be connected to what is happening in the world around them, and to be moved by the concerns and worries of the people within their parish bounds. Bill Hull suggests that Churches must assess people's needs and then attempt to meet them, but first this requires arousing their interest through our personal witness.[109] To be moved in evangelism, within these limits, means that the Church is compassionate about people and their needs. Power evangelism makes this possible, while emphasizing God as

---

Disciplemaking, 46. John Piper believes that the theology of Martyn Lloyd-Jones addressed power evangelism long before Wimber, which may suggest that it is a Reformed concept. Piper, "Passion for Christ-Exalting Power."

105. Wimber, *Kingdom of God*, 27.
106. Wimber and Springer, *Power Healing*, 104
107. Dever, *Nine Marks of a Healthy Church*, 137.
108. Lord, *Spirit Shaped Mission*, 18.
109. Hull, *New Century Disciplemaking*, 51.

the source of having all needs met. For a power encounter to be valid it must have a practical application, not just experiential. McLaren longs for a "power encounter" that results not just in spiritual gifts, but also in a changed attitude to the world around us.[110] Power evangelism, therefore, is built upon Evangelicalism and it is not a model to replace it. Wimber goes as far as saying: "Properly understood, power evangelism can make all the other approaches to evangelism more effective."[111] Power evangelism can slip in unnoticed and improve the other forms of evangelism without rejecting them entirely. It can be used with the other means to demonstrate the reality and the urgency of their emphasis.

Concerning the question of the completeness of the gospel without signs and wonders, Kendall notes that the gospel is complete.[112] Yet, power evangelism springs from a strong conviction in the power of the sacrificial death of Christ upon the cross, which released the greatest power in the world.[113] There appears to be a desire within the theology of Wimber for individuals to experience the full extent of the power of the gospel; to have their lives radically transformed through the Spirit's power in applying the gospel. Wimber states that power evangelism does not seek to add power to the gospel in any sense. Rather, power evangelism looks to the Holy Spirit, when believers consciously co-operate with him, as he reinforces the preaching with demonstrations of power.[114][115] He believes the gospel is completely sufficient for salvation, but God remains committed to the redemption of the whole person. So the gospel is telling people about Jesus and feeding the hungry and praying for the sick.[116] The mind of Wimber appears to be that this is part of the gospel; it is a logical outworking of the message, not an addition to it.

Despite this clear statement that the gospel is sufficient for conversion, there are some, such as John Woodhouse, who seem to suggest that

---

110. McLaren, *Church on the Other Side*, 31.

111. Wimber and Springer, *Dynamics of Spiritual Growth*, 176. "Power evangelism does not replace evangelistic neighborhood Bible studies or the Four Spiritual Laws: it makes them more effective. In other words, Evangelicals already have forms in which they can immediately practice power evangelism." Wimber, *Kingdom of God*, 27.

112. Cain and Kendall, *Word and Spirit*, 30.

113. Wimber and Springer, *Dynamics of Spiritual Growth*, 122–23.

114. Ibid., 177.

115. The notion of a physical and visual demonstration of the gospel is relevant to the post-modern audience, as Gibbs and Coffey note: "Even more than their parents, GenXers are influenced by television. Theirs is a post-literary culture for which sound and image have largely replaced the printed word." Gibbs and Coffey, *Church Next*, 127.

116. Wimber, *Way In is the Way On*, 227.

power evangelism does not have the confidence in the power of the gospel at all and is not Evangelical Christianity.[117] It appears unclear how he has reached this conclusion since it seems to be the emphasis of Wimber to demonstrate how the gospel affects people's lives and changes them completely, whether in regard to sickness or holiness. The view seems to be underpinned by a conviction that only the Bible is needed in evangelism, the same critique used in the definition at the start of this chapter. It is then implied that anything added to this questions the power of the Spirit to confirm the biblical message. What drove Wimber to consider power evangelism was a desire to see the people he ministered to released from the bondage by which they seemed to be controlled, even when the power of the gospel was proclaimed to them.[118] While some may want to theologically defend the gospel as the power to transform sinners and release them from God's wrath, in reality a powerful model is needed to see that victory applied within their lives. This sits with the "spiritual marketplace" that Hunt suggests exists in the Western world today.[119] Where there is competition for the spiritual devotion of people, a model of evangelism, which connects with their deepest needs and most fundamental problems, will be a powerful tool for the Christian Church.

Power evangelism begins, first, with a charismatic experience in the life of the believer, which launches them into ministry in explaining their experience.[120] While the discussion began by considering evangelism, the methodology is based upon discipleship and ministry models and, specifically, an emphasis on the empowering work of the Holy Spirit. This foundation means that only those who understand their position, regarding the Holy Spirit, will be enabled to minister in power evangelism. It is, therefore, important that models of ministry and discipleship that promote the work of the Spirit, or require the experience of "power encounters," are emphasized to enable power evangelism.[121] This could be seen as a circular argument in which the power of the Spirit is experienced in evangelism, but is also a prerequisite for ministering in power evangelism; the one cannot function without the other. This further underlines the outline of this book: that the three contextual applications feed into and support each other. There is also a sense in which, according to Warrington, as the Spirit empowers believers

---

117. Woodhouse, "Signs and Wonders," 37–38.
118. Wimber and Springer, *Power Healing*, 47.
119. Hunt, *Alpha Enterprise*, 32–33.
120. Wimber and Springer, *Power Evangelism*, 60.
121. Lord, *Spirit Shaped Mission*, 18.

for witness, believers become observers of his work in them.[122] This would certainly remove any pressure an individual may feel about operating in the supernatural, but it could be taken to mean that believers are nothing more than vessels through which God speaks, circumventing their personality and uniqueness.

Power evangelism is mostly connected with prayer for healing. This is repeated throughout the New Testament (Matt 9:18; Mark 5:23; 7:32; Acts 9:12). Quite often it can seem insensitive, and even inappropriate, to use people's suffering for our own agendas, especially if it appears that their illness is being used for the Church's theological ends. Ronald Allen believes that the reason Paul healed the sick was the same reason why works of mercy are practiced: not to authenticate the gospel, but to demonstrate compassion to people.[123] Gerstner believes that suffering, accidents and even sicknesses can be "God's way of screaming at people who pay no attention to conscience, nor His Word."[124] Yet, the essence of power evangelism is that the gospel has an application, even to these deepest of needs, as Wimber notes. If pain leads us to seek divine healing, then that healing ought to lead us to the cross.[125] It is this unwillingness to accept pain and suffering which drives human beings to seek a healing ministry so that they can see the deliverance of the gospel applied in reality to their lives. It is also significant to note that Wimber does not assert the physical healing of everyone, but he does assert that everyone can experience salvation.[126] Wimber does not make any promises of universal healing in this life, but that the gospel may provide physical healing.

This position is not without its critics, one of which is Dickinson who notes that power evangelism is not moved by the preaching of the Word, but the preaching of the Word is the result of power evangelism.[127] This criticism expresses the Reformed concern with anything that removes the pre- eminence of preaching from evangelistic activity. Dickinson believes that this methodology was "equally rejected" by Christ, because he warned people not to tell of what he had done, and on numerous occasions he rejected calls for a sign (Matt 12:28, 39; 16:4; Mark 8:11, 12; John 6:30), even

122. Warrington, *Message of the Holy Spirit*, 44.
123. Allen, *Missionary Methods*, 43.
124. Gerstner, *Repent or Perish*, 7.
125. Wimber and Springer, *Power Healing*, 33.
126. Wimber and Springer, *Power Healing*, 35. Warrington writes: "The Kingdom of God is not reflected on earth in its members enjoying perfect physical health but in demonstrating the life of Christ in all circumstances, whether in health or suffering." Warrington, *Healing and Suffering*, 27.
127. Dickinson, *Does God Heal Today?* 270–71.

going so far as to scold Thomas for demanding evidence of the resurrection (John 20:29). He concludes: "The method of publicly convening a great crowd of people by the promise or expectation of seeing or benefiting from a display of his divine power to induce mass conversions or Charismatic Renewal, would appear to have been utterly rejected by the Lord."[128] While it may be theology influenced by context, if the power of God can transform individuals' lives and provide an opportunity to preach Christ, then it may be a methodology that is powerful. As noted before, Wimber does not claim power evangelism replaces any other model. While it may challenge a proclamation-only model, it offers a practical experience of what is being preached.

Wimber's idea of power evangelism is based upon the idea of God's guidance of his Church to minister to certain people at a given time—a divine appointment.[129] These happen at significant moments in people's lives when they need it most.[130] In this sense power evangelism cannot be defined or predicted, as each situation provides an opportunity to share the gospel with people and have the Holy Spirit authenticate that proclamation. Power evangelism stresses the power of God over anything that humanity faces, and over the insecurities and lack of confidence that the believer can experience when confronted with gospel opportunities. It seems unclear how Wallace Benn and Mark Burkill evaluate Wimber's theology as lacking an appreciation of the sovereignty of God.[131] The sovereignty of God is seen in power evangelism with a demonstration of God's authority over every situation which the Church faces, whether sickness, demonic activity or simple rejection of the gospel message. This review does not take into account the teaching of Wimber in *Living with Uncertainty: My Bout with Inoperable Cancer*. He specifically states that "God is sovereign" and that "He determines whether to grant us what we ask for now—or later."[132] This review appears to come with a presupposition of its own rather than an objective consideration of Wimber's theology. Taking on board Wimber's statement, this would also harmonize with Reformed theology.

---

128. Ibid., 299–300.
129. Wimber and Springer, *Power Evangelism*, 101.
130. Ibid., 109.
131. Benn and Burkill, "Power Evangelism."
132. Wimber, *Living with Uncertainty*, 13.

Partial Conclusion

How the gospel is presented is an important question for the Church to consider. This chapter has considered different models of evangelism within the Reformed Church and reflected upon them, considering the teaching of Wimber. It has highlighted that the power evangelism model does not negate all other models of evangelism, but it complements them and even, according to Wimber, enhances them. Whether this assumption is true has not been answered by this chapter; indeed, it could not be answered apart from a practical investigation into an evangelistic practice. The criteria for success would also need to be defined, whether it is converts won, miracles performed or people presented with the gospel.

What this chapter has sought to answer is that there is more than one mold, and God can use the different theological emphases to the same end. Wherever evangelism begins from theology, the conclusion of the message is always Jesus, as Scot McKnight notes.[133] Should the means of our presentation discourage individuals from accepting the content of our presentation, then serious questions need to be asked. To aid this, Keller uses idolatry: giving "ultimate concern or some ultimate allegiance" to something other than God.[134] He suggests that this is the primary explanation of sinfulness today rather than the traditional message of sin as law breaking, something which he sees as endemic throughout all cultures.[135] This counters any relativism and makes sin personal. There needs, therefore, to be a sensitive presentation of the gospel that challenges thinking on this matter.

The issue is whether power evangelism is seen as a franchise to be adopted en masse? Eddie Gibbs and Ian Coffey note that "pre-packaged" models will not work, as there needs to be an altruistic element to our witness, because of the suspiciousness of our culture.[136] This will make the Church countercultural: not being aloof from the culture and not being so connected to the culture that there is no difference between Church and society.[137] This begs the question whether there is a place for preaching wrath in the contemporary world. The answer is both yes and no. Keller notes that emphasizing God's wrath, or his love, exclusively, is a misrepresentation

---

133. McKnight, "Gospel for iGens," 23–24.
134. Keller, "Talking About Idolatry."
135. Ibid.
136. Gibbs and Coffey, *Church Next*, 35.
137. "Instead of becoming a church that is simply absorbed by culture or that vainly endeavors to exist in isolation from the broader culture, the church must engage in a dynamic interaction with the culture in which it is immersed." Gibbs and Coffey, *Church Next*, 214.

when both are essential.[138] A balanced gospel must be presented, one that adequately describes the seriousness of sin, and yet extols the acceptance and love of God in Christ; a model that warns of the seriousness of God's judgment, but does so with acceptance and love of the sinner.

In commenting on balance in evangelism, Chalke comments how fear-based evangelism affects the Christian Church. It can make the Church seem superior and patronizing toward unbelievers, because of the belief that God does not "take to those outside the church."[139] There is also the matter of how a Church, which is exclusively gospel centered and focused in all of its worship, provides for the needs of its members.[140] Ryken notes that Church ought to be accessible to unbelievers, but that the primary focus of the Church is to worship God.[141] Thus, not only will unbelievers be challenged, but confessing believers will also be discipled and released into ministry service. Thus worship operates, as Chester and Timmis note, as a signpost directing worshippers, by explanation, to the truth of the gospel.[142] So worship, preaching, and the Spirit's presence work together in evangelism to challenge unbelievers and pastor members.

When the Church proclaims only the seriousness of hell, it places the gospel exclusively in the life yet to come and may make individuals wonder if there is any application to their contemporary situation. This is where power evangelism, side by side with proclamation evangelism, is the model that, I believe, is needed in the twenty-first century. Phil Moore comments on the present manifestation of the power of the gospel against the fact that everyone dies and, therefore, needs adequate preparation.[143] The heart of the gospel is experiencing this reality of the world yet to come, in the present. This is why power evangelism offers such a powerful model. It brings

---

138. Keller, "Advancing the Gospel."

139. Chalke and Watkins, *Intelligent Church*, 21–22.

140. Debate on the issue of hell has been prominent recently through the publication of Bell's book *Love Wins*. There are intricacies in his argument, but he seems to suggest that, on the basis of Lazarus, hell may be those who have oppressed others sharing eternity with them, watching them enjoying new life while their bitterness defines their eternity. In a sense it is a form of universalism, in that everyone goes to heaven, but he allows for different hells in eternity as there are different hells for people in this life. Bell, *Love Wins*, 77–79. The same theme is raised by Pearson who suggests that hell and heaven are states of consciousness, hell beginning and ending on earth, where inhumanity is practiced, but in eternity the love of God is supreme. Pearson, *Gospel of Inclusion*, 135. Power evangelism deals with the "hell" people live in everyday, and the hope that God's power can step in and change it.

141. Ryken, *City on a Hill*, 67.

142. Chester and Timmis, *Total Church*, 52.

143. Moore, "Healthy Theology of Healing."

the world to come into the present, in foretastes of healing and signs and wonders.

Yet a word of caution is needed; the Church "must be open to miracles but not dominated by it."[144] The possibility of miracles does not negate the importance of going through terrible situations with faith firmly anchored in God. It is important, however, not to reduce the gospel simply to what is done, even miracles, which Wimber calls "a gospel of performance."[145] There is a sense in which, when the gospel is proclaimed, the Church is doing exactly what it has been told to do. There is also a sense in which it is not putting people right regarding their true nature. Yet, as Wimber notes, there needs to be an awareness that it can come across as smug, and even aggressive at times, specifically regarding fear-based evangelism. Some may even tell others about hell with such passion and zeal that it almost seems as if they are glad they may be going there.[146] Evangelism insists that mercy is remembered, that Christians need mercy and that others need mercy. It is only when this truth is adequately understood that evangelism becomes compassionate.

The issue of relevancy also comes to the fore in evangelism, that of dealing with the question of how the gospel can be applied to a culture that can often be antagonistic to the teachings of the Bible. How relevancy is worked out is difficult, especially if, as Evangelicals, the assumption that the Bible is sufficient is axiomatic.[147] Dever writes of the need to be countercultural: to be separate from our culture, which is antagonistic to the gospel.[148] It may be that conversion may not always be immediate, yet the Bible encourages relevancy in gospel preaching. Even Paul became all things to his audience that they might believe (1 Cor 9:19–23). There is no need, as Dever

---

144. Fyall, *Charismatic and Reformed*, 12.

145. Wimber, *Everyone Gets to Play*, 34.

146. "We want to introduce the world to the God of love who is the solution to each individual's and every community's sin, isolation and dysfunction. The trouble is, rather than sending a message of hope around these issues, we've often ended up preaching, or being heard to preach, a debilitating and condemnatory message of judgment." Chalke and Watkins, *Intelligent Church*, 52–53.

147. "In exposing relevancy as a false criteria upon which to base evangelism we ought to ask, of course, what is meant by the term, for what relevancy amounts to in many cases is a story or some anecdote that gives the sermon a whiff of immediacy. Genuine relevancy, on the other hand, will take more seriously the modern condition of alienation, seeking to address it directly as well as transform it. Furthermore, we should be cautious about relevancy as a criterion for communication because in classical and biblical preaching there is an unashamed belief that the world of the text is relevant in itself." Stackhouse, *Gospel Driven Church*, 91.

148. Dever, *Nine Marks of a Healthy Church*, 27–28.

seems to suggest, to jettison those aspects of the gospel that are at odds with the general attitudes of people today[149], but a wisdom in how such truths are presented is required. Relevancy also means that people need time to come to faith because the widespread religious knowledge of prior generations may not be the norm today. Paul Beasley-Murray sees the developments in culture as encouraging because people to no longer make quick decisions, but weigh their plans carefully. He writes: "If the ordinary physical birth process takes nine months, then we should not be surprised if the spiritual birth process takes a number of months too."[150] Reformed Evangelicalism has emphasized the immanence of the gospel and the need to make an immediate response to its claims. While enlightenment may happen quickly, time must be allowed for people to respond to the gospel, even if it means annual statistics are not as high as other congregations.

There is also the need to be aware that some aspects of culture today are often antagonistic to direct confrontation with the gospel message. Fernando comments that this is partly due to the privacy with which many people choose to live their lives. People will not want a comment made upon their most intimate issues, and those who made such statement were often guilty of terrible prejudice and social sins.[151] The historical reasons why this mindset is prevalent in our communities today may be valid according to the criteria which Fernando sets down. What has resulted is a challenge to how the gospel message is proclaimed today. Yet, the fact cannot be ignored that the message of the cross causes an offence to people (Gal 5:11). As sin is challenged directly there will be opposition and charges of narrowness. However, when the Church demonstrates that it is not setting itself up to judge people and excuse itself, but that all are on the journey together, then the power of the message is seen. Mixed with the power of the Holy Spirit to overcome such inherent sinfulness, the message is relevant and practical.

What is needed, Wimber argues, is clarity of thinking concerning the relationship between the Church and the kingdom of God. He states that the Church is an avenue to salvation, but not exclusively so; neither is it the exclusive dwelling place of God's presence.[152] Power evangelism reminds Christians of the calling to be witnesses to the kingdom of God, and that kingdom is greater and more inclusive than their preconceptions and understanding. The result is a change in thinking regarding the power of God, as Don Williams notes. He considers it impossible to understand

---

149. Ibid., 58.
150. Beasley-Murray, *Transform Your Church*, 126.
151. Fernando, *Jesus Driven Ministry*, 124.
152. Wimber and Springer, *Power Evangelism*, 34.

the Bible apart from a supernatural worldview.[153] The connection between the kingdom of God that is coming and the heralding of that kingdom in evangelism, which demonstrates the power of that kingdom practically, is the essence of the Word and Spirit methodology.[154] Devenish writes that, if there is too great a separation between the kingdom and the Church, then some who focus on a prophetic ministry of transforming communities may become disillusioned with the Church. They may see it as irrelevant to their ministry because the Church is focused only on itself, and those who see kingdom primarily in terms of pastoral ministry will be frustrated by those who appear to have no commitment to the local congregation.[155] This sense of spiritual introspection on behalf of some members, and judgementalism on behalf of others, will hold back the work of the gospel. The answer is to marry the two: "Each local church is therefore to see itself as a community of people who are the agents of kingdom social action, and such social action projects are to be rooted in and accountable to the local church."[156] As the two sides of the one coin, the local congregation can seek community transformation, not just of social justice, but also for individual reconciliation of people to the kingdom of God.

Regarding the supernatural manifestations of the Holy Spirit's presence, O. Palmer Robertson believes that this is why the gift of tongues accompanied the Pentecost event: to demonstrate the universal nature of the gospel.[157] This, according to Wimber, is why Jesus performed miracles to "confront people with his message that the kingdom of God had come and that they had to accept or reject it."[158] When this understanding of evangelism is grasped, it is understood that the gospel is an ultimatum in which individuals must come under the power of the kingdom of God and accept its rule, as Keller says.[159] The challenge of the kingdom also ought to inspire the Church to reform her practices and reach out to the needy. This is what

---

153. Williams, *Signs, Wonders*, 48.

154. Williams also believes that the kingdom is the ecumenical glue that holds the varying positions together: "This book comes out of a deep conviction that God is restoring an understanding of his kingdom both theologically and experientially in his church today. Moreover, I am convinced that the kingdom provides the biblical key to the Pentecostal experience, the Charismatic Renewal, and the 'Third Wave' awakening which have influenced Christian life so dramatically and accelerated the tempo of world evangelism. I also believe that the kingdom will hold these movements on a proper biblical course." Williams, *Signs, Wonders*, xi.

155. Devenish, *What on Earth is the Church For?* 83.

156. Devenish, *What on Earth is the Church For?* 110.

157. Robertson, *Final Word*, 52–53.

158. Wimber and Springer, *Dynamics of Spiritual Growth*, 171.

159. Keller, *Ministries of Mercy*, 36.

Wimber calls "the first-fruits presence of the kingdom," where "the church acts as a counter-culture and social conscience, "salt" and "leaven" in the world-at-large."[160] This happens, according to Keller, in two ways: first as the "pilot plant" of the kingdom, living out the standards of the kingdom in every aspect of life; and, second, as agents of the kingdom, by "working for the healing of persons, families, relationships, and nations, it is doing deeds of mercy and seeking justice."[161] The power of a Christian testimony in this world is incredible and it ought to inspire even the most nominal believer to follow Christ wholeheartedly. Such a signs and wonders ministry opens hearts to the gospel as it visibly demonstrates the care and compassion of the Church. It also serves an eschatological function, pointing not only to the future, "they point to the fact that our compassionate King is here!"[162] Evangelism is the foretaste of the coming kingdom invading this dominion with power and might, not only to transform people spiritually, but also to see their situations changed, either through signs and wonders, or social ministries of mercy.

---

160. Wimber, *Way In is the Way On*, 75.
161. Keller, *Ministries of Mercy*, 54
162. Wimber, *Way In is the Way On*, 190.

5

Discipleship in a Reformed Church

Introduction

ONCE A PERSON HAS been incorporated into the community of faith, through evangelism, the next stage in our word and power ministry model is discipleship. This connects a personal experience of Christ with an ongoing commitment to the principles of faith.[1] Wimber argues for reproduction: when individuals are converted through power evangelism and integrated into the Church in discipleship.[2] In one sense discipleship is not an additional element in spiritual formation apart from conversion, but should be normative of all true Christian experience.[3] Alan and Debra Hirsch suggest that evangelism seeks to make disciples and, when it fails in this, it

---

1. Hughes suggests that this ought to mean a separation of believers from "the world" which would then minister to the world. Hughes, *Set Apart*, 17. Piper calls this connection "Christian hedonism" that states God is glorified when believers are satisfied in him, so the ongoing discipleship is the pursuit of that satisfaction. Piper, *When I Don't Desire God*, 13. Chapell connects the experience of the gospel to the attitudes that Christians have, which ought to be motivated and shaped by grace. Chapell, *Holiness by Grace*, 35.

2. Wimber, *Kingdom of God*, 15.

3. In a sense this discussion is one of terminology, and popular Evangelical culture has made a distinction between evangelism, that which is done to achieve new converts, and discipleship, that which is done with the new converts. Smallman defines this as a change from making "decisions for Jesus" to disciple making. See Smallman, *What is Discipleship*, 14–15. Brueggemann understands this ongoing work as what evangelism actually is, and that it will never be complete. Brueggemann, *Biblical Perspectives on Evangelism*, 94–95.

fails in its "primary mission."[4] They suggest this because they understand the gospel to be more than a personal experience and must have a wider implication through the Church and into society.

These positions are a critique of a Christianity that seems unconcerned with the wider world and whose primary focus is on individual redemption. This may be a product of an existentialist worldview that struggles to understand the world in which it lives. This may even be encouraged through religious experience.[5] There appears to be a movement away from individual spiritual development to community formation. There may be community elements in discipleship, as in the sacramental model to be considered later, and it is an issue that has been significant in Reformed circles. This is why Charles H. Dunahoo notes that the central aspect of the Church's mission is to make disciples and to transform these disciples into ministers, something that will be considered in chapter 6.[6] He further comments that part of this change is to apply the Word of God to every area of life.[7] This is why discipleship is not an addition to evangelism, but an integral part of it.

Discipleship seeks to bring a context for Christian living, enabling believers to make informed decisions on their actions from their understanding of faith. It may also be valid to say that the community can only be changed through the individual members' changing. This view seems to be opposed by Peterson who sees discipleship as developing a mature, personal

---

4. Hirsch and Hirsch, *Untamed*, 23–24. L. Green and C. Forester state that discipleship needs to be central to the Church's identity: «The Church is the community of discipleship." Green and Forster, *Small Church*, 41.

5. Solomon, *Existentialism*, 1–2. "It is an attitude that recognises the unresolvable confusion of the human world, yet resists the all-too-human temptation to resolve the confusion by grasping toward whatever appears or can be made to appear firm or familiar - reason, God, nation, authority, history, work, tradition, or the "other-worldly," whether of Plato, Christianity, or utopian fantasy. The existentialist attitude begins with a disoriented individual facing a confused world that he cannot accept. This disorientation and confusion is one of the by-products of the Renaissance, the Reformation, the growth of science, the decline of Church authority, the French Revolution, and the growth of mass militarism and technocracy."

6. "What is religion but relegation - a knitting together of hearts? Faith knits us to God and love knits us one to another." Watson, *Godly Man's Picture*, 139; Dunahoo, *Making Kingdom Disciples*, 3.

7. "The primary objectives of the kingdom approach of disciple making include knowing, understanding, and applying God's Word to all of life. It also involves living lives more obedient to God's commands. Transforming the way a person thinks and lives is a key in serving and ministering to those who are the image bearers of God both inside and outside the church community. Bringing all thoughts captive to Christ is also essential. This kingdom model produces Christians with a self conscious understanding of an all pervasive philosophy of life." Dunahoo, *Making Kingdom Disciples*, 11–12.

relationship with a personal God.[8] Peterson does root this in the pastoral ministry, which is a manifestation of the community. Discipleship could, therefore, be defined as that movement by which individuals grow in their personal relationship with God and become committed to congregational life in the Church.

Discipleship provides a medium for the congregation to rear, spiritually, those who have come to faith and need guidance on how they ought to live the Christian life. There are different ideas on what is meant by this ideal of spiritual growth. In this discussion, I will adopt the definition given by Wimber:

> Spiritual growth is more difficult to define and chart than physical growth. But I think it can be summed up in one statement: Spiritual growth is the process we go through here on earth of becoming more Christlike.[9]

This takes not only new converts, but those who exist on the fringe of congregational life, into a deeper relationship with Christ and a greater degree of commitment to the local congregation. It is an all of life definition.[10] Wimber compares this to the weaning and rearing of natural children—hard work.[11] Part of this rearing is encouraging and equipping them to withstand the attractions of the world, which will only be accomplished through prayer, Bible study, and spiritual disciplines.[12] It is encouraging the believer to pursue a relationship with Christ, beyond the "mediocre level of the world," and not fall into the individualism of Evangelicalism noted earlier.[13] This fellowship includes a connection with people and a commitment to spend time together growing in the understanding of their faith.

8. Peterson, *Five Smooth Stones*, 157.

9. Wimber and Springer, *Dynamics of Spiritual Growth*, 3.

10. "The word disciple is used more frequently than Christian to refer to believers in the Bible. This repeated usage tells us that disciple is a fundamental category for Christians. We are disciples first and parents, employees, pastors, deacons, and spouses second. Disciple is an identity; everything else is a role. Our roles are temporary but our identity will last forever." Dodson, *Gospel Centered Discipleship*, 29.

11. Wimber, "Leadership and Followership." This process of growth never ends: "Adults reach full height, a point beyond which they will grow no taller. But Christians never reach a point beyond which they cannot still grow." Wimber and Springer, *Dynamics of Spiritual Growth*, 4.

12. Wimber and Springer, *Power Evangelism*, 40: "Fellowship with other Christians in local Churches—outposts of the kingdom—is a primary defense against being taken in by the world. Prayer, Bible study and spiritual disciplines such as fasting are necessary not only to gain God's power and insight but also to equip us to resist the world."

13. Bonhoeffer, *Cost of Discipleship*, 13.

Discipleship, therefore, could become adherence to the rules of the local or denominational community and how they understand the world. It may be more helpful to understand discipleship as aiding the convert to understand the implications of their conversion rather than their opposition to the world.

This chapter considers how discipleship is practiced within the Christian Church and reflects upon the challenges that Wimber's theology has to a traditional Reformed approach. There appears to be a paucity of literature seeking to integrate the Reformed and Charismatic models of discipleship.[14] This chapter seeks to bridge this gap through considering three contextual examples: the behavioral approach, in which the local congregation becomes the discipleship educator; the proclamation model, in which the emphasis is placed upon listening to preaching and Bible studies; and the sacramental model, in which baptism and communion are central to the discipleship process. I have chosen the models, outlined below, for a number of reasons. Robert Warner speaks of an experiential element (behavioral), a relational element (sacramental), and a doctrinal element (proclamation).[15] The same pattern is seen in David Watson's theory of creating community through "human interactions" of covenant love (behavioral) and aiding growth through ministry gifts (proclamation) on the basis of our fellowship, which is holy communion (sacramental).[16] Kathryn Tanner speaks of discipleship as listening to the Word of God (proclamation), being inspired by the actions of others (behavioral) and experiencing Christian practices (sacramental).[17] Dallas Willard speaks of conformity of lifestyle (behavioral), formal association (sacramental) and being taught (proclamation).[18] These models will be compared with Wimber's suggestions and I will be asking whether his Charismatic model is in sympathy with, and complementary to, these other models.

---

14. Hull, *New Century Disciplemaking*; Hull, *Disciplemaking Church*; Dunahoo, *Making Kingdom Disciples*; Camp, *Mere Discipleship*. There is a wider corpus of material on the issue of discipleship from both Charismatic and Reformed positions, as is seen in this chapter. My contribution is to attempt to connect the Reformed and Charismatic models through Wimber.

15. Warner, *I Believe in Discipleship*, 153–54. Warner stands in the charismatic Baptist tradition.

16. Watson, *Discipleship*, 59–61. Watson stands in the charismatic anglican tradition. This has significant bearing on the discussion with Wimber as Watson hosted the first Vineyard conference in England in 1980.

17. Tanner, *Theory of Culture*, 138. Tanner represents the mainstream anglican position.

18. Willard, *Divine Conspiracy*, xv. Willard represents the evangelical position.

Discipleship is closely linked to evangelism because the Church is not just to reach "people with the gospel message and bring them to a decision for Christ," but to make them disciples.[19] This implies change from living in one way to living for God. As Wimber notes, this is more than making a decision and waiting for Christ's return. Wimber argues that this experience affects every aspect of the believer's life, including morality, relationships, decision-making and even emotions.[20] What he is arguing for is an experience of Christianity that is more than a hope of eternal life, but an experience of eternal life in the present. This experience consists of spiritual gifts that are open to all believers. Wimber wants committed Christians who are eager and willing to follow Christ as disciples in every aspect of their lives. It is a critique of nominalism. Discipleship, therefore, roots the believer in the present, by their experience of salvation, and focuses them on the future, when they will go to be with Christ. This living relationship with Christ is what Dietrich Bonhoeffer understands as the essence of discipleship. This understands Christ not as an abstract truth, but as a living reality.[21] Evangelism ought to have introduced this idea, and a conversion experience should have ratified it. Discipleship is seeking to take this to the next stage of relationship. This dovetails with Wimber's Charismatic model in which a dynamic and living relationship with the Holy Spirit is birthed in discipleship. Yet, as Bonhoeffer notes, it is a relationship with Christ and, so, this may be one area in which Charismatic discipleship fails.

When trying to define what discipleship is, a number of different models come to mind. Some think of the Discipleship Movement, of the 1970s and 1980s, and have rejected any form of discipleship because of its extremes.[22] This is balanced against an apparent individualism in the Chris-

19. Wagner, *Leading Your Church to Growth*, 21.

20. Wimber, *Kingdom Living*, 6–7. Tozer makes some of the same comments about living for God in the world when believers think of their lives less as being at war with all that is opposed to God and more of being at play, enjoying the world around us. Tozer, "This World," 4–5.

21. Bonhoeffer, *Cost of Discipleship*, 17.

22. The Shepherding Movement refers to the Fort Lauderdale Five (Don Basham, Ern Baxter, Bob Mumford, Derek Prince and Charles Simpson) who pioneered a discipleship model in which every believer was to have a "personal, definite, committed relationship with a shepherd" to enable personal pastoral care and this relationship defined whether the individuals were joined to the Church. This relationship, or personal covering, referred to every aspect of the individual's life, not just their spiritual development, including «etiquette, personal dress, management, budgeting, and basic home, yard and automobile care.» See Moore, *Shepherding Movement*, 73–75. Harper called this "the most disturbing controversy to hit the Charismatic Movement." He acknowledges the need to integrate believers into local Churches. He seems to suggest that the real issue was how people related to confrontation. Harper, *Three Sisters*,

tian world where only what is personally wanted or desired matters. Any idea of an objective standard, regulated by either an individual or the community of faith, is rejected.[23] Hope states that the power of discipleship is a change of focus from self to serving the cause of Christ and being obedient to him. This is a movement away from being a child who demands that all of our needs are met, to being a servant who seeks to live out our commitment to Christ in the world. Hope is careful to state that this springs from love for God and that it is not a cold relationship with God that is seen only in obedience to divine demands.[24] This moves the believer and Church from a self-focused gospel message and response, to an individual and corporate commitment to serving God in their world. Matthew's record of the Great Commission, to go and make disciples (Matt 28:19), means that responsibility does not end once a profession of faith is made, it is only the beginning.[25] When the gospel is taken personally into our hearts and made part of daily existence it produces growth, which is the natural outcome of evangelism.[26] This would require a change in message, from "come to faith" to "take up your cross" in all witness and worship. This is why discipleship could be seen as a deep and loving commitment to God. Some of these themes were considered earlier and it seems that, in this context, discipleship is a movement away from personal emphasis to a degree of corporate responsibility.

91–92. Problems arose with the abuse of this relationship when a pastor disciplined a family because the wife left town without his permission. This led to Pat Robertson of CBN and the Presbyterian Charismatic Communion raising issues about the validity of this emphasis. Moore, *Shepherding Movement*, 93–96. Barrs believes its intentions were good: to address low commitment, poor sense of community and worldliness. Yet the outcome was dangerous: "Advice may be sought, community and support must be encouraged, but no single individual has a right to claim to know God's particular will for another believer. Discipline must be applied only for doctrinal and moral disobedience to Scripture, not for questioning prophecy or "covering." Spiritual immaturity rather than true discipleship results from excessive authority." Barrs, "Shepherding Movement," 639–40.

23. This may be the result of contemporary Evangelicalism in which people experience a personal conversion and the result is that they become "self-obsessed." Tomlinson, *Post Evangelical*, 48. An evidence of this is suggested as being the lyrics of some contemporary Christian worship in which individual experience and fulfillment are centrally placed. Stackhouse, *Gospel Driven Church*, 55. Individualism has led some to believe that Evangelicalism does not have an ecclesiology, only a means of personal salvation. Carter, "Beyond Theocracy and Individualism," 173.

24. Hope, *Mission Shaped Spirituality*, 17.

25. Chalke and Watkins note that we are called both to go out proclaiming and invite people in to hear: "Our mission is both come and go, never either/or, always both/and." To this end they suggest that our "buildings can become our greatest assets." Chalke and Watkins, *Intelligent Church*, 42.

26. Keller, *Prodigal God*, 115.

Hull believes that discipleship has been the forgotten activity of the Church, or the "primary matter of negligence."[27] Hull seems to be making the same comment on the individualistic emphasis of the Church in gospel ministry. His suggestion is a change of emphasis in which corporate responsibility is emphasized. Believers are to be impressed with their part in witnessing to the gospel. In that sense, it may be considered to be the primary focus of the Church. This would move the Church, from being something that is joined, to becoming something that is served. This is what David Watson seems to be suggesting. The Church is not to be viewed as a club in which all needs our met, but a body, building, family, or army in which all Christians have a part to play.[28] This is the change that an emphasis on discipleship may make. This may be more of a comment on the social nature of the Church rather than a critique of the theology of discipleship. It may also be a comment on the missional nature of the Church, which may be better suited to chapter 6. Yet, it does deal with the issue of how Christians can move from a place of decision in evangelism to commitment in discipleship.

Wimber comments that people who come to Church will stay only if they have a sense of the reality of their faith, which directs them throughout their lives.[29] Applying this to a Reformed context aids not only those on the fringes of the congregation to grow spiritually, but also for those who join the congregation to feel part of the local Church community.[30] This encourages movement beyond any emotionalism of the initial conversion experience, to seeing quality commitments, not only to God, but to the local

27. Hull, *New Century Disciplemaking*, 10. He comments elsewhere: "Unless the church makes making disciples its main agenda, world evangelism is a fantasy. There is no way to reproduce, multiply, and decentralize people and the Gospel without first diligently making disciples." Hull, *Disciple Making Church*, 11.

28. Watson, *Discipleship*, 32–33. These distinctions are particularly applicable to the "traditional" churches where individuals have been connected to congregational life through long family lines rather than a conversion experience that may typify many of the newer congregations.

29. Wimber, "Leadership and Followership."

30. There has been some debate whether conversion is to Jesus as Savior but not as Lord, mostly from a dispensational position. Ryrie questions lordship on the basis of compulsion, suggesting that it is grace which motivates devotion and commitment, not legalism. Accordingly, separating lordship from salvation makes discipleship legal and not of grace. Ryrie, *Balancing the Christian Life*, 168. Chafer comments that true Christianity allows the believer to do exactly whatever they may want because it is of grace. Chafer, *Grace*, 345. Hodges suggests that this is simply accepting Christ at his word, with no conditions. Hodges, *Gospel Under Siege*, 14. Reisinger responds to this view, from a Reformed perspective, by stating that without lordship Christianity is "bankrupt." Reisinger, *Lord and Christ*, 6. Lordship would state that discipleship is part of accepting Christ as the Lord of life as well as Savior; the opposing view believes that this is legislating discipleship which is contrary to grace. See also McKnight, *King Jesus Gospel*.

Church.[31] Discipleship is not, therefore, just about the theological orthodoxy of a confession of faith, but how that confession affects a Christian's life. Discipleship is concerned, therefore, with the application of the conversion experience to the daily life of the believer, moving from observation to participation in ministry. This is the idea of this chapter, that it bridges the evangelism and ministry models.

Discipleship means, according to Hull, not accumulating skills or knowledge. Rather, it is the preoccupation with every aspect of the local Church's ministry, where gifts can be exercised and networked to produce mature Christians.[32] Discipleship is the absorption of every element of the Church's ministry and every aspect of the Church's activity. This model also challenges the message presented in evangelism, salvation from eternal death, to not living lives on our own, but serving God's purposes.[33] Discipleship, then, is not a surprise to the new convert. It is the logical outworking of their acceptance of faith. This works with the leadership of the local Church, to develop further what began in embryo at the moment of conversion. In one sense, this comment on discipleship could also be seen as a critique of evangelism methodology. Yet, what Wimber is seeking to address, and indeed this chapter seeks to address, is that which happens after the conversion experience.

The rooting of discipleship, within a specific local congregation, is another issue raised in this discussion. Gunter Krallman suggests that this life connection is based on Christ's relationship with the disciples, a "witness" that sought to develop maturity and train for leadership.[34] This sees the purpose of discipleship as more than numerical growth, but quality growth. It may suggest a symbiotic relationship between the people of God, as they invest their lives into each other, with the aim of release into service. Driscoll believes that this implies discipleship ought not to be left to para-church organizations because it is so central to the Church's ministry.[35] This would

31. Chantry, *Today's Gospel*, 15–16.
32. Hull, *Disciple Making Church*, 59.
33. Wimber, *Way In is the Way On*, 29.
34. Krallmann, *Mentoring for Mission*, 13.

35. Driscoll, *Radical Reformission*, 21. Driscoll believes such organizations are often age specific and ethos specific unlike the local Church which has many different ages and opinions, and which cements family relationships. Hull believes that the root cause of this abdication of responsibility is because the Church focuses on what Jesus did rather than the changes the apostles instituted and experienced. Hull, *Disciplemaking Church*, 30. The reason for abdicating responsibility to para-church organizations may be historical, with the rise of independent faith missions in the nineteenth and early twentieth centuries in response to the perceived liberalism of many mainstream denominations. Stanley, "Future in the Past," 115.

imply that being part of a local church enables believers to understand what being a follower of Christ means, and to grow in their understanding of the Christian faith. The Church, as a community of faith, is important because it roots believers in a multi-generational, multi-perspective context. This will not only challenge theological convictions, but also practical and cultural assumptions of how Christianity ought to be practiced. This emphasizes a corporate element within the discipleship process, where responsibility is taken for one another. Driscoll does not outline how this is to be implemented fairly and equally so that it avoids the extremes in the Discipleship Movement, as noted previously.

According to Wimber, spiritual growth develops with "certain crucial moments," which he calls "powerpoints."[36] These experiences teach commitment and devotion to Christ while, at the same time, challenging how lives are lived. They are both facilitative, as they are the access though which power is reached, and episodic, as they are the events by which power effects change.[37] They hone the manner in which Christians relate vertically, towards God, and horizontally, towards others. Powerpoints determine the extent of spiritual growth because they challenge assumptions about the Christian faith. It is often during these times of trials and difficulty that many believers begin to question their faith and ask some difficult questions about the reality of that faith. There may be a danger of seeing these events as being purely subjective. However, Wimber asserts that they are "rooted in objective truth about God," and the "heart of each powerpoint is biblical truth."[38] This means that however the individual believer may feel, or whatever difficult questions the experiences may make them ask about God, their purpose is never to drive them away from faith. There may be a sense in which the end is justifying the means here. As long as there are positive, spiritual outcomes in discipleship, then it could be deemed to be authentic.

---

36. Wimber and Springer, *Dynamics of Spiritual Growth*, 4.

37. Percy, *Power and the Church*, 10. This sits in context with the experiences recorded in 2 Cor 11:24–28.

38. Wimber and Springer, *Dynamics of Spiritual Growth*, 5. The issue of subjectivity needs to be noted because these powerpoints are not simply unregulated personal experiences. There are criteria that, Wimber notes, define these experiences in terms of spiritual development. The results are also evident in producing a Christlikeness in the believer. The evidence is, in a sense, the justification of the authenticity of the experience.

The Behavioral Model

One discipleship model emphasizes right behavior as an evidence of spiritual growth. Pawson defines what a behavioral model means for aggressive evangelism, on the street and on television.[39] Often this model of evangelism encourages believers in gospel witness through tract distribution, open-air evangelism and personal witness. In this model, disciples are encouraged to give themselves to God so that he will mold their behavior (Rom 12:1, NLT). Devenish writes that conversion is more than an individual's act of conviction and commitment; rather, it is a movement of that individual into the life of the local Church, demonstrating personal holiness.[40] When Christ's call to conversion is considered, not just of belief but also of lifestyle, then the essence of being one who values spirituality is grasped.

The notion of sacrifice is implicit within this model. Ryken comments that the Christian life is one of sacrifice, from its inception to its end. This understanding places Christianity, not as an element of a disciple's life, but as the defining characteristic of the disciple's life.[41] This can be positive, as Christians make their faith the central axiom of their lives. Yet, taken to an extreme, it can produce a performance-based discipleship model that is about doing and not being. This tends to be the pattern of the more fundamentalist believer who relies upon their minister or pastor to give them a set of rules by which to live. Wimber states that our behavior is never quite as good as Christ's standards.[42] Wimber, however, understands these works as God's Works, which he performs through believers as they listen to him through prayer and Bible study, not as they obey a set of rules and regulations. The result of this is that the Holy Spirit strengthens the Church to do these acts.[43] Discipleship cannot be watered down to a list of behavioral norms, because these norms would differ from culture to culture.

A historical example from the Reformed tradition is that of John Bunyan in his work *Christian Behavior*. William P. Farley notes that Bunyan's life was characterized by persecution and suffering because of his theological principles.[44] There may be some sense in which the behavioral model is a product of the proclamation model. Bunyan was a self-educated man, and

---

39. Pawson, *Word and Spirit Together*, 68.
40. Devenish, *What on Earth is the Church For?* 38.
41. Ryken, *City on a Hill*, 112–13.
42. Wimber and Springer, *Power Evangelism*, 42. Good works, are to be seen as the necessary outcome of salvation by grace and faith (Eph 2:8–10).
43. Wimber and Springer, *Power Evangelism*, 42.
44. Farley, "John Bunyan," 93. He further notes that through his imprisonment he was enabled to write books and spend time in Bible study (94).

this may be why his emphasis was on a behavioral model, because he had to work out his theology practically rather than academically.[45] He addressed how believers are to act, specifically new converts, so that they may live correctly for God, in every aspect of their lives, becoming flowers "that stand and grow." He outlines four principles concerning good deeds: they flow from faith; Christians ought to be careful that their works are good; they must maintain their good works; and, their good works will affirm justification by faith.[46] Bunyan's emphasis on good works may have sprung from his own experience of the Bedford Independent Church where, according to Raymond Brown, he experienced Christians whose lives were an evidence of their beliefs.[47] Bunyan is not suggesting that these good works are salvific, but that they are the evidence and focus of the justified life: "put yourself into a conscientious performance of them."[48] John Owen adds the caveat that it is not just what Christians are doing, but their intention in doing them.[49] J. C. Ryle uses the example of the Christian as a soldier who never ceases fighting and, so, must not become weary in doing good.[50] These examples highlight the emphasis, in many Reformed Churches, on behavior and obedience seen in action. This may mean that the emphasis on doing becomes greater than the emphasis on being, as the spirituality of believers is determined by their activity. This can lead to personal exhaustion and judgment toward others who do not appear as active.

Within the behavioral model there is an emphasis upon fellowship together. The notion of community takes the spiritual truths of Christianity, the "ethereal heights" that Snyder speaks of, and anchors them in the "nitty-gritty business of Christians living together, sharing a common life"; this, he believes, is essential for effective witness.[51] This demonstrates the connection between the contextual applications of the research question. Our model of evangelism affects our model of discipleship and our model of ministry. According to Liam Goligher, this evangelistic element means that, when considering the claims of Christianity, people will consider the Church's care for each other. If they see community, as it was intended, they

---

45. Greaves, "Tinker's Dissent," 8. D. Wenkel writes that Bunyan's theology «was not driven by exegesis or by expanded interaction with scholarship.» Wenkel, «John Bunyan's Soteriology," 352.

46. Bunyan, *Christian Behaviour*, 550.

47. Brown, *Four Spiritual Giants*, 136.

48. Bunyan, *Christian Behavior*, 555.

49. Owen, *Nature, Power, Deceit*, 314 and 316.

50. Ryle, *Holiness*, 73 and 100.

51. Snyder, *Community of the King*, 59.

will have that sense of belonging and acceptance they crave.[52] The power of including people, through a community of love and acceptance, cannot be underestimated. Chester and Timmis note that what is needed to be seen is to be communities of love, as the Church builds relationships with those outside of its membership. People are attracted to the community before the message of the community.[53] This approach takes the community beyond a place that is attended for an allotted time on a specific day of the week, and becomes a community in which Christians relate to one another in love and acceptance.

The issue of belonging to a community, Chalke believes, brings a sense of identity, security and accountability. This fulfills humanity's need for relationships, releasing humanity's creativity and developing something that will endure.[54] With many people feeling unconnected to anyone, the Church can offer something countercultural with an emphasis on community. Ronald J. Allen comments that an emphasis on community connects with the desire of many postmodern people who see relationships as constituting their identity.[55] It will change the identity of people, from thinking about race, culture, economic status and even educational achievements, into a new identity as members of the Church, and this will offer a sense of belonging to those who feel lonely and isolated in their present situation.

How discipleship works out practically, in the behavioral model, is also significant. Hull suggests that every Christian ought to have a core group with whom they can spend time and grow spiritually.[56] To do this he suggests weekly meetings, over a fixed time, to aid in discipleship. When a context is one of nominalism, moving people from Sunday worship to discipleship groups can be difficult. Yet, it is one that Beasley-Murray states is essential for Church life.[57] Banister points out that the use of small groups is something that is practiced amongst Evangelicalism, for in depth Bible

---

52. Goligher, *Fellowship of the King*, 52.
53. Chester and Timmis, *Total Church*, 56–57.
54. Chalke and Watkins, *Intelligent Church*, 138.
55. Allen, "Individual and Community," 140
56. Hull, *New Century Disciple Making*, 22.

57. "Sadly, unless a church is prepared to structure its life around small groups, true fellowship will never really be possible. Honest conversations, meaningful relationships, will be the exception rather than the rule. It is only within the privacy of a small group, where people have begun to trust one another, that we can make ourselves vulnerable and so become real with one another. Small groups should not be optional extras in any church – they are an essential to being church." Beasley-Murray, *Transform Your Church*, 46.

study, and amongst Charismatics, for practicing spiritual gifts.[58] They may, accordingly, provide a bridge between an Evangelical and Charismatic discipleship program. The behavioral model, therefore, can be both pastoral and missional. Watson writes that the age in which the Church lives is one of loneliness and personal insignificance, so the notion of the Christian community is something countercultural.[59] This thought of belonging is something that keeps arising in the behavioral model as community standards are an important element in judging behavior.

When discussing discipleship, spiritual development and growth are often emphasized from a position of personal faith in Christ. Yet, as the Church pastors and disciples its own people, this will also have an evangelistic function to those outside of the Church. They may see the sense of belonging that individual members have, and the interest that is invested in each person.[60] Non-Christians begin to see the gospel as more than a set of propositions to be assented to and begin to experience the power of God to bring wholeness.[61] While behavior is only one aspect of the Christian life, it demonstrates what is significant to individuals; namely, their personal evangelical experience.

There is, within the behavioral model, an emphasis on believers being present at the Sunday worship services, to hear the Word of God and be discipled, harmonizing with the proclamation model. Wimber writes that fellowship is more than socializing, but living our lives in common and demonstrating that commonality through generosity toward one another.[62] This may be seen as building a dependence upon an individual or institution

---

58. "Evangelicals and Charismatics have used the small group for different purposes. Charismatics have found the small group a perfect climate for prayer and ministry in the charismatic gifts, while evangelicals have found the small group a great place for accountability and the study of the Scriptures. Word and power churches expect that both benefits will result from the small group." Banister, *Word and Power Church*, 62.

59. Watson, *Discipleship*, 36.

60. "When the church commits itself to a pattern of corporate life based on radical biblical principles, it immediately challenges the moral, political, economic and social structures of the world around it. In this way, by its very existence, the church is both prophetic and evangelistic. And only in this way will the proclamation of the gospel make much impact amongst the vast majority of people who, at this moment, are thoroughly disillusioned by the church as an institution. For this reason it is impossible to separate the call to discipleship, the call to community and the call to mission. Without a strong commitment to discipleship, there can be no authentic Christian community; and without the existence of such a community, there can be no effective mission." Watson, *Discipleship*, 42.

61. Chester and Timmis, *Total Church*, 64.

62. Wimber and Springer, *Dynamics of Spiritual Growth*, 148.

for spiritual security. If that individual or institution should fail, then the spiritual world of the believer will be detrimentally affected.

Worship is also greater than a service on a specific day. Wimber believes that it encompasses every aspect of our lives, giving us a sense of purpose and reason.[63] This is a common theme with Tchividjian who believes that worship connects believers with their true identity, as citizens of the kingdom of God.[64] When believers understand that their discipleship gives them a sense of participation in a purpose greater than their own lives, it also aids bridging the gap between evangelism and ministry. Part of growth in discipleship is an understanding that more is needed than that which can be provided for in a Sunday worship service. Rick Bundschuh comments that this would produce "spiritual malnutrition" because, although adequately fed on Sundays, they are not feeding themselves throughout the week.[65] There needs to develop a weekly diet of worship that practices fellowship throughout the week, and encourages the sense of community that exists within the local Church.

One means of developing spiritual growth within a congregation is through home/fellowship groups. Gibbs and Coffey see it as evangelistic as much as it is didactic, encouraging Christians to get to know unbelievers intimately so that the gospel can be communicated relevantly and clearly.[66] To develop a sense of community is a positive matter in Christian growth because it not only develops a sense of belonging, but also a sense of mutual accountability. There is potential for spiritual discipline to be exercised as the members of the groups invest time and energy in each other. Discipleship may take time, as White states, but it is a worthwhile activity.[67] This happens as individual members feel they matter and they can contribute to the group through, as Richard Peace suggests, the sharing of their own personal histories and stories.[68] This may produce an "authentic Christian community," which Ryken believes would speak clearly for God's standards through preaching and worship, even if the world around them rejects such

---

63. Wimber, *Way In is the Way On*, 131.
64. Tchividjian, *Kingdom of God*, 3–4.
65. Bundschuh, *Church*, 143.
66. Gibbs and Coffey, *Church Next*, 197.
67. "While discipleship takes time, it is not merely a product of time or a by-product of mere 'exposure' to the Christian subculture. Churches are full of individuals who have spent years as Christians yet live lives that reflect little of the fruit of the Holy Spirit. The reason for this is simple. Life change is not a question of time as much as intentionally." White, *Rethinking the Church*, 72.
68. Peace, *Small Group Evangelism*, 89.

community.[69] Such a sense of community not only aids spiritual growth and discipleship, but also provides a means for evangelism by creatively showing the world that humanity is about interpersonal relationships.

When the personal renewing of the Holy Spirit is added to the formation of small groups, then the experience is heightened and intensified, as J. Rodman Williams describes. A new enthusiasm and sense of joy invades every aspect of Church life as the Church ministers to its own needs.[70] As this passion grows, what results is an increased attendance at public worship and commitment to the spiritual life of a congregation. Not only is the behavioral model helpful concerning spiritual discipline, it is also helpful concerning Christian relationships.[71] Wimber writes that commitment to God is commitment to his Church, as Christians love what Christ loves (Gal 2:2; Tit 2:14).[72] He further notes that Christ often sees the Church differently from humanity; he sees it as a bride preparing for marriage and for which he will return. If people become connected to one another in this family atmosphere, then they are more likely to stay the course because they are seeking relationship and identity that will aid them through life's trials.[73] When it is demonstrated that Christians are prepared to be committed to God through commitment to his Church, learning to "love the people we would not necessarily even like"[74], both ecumenically and locally, it may be not only a discipleship tool but also an evangelistic tool.

This model reminds us of the importance of the Law for the Christian. Bryan Chappell believes that the Church has misrepresented God because it has not presented properly a life ordered by his law.[75] Chappell further comments that, in the context of the two congregations he had pastored, both of which were historical congregations, he did not observe any obvious prob-

69. Ryken, *City on a Hill*, 32.
70. Rodman Williams, *Renewal Theology*, 2:317.
71. "When people find their niche in a church and stay there, they enter the comfort zone. Nothing challenges their fears, confronts them with their weaknesses, or asks them to expand their strength. The key word is *sameness* . . . Though comfort zone Christians may dream about change, they awake to major realities that prove too tough to battle. They resist the push to expand or be creative by answering calls to fine tune the institutional machinery. People become too comfortable with their leaders, roles and mediocrity. Keeping the vision before the people breaks the back of institutionalism. Challenge them to face their fears and work on their strengths – and more important, to find and develop their strengths. Encorage them to move into their strong points, and keep the organisation in motion." Hull, *New Century Disciple Making*, 91.
72. Wimber, *Everyone Gets to Play*, 34–35.
73. Ibid., 45.
74. Ibid., 118–19.
75. Chapell, *Wonder of it All*, 101.

lems with Christian behavior. Church members knew how to act, yet their internal attitudes, depression, coldness toward one another and intolerance permeated their lives.[76] This is a danger with the behavioral model: that only the actions that are visible are focused on, whereas the internal attitudes and thoughts are permitted.

While the behavioral model alone may not be enough for spiritual growth, there appears to be some element of truth in the fact that Christians must be accountable for their spiritual development and must see a change in behavior. This is what Wimber calls "spiritual acumen": not just whether people exercise any spiritual gifts they may use, but it is the degree to which Christians act on what they believe.[77] The behavioral model tells us that discipleship is not just what is done, but what inspires people to do it. This is how David Jackman defines maturity: not whether Christians do specific things, but how our beliefs interact with our lives.[78] This will mean that a passion for spiritual growth will be evident, as will a love and commitment for the Church, a passion for missions, and a common love for the people of God. Where these are absent it may rightly be asked if the discipleship model, in general, has failed.

The Proclamation Model

One of the most widely used methods, amongst Evangelical Churches, is that of proclamation. It places the preaching of the Bible as central to all aspects of the Church's witness.[79] Hull believes that preaching is the primary means of effecting discipleship because the pulpit sets the agenda for the

---

76. Chappell, *Wonder of it All*, 143–44.

77. Wimber, *Everyone Gets to Play*, 53. He further states: "Gifts are to character as adornments are to a body . . . So it is with spiritual gifts. They are to be adornments to a well formed character, which is the foundation for properly displaying them." Wimber, *Kingdom Living*, 9–10.

78. Jackman, *Understanding the Church*, 23.

79. Adam notes that the emphasis of preaching ought to be corporate and not exclusively individual: "But the Bible's main address is to the community of faith, the church . . . Preaching, in our definition, is a public presentation of the truth." Adam, *Speaking God's Words*, 70–71. Old writes: "With the sixteenth century Reformation, biblical preaching once again took a prominent place in the regular worship of the church." Old, *Worship Reformed According to Scripture*, 70. N. Lee writes: "Preaching is part of the Reformation heritage . . . Yet nowadays we inhabit a culture in which learning from words, whether printed or spoken, is increasingly difficult. There is a growing disillusionment with the kind of expository preaching that has been so crucial to the Reformation tradition. It is held to be less and less appropriate in a visually oriented, post-literate society." Lee, "Trouble with Expository Preaching," 1.

rest of the Church.[80] He argues that preaching determines the character and ethos of congregational life. Understood in this light, it will have an impact upon the spiritual development of believers.

The Reformed model I have chosen to reflect upon is that of Martyn Lloyd-Jones, minister of Westminster Chapel London from 1939–68. Lloyd-Jones professed and practiced the centrality of preaching in Christian worship. He devotes a whole book to the subject of preaching and, while most of his advice is for those who are practitioners, he does outline a close connection between preaching and revival.[81] The effect of preaching is to enliven the Christians who hear and to connect them to the power and presence of God. Martin Downes notes this when he comments that Lloyd-Jones saw preaching as "a transaction between the pulpit and pew . . . coupled with the expectation that God is present and is dealing with people."[82] This reminds Christians of what has been recorded in the Bible as the standard for their Christian living. This connection between revival and preaching is a significant theme in Lloyd-Jones. Robert V. Rakestraw writes that, while people may claim Church to be boring, not to preach the truth in the power of the Spirit is much worse.[83] The effect of preaching is always more important than the entertainment of the listeners because its purpose is to produce an obedience to what the Bible says, so that discipleship may grow.

Ryken suggests that proclamation involves engaging the believers' minds, so that their thoughts influence their actions to such an extent that what is done is what is believed.[84] Believers are encouraged to be present at Sunday worship, where the majority of the service is devoted to exposition of biblical texts. This pattern is continued throughout the weekly Church activity, in midweek meetings or fellowship groups.[85] What this model hopes to produce is, not just Christians who know the teaching of

80. Hull, *Disciple Making Church*, 41.

81. Lloyd-Jones, *Preaching and Preachers*, 24–25. "What is it that heralds the dawn of a Reformation or of a Revival? It is renewed preaching. Not only a new interest in preaching but a new kind of preaching. A revival of preaching has always heralded these great movements in the history of the Church."

82. Downes, "Review Article," 55.

83. Rakestraw, "Power of the Holy Spirit."

84. Ryken, *City on a Hill*, 113.

85. Some see a distinction between preaching and teaching, however, it is unclear whether such a distinction is viable. MacArthur writes; "I've put preaching and teaching together because they are both related to the proclamation of biblical truth. Proclaiming the Word of God is a primary function of the church . . . But the church's most important function is to proclaim the Word of God in an understandable, direct, authoritative way." MacArthur, *Master's Plan for the Church*, 57. To avoid any confusing I use the term proclamation.

the Bible, but Christians who are obedient to the teaching of the Bible. As Chappell notes, they have their hearts molded and broken by the Word.[86] Preaching is not only the gospel, but also the law of God and his requirements from humanity (Matt 5:17–18; Gal 3:24–25).[87] It would generally be assumed, amongst the proponents of this model, that the Bible is the only means by which God's voice is heard.[88] John MacArthur notes that the Bible is so "comprehensive in its diagnosis and treatment of every spiritual matter" that, when "energized" by the Holy Spirit, it is all that is needed.[89] This expresses the high doctrine of the Bible that is held in many Reformed circles, and their understanding that to listen to the Bible is to listen to God. This attention to preaching requires, as shall be considered in chapter 6, an academically trained preacher to properly educate the congregation.

Wimber desires that people would know God and hear his voice through the Bible, being not only biblically "literate," but also biblically "obedient."[90] When moving from listening to practicing, discipleship is doing what it is meant to do. In this model obedience comes through adherence to the guidebook; namely, the Bible. As Christians read and digest its teaching, they aim to practice what it says. Wimber comments that it is not how much time is spent in Bible study that matters, but the impact that the Bible has on Christian's lives which is significant.[91] Without such a commitment to the Bible, therefore, a Christian would be undisciplined and could possibly slide into heresy.[92] Wimber notes that if Christians are

---

86. Chappell, *Wonder of it All*, 20.

87. "It is not faithful to either the Scriptures or the Reformed faith to adopt a naïve, biblicist approach to the proclamation of the word. Yes, the minister must preach the word, but, according to Scripture as understood by our confessions and theologians, the word has two moods—law and gospel. At any moment, the minister is preaching either law or gospel. It is not possible to "preach the word" indiscriminately. The faithful minister will be conscious of that fact and adjust his preaching accordingly." Clarke, "Letter and Spirit," 352.

88. "The *fact that revelation has reached its end or goal in the coming of Jesus Christ does not mean that God has stopped speaking and communicating with men through the Scriptures*. The Spirit of God continues to illuminate the truths of the Bible so that the hearts and minds of men can understand and believe. Affirming that special revelations about Jesus no longer occur does not mean that God no longer communes and communicates with his people. By the work of the Spirit in the hearts of men, millions of people all over the world daily come to a better understanding of the truth of God as found in the Bible." Robertson, *The Final Word*, 55.

89. MacArthur, *Our Sufficiency in Christ*, 58.

90. Wimber, *Everyone Gets to Play*, 17.

91. Wimber, *Way In is the Way On*, 112.

92. Pawson comments that believers are considered "sound" in some circles because they know certain proof texts for their beliefs, making faith an intellectual exercise, and

to live an obedient life to God, then that life must be true to the Bible.[93] This is one of the reasons why I believe it is important to reconcile the ethos of Wimber with that of a Reformed and Evangelical congregation, because of the apparent similarities.

The proclamation model claims to provide a firm foundation upon which to build Christian experience. However, something more is required—a submission to doctrine.[94] It is possible to be a Christian who is very well taught on matters of Christian doctrine, yet live in a way that appears to contradict that doctrine. Wimber wants believers to interact with something more than information; if discipleship is solely information, then, he believes, it leads to "dead orthodoxy."[95] Philip Jensen calls this the technological triumph over theology, where the text is argued away or coldly applied.[96] There is also a tendency to look for a Bible verse only when things go awry in life. Wimber likens this to taking medication rather than the daily nourishment that is needed to grow and develop.[97] Wimber's assessment appears correct, not only regarding Evangelicalism, but also some elements of the Charismatic Movement in which claiming biblical promises is encouraged when life's trials come along.[98] While this is a challenge to the proclamation-based model, it is a wider problem when people turn to God as a last ditch attempt to find reason for their trials.

For the proclamation model to work it has to move beyond Sunday services and become a daily experience of feeding upon the Word of God. Wimber notes that the knowledge of God is progressive and, as believers grow in that knowledge, opportunities for service become evident.[99] Bill and Lynne Hybels believe that there is some confusion about the nature of leadership because the Church has been directed by teachers and not leaders. This needs to change from the focus of communicating knowledge to impressing the need to get behind a specific goal or aim.[100] It is, however,

---

the result is separation from all considered not "sound" in doctrine: "This tendency to divide is sometimes extended to the point of isolating those who may be orthodox themselves but who relate with those who are not, a practice known as "guilt by association". The result is that circles of fellowship become progressively smaller and more exclusive." Pawson, *Word and Spirit Together*, 113.

93. Wimber, *Way In is the Way On*, 51.
94. Wimber and Springer, *Dynamics of Spiritual Growth*, 6.
95. Ibid., 9.
96. Jensen, "Preaching the Word Today," 165.
97. Wimber and Springer, *Dynamics of Spiritual Growth*, 45.
98. Savelle, *If Satan Can't Steal Your Joy*.
99. Wimber and Springer, *Dynamics of Spiritual Growth*, 145.
100. Hybels and Hybels, *Rediscovering Church*, 149.

unclear how a passionate teaching ministry will not also accomplish what Hybels suggests. The issue is that the proclamation model must be focused on releasing people into ministry, themselves. To take on board the challenge of Hybels and Hybels means that the Church will begin to release people from dependence upon clergy for spiritual direction, and enable them to interact with God themselves. When the proclamation model works well it accomplishes these ends and the effect of the Holy Spirit, applying the exposition to the believer's heart, will be evident.

Listening to preaching alone would not be significant for spiritual development; there is a need for something more. Chester and Timmis write that this is experiencing God through the Word, as his Spirit applies that Word to our lives, leading us into action proclaiming that Word.[101] This is the ministry model connection that I am suggesting: evangelism leads to discipleship and releases into ministry. Proclamation-only models of discipleship produce scholastic believers who, although they may know the truth of the Bible, may struggle to have that truth affect and change their lives. Head knowledge is no substitute for heart experience, and simple knowledge of truth does not necessarily equate with spirituality.

While it will rarely be admitted amongst Reformed believers, there may be a tendency toward bibliolatry.[102] Wimber reminds us that the focus of Christian worship is the Triune God, not the Bible: "the Bible is the menu, not the meal."[103] A. W. Tozer notes that some have claimed Evangelicals to be "bibliolaters" and, he comments, that a book can only ever give the letter of the law. It is the Holy Spirit who takes things further, so not only is the Bible to be known, but also there is a need to be enlightened by the Holy Spirit.[104] There is a need to be more than biblically orthodox in doctrine, knowing proof texts for what is believed and against what is rejected. For Reformed Christians this means, not only a devotion to Scripture, but also a passion for experiencing that which is spoken of. Word and Spirit comple-

---

101. Chester and Timmis, *Total Church*, 31.

102. This is a view of the Bible that understands it not as the ultimate source of knowledge but the sole source of authority. This view has been formed in reaction to changes in the educational system in which matters of religion or ethics are considered as private matters. This is different from the notion of a unified curriculum "grounded in a monotheistic God, and in which knowledge and truth was present in all areas of study. The Church has reacted to this by extolling the Bible above all other means of understanding God, and so guidance or revelation through prophecy, words of knowledge and wisdom have been ignored. The final aspect has particular bearing on this discussion as it seems to suggest this position rules out any charismatic guidance." Moreland, "How Evangelicals Became Over-Committed," 4–6.

103. Wimber, *Way In is the Way On*, 99.

104. Tozer, "Bible Taught or Spirit Taught?" 38.

ment each other, leading to a greater degree of commitment and devotion to each other.[105] There needs to be an interaction with the Spirit, of whom the Bible speaks, and who is claimed to have inspired the text. This discipleship will mean an orthopraxy as well as an orthodoxy of theology.[106]

This model could be understood as an educational model in which the congregation is educated in theological belief. Banister comments that the emphasis on Bible knowledge was turning his Church into a "classroom" in which the congregation knew about God, but did not experience his presence: "We were getting to know him *propositionally*, but we were not meeting him *personally*."[107] This may be a danger when spirituality is judged upon how much is known, not how deep is a relationship with Christ. Yet, there is also a sense in which knowledge of God, through the Bible, is an expression of love for God. The motivation, therefore, for the proclamation itself ought to be love for God.

Kendall comments that there appears to be a lack of confidence in the Bible. He believes that the power of the Spirit will only be manifested in the degree to which the Word of God is loved.[108] When the proclamation model is used as a means of drawing believers further into relationship with Christ, the foundation is laid upon which a dynamic experience of the work of the Spirit may be built. This will provide a confidence in the Bible to accomplish exactly what is promised within the text; namely, a powerful experience of God through the Holy Spirit.

A marriage between the Word and Spirit is suggested as necessary for balanced Christian growth. Pawson notes that there must be both experience and theology for discipleship to be true and valid, otherwise it will

---

105. The focus of preaching to postmoderns must be community awareness: "Postmodern preaching intends to form the church as community. A Christian is more than an individual with a relationship with God (and consequent personal ethical responsibilities) mediated through Jesus Christ. A Christian is an expression of a world shaped by the awareness of gracious Transcendence. And the church is more than a collection of individuals. It is a body of persons who are related to one another and to God on the analogy of the parts of the body." Allen, "Individual and Community," 142.

106. Praxis refers to the epistemological view that united theory and practice as inseparable and mutually informing. Archer, *Gospel Revisited*, 11. Wimber writes: "As leaders we need to remain congruent with orthodoxy and orthopraxy, to maintain our focus on the "main and the plain" in Scripture." Wimber, *Way In is the Way On*, 143–44.

107. Banister, *Word and Power Church*, 15.

108. Cain and Kendall, *Word and the Spirit*, 35. See also "Such manifestations of the Spirit were often valuable when accompanying and complementing the preaching of the gospel, for they enabled believers to powerfully engage in the task of presenting the supremacy of Christ and of authenticating the gospel, especially in the context of other power based religions." Warrington, *Message of the Holy Spirit*, 129.

become barren or dangerous.[109] Experiencing God and knowing the truth requires the Bible, yet more is needed: an experience of the God of the Bible. Kendall gives a word of caution: he believes the reason more signs and wonders are not seen is because there is more interest in them than in the Bible.[110] Understanding the Bible as the central axis of our faith may be positive, but there is more to experiencing God than just the words on the page. This happens through personal experience with the Holy Spirit who inspired the writing and makes it come alive.

Practically speaking, there may also be a need for cross-pollination between the Charismatic and Reformed streams. Fyall comments that the Charismatic practice of reducing the sermon to a homily, "reinforces the idea that preaching is something which interrupts worship" when it ought to lead us into deeper worship.[111] This blending of the ethos of the two streams may be healthy and positive. The central role of the Bible in worship and spiritual formation is emphasized by Reformed and Evangelical theology, as has been noted. Even amongst those who profess the strongest adherence to the Bible, there is an attitude that likes to keep things in their prescribed order. So, keeping biblical preaching central, but encouraging a Charismatic response to it, may be a positive alternative.

Fyall argues that preaching needs to be understood in a Charismatic manner—prophetically. The fundamental approach to preaching, he argues, must be expositional, and the twin errors of emphasizing only those passages that reference spiritual gifts, or "preach the gospel only" sermons, should be avoided. He concludes: "In all church the declaring of the whole of the Scriptures is a prerequisite of the power of the Spirit."[112] This is the true ecumenical spirit of the Reformed/Charismatic model of ministry in which inspiration is sought from many texts of the Bible to direct an understanding of the Holy Spirit's work.

The Sacramental Model

The sacramental model of discipleship emphasizes baptism and communion as integral parts of spiritual development and a more liturgical form

---

109. "Charismatics without evangelicals become vulnerable to being "blown here and there by every eddy of teaching" (Eph 4:14). Evangelicals without Charismatics are of equal concern. Sound doctrine does not ensure spiritual dynamic. Exegesis is no substitute for experience. The church is meant to be powerful as well as pure." Pawson, *Word and Spirit Together*, 10.

110. Cain and Kendall, *Word and the Spirit*, 42.

111. Fyall, *Charismatic and Reformed*, 2–3.

112. Ibid., 3.

of worship. Baptism is a central aspect of the theology of the Reformed Churches, and the WCF notes that "it is a great sin to contemn or neglect this ordinance."[113] According to Bradford, there is a developing theology that equates water baptism with Spirit baptism as an initiatory rite into the Christian community.[114] If the Spirit is understood to be received at baptism, it would make the rite more spiritual than a naming ceremony. If a rite of confirmation were to be introduced then it could fulfill the place of a second blessing to some charismatics. This may be a form of baptismal regeneration, in which the spiritual reality of faith is linked to the physical act of baptism. This has not been the traditional view in Reformed Churches.[115] For Reformed Churches the connection between baptism and Church membership is important, however.[116] Within this model, the notion of the community of faith is significant because that community of faith gives meaning to the individual member of it.

113. WCF 28:5. This symbolically illustrates an element of the gospel, the washing away of sin, and when publicly administered presents an object lesson of spiritual truth. While accepted into the Church in baptism, there is a further element in spiritual development when the baptized makes a personal profession of faith.

114. This associates the means of entrance into the visible Church through baptism, whether as an infant or believer, with entrance into the Invisible Church through the reception of the Holy Spirit. Bradford, *Releasing the Power,* 12–13. In recent years this view has developed into a loosely held theological group called the Federal Vision or Auburn Avenue Theology. See Waters, *Federal Vision and Covenant Theology.* Jeschke believes that this association between baptism and membership of the Church in the Anabaptist Community has been detrimental to the doctrine of baptism itself separating it from personal faith. Jeschke, *Believers Baptism for Children,* 52–53.

115. "Therefore, the children of Christian parents benefit by that which baptism signifies. It signifies that, as water washes away the dirt of the body, so Christ's blood washes away the sin of the soul . . . Although these promises are not fulfilled in infants at the moment at which baptism is ministered, the Lord Jesus will effectually work by the power of His Holy Spirit in the hearts of His chosen all that is signified in baptism, in His appointed time." Dale, *Reformed Book of Common Order,* 18–19. The view of Presbyterians has been called "presumptive" regeneration, that the children of believing parents are baptized because they are presumed to be regenerate. Schenck, *Presbyterian Doctrine of Children,* 135. Murray also notes that there is no connection in Reformed theology between baptism and regeneration but there is between baptism and union with Christ. Murray, *Christian Baptism,* 4–5.

116. "In the New Testament, it was baptism that marked people off as being members of the visible church . . . Repentance and faith in Jesus by people who have not been previously baptized, leads to baptism, which leads to admission to the visible church. It is through baptism that we are brought within the fellowship of God's people, the visible Church. It is important to stress this because some Christians tend to divorce baptism and admission into the fellowship of God's people. They are prepared to baptize people without incorporating them into the visible church." Crooks, *Salvation's Sign and Seal,* 30–31. The Presbyterian position has emphasized the faith of the parents in baptism, not the regenerative power of the sacrament. Murray, *Christian Baptism,* 77; WCF 28:4.

Wimber notes that evangelism not only focuses on individual disciples, but also building bodies of people, because human beings were created for fellowship, as has been seen in the behavioral model.[117] The connection between the Spirit and the sacraments is supported by Ellen T. Charry who notes that the Spirit works as the agent of "Christianisation" in the sacraments.[118] This requires a higher view of the sacraments than may be common in many Evangelical Churches, but a view that appears to be in sympathy with the teaching of the Reformed Churches. In conceding that the Spirit makes water, bread and wine something spiritual, there may be merit in asserting, as has been noted previously, that miracles as a result of prayer may also be included. This places the idea of the community of faith, as an interpreter of faith, central to Christianity.

A historical example for this model is John Williamson Nevin, a nineteenth-century theologian and convert from Scot/Irish Presbyterianism to the German Reformed tradition, who eventually taught in their seminary in Mercerberg, PA.[119] Nevin's primary work on the sacraments was *The Mystical Presence: A Vindication of the Reformed or Calvinistic Doctrine of the Holy Eucharistic*. His thesis is that the nineteenth-century practice had fallen away from the sacramental doctrines of the sixteenth century, and that there was a need to return to the "externalization" of the Christian faith.[120] He restates the doctrine of the real presence of Christ in the Eucharist, but takes it to an eschatological conclusion, where its consummation is heaven.[121] Nevin sees the celebration of the Lord's Supper as a central aspect in the spiritual formation of the believer, and an ongoing experience of spiritual growth that leads into eternity. He also believes that this is different from the Roman Catholic position in that believers do not eat Christ, but are mutually connected to him.[122] Although a Reformed position, it was not without its critics. Charles Hodge, coming from a scientific and realist

---

117. Wimber and Springer, *Power Evangelism*, 105.
118. Charry, "Sacraments for the Christian Life."
119. For a full discussion of Williamson's life see Hart, *John Williamson Nevin*.
120. Nevin, *Mystical Presence*, 1–2.
121. "Thus, the sacramental doctrine of the primitive Reformed Church stands inseparably connected with the idea of an inward living union between believers and Christ, in virtue of which they are incorporated into his very nature, and made to subsist with him by the power of a common life. In full correspondence with the conception of the Christian salvation, as a process by which the believer is mystically inserted more and more into the person of Christ, till he becomes thus at last fully transformed into his image, it was held than-nothing less than such a real participation of his living person is involved always in the right use of the Lord's supper." Williamson, *Mystical Presence*, 27.
122. Nevin, *Mystical Presence*, 31.

view, who had been Nevin's professor at Princeton Seminary, disagreed with his position because he distrusted anything speculative. He saw Christianity primarily as a system of doctrine, whereas Nevin understood it as a life to be lived.[123] Nevin's position may lend itself to a Charismatic approach in which the experience of spiritual life is as important as the understanding of spiritual life; that is, the equality of orthodoxy and orthopraxy.

Sacramentalism could also offer a relevant and modern approach to faith when an emphasis is placed on the aesthetics of sight, taste, sound, and touch. Stackhouse comments that sacramentalism, which emphasizes the distinctiveness of Christian worship, is visibly displayed weekly in communal worship.[124] Dave Tomlinson agrees with this view because there are many who have become disillusioned with the reductionism of the Evangelical and Charismatic Movements, finding their spiritual home in a sacramental tradition.[125] The sacraments are both pastoral and evangelical, in as much as they proclaim the essential elements of the gospel and offer a sense of belonging to the people of faith.

This emphasis on the sacrament, with its understanding of Roman Catholicism,[126] may be difficult to relate to the Reformed position. Yet, as Wimber states, the Church's goal is to be aware of our worldview and to change it so that those elements that are contrary to our faith are excluded.[127] Anything that encourages hatred of another individual because of their culture, politics or religion is a worldview that can be challenged and, therefore, is open to the challenge of community. The community of the Church is a community of grace, as Donald G. Bloesch notes, and this grace works, not from the leadership down but from the membership upwards.[128] Sacramentalism teaches the Church to sanctify every aspect of its individual lives and have that holiness affect all relationships of their lives.

There may be an argument that the sacraments need a greater emphasis amongst the Evangelical and Reformed Churches today than is generally given. Abraham comments that the Church needs to rethink the connection

---

123. Bonome, *Incarnation and Sacrament*, 7–17. There are also areas of commonality between Nevin and Hodge including a distrust of the growing revivalism of the nineteenth century. P. J. Wallace sees a movement in Nevin away from his Scotch/Irish background toward a more continental Reformed position where he becomes more Reformed than the German Reformed Church of his day. Wallace, "History and Sacrament," 175–76.

124. Stackhouse, *Gospel Driven Church*, 131.

125. Tomlinson, *Re-Enchanting Christianity*, 78.

126. WCF 25:6.

127. Wimber and Springer, *Power Evangelism*, 131.

128. Bloesch, *Church*, 209.

between evangelism and baptism, thus connecting salvation and initiation into the Church.[129] This has led some Reformed theologians, in North America, to develop a salvific theology that includes baptism and communion, calling themselves the "Federal Vision." Norman Shepherd writes that the "covenant sign and seal" marks an individual as converted and a member of the Church, so that, from a covenantal perspective, individuals are united to Christ from the moment of baptism.[130] This theology sits more comfortably with paedobaptist Churches than credobaptist Churches.[131] If too close a relationship between sacrament and evangelism were professed, then evangelism may simply be administering the sacraments. There may, however, be a positive way of considering this theology that sees Baptism in the Holy Spirit, along with baptism in water, as part of the conversion and initiation process.[132] Baptism in the Holy Spirit, therefore, points back to a previous sacramental experience.[133] Lines of division between Evangelical, Charismatic and Sacramentalist could, therefore, become blurred. So, this tradition may also develop a Charismatic ethos that blends the two streams.

There may be an assumption that a defined format of worship, and a sacramental theology, rule out the extempore work of the Spirit. Wimber attempts to answer this criticism by emphasizing the appropriate kind of order that is necessary: the kind of order that separates the living from the dead, for both are highly organized.[134] To apply his theology to a Reformed context does not necessarily imply that form and ritual need to be purged. There may be a need to have a semblance of order; otherwise worship may descend into extreme individualism without any idea of corporate identity.

129. Abraham, *Logic of Evangelism*, 118.

130. Shepherd, *Call of Grace*, 94. While not directly related to the Federal Visions his influence is seen in their theology. "One would also have to identify Norman Shepherd as a fountainhead of the central teachings of the Federal Vision." Waters, *Federal Vision and Covenant Theology*, 301.

131. Paedobaptism refers to the baptism of children, see Crooks, *Salvation's Sign and Seal*. Credobaptism can be defined as follows: "In fact, I believe that the Bible authorizes the baptism of disciples alone. This position may also be called credobaptism from the Latin verb credo, meaning believe or trust. Other designations are believer's baptism, confessor's baptism or professor's baptism, all synonyms describing the baptism of disciples alone." Malone, *Baptism of Disciples Alone*, xiii.

132. This view sees a process in individuals coming to faith, beginning at their baptism, leading to personal profession of faith, and then becoming a functional member of the Church. As we shall see Wimber believes that at conversion the Spirit is received, so to add other elements in what leads up to and precedes this event may be part of the initiation process. Baptism in the Holy Spirit is defined further in the Charismatic model.

133. Cartledge, *Encountering the Spirit*, 109.

134. Wimber and Springer, *Power Evangelism*, 64.

It can be concluded, therefore, that sacramentalism alone is not necessarily incompatible with Wimber's theology, but could be understood as a Charismatic model also.

Wimber notes the purpose of the sacraments is to point us away from ourselves and towards Christ and our salvation experience in him.[135] Sacramentalism, that builds a dependence upon the sacraments themselves, is a self-defeating model. However, when explained through the power of the Spirit and biblically, what they signify becomes a promise to believers.[136] A sacramental emphasis may be something very helpful; when people see the sacrament observed, and hear the explanation of what it means, they experience the grace of God illustrated by the sacrament. This will add faith to the sacrament and enable observance to become participation. In the essence of what the sacrament signifies, Peterson sees the sacrament of communion as having a threefold focus: the past, with what happened on the cross to effect salvation; the present, in which the faith of the people of God is expressed in worship; and the future consummation at the return of Christ.[137] This would link the sacramental to the proclamation model as the meaning of the sacrament is explained and the experience encouraged.

The sacramental life, specifically baptism, may have a powerful effect upon a person's life. Within the Reformed Churches the majority practice is that of infant baptism. Yet, when the message of covenantal faith is remembered, the understanding changes.[138] Wimber believes baptism needs to be rethought. He suggests removing the sentimentality and nostalgia associated with it, and beginning to understand it as a matter of obedience and "a declaration of war."[139] Whether paedobaptist or credobaptist, both views are based upon the conviction that their practice is obedient to the Bible.[140] So there can be great power in being told that you are accepted by

---

135. Wimber and Springer, *Dynamics of Spiritual Growth*, 149–50.

136. WCF 27:3.

137. Peterson, *Five Smooth Stones*, 62–63.

138. It is beyond the remit of this work to debate the rectitude of baptismal theology. The Reformed understanding of the sacrament, as held within PCI, is based upon the promise to Abraham (Gen 17:7) and Peter's sermon at Pentecost (Acts 2:38–39). It is further enshrined in the WCF: «The efficacy of Baptism is not tied to that moment of time wherein it is administered; yet notwithstanding, by the right use of this ordinance, the grace promised is not only offered, but really exhibited and conferred, by the Holy Ghost, to such (whether of age or infants) as that grace belongeth unto, according to the counsel of God's own will, in His appointed time." (WCF 28:6).

139. Wimber, *Way In is the Way On*, 169.

140. Allen, *Theology for a Troubled Believer*, 175. "Our union with Christ is strengthened and renewed with every celebration of Jesus' death, resurrection, and ascension in the Eucharist («thanksgiving»), or Holy Communion. Both baptism in

God, and that once faith is added to the baptismal promises, then you are ready for war.

The Charismatic Model

Wimber stands within the Charismatic model and suggests an ongoing development of discipleship through the Holy Spirit. A Charismatic model of discipleship remind us, as Hull notes, that programs and strategies, while helpful, cannot ever replace what the Holy Spirit does in a human heart.[141] This ongoing charismatic experience is mirrored in the ongoing battle ethos of the Christian who, according to Wimber, does not recognize that Christ's victory is applicable to everyday life.[142] In the Reformed context this takes theological principles and places them within the practical life of believers, producing orthopraxy as well as orthodoxy.[143] It demonstrates that what is believed has a direct impact upon how life is lived. Unless this impact is seen, what is believed could be challenged because Christian theology ought to produce practical change. Indeed, it could be claimed that this is a spiritual work.[144] This is similar to the principles of the Reformed tradition.

Wimber does not see discipleship, exclusively, as being about spiritual gifts, but the spiritual fruit that spring from a "repentant, born-again heart."[145] This moves the debate beyond prophecy, tongues and interpretation, and looks for what is changing in the convert's life.[146] Wimber seems to be looking for a change in attitude, rather than an experience of spiritual gifts, in which "habits of righteousness," like caring for others, repentance, prayer and Bible study are practiced.[147] If a cessationist position were taken

---

the name of the Father, Son, and Holy Spirit and the celebration of Holy Communion were instituted by Jesus. Hence, they constitute the sacraments for the churches of the Reformation."

141. Hull, *New Century Disciple Making*, 44.

142. Wimber and Springer, *Power Evangelism*, 57–58.

143. Johnson, *When Grace Comes Home*, 16. He suggests that many believe Reformed doctrine are "irrelevant theological abstractions without any practical relevance at all." Yet, the focus of his book proves their practical application for Christian living.

144. "The modern devotion sought a deeper and more Christocentric spirituality based on a firm commitment to the bible." Jones, *Great Reformation*, 22.

145. Wimber and Springer, *Dynamics of Spiritual Growth*, 10.

146. Generally speaking, any conversation on spiritual gifts centers around tongues, prophecy and healing, as Pawson notes: "While all the "gifts" are believed to have been available to the whole church for the whole of her history on earth, some are more prominent, or at least more frequent, in Charismatic circles today. Prophecy, tongues and healing tend to dominate the scene." Pawson, *Word and Spirit Together*, 34.

147. Wimber and Springer, *Dynamics of Spiritual Growth*, 11.

then Wimber's ethos would be readily accepted. It does not deal with believers' experiencing spiritual gifts, or even if they ought to experience them. Rather, he suggests a change of attitude through the Holy Spirit's action. The issue of spiritual gifts remains to be dealt with.

Not only is this a common foundation, but Wimber criticizes those who place their experience on the same level as, or above, the Bible as a subjective truth, because personal revelation must always conform to biblical accuracy and values.[148] Wimber's Charismatic model desires a Bible-based Christian, thinking and acting in a biblical manner. This roots the believer in the things of God and places firm foundations within the Christian life, through a foundational knowledge of justification and how the gospel is to be ministered.[149] This happens as Christians listen to the Bible, study, and apply it, both personally and corporately. Wimber does not exclude alternative means of God communicating to people apart from the Bible. He sees the Old and New Testaments as "our final court of appeal," but God continues to speak through creation, conscience and continuing providence. In the New Testament he speaks through supernatural means such as dreams, prophecies, and visions.[150] This is the emphasis that Wimber brings to discipleship: spiritual gifts that add a new dimension to discipleship. This may have a powerful effect upon those who are involved in traditional models of discipleship, bringing an abstract theology about spiritual gifts into the reality of their Christian lives.

This experience will speak to the fact that every believer is valued and is significant to the witness and worship of the Church, and should they not understand the role they are called upon to play, then the Church would suffer. Wayne A. Mack and Dave Swavely believe that ignorance of spiritual gifts harms the Church as a whole because gifted individuals feel that they have no function to perform and are useless. If individuals believe God has given them spiritual gifts, then they will make a contribution to the Church and develop a sense of personal fulfillment.[151] Discipleship reminds believers that their contribution to the work of the kingdom is not to be seen as observance, but participation. Should individuals question their ability to participate, then the sovereign work of God in distributing spiritual gifts will encourage their participation in the active ministry of the Church. This needs the work of the Holy Spirit who, as Horton notes, "now fills the eschatological end time temple: the church as Christ's body" and "is the one who

---

148. Ibid., 43–44.
149. Wimber, *Way In is the Way On,* 49.
150. Wimber and Springer, *Dynamics of Spiritual Growth,* 55.
151. Mack and Swavely, *Life in the Father's House,* 145.

turns a house into a home."[152] Rather than listening in the proclamation model, becoming in the behavioral model, or observing in the sacramental model, this model emphasizes the active participation of believers in their spiritual development.

Underpinning the methodology proposed by Wimber is the notion of "kingdom conversions." Believers undergo a radical change when they come to faith in Christ and become citizens of the kingdom of God. This is also present in Reformed theology where the emphasis is placed upon the change that happens in the believer's life.[153] This brings an understanding that both supernatural experiences and ministry are available, as they rely on Christ to confirm the gospel with miraculous signs (Mark 16:20).[154] For Wimber, the idea of conversion better expresses the notion of a Christian experience, perhaps, than an emotional response to evangelistic activity. Graham Tomlin comments that the Church, which lives under the kingdom of God, cannot but provoke questions from others, which gives opportunity for evangelism.[155] The kingdom of God is, therefore, a dominant theme and, according to Cartledge, could be said "to encapsulate the others." This contains all the emphasis on signs and wonders, miracles, healing and the like that are connected to Wimber's theology.[156] In reflection upon the Great Commission (Matt 28:18ff), discipleship will only work when evangelism promotes the becoming of disciples, emphasizing the corresponding character changes necessary for conversion to be genuine (Eph 2:8–10).[157] Kingdom conversions, as Devenish notes, mean a commitment to a way of life that is "dynamic not static"—a way of life in which the moving of the Spirit in the world is witnessed as the extending work of God's kingdom. If the sick are healed, the demonized delivered, good news brought to the poor and justice triumphs over injustice, then the kingdom of God is

---

152. Horton, *People and Place*, 15–16.

153. "My desire is to show the connection between the kingdom of God and the Christian life so that Christians will once again see themselves first and foremost as citizens of God's kingdom, allowing the transforming presence of that kingdom to mould and shape them into the image of its King." Tchividjian, *Kingdom of God*, 6. He further notes the change in operation within the Christian life to new standards that reflect the "different goals, desires, motivations, and perspective on life and humanity altogether." This makes Christians "resident aliens" in this world. Tchividjian, *Kingdom of God*, 16.

154. Wimber and Springer, *Power Evangelism*, 87.

155. Tomlin, *Provocative Church*, 14.

156. Cartledge, *Encountering the Spirit*, 28–29.

157. Camp suggests that the Kingdom of God ought to be the primary identity for all the people of God, however, it is often the world in which we live that forms and molds Christian discipleship. Camp, *Mere Discipleship*, 48.

extending.[158] Commitment to Christ means a commitment to the advance of this kingdom; not a passive observance of what is happening, but an active participation in the work.

As the name suggests, there is an emphasis upon the role of the Holy Spirit within the Charismatic model of discipleship: specifically, that of experiencing a "baptism" in the Holy Spirit. This can be taken to define a two-tier Christianity of those who have the Spirit and those who have not. This can be difficult, in a traditional Reformed congregation, because phrases like "Baptism in the Holy Spirit" are often beyond the frame of reference of the people. It can also be offensive to tell such people that they do not have the Holy Spirit.[159] It has also been theologically questioned as a valid means of defining what Charismatics claim to have experienced.[160] It is in this area that the Charismatic Movement may be more acceptable, pastorally, to Reformed Churches than to the Pentecostal. This is a commonality, which Colin Craston points out, that argues for an openness to the Holy Spirit and his gifts, rather than a theological modus operandi, as in some Pentecostal traditions.[161] Whatever terms may, therefore, be used to describe the work of the Holy Spirit, it is helpful to remember, as Bloesch points out, that "the Holy Spirit is not uniform but multiform," moving in many different ways, giving many different gifts, and being consistently surprising and unexpected.[162] This need not, therefore, become bound by terminology, as long as the experience is there. Often the terms themselves, as has been seen concerning the communication the gospel exclusively through a fear-based model of evangelism, can be off-putting.

158. Devenish, *What on Earth is the Church For?* 80.

159. "Now this Pentecostal viewpoint often comes as a shock when the evangelical first encounters it . . . Accordingly, the Pentecostal position on Spirit-baptism often rouses the antagonism of the evangelical." J. Rodman Williams, "Neo Pentecostal Viewpoint," in *Perspectives on the New Pentecostalism,* 78–79. Lucas states that the doctrine of the Baptism in the Holy Spirit came into American Presbyterianism through the influence of D. L. Moody and, specifically, through Charles G. Trumball and A. T. Pierson. It was not a Pentecostal understanding of the doctrine, but a holiness one. See Lucas, *On Being Presbyterian,* 208–09.

160. Brown, *Follow the Wind,* 177. He states that while he does not doubt the validity of the charismatic experience he questions the rectitude of defining it as Baptism in the Holy Spirit and suggests that words such as filling, experience or demonstration may be more appropriate.

161. Craston, "Pastoral Implications," 31. "When one becomes a believer, one receives Christ *and also the Spirit.* Conversion is about a change in direction, a transformation, a judicial declaration including the forgiveness of sins. However, it is also about a commencement of a relationship with the Spirit." Warrington, *Message of the Holy Spirit,* 88 (emphasis mine).

162. Bloesch, *Holy Spirit,* 285.

Wimber sees salvation as the "one Lord, one faith, one baptism" model (Eph 4:5), yet continues to ask how Christians experience Baptism in the Holy Spirit. He stands in sympathy with the Reformed tradition, arguing that conversion and Baptism in the Holy Spirit are the same: "The born-again experience is the consummate charismatic experience."[163] This view dovetails with that of Bradford who states that, for Reformed Christians, being baptized in the Holy Spirit is the same as being born of the Holy Spirit. For Bradford, conversion would also be the consummate charismatic experience.[164] In this context Wimber appears to be within the Evangelical camp in his theological views; therefore, when explained to a Reformed congregation, his views are much more accessible than those of Pentecostalism. Pawson agrees that Charismatics need to stop thinking of a two-stage Christianity, because this has made Baptism in the Holy Spirit an optional extra for Christians and irrelevant to citizenship in heaven.[165] I would argue further that it creates a two-tier Christianity between those who have experienced the Baptism in the Holy Spirit, who would of necessity be more spiritual, and those who have not. This would defeat any notion of all Christians being able to contribute to the work of ministry and being released into evangelism. While this will be a challenge to traditional Pentecostal and Charismatic theology, it is a revelation that aids the inclusion of traditional Church believers. Whether it is accepted or not, a two-stage initiation process can make some believers feel useless unless they experience Spirit baptism.[166] I would suggest that it matters little how the experience is defined, but that the experience itself is the most important thing. If it can be made more accessible to more believers then ought that not to be so?

Wimber further comments that the experience of salvation, and being born-again, produces significant changes in human lives and forms the basis for all spiritual healing.[167] This seems to suggest that salvation initiates cataclysmic change in believers, so that the moral struggle to live the Christian life is lessened in the degree to which the power of the Holy Spirit is experienced.[168] This may be a challenge to those who see the Reformed faith as a theological assent to certain doctrines, and not engaging with the heart. The life that Wimber outlines will stand out as different to this notion.

---

163. Wimber and Springer, *Dynamics of Spiritual Growth*, 139–40. Wimber cites 1 Cor 12:3 and Rom 8:9 as justification of his position.

164. Bradford, *Releasing the Power of the Holy Spirit*, 12.

165. Pawson, *Word and Spirit Together*, 143–44.

166. Pawson, *Word and Spirit Together*, 150.

167. Wimber and Springer, *Power Healing*, 87.

168. Ibid., 90.

It will also challenge a legalistic understanding of Christianity, one that the proclamation model may lean to, which sees the faith as what is done or not done, something that Wimber calls "over-scrupulosity." A Charismatic model of discipleship offers a clear alternative.[169] This is a model that engages the heart as much as it engages the head, and encourages a correlation between the heart and the head in lifestyle.

The issue of tradition also affects discipleship. The memories of past failures can become a formative force. Part of Wimber's emphasis in Charismatic discipleship is the healing of these bad memories, so that they are no longer factors in how the Church views itself or the world, but their identity becomes what Christ has made them through faith.[170] The power of the Charismatic model of discipleship is that it does not make the believer feel worthless and unable to change. Like the model of evangelism, which emphasizes fear as the primary encouragement to repentance, there is a fear-based discipleship program that is creating legalistic Christians who condemn others who do not live up to a perceived community standard. It is through Wimber's emphasis on the work of the Holy Spirit that our appetites are changed through the Spirit, and Christians "live for our center" that is the righteousness of God in Christ.[171] This works out as lives are lived with honesty and sincerity, applying God's truth to every aspect of existence.[172] This will produce healthy Christians without an excessively oppressive sense of guilt, and this, in turn, will be attractive to unbelievers also.

One criticism of the Charismatic model of discipleship is linked to the emphasis on prayer for healing in evangelism. The initial purpose of these miracles, it is proposed by Edmund Clowney, was to seal "the final revelation given in Christ, preserved in the New Testament Scripture."[173] This could mean that there is no need for such miracles today. It reminds us, however, that prayer for healing is still connected with the gospel, and may be understood as still authenticating the gospel message. It is claimed that this devalues sickness and suffering in the Christian life as performing a spiritual function in discipleship. There are examples in the New Testament of believers struggling with illness: Trophimus (2 Tim 4:20), Timothy (1 Tim 5:23) and even Paul himself (Gal 4:15). Wimber does not understand sickness as a hindrance to spiritual development, but he concedes that it

---

169. Ibid., 97.
170. Ibid., 102.
171. Wimber, *Way In is the Way On*, 92.
172. Wimber and Springer, *Power Healing*, 134.
173. Clowney, *Church*, 243.

can be a great aid.[174] Wimber believes that suffering and sickness can play an important role in spiritual development, as believers trust and rely on God exclusively.[175] It is on this matter that Wimber's theology appears more accessible to a traditional congregation than the apparent triumphalism of traditional Pentecostalism, which asserts that Jesus died for our sickness; therefore, divine healing has been provided for in the atonement.[176] From this understanding, it may be possible to develop a faith-based methodology that asserts the principles of divine healing, yet allows for the formative role of sickness and suffering in Christian discipleship.

James 4:13–16 encourages Christians to depend upon the Lord's will for their plans, which sits very comfortably with the Reformed understanding of the sovereignty of God. Also, an emphasis on healing springs from a corporate element in worship because, as Wimber suggests, it can be an opportunity for healing. This happens because in worship, the sacrament and preaching open the door for the manifestation of God's power.[177] This corporate element reminds disciples of their place within the local community, that their spiritual growth and development is grounded within that local community and, out of that corporate experience, something spiritual arises. This will produce a sense of anticipation for divine worship that transcends and replaces the notion of routine that pervades many minds in a traditional setting.

Partial Conclusion

Discipleship appears to be the goal of evangelism. At Pentecost the converts were added to the Church (Acts 2:47b). Discipleship is not exclusively the preserve of individual converts: it has a broader function also with the body politic, as Wimber notes. Evangelism produces right relationships between individuals, which are part of God's plan for our lives. This requires a change of focus from individual conversion to membership of a social grouping.[178] To the Reformed Church, this would evoke stories of the Reformation in

---

174. There is some confusion as to exactly what Wimber believes on this area as other references from his works seem to suggest that he sees no benefit in sickness: "Their attitude indicates to us what Christian ministry is supposed to be like. Jesus never saw benefits in illness for sick people; he healed people wherever he went. If he is our model of faith and practice, we cannot ignore his healing ministry." Wimber and Springer, *Power Healing*, 58.

175. Wimber and Springer, *Power Healing*, 34.
176. Fundamental Truths of the Assemblies of God.
177. Wimber and Springer, *Power Healing*, 186.
178. Wimber, *Everyone Gets to Play*, 131.

which God reformed doctrine and practice. Discipleship seeks to encourage and inspire spiritual passion. Mittelberg believes that the key is to keep spiritually alive and responsive to God, and to express that through the way others are served, making the Church contagious.[179] Discipleship ought to encourage believers to develop a deep and consuming passion for God and for the people of God, which will in turn draw people in an engaging manner to the Church and to the Savior.

This chapter has sought to outline three models of discipleship within the Reformed tradition and to evaluate them, considering the Charismatic model of Wimber. There has been a connection between all three, as the behavioral model listens to the proclamation model, which encourages experience through the sacramental model. None of these clearly contradicts a Charismatic model. All of the models emphasize the need for converts to change how they relate to each other.[180] Discipleship can offer a new identity for "those who have made a decision for Jesus Christ which may not be accepted or approved of by their relatives, friends or neighbors."[181] This may mean that the designations of Reformed or Charismatic become defunct because of a new relationship to each other.

Discipleship suggests a submission to God's call to change attitudes. Wimber notes that discipleship means that God has the right to ask Christians to make any changes and sacrifices. This works out in the economy of the kingdom that every step forward a Christian takes, it costs them everything they have, even "reputation and security." Essentially, it is a heart that is a constant learner.[182] It is a challenge to leave everything and become a follower of Jesus (Mark 8:34–47). A gospel of belief only, where assent

---

179. Mittelberg, *Becoming a Contagious Church*, 33.

180. McLaren gives a contextual goal of discipleship within the North American culture: "There the challenge will be to turn a secular atheist (or a secular nominalist for that matter) into an enthusiastic student of the wisdom and ways of Jesus Christ. The challenge will be to take a young woman who has been abused by her incestuous father and brothers and help her regain her sanity and learn to laugh again—with the laughter of God. The challenge will be to take a right-wing Republican and teach him a love that bonds him to the left-wing Democrat (or whatever either party's descendants will be called as the new world unfolds). The challenge will be to take good middle-class dentists and accountants and help them emerge from their suburban cocoons to care for their neighbors, in Jesus' name. The challenge will be to get black folk who resent whites and white folk who resent blacks to come together as brothers and sisters who see their humble, barrier-bridging friendships as a form of quiet, powerful revolution." McLaren, *Church on the Other Side*, 32. This radical transformation is the essential goal of all discipleship.

181. Green and Forster, *Small Church, Big Vision*, 51–52.

182. Wimber and Springer, *Dynamics of Spiritual Growth*, 124–25; See Wimber, *Everyone Gets to Play*, 42.

to a doctrinal position on fear of hell, as considered in chapter 1, appears to be an incomplete gospel, and the challenge of allowing God complete control can remain an unanswered message. This is not a synergistic theology of Christian discipleship, but an emphasis on the part being played in growing spiritually through the empowerment of the Holy Spirit, and our co-operation as our minds, wills and emotions are engaged.[183] A criticism of Reformed theology has been that it places little emphasis upon personal responsibility and, instead, is passive in allowing God to work sovereignly. Yet, true Reformed theology is not passive, and there is convergence with Wimber, as the Holy Spirit works upon humanity to transform us spiritually.

There is also a sense with discipleship that perfection will never be reached. Discipleship is to take place within the local Church where the struggle with worldliness and sinfulness is confronted. In the New Testament this battle continued, and the disciples did not appear to understand (John 14:9). Wimber comments: "They so thoroughly and so consistently failed to grasp what He meant that the spectacle is almost comical."[184] This reminds us that discipleship is a long-term aim that cannot be accomplished without significant investment in the believers' lives. It is important to "encourage the fainthearted" (1 Thess 5:14) so that the bumps along the way do not discourage the goal, but encourage reflection on the Bible and assurance of success.[185] The local Church needs to build discipleship upon an encouragement to change, through listening to the Bible, participating in the sacraments, and experiencing the reality of the Holy Spirit.

---

183. Wimber and Springer, *Dynamics of Spiritual Growth*, 144.
184. Wimber, *Way In is the Way On*, 23.
185. Ibid., 50.

6

Ministry in a Reformed Church

Introduction

HAVING EXPERIENCED THE GOSPEL in the Church's evangelism, and been disciplined to understand the power of the Holy Spirit in the believer's life through discipleship, the third stage in the word and power methodology is releasing members into ministry.[1] Underlying our discussion of this methodology is the assumption that, as Williams points out, the main purpose that the Holy Spirit was given was that the Church might witness to Jesus and the gospel be demonstrated in word and deed.[2] Wimber's theology of ministry was developed through his teaching at Fuller Theological Seminary. Bill Randles notes that the seminary was part of the wider Evangelical tradition and not specifically Charismatic or Pentecostal.[3] I

---

1. "A disciple of Jesus is someone who learns the gospel, relates in the gospel, and communicates the gospel. This definition of disciple shows us that the gospel both makes and matures disciples." Dodson, *Gospel Centered Discipleship*, 38.

2. Williams, *Renewal Theology*, 2:311–12. Acts 1:8.

3. Randles, "John Wimber and the Vineyard." "Fuller Theological Seminary, embracing the School of Theology, School of Psychology, and School of Intercultural Studies, is an evangelical, multidenominational, international, and multiethnic community dedicated to the equipping of men and women for the manifold ministries of Christ and his Church. Under the authority of Scripture we seek to fulfill our commitment to ministry through graduate education, professional development, and spiritual formation. In all of our activities, including instruction, nurture, worship, service, research, and publication, Fuller Theological Seminary strives for excellence in the service of Jesus Christ, under the guidance and power of the Holy Spirit, to the glory of the Father." http://www.fuller.edu/about-fuller/mission-and-history/mission-beyond-the-mission.aspx.

have argued earlier that Wimber occupies "the radical middle," somewhere between Evangelicalism and Pentecostalism, as well as wanting to combine elements of the two. Should Wimber have come from a distinctly Pentecostal institution it may make his comments appear to be from a distinct tradition that may not be readily accessed by Reformed Churches.[4] This chapter seeks to explore the question of whether Wimber's model of releasing for ministry is limited to one traditional setting, or whether it can be applied more widely, including a Reformed context.

Building on the previous two contextual applications, I want to ask whether Wimber's suggestions about ministry training, or formation, would be applicable within a Reformed Church. Specifically, this will look at whether the historical and contemporary methods used within a Reformed denomination would be compatible with a Charismatic model of ministry. In doing this, I will consider a training or college/seminary-based model, an apprenticeship model and an in-house model, before reflecting on Wimber's own teaching. These three models are chosen as representing the elements within the ministry training of the PCI. Those who wish to train as ordained ministers start theological training in a college, then moving to an unordained student assistantship and, subsequently, an apprenticeship as assistant to a parish minister.[5] There is also further in-house training in which Licentiate ministers undertake a written project on their congregational involvement that performs an in-house training element for ministry.[6] These three elements will be considered and reflected upon in the light of Wimber's theology, and a possible alternative suggested that brings the three together.

Wimber believed his teaching applied to everyone irrespective of age, gender, or position within the Church.[7] Wimber is arguing what Reformed Churches have believed about the priesthood of all believers (1 Pet 2:9).[8] Fyall notes that there appears to be a "minister-centered" approach in the Reformed Churches. This implies any meaningful body ministry is

---

4. It is difficult to say with any certainty that Wimber's theology would be any less compatible with the Reformed Churches had he come from one of the traditional Pentecostal seminaries.

5. *Code*, chapter 16, paras. 214–18.

6. Ibid., chapter 16, para. 219.

7. Wimber and Springer, *Dynamics of Spiritual Growth*, 137.

8. The priesthood of all believers reflects the "church's witness of praise' linking it to training for evangelism. See Clowney, *Church*, 163. This is an inclusive theology: "In the wider context of Scripture the keys of the kingdom are in the hands of all Christians, since we are all priests and kings in Christ . . . and we are all assigned an evangelical mandate to preach the gospel to all nations." Bloesch, *Church*, 91.

defunct "and the minister too easily becomes a convenient scapegoat or the object of uncritical adulation."[9] I do not assume that this is practice within Reformed congregations. As Pope says, what is needed is a new reformation, building on the first Reformation, which put the Bible in the hands of the people. Now the work of God needs to go back into the hands of the people.[10] In this sense, I am arguing that the Reformed Church needs to embrace both the theology of Wimber and its own theology. Wimber appears to be reminding the Reformed Churches, perhaps unconsciously, of their own tradition, or perhaps he has been influenced himself by the Reformed view. This may suggest a cross-pollination. In the context of a traditional Reformed congregation, where there is a clear distinction between the minister and the members of the congregation, a model that releases every member into ministry may be a necessity to adequately fulfill the need of ministry today.[11] With the central role that a minister plays, it enables molding of the congregation into a Charismatic model. Percy states that Charismatic churches are driven by personality.[12] This may be a criticism; however, it is also an opportunity, even a "powerpoint," because it uses the present condition of things to effect change. It can be used in a minister-centered Church to bring renewal from the top down.

Wimber wants to deflate a superior understanding of ministry. He sees believers as being servants of God, who has much work for them to do throughout the world. This also affects how ministry is viewed, for Wimber believes it is wider than a professional class.[13] Charismatic theology speaks of this theme and seeks to "democratize spiritual power" amongst all the members of the Church.[14] In this sense a minister-centered approach is seeking to erode its own centrality. A word of caution is needed: if this theology of ministry is to become the norm in the Church, there may be some who do not feel able to speak out in evangelistic activity. It is a presupposition that ministry is evangelistic, yet not everyone may feel able or equipped

9. Fyall, *Charismatic and Reformed*, 9.

10. Pope, *Intentional Church*, 131.

11. This is needed for adequate pastoral care also because if a one-person ministry remains the norm within PCI, those in need will consequently fall by the wayside, as Goligher states: "In every congregation there is a need for better and more personal pastoral oversight. The fact that no one can adequately pastor more than ten people raises a question about the traditional role of the minister. The gift of pastoring must obviously be more widespread than individual ministers; the responsibility for pastoring falls on us all. *Episcope*, or oversight, is not the job of only a few; it is entrusted to all of us." Goligher, *Fellowship of the King*, 83–84.

12. Percy, *Power and the Church*, 11.

13. Wimber, *Way In is the Way On*, 30–31.

14. Cartledge, *Encountering the Spirit*, 59.

for this activity. Prior comments that, if evangelism is "new ground and directly confronting non-Christians with the gospel," then it may not be a gift shared by everyone.[15] To some this may be interpreted as an excuse for not evangelizing; yet the Charismatic model of ministry takes the pressure off individuals and unto service in the Spirit's power. My argument is that the three models flow into each other so that the believer is charismatically equipped to evangelize, to incorporate the convert into the Church, through discipleship, and see the convert trained in ministry.

Peterson explains this by contrasting corporate worship, which includes the proclamation of the Word of God, with pastoral work amongst people. He sees "that the story of God's revelation is a comprehensive narrative that includes everyone," and so encourages each individual to become active in writing their own page in sacred history.[16] As Warrington notes, this inclusion affected gender, age, race, culture and nationality, making the Church "a medley of people who are privileged to stand with each other, to relate to each other, to minister together on behalf of the Spirit and, thus, to reflect God and his purposes."[17] There are many ideas of what ministry is and many preconceptions of how a Christian ministry ought to be exercised. These can come from a few dominant personalities within a congregation or denominational leaders following a specific model.[18] The key is how disciples are to be released into their ministry, how we are to train and prepare them for the work of ministry in an inclusive and affirming manner. These ideas emphasize the fact that each individual has a role to play and it is how we equip them to fulfill that role which we are considering.

How to release members into ministry within the local congregation builds upon our models of evangelism and discipleship as outlined before. It is a challenge for the Christian Church to begin to think missionally about its own location.[19] This may lead to understanding the needs that once

---

15. Prior, *Gospel in a Pagan Society*, 50–51. Dever suggests that one of the characteristics of a healthy Church is a passion for evangelism amongst the membership: "Christians often leave evangelism to 'the professionals' out of a sense of inadequacy, apathy, ignorance, fear, or simply feeling that it is inappropriate for them to do it. Perhaps they're not sure of what evangelism entails and how it should be done. And this situation is tragic. I'm convinced that one of the distinguishing marks of a healthy church is a biblical understanding and practice of evangelism." Dever, *Nine Marks of a Healthy Church*, 120.

16. Peterson, *Five Smooth Stones*, 76.

17. Warrington, *Message of the Holy Spirit*, 141.

18. Long et al., *Growing the Church*, 29. These are contrasted with leaders who seek God's agenda for their congregation.

19. This is a difficult term to define. There is confusion over whether the Church is the object or instrument of mission. Does it mean to start new Churches or to become

were described as being overseas, as now in our own parishes.[20] Keller notes that the gospel is more than challenging outsiders so that they will embrace the message, but teaching and shepherding believers, so that the gospel molds their lives as they live out their living faith.[21] This takes evangelism beyond making a profession of faith and redefines it as a commitment to discipleship, the outcome of which will be a release into ministry.

This means that the Church needs to be outward looking toward those to whom it ministers.[22] It also means that each believer understands God has "signaled" them out for a gift that is "supernaturally endowed."[23] The theme of this chapter is that every member has a spiritual gift, and part of the Church's calling is to provide a way in which they can receive appropriate training in the skills to carry this gift out.[24] This offers an inclusion of every member ministry. Wimber uses the analogy of a cruise liner in comparison to a navy vessel. Some see their faith as a holiday for enjoyment, others as enlisting in God's service.[25] There is no place for nominalism or inactivity; all are enlisted to fight from the moment of conversion until the day of death. Christians ought never to expect the battle to cease.[26] This notion, of releasing members into an active role in ministry, can be difficult where the traditional roles of clergy and laity have been preserved. Yet, it offers something more than observation of mission and encourages participation.

Wimber calls the Church "Christ's co-belligerents,"[27] those who are aware that our conversion is to the kingdom of God, and because of that: "we

---

intentionally evangelistic as the Church. See, Hull, *Mission Shaped Church*, 1 There is implied meaning of the two words. Mission is something that the Church does as part of its life and programs. Church is the building that people go to to have their spiritual needs provided for, something for insiders. "The words mission and church are, therefore, used together to define a church that attracts, worships, equips, and then sends. And of course the sending has the purpose of bringing back more people to the attractional event." See Roxburgh and Boren, *Introducing the Missional Church*, 30.

20. Prior, *Gospel in a Pagan Society*, 30.

21. Keller, "Gospel and the Poor."

22. This will in itself provide an evangelistic tool: "Each time your church meets someone's need, a good rumor about the church begins travelling the interpersonal network of your community. When enough of those good rumors get spread around, your church will begin attracting people no visitation program could possibly have reached." Warren, *Purpose Driven Church*, 222–23.

23. Brown, *Follow the Wind*, 122–23.

24. Odgen, *New Reformation*, 115.

25. Wimber and Springer, *Power Evangelism*, 38.

26. Ibid., 40. The themes of battle are seen throughout Wimber's writings and his emphasis on release from the demonic is one manifestation of power evangelism.

27. Ibid., 43.

are now members of a new kingdom that is opposed to virtually everything the world around us says is important."[28] This theme, of opposition to the kingdoms of this world, is similar to the subversive ministry philosophy espoused by Peterson. It sees the work of the Church as "subversive" to the culture in which people live. It encourages Christians to work for the secret kingdom of God that is now beginning to replace the kingdoms of this world.[29] John Christopher Thomas notes that this will be accomplished as the Church understands the kingdom is God's. It is his power to consummate that kingdom. This reminds the Church of what has been considered in the discussion of evangelism: that it is God's power and the Church is the vessel.[30] Although the Church is bringing stability to society, when it challenges the social institutions that matter to people, the Church then becomes a prophetic voice.[31] The Church speaks with a relevancy that people can understand, but with a challenge to what is seen around them, so the world is transformed through individuals following the gospel.

The concept of the Church as a body is central to this thinking; that the Church now performs the function that the physical Jesus did while on earth.[32] Newbigin writes that the Holy Spirit is the true missionary, going ahead of the Church and using different methods to open people's hearts. To do this, he equips people with the gifts that they need, irrespective of their educational background. This will lead to less of a dependency on outside sources for effective ministry.[33] Ministry does not, therefore, rest upon the principles of popularity or promotion from another office in the Church; rather, it is the gift of God to that local community for a missional purpose.

---

28. Wimber and Springer, *Dynamics of Spiritual Growth*, 182.

29. Peterson, *Contemplative Pastor*, 27–28.

30. Thomas, *Ministry and Theology*, 31.

31. "Only the church can minister to the whole person. Only the gospel understands that sin has ruined us both individually and socially. We cannot be viewed individualistically (as the capitalists do) or collectivistically (as the Communists do) but as related to God. Only Christians, armed with the Word and Spirit, planning and working to spread the kingdom and righteousness of Christ, can transform a nation as well as a neighborhood as well as a broken heart." Keller, *Ministries of Mercy*, 26.

32. "In other words, that which is human about *Jesus*—visibility, temporality, fleshiness—is now transferred to the *church* as a historical body. Jesus proclaimed himself as Jacob's ladder (John 1:50–51), but in his bodily absence the church offers itself for that mediation. The history of Jesus in the flesh is at least implicitly replaced by the history of the church as the kingdom of God. The deity of Christ remains transcendent, but his incarnate existence is 'fleshed out' by and as the church." Horton, *People and Place*, 6.

33. Newbigin, "Pattern of the Ministry in a Missionary Church."

Wimber points out that the decision making on appointments to leadership need to be challenged in terms of spiritual value, along with the role of leadership.[34] Ignoring the charismatic dimension in ministry, any understanding of the roles in which members may operate may be limited because of the clergy/laity divide. There may be a lack of understanding of how the Holy Spirit empowers believers in their ministries.[35] In this book, I would contend that a marriage of Reformed theology and Charismatic experience equips the Church to be effective ministers and releases individuals to pursue their calling. This emphasizes a deep theological understanding of the sovereignty of God, coupled with a contemporary dependence upon the Spirit's unction.

It is also important to remember the central role that the local Church is to play in ministry. Evangelism and discipleship are not optional extras that can be left to para-Church organizations, but need to have their roots and focus within the local congregation.[36] Mack and Swavely comment that the Church is the primary means by which God accomplishes his will in the world, through evangelism and discipleship ministries, so a deep commitment to the Church is necessary.[37] This ministry needs to be anchored within the local congregation whose role it is to equip the members, through the leadership, to minister for Christ (Eph 4:11–12). This will also affect the local congregation's focus because, as Mack and Swavely note, the energies of the Church ought to be directed "toward the edification and growth" of local Churches, not para-church organizations. It is the Church that God has promised to bless, so other ministries may not have the same lasting influence.[38] The implementation of these ministry models will aid the local congregation in seeing the Church being built. It will be a challenge to their priorities and foci, but the Church needs to fulfill its responsibility to minister biblically, effectively, relevantly, and confrontationally.

---

34. Wimber and Springer, *Power Evangelism*, 58.

35. Wimber, *Way In is the Way On*, 175.

36. Reid comments: "The church is not a vacation spot for saints; it is an emergency room for sinners. We must teach people that the primary place of ministry for the church of the Lord Jesus Christ is outside the church building." See Reid, *Introduction to Evangelism*, 283. Warren also notes: "The church exists to communicate God's Word. We are ambassadors for Christ, and our mission is to evangelize the world." See Warren, *Purpose Driven Church*, 104. Stackhouse suggests that this priority ought to effect a change within the Church's preaching so that the distinctions between preaching and teaching become irrelevant because of the mixed nature of contemporary congregations. See Stackhouse, *Gospel-Driven Church*, 94. Regarding discipleship this point was made by Driscoll and Hull in the last.

37. Mack and Swavely, *Life in the Father's House*, 21.

38. Ibid., 31.

The Training Model

Most denominations have some model of training in which individuals absent themselves from their local Churches, becoming part of an academic community, to study theology, in preparation for ministry.[39][40] In historic traditions this theological model has developed over many years.[41] Within PCI, for instance, ministry students must undertake at least one year of study at Union Theological College before becoming an assistant to a minister.[42] The college system, therefore, is working alongside local congregations. Gibbs and Coffey suggest that it is the task of a theological college to equip students with the necessary missionary tools for their changing context. This is a challenge to students because the congregation needs relevance, whereas the college emphasizes theological accuracy and evaluation.[43] The training is often conducted by professional theologians

---

39. Tozer notes that this model does not mean that the trainee is even a believer: "It is altogether possible to be instructed in the rudiments of the faith and still have no real understanding of the whole thing. And it is possible to go on to become expert in Bible doctrine and not have spiritual illumination, with the result that a veil remains over the mind, preventing it from apprehending the truth in its spiritual essence." Tozer, "Bible Taught or Spirit Taught," 36.

40. Banks notes a distinction between seminaries, whose aim it is to train the professional clergy through divinity degrees, and Bible colleges who aim to train lay people for mission or education through offering a baccalaureate degree. Banks, *Re-envisioning Theological Education*, 4–8. This distinction appears to relate to the North American context more than the British context. In Ireland the designation "seminary" would specify a training institution of the Roman Catholic tradition e.g. Seminary, St. Patrick's College, Maynooth.

41. McLaren places his ministry philosophy within an already organized Church: "The renewed church is an old church that, after having lost touch with its own people, goes through a process of change in order to relate to them and better meet their needs." McLaren, *Church on the Other Side*, 22. This is the process that I am attempting to reflect upon. He further comments: "The new church can be on any age, any denomination. It goes through a process of peripheral change similar to the renewed and restored churches, a process of radical self-assessment, of going back to roots, sources, and first things. But the new church does not try to draft a new blueprint. Instead, it comes up with a new philosophy of ministry that prepares to meet whatever unforeseen changes are to come." McLaren, *Church on the Other Side*, 24.

42. All ministry candidates under 40 years old must have a primary degree in another discipline, and then study for the theology degree (which includes both Hebrew and Greek) at Union Theological College for at least two years. *Code*, 117–21. This is what separates ministry in PCI from other denominations in Ireland. It may have its source in the training required for Scottish Advocates, in which two years of academic study were required before admission to the Faculty of Advocates, unlike the English Barrister system which is entirely apprenticeship based. See Herman, *Scottish Enlightenment*, 86.

43. Gibbs and Coffey, *Church Next*, 94.

who are highly trained and academically qualified.[44] It could be claimed that this training has molded the ministry of the Reformed Churches and places theology at the center of ministerial training.

The Reformed model I have chosen to reflect upon is that of J. Gresham Machen and, particularly, the establishment of Westminster Theological Seminary. Machen was initially a faculty member of Princeton Theological Seminary (1915-29). When the Presbyterian Church of the USA decided to restructure the seminary, appointing a President rather than allowing the faculty to control affairs, Machen withdrew. He opposed not only an appointed President, but also a more practical educational method, favoring courses in systematics and languages over practical theology.[45] The result was the foundation of a new seminary, following the path of old Princeton, with a dual commitment to scholarship and the Church.[46] One of the key issues was that the faculty would control the new institution and elect a chairperson, so no denomination could control the seminary through appointment of a President.[47] Machen's desire was theological education that fused solid biblical scholarship with spiritual piety.[48] He believed that to be equipped for ministry it was important to know the basics of theology.[49]

---

44. Emphasizing the place of people in the educational and training process of the Christian ministry is something that is practiced in many different denominations. Yet a word of caution needs to be raised: "The desire to be taught by someone who knows what he or she is talking about is deeply ingrained in humans. But that authority needs to be given to the only one who can teach us truthfully—Jesus Christ. So the first step is that we must become less enamored with people. We must become less dependent upon being told what to believe or to do and become determined to follow directly the teachings of the Bible." Bundschuh, *Church*, 99.

45. Hart, *Defending the Faith*, 124. Machen believed that his approach was practical: "But if knowledge is necessary to preaching, it does seem probable that the fuller the knowledge is, the better the preacher will be able to do his work." Machen, "Christian Scholarship and Evangelism, 137.

46. Nichols, *J. Gresham Machen*, 33, 53–59. Nichols further writes: „What Machen was searching for was neither an intellectualism devoid of faith nor a faith devoid of intellectual merit. Nor was he after either a rigorous scholarship without piety or a vital piety without roots in scholarship. He longed for piety and intellect fused into one, an intellectually informed and compelling faith."

47. Stonehouse, *J. Gresham Machen*, 452.

48. Nichols, *J. Gresham Machen*, 175–76. Hart notes that while many fundamentalist colleges reduced the educational standards of their training in reaction to the perceived liberalism of professional theologians, Machen maintained high academic standards and the prerequisite of a liberal arts education previously. Hart, *Defending the Faith*, 134.

49. Ibid., 106–07. What underlined this ideal was Machen's conviction that God reveals himself exclusively through the Bible, and learning to deal with the phenomena of religion is misdirecting students from hearing God's voice. Machen, «Westminster

This emphasis on the biblical languages and systematic theology forms part of the Reformed understanding of ministerial education.[50] It roots the practitioner in the scholastic tradition, but does not necessarily emphasize how ministry is to be practiced congregationally.

In this context, as Ryken outlines, ministers are trained to be systematic expositors and that ministry is to guide and form every aspect of the Church's witness.[51] A Reformed approach to theological education may exclude a specifically practical element, in the sense of non-academic disciplines. An unwillingness to submit to theological training, therefore, ought to exclude someone from ministry.[52] This is a view criticized by Banks who believes that the spiritual formation of the minister is paramount over the educational training.[53] Yet, if many Reformed ministers are truthful, it is often a challenge to keep such ministry engaging and, while the power of the Scriptures are professed, many lives are not as liberated as they could be. This may be because of the abstract nature of the training, which often produces theologically competent preachers but not competent practitioners, as David Haywood notes.[54] This may lead to discouragement in ministry, and a frustration that the members of the congregation are not personally appropriating the effects of the theological truths learned in college.

Wimber notes that he assumed that being equipped to preach the Bible was a key to the spiritual empowerment necessary to work for God. He defines Christians who minister this way as "Word-workers": those who seek to apply the Bible to every aspect of their lives and theology.[55] He does not belittle the importance of such work, but believes there is something more. He came to understand that there were also miracles. As an Evangelical he saw faith in two ways: doctrinal faith and faithfulness. There was

---

Seminary," 188.

50. PCI requires all ministers to study Hebrew. The practical element is elocution. *Code,* para. 27, 1.b.ii., 2.b.

51. Ryken, *City on a Hill,* 25–26. MacArthur comments regarding Christian testimony: "A Christian's testimony should never be independent of God's Word. It should only be an echo of God's truth. An echo always repeats what is originally spoken. God has put His voice in you—the Holy Spirit. He doesn't want you to create your own words; He wants you to echo His truth." MacArthur, *Master's Plan for the Church,* 99.

52. "If a student is not interested in learning, if a student has no genuine intellectual interest, if a student is not willing to read, learn, dig, and research then he will almost certainly be a mediocre preacher and minister." Clark, "Who Should go to Seminary? Part 2."

53. Banks, *Reenvisioning Theological Education,* 25.

54. Haywood, "New Paradigm for Theological Education?" 16.

55. Wimber, *Witnesses for a Powerful Christ,* 33–34.

also the charismatic dimension.[56] Some have criticized the relationship of Wimber's beliefs to the Bible.[57] The training model of ministry emphasizes doctrinal truth and orthodox theology as being of paramount importance to ministry. Yet, practical needs for ministering to people are not necessarily implied in this educational model.[58] This is something that Wimber was accused of: not marrying his Conservative Evangelical doctrine with orthodox practice.[59] There may be a notion here that Wimber was more focused on the practice than the doctrine that formed the practice. We have discussed the apparent divergence between doctrine and practice, earlier. It may appear that Wimber's focus was more pragmatic than intentional; he looked for simply what worked. There may also be the issue of context—that different manifestations of the same theological conviction work out differently in each locale.[60] It also allows for different applications of the same theological truths because Wimber does not apply his method exclusively to one context. This highlights how his theology can be applied to a Reformed context, because the doctrine appears to fit with that of the WCF. It maintains a confessional doctrinal position, but a fluid practice within a local context.

For this to happen there needs to be a change of emphasis in which, as McLaren notes, "creativity and problem solving" are emphasized, resulting in "life," because "if everything worth saying has been said as well as it can be, then theology is dead, whether God lives or not!"[61] McLaren seems to suggest that what is needed is a rethinking of how Christians view the world, from being the enemies who are fought and who fight back, to being

56. Wimber and Springer, *Power Evangelism*, 91.

57. Friesen, "Wimber, Word and Spirit," 36.

58. Stackhouse notes a "discernible shift" in seminaries from the theology of ministry to the praxis of ministry, healing the split between college and church. Stackhouse, *Gospel Driven Church*, 225. McLaren comments that the title "evangelical" carries with it in the mind of some either a right wing political position or a "narrow-minded and arrogant attitude" toward others. McLaren, *Generous Orthodoxy*, 128–29. Defining Evangelicalism in terms of practice as well as belief has led some to question whether the position itself has an image problem? Deen, "Do Evangelicals have an Image Problem?" 1. This has even led some to define themselves as "warm-hearted" Evangelicals to distance themselves from the narrow and cold doctrinal orthodoxy. See "Patton Elected as Next Moderator."

59. Thompson, "Spiritual Warfare 1," 19.

60. In the Reformed tradition this is seen in the debate over exclusive Psalmody or the use of other sources for public worship. This has also been popularized by the 2010 decision of the Free Church of Scotland to permit the singing of hymns and use of music in their public worship for the first time since 1843. http://www.christiantoday.com/article/ free.church.of.scotland.allows.singing/27114.htm.

61. McLaren, *Church on the Other Side*, 67.

the needy neighbors who have not yet found Christ.[62] This seems to be commenting on the world from a North American perspective in which conservative politics and Evangelical religion appear to be closely connected.[63] This may not necessarily be the case in Great Britain.[64] Believers are encouraged to stand against accepting the world and its attitudes. There is, however, a need for positive engagement with the world, as has been noted in the incarnational model outlined in chapter 4. What McLaren perceives developing is an ecumenism of the trenches, including all people of Christian faith from every background.

The question arises whether seminary/college education adequately trains ministers. R. Scott Clark agrees that seminary/college education does train ministers, and that a desire to know biblical language may indicate that someone is called to pastoral ministry.[65] Banks believes that this model practically hinders the local Church because it increases the divide between trained clergy and laity.[66] Keith Warrington appears to disagree with the traditional model of Bible college/seminary education. He believes that it needs to be reconsidered because of what potential pastors need to learn for their calling, which is not the same as an academic theologian. What is needed is a "dynamic response to contemporary questions," such as gender issues, premarital sex, etc.[67] Both McLaren and Warrington suggest that there needs to be a change in our understanding of the nature of the theologian. McLaren understands this change in terms of creative thinking; pursuing truth rather than repeating and defending "old formulations." The Church then becomes missionally incarnate in its own setting.[68] Seminary-based education, however, may not produce such creative thinking. Rather, it may continue to perpetuate the same principles to another generation.

This model can also prove difficult if those who are non-academic, yet want to apply for ministry, as the academic rigors may discourage them.

---

62. Ibid., 33.

63. Mansfield, *Faith of George W. Bush*.

64. For a connection between Socialism and Christianity, see: Bryant, *Reclaiming the Ground*.

65. Clark, "Who Should go to Seminary? Part 1." He goes on to state, somewhat sarcastically, that seminary is only needed for those who are not receiving divine revelations because learning biblical languages, systematic theology, church history would bore such a person.

66. Bank, *Reenvisioning Theological Education*, 135.

67. Warrington, "Would Jesus have sent his Disciples to Bible College?" 38. He contends that Pentecostals have traditionally viewed Theological/Bible Colleges as venues for short-term ministry preparation "not as places for exploration and contemplation." Although this notion is changing. Warrington, *Pentecostal Theology*, 152.

68. McLaren, *Church on the Other Side*, 68.

Such an academic emphasis may fail to recognize the work and effort that many non-academics put into their professional qualifications. Nor is there any guarantee that right theology will make someone a good pastor or evangelist.[69] Such an emphasis on supernatural ministry may seem to undermine any need for theological training at all. For a stream that is deeply connected to its theological statements, like the WCF, this could be a liability to its acceptance.

Gibbs and Coffey comment that the system, as it presently stands, is too narrow and takes little account of previous experience, gifts or calling. They suggest a customized learning system that is specific for each student.[70] There is also a challenge to the notion of a residential collegiate community exclusively for the training for ministry. They suggest that this is not relevant because of the older age of many students. The solution is cohort-based learning, through intensives and discussions, with one another and the teacher.[71] This may seem to be an effective alternative. Yet, it is a local response to a wider issue than simply that of who will lead a local congregation. It may train effective practitioners in one context, but produce little understanding of other contexts. This may limit the pool of resources to the local congregation because of a lack of awareness of the wider Church scene.

These challenges to the seminary model have a practical application as students may be mature and married with children. Such training demands leaving work and often sacrificing family time for theological study. It is also noteworthy that many clergy see the benefit in postgraduate professional ministry study based on a cohort system, such as the Doctor of Ministry programs. This may suggest a gap in the current educational model for ministry training. Miroslav Volf outlines some of the issues that theological institutions face: financial constraints, institutional cohesion considering dominant individual teachers, and even the pedagogical pattern itself is questioned in the light of individualism.[72] This may be why many streams

---

69. Merrette writes that German managers in industry are better qualified than their British counterparts. Many of them having doctorates (fifty to one) which makes their industry more stable than their British counterparts, but not as easily transferred to entrepreneurial skills. Edwin Merrette, "Company 'Doctors.'"

70. Gibbs and Coffey, *Church Next*, 117.

71. Ibid., 103. With regard to the older nature of many students, the point is made that they often do not integrate completely into the seminary/college community. This is because they often remain at home and travel into classes. This also means that they continue attending their home congregation and find pastoral care there. A younger student may choose to live in or near their college, making them a more visible part of the community and looking to that institution for their pastoral care.

72. Volf, "Dancing for God," 2–3.

seek to implement more than one model of ministerial training to effectively equip leaders. Perhaps the training model offers an element of ministry preparation; however, other elements can complement it.

Power evangelism may be a challenge to this model. Wimber writes that power evangelism is not anti-rational because there is a deep need for a firm theological and doctrinal foundation. While telling people about their spiritual needs will no more effect conversion than signs and wonders, it will demonstrate the power of the gospel and support the message.[73] Power evangelism still rests upon a proclamation of the gospel and, to be able to do that properly, an understanding of what is believed is important. The training of ministers does not preclude any emphasis on power evangelism, but can and ought to complement it.

The model of training often used in colleges to prepare people for ministry in Reformed Church relies on one emphasis of study. Wimber calls this the "scientific Bible study" method, in which attention is given to the original languages and the original context of the texts; yet, it does not teach how the Church can apply relevantly that which is preached.[74] Wimber levels three criticisms of this model of ministry preparation. First, it creates an intellectualization of the faith that is different from the small group, "learn while doing," methodology of Jesus and the disciples.[75] While it is important to understand what is believed and why it is believed, simple knowledge is not enough. There must be something internal and inward also. This could possibly lead to highly educated, yet unconverted clergy, whereby all that is understood to be important is education. Yet, without the rigors of this understanding, leadership can make simple yet heretical mistakes in Bible study.

Second, Wimber challenges this method as the exclusive means of presenting Christianity because it can lead to an intellectualization of the faith.[76] Perhaps what Wimber is pointing to here is a Christianity that is theologically accurate, but lacks passion and vitality; or one that is completely orthodox in theology, but cold of heart towards people. Hull comments that, while Christians may know correct doctrines and methods, it is only when people see the depth of our care for them that they will respond to the gospel.[77] This is what Mittelberg appears to be suggesting: that believers must "Let the love of God and your love for people motivate

---

73. Wimber and Springer, *Power Evangelism*, 108.
74. Ibid., 191–92.
75. Ibid.
76. Wimber and Springer, *Power Evangelism*, 192.
77. Hull, *New Century Disciple Making*, 53–54.

you."[78] This will become an educational and inspirational tool as others are shown how to minister with compassion. On this matter, I would concede that Wimber makes a valid challenge.

Third, Wimber notes that this method of communication relies upon the intellectual rigor of the study itself rather than the leading of the Holy Spirit. This is different from Christ's emphasis, which sought to teach the disciples how to hear God's voice and obey the Spirit's leading.[79] This criticism seems more polemical than reflective. The Bible seems to encourage rigorous biblical study (2 Tim 2:15). If it is understood that the Holy Spirit works through intellect and directs studies, then the deeper the understanding of the teaching of the Bible, the more understanding of God will result.

Consideration also needs to be given regarding why God has given the Bible, the purpose for which training in doctrine is given. The training model suggests that the Bible is given to be preached, in an expositional manner, to others. Dever notes that some believe a new approach is needed in which there are more interactions through video, drama or even art, rather than one person speaking. Preaching may then be countercultural to these suggestions.[80] It may be that Dever is arguing for a strict interpretation of the regulative principle in worship, or that he simply does not personally like the other means he notes. There may even be a sense in which these means distract from preaching. Ryken comments that preaching is not intended to be an opportunity for a minister to preach their opinions, experiences, politics or theological tradition, but simply the Word of God.[81] The Church is to proclaim the teaching of the Bible that is given to equip the believer for service (2 Tim 3:16–17). Wimber notes that the Bible enlightens us so that the Church may pass on our blessing to others, and share with them.[82] This is the circular argument of this work: the gospel is proclaimed to challenge individuals to become disciples, and in becoming disciples they become active in ministry, bringing us back to where the gospel is proclaimed. Bible knowledge and doctrine is given to pass on.

Wimber issues a word of caution. Biblical and theological knowledge are important, yet it needs to be spoken in a spirit of love. The absence of love, he believes, is the "new Pharisaism" that expresses itself in "heartless" ministry. When this is put into practice, especially when challenging sin,

78. Mittelberg, *Becoming a Contagious Church*, 44.
79. Wimber and Springer, *Power Evangelism*, 192.
80. Dever, *Nine Marks of a Healthy Church*, 53–54.
81. Ryken, *City on a Hill*, 42. Dever further expounds this point: "A preacher should have his mind increasingly shaped by Scripture. He shouldn't just use Scripture as an excuse for his actions."
82. Wimber and Springer, *Dynamics of Spiritual Growth*, 48.

needy people are injured. It can appear that the Church is "attacking the sinner rather than the sin."[83] This could be taken to mean that theological training may not aid ministerial practice. I do not think that Wimber is saying this. Rather, he is saying that divorcing belief from practice is a misnomer. This theme of belief informing practice—either causally (theology to practice) or indirectly (practice to theology)—is one that both Wimber and the Reformed tradition emphasize in one way or another. John Piper writes that the Church cannot invest its life in others, with all their faults and shortcomings, if it is unforgiving. This will lead to a preoccupation with people's failures and offences, and not their joy in the gospel.[84] Chappell notes that the gospel must be connected to the individual's brokenness whose hurt can only be healed by God.[85] This will happen only as the root problem is dealt with: "We are all sinners in need of the Savior."[86] The use of the gifts that God has given us, as Eric Wright suggests, makes us more Christlike and has the same end in others also.[87] Ministry trains the Church to have compassion and love for others and, if that is lacking, then it ought to seek to ignite such a passion within us. Calian notes that this vision for service needs to be implanted within those in training by theological educators, thus enabling a visionary leadership within the local congregation.[88] Without such compassion, ministry will never accomplish what it ought to. It will have good theological knowledge but limited understanding of how to put that knowledge into practice.

There can also be a danger for those who are trained in the proclamation model to think that they now have access to all the answers. John Drane notes that the Church is not just about marketing. The nature of human lives means that there will be many issues that cannot be tied up neatly, in a business-like fashion. Meaningful spirituality must interact with this fact and not give slick, polished answers that do not take account of the individual issues that people face.[89] A disservice can be done to the journey of

---

83. Wimber, *Everyone Gets to Play*, 32.

84. Piper, *Don't Waste Your Life*, 99.

85. Chappell, *Wonder of it All*, 30. To this end there may be some merit in the suggestion that we make our services more accessible to the unconverted: "We want our life together to be gospel-saturated. We want to live and talk the gospel as part of our shared life. At the same time we try to make our meetings less strange to unbelievers. We work hard to ensure that everything we do is explained. We want unbelievers to feel comfortable." Chester and Timmis, *Total Church*, 62.

86. Chappell, *Wonder of it All*, 38.

87. Wright, *Church*, 59.

88. Calian, "Building a Visionary Church," 486.

89. Drane, *McDonaldization of the Church*, 37–38.

faith if it is believed that the Christian minister will be able to answer every question. People have issues to work through and problems that do not go away when they pull up to the drive-through window of Sunday worship, to draw on the analogy of the title of Drane's book. The wisdom of others, those who have trodden the path of faith before, can be offered. Yet, the challenges of our own generation, and the unique issues they face, must also be taken up, and these may not so easily be answered.

The Apprenticeship Model

One suggestion is that ministry development could be organized in a similar way to that of an apprenticeship: when individuals learn by spending time with and assisting experienced ministers to learn how to be a minister. Learning by doing can be a valuable educational tool, particularly in a profession in which the emphasis is as much upon what is believed as what is done. The one difficulty is the rather high damage rate when working with people. Practitioners learn from their mistakes; however, pastoral mistakes may have a deep effect upon people. Releasing the ministry apprentice, therefore, to make these mistakes, may not come easily to the supervising leader. Within PCI, ministers serve between 18 and 30 months working as an assistant to an ordained minister, before seeking a call of their own. This is to provide the practical experience that theological training may not cover.[90] While there appears to be little reflection upon this model historically, perhaps due to the long-standing seminary/college tradition, there has been some contemporary reflection upon it within the Reformed tradition.

Reflection on this area comes from Australia, as the Ministry Training Strategy (MTS), and has been tried throughout the world. It emphasizes seven areas before entering theological education.[91] The MTS emphasizes the personal development character of apprenticeship training, which is "not a barren educational exercise" and more than a transfer of information

---

90. Theological training within PCI covers five core areas: Old Testament, New Testament, Church History, Systematic Theology and Practical Theology. The purpose of this is to ensure that ministers are "spiritually mature and pastorally sensitive, as well as being intellectually competent." Union Theological College Management Committee, 204.

91. Marshall and Payne, *Trellis and the Vine*, 143–46. They note the following areas: 1. Apprentices learn to integrate word, life and ministry practice; 2. Apprentices are tested in character; 3. Apprentices learn that ministry is about people not programs; 4. Apprentices are well-prepared for formal theological study; 5. Apprentices learn ministry in the real world; 6. Apprentices learn to be trainers of others so that ministry is multiplied; 7. Apprentices learn evangelism and entrepreneurial ministry. Marshall has also produced a handbook for apprenticeship: Marshall, *Passing the Baton*.

or skills; rather, it is an impartation of relational ministry. It seeks to provide conviction in the Bible, character which ministers in accordance with the Bible, and competency to proclaim the Bible.[92] What separates this from the on-the-job training of the third model in this chapter is that it takes place before formal theological education. This is not an alternative to theological education, but seeks to complement it. For denominations that stress the college/seminary aspect of ministry training, this may be suitable. Unless it is done as a part-time model, however, it would dramatically increase the time required to study. It may be better to marry the two together and include the apprenticeship element within the formal theological education.

Wimber believes that this is based on the model of Jesus who trained the disciples to do signs and wonders through apprenticeship.[93] He sees it as an ongoing model in which the first disciples were trained over three years and, in turn, they were sent on to train others, and so on.[94] Apprenticeship training means that the apprentice learns by doing and, in turn, becomes a mentor from whom new apprentices can learn. MacArthur believes that this is a valid apprenticeship model whereby people find someone to teach who knows less than them, and someone more knowledgeable than them to be their personal teacher.[95] The weakness with this model is the emphasis it places upon individuals teaching each other. If there is a personality clash with the teacher, then the apprentice can suffer as a result of that. Yet, accountability to someone for ministry is important, and it may be appropriate that a calling be judged by the Church to see if it is valid.

Difficulties might arise if the trainer does not quickly release the opportunities to practice the skill, or does not accept that there is a place for anything beyond their own practice. Wimber addresses this and suggests that an integral part in this model is that of releasing the apprentice to do the job themselves.[96] Despite the negatives, an opportunity to see how ministry functions will prove far more valuable, when dealing with the complications of people, than abstract knowledge of how things ought to

---

92. Marshall and Payne, *Trellis and the Vine*, 71–72, 78.

93. Wimber and Springer, *Power Evangelism*, 194. Wimber calls disciples followers, acolytes, students or apprentices and this manifests itself in a willingness to become a learner over and over: "If there is anything that characterizes Christian maturity, it is the willingness to become a beginner again for Jesus Christ. It is the willingness to put our hand in His hand and say, 'I'm scared to death, but I'll go with you. You're the Pearl of great price.'» Wimber, *Everyone Gets to Play*, 42–43.

94. Wimber and Springer, *Power Evangelism*, 196.

95. MacArthur, *Master's Plan for the Church*, 63.

96. Wimber and Springer, *Power Healing*, 183.

function.[97] Theological education paints the broad picture of what Christian ministry believes and aims to achieve, and the practical experience offers opportunity to put that knowledge into practice.

To apply the apprenticeship model to power evangelism may be difficult because of a lack of people able to train in this area. Wimber suggests that reading Christian books, attending conferences and learning from those effective in power evangelism, coupled with a connection to Christ, are the key means of training.[98] This is one of the recurring dangers amongst some Charismatic ministries—the "lone ranger" approach. Richard J. Krejcir defines accountability as a check and balance system, protecting us from harming ourselves and others. This develops an openness to our thoughts and actions, enabling encouragement and reproof.[99] Scott Thomas suggests five areas for accountability in leadership that encompass all of the practitioner's life.[100] Such transparency, as Scott notes, would be difficult in a traditional hierarchal leadership system, as honesty may cost someone their job. In a wider relationship, however, it may be very worthwhile, providing confidentiality can be secured. This may be one of the most important roles that existing leaders can be involved in: training the next generation of leaders to do the work of the gospel.

This may be based upon a different understanding of ministry than that which is perceived to be a traditional Reformed cleric.[101] A model in which leadership gifts are given to equip members to be ministers is implied (Eph 4:12). Bill and Lynne Hybels note that leaders involve people "in the thrill of doing ministry" and, to accomplish this, they "discover, develop and deploy" their gifts.[102] The notion of widening the focus of ministry,

---

97. In my own experience, I was ordained to a pastorate without serving an assistantship and when I transferred to PCI had, after five years of ministry, to serve that assistantship. During the period of apprenticeship I saw that how we deal with people was equally as important as what our theology is and the mistakes I made when I did not grasp this fact.

98. Wimber and Springer, Power *Evangelism*, 213.

99. He suggests that accountability can help prevent burnout and stress specifically. R. J. Krejcir, "Understanding and Developing Christian Accountability."

100. Thomas, "Five Basics for Accountability." He notes that it begins with the grace of God, openness with men who know our lives intimately, interacting with those of the same gender who are not employed in the same congregation, insisting on absolute openness and even prove their commitment, and dealing with sins in the head by asking questions of motivation.

101. "The special calling of the minister is the ministry of the Word, in public and private, the conduct of public worship, the administration of the Sacraments, the instruction of the young and the pastoral care of souls." *Code*, 36.

102. Hybels and Hybels, *Rediscovering Church*, 150.

from accurate communication of biblical and theological truth to releasing people into the work of ministry itself, may require a shift in the Church's thinking. Wimber agrees that training and equipping future leaders for ministry is one of the key jobs of existing ministry.[103] Not only does this perpetuate the ministry of power evangelism, it also develops discipleship and moves people from observation to active participation in the work of ministry in the local congregation.

This apprenticeship relationship is, essentially, a mentoring relationship. Max C. Wright outlines the role of the mentor: that they see life as a journey. Success in the journey, throughout the high and low times, is what really matters most. This emphasizes character, specifically in how those around us are engaged with.[104] A mentor allows individuals to become associated with other individuals from whom they can learn valuable lessons in life, ministry and character development. Character is an essential element if believers are to become, not only the disciples, but the ministers that God desires us to be. Wright defines character as a mix of our commitments, beliefs, passions and assumptions. These define our identity and are expressed in the values brought to leadership and life.[105] If the Church is to be an effective instrument in God's hands, then character matters more than any gifting. Further, Wright notes that character forms theology as it reflects the faith, beliefs and commitments of the believer, as well as the mentor from whom they learned.[106] If the mentoring model is allowed, then those from whom education and formation is looked will further develop that character and mold the mentored into effective ministers. It is not surprising that often people become like their mentors, in some of their attitudes and actions, and even in the way they communicate.

Consideration is also needed concerning how, in an apprenticeship/mentoring model, the inevitable disagreements and disappointments will be dealt with. This is seen in Acts' description of the relationship between Paul and Barnabas, who seemed to be the mentor to the newly converted Paul, bringing him to the Church at Antioch. (Acts 11:19–30). When they set off for their first missionary journey, they took along another young man called John Mark. At the very beginning of this mission he returned home (Acts 13:13). When Paul and Barnabas were planning their second missionary journey, Barnabas wanted to include John Mark (Acts 15:37–40). This divergence of opinions and ideas meant that the two men did not minister

---

103. Wimber and Springer, *Power Healing*, 189–90.
104. Wright, *Mentoring*, xxvi.
105. Wright, *Mentoring*, 4.
106. Ibid., 8.

together again.[107] Wright comments that mentoring is not a cloning process and so the mentored person "needs to cultivate the independent objectivity to choose different paths from their mentor" so that they think for themselves.[108] This reinforces the need to see mentors as human. He further notes that there will be an emphasis on forgiveness with mentors, because they are human; yet, this is the nature of relationship.[109] This means the apprenticeship model is more than that of repeating or adopting a pattern; it is learning practical lessons to enable the apprentice to be equipped to serve in ministry.

It is reasonable to deem mentoring successful, not only if the individual emulates the successes of the mentor, but also if they learn from and avoid their failures. If the aim of mentoring is to produce effective ministers, then that will produce a maturity that is not dependent upon popularity or success. As faith develops, a dependency upon people to define and strengthen lessens. This may happen, particularly, when people are disappointed with their leaders. When the mantle of leadership is taken, an understanding of how people will be disappointed develops. Mentoring, therefore, breeds self-awareness and spiritual maturity. This may be a benefit for a congregation as the effect will be quality as well as quantity of growth. It will be a relevant evangelistic community of faith that produces healthy and integrated disciples.

The In-House Model

This model asserts that training ought to be done within the context of a local Church. In this model, if someone wanted theological education to degree level, it would be done in a college/seminary setting. If they wanted to be trained for ministry, then it would be done within a local Church. This could be considered a complementary method to the training model. This is also significant, when considering Wimber's theology, because the Vineyard Churches have established their own training centers.[110] This may signal a

107. There seems to have been a melting of opinions later on in Paul's life (2 Tim 4:11).

108. Wright, *Mentoring*, 32–33.

109. Wright, *Mentoring*, 66–67.

110. The Vineyard College of New Zealand began offering night classes in 1996 and now is a full-time in-house college. See http://www.vineyardcollege.org.nz/index.php? option=com_content&task=view&id=12&Itemid=2. There is also the Vineyard Leadership Institute in the USA, which offers courses to "integrate hands-on training, ministry experience, spiritual formation, and academic understanding with an uncompromising commitment to excellence in biblical-theological, ministerial and

move away from an informal style of ministry to a more denominational ethos within the Vineyard Churches.[111]

One model that has emphasized in-house training has been Bild International, whose aim is to train and release Church-planters.[112] Jeff Reed, their CEO and Founder, has suggested a Church-based form of theological education. This model seeks to work in conjunction with colleges/seminaries and local congregations, to create a new paradigm. As with the apprenticeship model, Reed is keen to state that this model will not replace the training model; rather, it will complement it.[113] This change, he asserts, has been heralded by the Theological Education by Extension Movement and satellite colleges, including Doctor of Ministry programs, and offers "various non-formal theological education programs."[114] This model is also followed by the Porterbrook Network in the UK. It offers two models: either local congregations or regional gatherings, which are used to follow a study program.[115] For someone whose commitments may keep them from being able to leave home and become part of an academic community for a given amount of time, this may offer a possible training model. How the course would be taught is an issue. If it were to be communicated through the internet or DVDs, then there would be no difference from the "undisciplined, unaccountable study and poor mentoring" of existing extension theological

---

spiritual- formation training." See http://www.vli.org/pages/about.asp.

111. "The Association of Vineyard Churches, for better or worse- is a denomination. We see this primarily in the area of relational structure, that provides accountability, cohesion, and encouragement." Although Wimber acknowledges this he claims that it was never his goal to begin a new denomination, but with 99 percent of the Churches using the title Vineyard it is a reality. The movement toward a denomination received some criticism in 1992, mainly over the issue of control, but Wimber argues that because the Church is involved in spiritual warfare control is necessary. Whether Wimber would have been happy with a training institution is unclear. He writes: "If twenty years from now, the leaders of the Vineyard turn inward, and become self-serving, shame on them. They need to take risks and continue to grow in the same way we took risks and continued to grow. If they don't God will hopefully raise up some other Renewal Movement, and they will be seen as irresponsible radicals, in much the same way some parts of the institutional church regard the Vineyard today." Perhaps the college is a means to taking a risk or admitting that they need to serve themselves. See Wimber, "To Be or Not to Be."

112. http://www.bild.org/aboutUs/MissionAndVision.

113. Reed, "Church Based Theological Education," 2.

114. Ibid., 5.

115. http://www.porterbrooknetwork.org/porterbrook-learning/using-porterbrook/. What is significant about this model is that it springs from a Reformed source and is under the leadership of Chester, who defines himself as Reformed and Missional. http://timchester.wordpress.com/about/.

education.[116] If it were taught personally, as in a college setting, it would require appropriately qualified local clergy who could teach the courses and have sufficient time to devote from other pastoral duties.

Wimber uses the term "homesteaders" to describe such a model: one that invests in future generations by educating them at home.[117] This is similar to a home-schooling methodology. Pastors train up their successors and hand over the reins to them, personally, in context. This may be more applicable to a North American context, in which home schooling is more widely used, than in the current British context where about 17 percent of children are educated like this.[118] This does invest in the local context, where the next generation of leaders is trained in their own congregations. Yet, that training may not be transferable to a different context, which may limit where that individual could serve. To apply this model within PCI would be impossible as the rules state that, when a minister leaves and a vacancy is declared, anyone wishing to be considered for that vacancy cannot minister in the congregation.[119] It does, however, offer a degree of continuity from which other Presbyterian denominations may have benefited.[120] There may also be a difficulty if the outgoing pastor does not vacate the leadership role easily.

The benefit of the "In-House Model" is that it provides a grassroots approach to ministry and evangelism. It allows those, in the context, to determine how best to minister to the communities that surround them, and how best to train others to minister to those communities. Green and Forster believe that, because a local congregation knows its own missional context, it is best suited to train others to minister in that context.[121] This builds on the assumption that there is no one better suited for ministry, in a local context, than those who live in it. Yet this could also possibly be a disadvantage. To be so connected to one local context, without having experience of another context, could produce a narrowness of vision. Also, the congregation must reconsider how they understand the minister, from being someone whom they have known as a contemporary, to someone making leadership decisions. It may be true that such familiarity could be

116. Reed, "Church Based Theological Education," 1.
117. Wimber, *Everyone Gets to Play*, 25.
118. http://www.home-schooling-uk.com/.
119. *Code,* para. 190:2 (b), p.57.
120. Rev. Dr. P. G. Ryken succeeded Rev. Dr. J. M. Boice, to whom he had been assistant, in 2005 in 10th Presbyterian Church, Philadelphia, in the Presbyterian Church of America.
121. Green and Forster, *Small Church, Big Vision*, 81.

detrimental to making difficult decisions that affect those with whom the minister is intimately acquainted.

Chester and Timmis note that the majority of gospel ministry is people living their own lives, honoring God and seeking to share that gospel with others. They call this "gospel intentionality." It is this preoccupation with the gospel that separates such lifestyles from social reform.[122] The nature of this model is that it allows people to keep consistent connections with those around them, their colleagues, neighbors and friends, and trains believers to minister the gospel, in this context. A shift is needed in the understanding of a minister as a professional, who is trained in one location and ministers in a different location, to local believers ministering locally for Christ. This model dovetails with the behavioral discipleship model in that it emphasizes the importance of the local Christian community. They continue and connect the proclamation of the gospel with the Christian community. That community is created and nourished by the gospel and, in turn, becomes the prophetic voice to the world for the gospel.[123] Those trained in these methods are able to proclaim the message of the gospel, effectually and practically, in their local communities. This may reduce the amount of time that new ministers take, when they are installed, to learn about the needs of a local congregation.

There are, also, some drawbacks to the In-House Model. Gibbs and Coffey point out that it can lead to a narrow vision that produces leaders who are doing what is already being done. This means "leaders require theological and missiological preparation as the development of ministry skills is prepared."[124] There is also a narrowness to this model of training. It may be assumed that leaders, who were trained in this manner, would be contextually and culturally aware of their ministry setting because they were educated and work within it. Yet, that is not necessarily the case. People can become a product of their context, rather than a critic and challenger of it. This model can also be narrow in its vision because there may not be any sense of mission beyond that of the local congregation. On a personal level, members of a congregation may have difficulty in altering their relationship with an individual, who was a contemporary and who is now a trainee leader. A better idea may be to include this model as an element alongside other models of ministry training.

---

122. Chester and Timmis, *Total Church*, 61.
123. Ibid., 53–54.
124. Gibbs and Coffey, *Church Next*, 88.

The Need Model[125]

The need model seeks to encapsulate the methodology of Wimber, in which individual members are equipped to satisfy the needs that they experience in the world in which they live. His primary concern was to see what God could do with people who would obey him and who were equipped to minister for him.[126] Through this model, believers are encouraged to believe that they can make a contribution to the work of ministry; when they are confronted with situations in their own lives, expecting that God will demonstrate his love through his Church, as Bennett says. They, therefore, satisfy the needs of the people around them, whether spiritual or practical, through the Holy Spirit's gifts.[127] The work of the Holy Spirit is there to move the Church forward in this evangelistic task. Lloyd-Jones sees this as a key to understanding why the Holy Spirit was given. It was not for spiritual experiences or sensations, but to move the Church forward in mission.[128] It is the circle connection—of evangelism through discipleship, and into ministry, and back to evangelism—that this work suggests. It also connects any notion of a charismatic experience with a clear objective; namely, world evangelization.

Connecting the work of the Holy Spirit to evangelism means that any gifts that may be given come to all the congregation, and not just professional clergy. This is a new reformation, worked by the Holy Spirit, in which, as Bruce Bugbee states: "God is placing ministry back into the hands of every believer across denominational and geographical boundaries."[129] This would mean that ministry training is not exclusively for those who are becoming pastors or ministers, as a specific office.[130] There may be issues in transferring this ministry to traditional training models because it interprets ministry as being wider than clergy, to include church members. It may prove very beneficial for encouraging participation in local aspects

---

125. I have taken the name for this ministry model from Lloyd-Jones' comment on the need for spiritual life within the Church: «With the church as she is and the world as it is, the greatest need today is the power of God through his Spirit in the church that we may testify not only to the power of the Spirit, but to the glory and the praise of the one and only Savior, Jesus Christ our Lord, Son of God, Son of Man." Lloyd-Jones, *Joy Unspeakable*, 160.

126. Wimber and Springer, *Power Healing*, 63–64.

127. Bennett, *Holy Spirit and You*, 86–87.

128. Lloyd-Jones, *Joy Unspeakable*, 257.

129. Bugbee, *What You Do Best*, 33. This is similar to the point made by Pope earlier in the chapter, 166, n.10.

130. The traditional position of minister is often predicated by the title Reverend or Pastor. This is not used by other members of the congregation.

of congregational ministry, such as visiting, lay preaching, evangelism or youth ministry.

Not only is this model applicable for every member of a local congregation, it also has a wider effect than training for preaching and pastoral visitation. Keller comments that Christianity is a materialistic faith because the Church is passionate, not just about spiritual salvation, but also changing social structures, influencing culture and working against injustice.[131] Miracles, in this context, whether laying hands on the sick to pray for healing, or allowing God to use us to broker peace between the two communities in a small town, are the essence of the gospel and cannot, as Watson laments, be ignored or left to the lunatic fringe.[132] They are not just about personal experience, but effecting global transformation.[133] Abraham argues that the initial forays into ministry within the early Church happened because the Holy Spirit was already at work in the community. What the people observed happening to the believers raised questions, which gave an opening to share the gospel.[134] Having understood the needs of people and the part to be played by every believer, through the resources of the Holy Spirit, a model of ministry that allows no place for nominalism or observation is developed, and believers are no longer passive.

An emphasis on the miraculous may be discouraging because of an apparent lack of miracles. This may lead, as Jackman points out, to a polarization of either extreme cessationism or hyper-charismaticism. He notes that the evidence of miracles on the scale that Jesus did them is not around today. If they were, the crowds would be overwhelming. He also suggests that this may be an underestimation of the miracle of the new birth.[135] Arguing from a position of contemporary silence, to that of theological axiom, may be a problem because only one exception needs to be noted to disprove the theory. What may lie behind this idea is a discomfort with some of the elements of the contemporary Charismatic Movement, and its apparent extremes, rather than theologically ruling out all miracles.

The challenge is to deal with the issue of spiritual gifts. As noted in chapter 2, there has been a strong consensus, within the Reformed tradition,

---

131. Keller, *Prodigal God*, 112–13.

132. Watson, *Discipleship*, 100–01.

133. Green sees prayer for healing, not just in terms of individual believers, but also the corporate body: "Every congregation should be a community of "salvation", that is to say of healing in every sense; and it is to our shame that until recent years we have not really expected God to heal in answer to the united, believing prayer of the congregation." Green, *I Believe in the Holy Spirit*, 266.

134. Abraham, *Logic of Evangelism*, 37–38. See Acts 2:12–16.

135. Jackman, *Understanding the Church*, 57.

that these gifts have ceased. Watson says: "It was through the power and gifts of the Spirit that this promise was fulfilled."[136] Spiritual gifts come, primarily, from the list in the New Testament (1 Cor 12:4–5). When an individual is blessed with a specific spiritual gift, it may lead to superiority and arrogance when they meet someone who seems to have no specific spiritual gift.[137][138] In one sense, spiritual gifts can be intimidating, especially if someone feels that they do not have a spiritual gift at all. It is, therefore, important to demythologize these gifts. Bugbee sees that these gifts are often easy to grasp because they connect to what is cared about the most, how personalities function and what style of ministry sits best with these two.[139] Part of the demythologizing of spiritual gifts is to see them, not only as ministry focused, but also as complementary to our personalities and passions. To claim a spiritual gift, but to have no passion or love for people, appears inferior. Spiritual gifts are not all that is needed; for they cannot make us into something that is different from the personality God has given us (1 Cor 13:1–3, 13).

An ongoing work of the Holy Spirit, through the release of spiritual gifts, is the challenge of this model. According to van der Kooi, this underlines the Spirit's wider role in the world today, in creation and providence. This suggests an ongoing work in the Church that opens the hearts and lives of the congregation to receive these gifts.[140] This would require the Church to understand a continual, rather than static, work of the Holy Spirit. This could then lead to an openness to receive whatever spiritual gifts God sovereignly chooses to give to his people. It may lead a Reformed congregation away from cessationism and into a more Charismatic theology. Any sense of exclusion, because a specific gift may not be present in an individual life, is removed by emphasizing the sovereignty of God.

---

136. Watson, *Discipleship*, 107.

137. "One obvious by-product of this idea that the possession of spiritual gifts confers some kind of superiority is that it divides people into *haves* and *have nots*. As a result, divisions increase between parts of the body of Christ. People are divided into the Spirit- filled and those who are not Spirit-filled, or the gifted and the ungifted . . . It is a tragic irony whenever the gifts of the Spirit, which are given for the common good and for serving others, are used to delineate points of division in this way, I believe that it shows a deep misunderstanding of the nature and meaning of the gifts." Wimber and Springer, *Dynamics of Spiritual Growth*, 158.

138. Keller notes two extreme positions that demonstrate the potential danger of spiritual gifts, one says that they do not have a specific gift and so evades ministry the other feels totally condemned, because they do not have that gift. Keller, *Ministries of Mercy*, 75.

139. Bugbee, *What You Do Best*, 15.

140. van der Kooi, "Wonders of God," 43–44.

Mack and Swavely believe that every Christian plays an important part in the Church's work and, when they are not active in this, not only do they suffer individually, but the body politic also suffers. The conclusion is that one ineffective Christian can hinder the Church.[141] It is not just good pastoral practice to remind people of their significance and their value both to God and to the Church, it is also a serious matter. The ministry of the Church needs people, not only to understand their gifts, but also to use them. This will be the determining factor, not only in quantity, but also in quality.[142] Spiritual gifts can be incredibly encouraging when it is seen that God is interested in healing and transformation. They can, however, be discouraging when operated in the wrong way. This reminds the Church that the behavioral model of discipleship has a significant role to play in the need model of ministry.

Wimber's argument is that spiritual gifts need to be understood, taking into account the corporate body rather than focusing on the individual possession. This would counter any notion of superiority. The purpose of the gifts is that they are given for the blessing of the Church and for a specific situation.[143] Wimber brings the emphasis right back to the local congregation. These spiritual gifts, he argues, are not talents or personality traits, as Bugbee has argued, but "supernatural manifestations of the Spirit of God, given momentarily, so that God's love, charity, kindness and grace may be shed abroad among his people."[144] Spiritual gifts are given to individuals, for a specific time, so that the work of the Church may continue.[145] Understood in this manner, it encourages believers to believe that God will give them the gifts that they need, at the time they need them. Yet, it reminds them that they are not indispensable, and that their gifts are not their own,

---

141. Mack and Swavely, *Life in the Father's House*, 151.

142. "When the members of the body fulfill the unique roles of service for which God has gifted them, the church will grow. It will grow qualitatively in the effectiveness of its ministries, and in most cases it will also grow quantitatively by adding people who are being saved through hearing the Gospel or being served in some way by the body. On the other hand, the church is like a human body in that it cannot work effectively when its individual parts are not performing their function." Ibid., 159–60.

143. Wimber and Springer, *Power Healing*, 201.

144. Wimber and Springer, *Dynamics of Spiritual Growth*, 160.

145. "The Spirit also equips us with the peculiar gifts needed for the accomplishment of the church's mission. Each member of Christ's body has received from the Spirit of God a particular gift, and with it an obligation to use that gift in the service of others within the body (Rom 12:3–8; 1 Cor 12). As each member uses his gift, the church matures and grows up into Christ (Eph 4:1–16), living in righteousness and holiness and fulfilling the mission that God has given His people in the world." Leithart, *Kingdom and the Power*, 243, n.10

but transitory.[146] Even in a context where many Church offices are held long term, as may be the case in Kirk Sessions, such an understanding of spiritual gifts may aid the Church's overall ministry.

How to understand what these gifts are, also requires effort. Keller helps by offering a threefold formula: desire to act, ability to do, and opportunity to perform. When all three come together, it constitutes a call.[147] Some may not want to lead from the front in evangelism, but have a clear gift of mercy to help others in their time of need. Wimber does not believe it appropriate to speak of owning a spiritual gift. Rather, it is the gift that God has given him, to give away.[148] This is because he believes that spiritual gifts can be momentary. They are not permanently held manifestations of the Spirit's presence, but "can come and go in milliseconds"; something that, he accepts, challenges a Church in which the members are passive observers.[149] Such an emphasis moves the focus away from the individual and onto the people. It encourages every Christian to believe that they all have a gift to share in the work of ministry, and challenges those who "are just too dull and lethargic about our Christian witness and responsibility."[150] They may receive a gift for the use of the congregation, which will move them from observation to participation.[151] This is helpful if the local Presbyterian congregation is to move from observation of ministry to participation in ministry. The culture, which reacts against strong individual ministries, will be challenged to find their place of contribution to congregational life by a charismatic, need-motivated ministry model.

There may also be a need for caution when ministering spiritual gifts. If it is accepted that God is revealing information about individuals to other

146. Bugbee comments that unity springs from this understanding of spiritual gifts when we see that we all have something to contribute: "There *is more unity and harmony in churches that teach and develop gift-based ministries.* Confusion and disharmony exist in church where there is a lack of appreciation for the unique contributions of individuals. We often observe the differences in others as obstacles. But God views them as opportunities to serve one another in a variety of ways, meeting diverse needs in the church and in the world." Bugbee, *What You Do Best,*. 40.

147. Keller, *Ministries of Mercy,* 76.

148. Wimber and Springer, *Power Healing,* 201.

149. Wimber and Springer, *Dynamics of Spiritual Growth,* 151–52.

150. Wimber, *Way In is the Way On,* 252.

151. When speaking to a PCI congregation concerning spiritual gifts we often are using a language few of them have heard before. Wimber gives some examples which may help to contextualize what we mean, and de-mythologize charismatic phenomena: To be suddenly able to apply Scripture to the private life of someone we are talking with, walking into a room and suddenly know secret facts about people in the room, that knowledge is a spiritual gift. He further comments: "We may not have names for all the gifts, but we can see them functioning." Ibid., 253.

individuals, such information is to be treated sensitively. Wimber believes this kind of prophecy must be personally delivered, not publicly, and ought to be overseen by the congregational leadership to avoid individuals controlling other individuals. Also, major decisions ought not to be made from such prophetic utterances.[152] Much of this appears to be common sense. It is accepting the frailty of humanity—that things will be done wrongly and that mistakes can be made. It respects the authority of the leadership, within the local congregation, and limits any natural human propensity toward controlling others. With these provisos, the damage that could potentially be done in using spiritual gifts, and negative experiences, may be limited.

Focusing on spiritual gifts rather than on character "bypasses a fundamental principle of the Christian life: gifts and abilities, no matter how magnificent, are either limited or enhanced by character."[153] To aid this, Wimber suggests that Christians seek the fruit of the Spirit, before the gifts of the Spirit, because fruit is a product of time and maturity. Although converted, there is still the need to go through a process of maturing and formation of character to become the people who can operate in spiritual gifts, without our lives compromising our ministry.[154] What this shows is that spiritual gifts are not a substitute for Christian character. Rejection of charismatic experience may be because of the inconsistency seen in the lives of charismatic believers and ministries. Emphasizing the matters of character may limit this drawback.

Partial Conclusion

In this new model for ministry, the Church is moving beyond individual and tribal history and into a new history that draws identity, not from what separates, but from what unites. The paradigm of theological education needs to become more practical, with even a degree of experimentation in how leaders are trained within a college setting.[155] Perhaps the Charismatic model of Wimber may provide such an alternative. Chalke believes that the Church must reach out indiscriminately to any whom it may meet. This will be an inclusive Church that welcomes all people, at all levels of faith, with all the social issues that the contemporary world faces and lives with.[156] This would be the ministry that the Charismatic model seeks to empha-

152. Wimber and Springer, *Dynamics of Spiritual Growth*, 57.
153. Wimber, *Everyone Gets to Play*, 51.
154. Wimber, *Everyone Gets to Play*, 51.
155. Haywood, "New Paradigm," 6.
156. Chalke and Watkins, *Intelligent Church*, 39.

size, in which the Baptism in the Holy Spirit begins to attract people to the Christian community through empowering the Church to be witnesses. It also implies an openness to the communities in which the congregations are ministering, even when that may challenge the accepted cultural norms of that congregation.[157]

Christian spirituality, as espoused in the Reformed tradition, is introspective, not condemnatory.[158] The Church seeks, as Chalke notes, to be an incarnational institution that is made up of individuals working out the power of the gospel in their own lives. It reaches out with passion and acceptance to those who would normally be ignored. Failure to do so is to be irresponsible to the biblical mandate of Church.[159] Keller comments that, while Jesus offended the religious establishment, our Churches generally attract them, resulting in the fact that many broken people avoid Church.[160] This identifies the Church with those who are often not currently in the Church. Yet, it cuts across theological, cultural, racial, economic, and even class barriers that may prevent people from joining a congregation.

The effect that this may have on the Church is that individuals find their identity in the wider community. McLaren comments that this will lead to a new ecumenism, in which private denominational histories will become less significant, because the same issues were at work in all our common history.[161] McLaren is correct about the need to see Christianity as wider than our current experience and personal histories. I would want to modify his statement, by reinforcing the need to be identified with a personal and religious history, to that which connects us to where believers have come from

---

157. One example of this was the Calvary Chapel of Costa Mesa, CA, who under Chuck Smith effectively reached out to the hippie youth culture of the 1970s. Smith speaks of those in the Church, "who represented mainline America," being challenged to accept the youth from a different culture and the result was that both elements grew in the Church. He writes: "Our challenge was to overcome what most churches had not: namely, their insistence on respectability, conformity, and a judgmental attitude toward anything that departed from the norm." This happened when hippies came into the building barefooted and a sign was placed upon a new piece of carpet resulting in a board meeting in which the carpet was removed so that the young people could come into Church. Thus, Calvary Chapel reached outside of its natural frame of reference. See Smith with Brooke, *Harvest*, 23, 46 and 49–50.

158. WSC, Q.97.

159. Chalke and Watkins, *Intelligent Church*, 59–60. We are not called to accept sin without comment: „Generous churches acknowledge the issue of sin in each individual's life, but they do so within the context of recognising their own daily battle in this area.» Chalke and Watkins, *Intelligent Church*, 99. Rather we reach out in a spirit of dependence upon God's grace.

160. Keller, *Prodigal God*, 15–16.

161. McLaren, *Church on the Other Side*, 57.

and anchors us in the present. This would permit Christians from different backgrounds to hold on to their traditions and respect the diversity that is the journey of faith. New memories and identities will be forged, as a new identity is found in the context of the ministry in which Christians are now involved: a ministry that releases individual believers and local Christian communities, to demonstrate the power of the gospel in the world.

There may also be a need to see the beginning and end of the Church's gospel ministry of presenting a gospel that integrates, and then releases, disciples into a gospel and missional ministry. Devenish defines a local Church as a group of grace-motivated, Spirit-filled people from diverse backgrounds, committed to one another and their leadership, and reaching out missionally to their community.[162] This issue is central to the community of faith. The Church must not only understand the theology of evangelism, but disciple, train and release local congregations into missional activity. Wimber believes that there needs to be a release of spiritual gifts, which are freely distributed to all believers, as the norm and not the exception.[163] Every Christian can experience spiritual gifts, not just a few super spiritual people. This will bring a new understanding, that all members are equipped to play a part in ministry. It could see a congregation turn membership into active participation. This dovetails with Hull's concept of "corporate teamwork," in which everyone works "together for the common good."[164] Wimber's position appears to be relatively simple. He notes the gospel of forgiveness of sins and hope of eternal life is: "more creative than your best idea; it contains more wisdom than your deepest insight; it brings more healing than your most solicitous care."[165] This conviction, that the simple message of the New Testament is all that the Church needs, may strike a chord with Reformed believers who emphasize the regulative principle in all of witness and worship.[166]

Wimber offers a synthesis of the different models that have been considered, taking them on board and adding his own specific emphasis for their benefit. He writes that Jesus' method of training was to encourage the disciples to become practitioners who pass on the training to others. This was equipping, rather than education, and while this does not dismiss the

---

162. Devenish, *What on Earth is the Church For?* 60.
163. Wimber and Springer, *Dynamics of Spiritual Growth*, 153.
164. Hull, *Disciple Making Church*, 31.
165. Wimber, *Way In is the Way On*, 35.
166. "But the acceptable way of worshipping the true God is instituted by Himself, and so limited to His own revealed will, that He may not be worshipped according to the imaginations and devices of men, or the suggestions of Satan, under any visible representations, or any other way not prescribed in the holy Scripture" (WCF 21:1).

need of theory, theory by itself cannot replace it.[167] Often, the prestige of ministry and the position may take over. Having studied for a number of years and gained academic achievements, then having assisted ministers of larger congregations, PCI ministers may have a sense of superiority, of having arrived. Yet, the evidence of good ministry preparation is the ministry to which the students are called and released. Theology must inspire us to do the works of Christ in this world; it must inspire us to have the confidence to believe that the Church can make a difference through serving God and see people's lives changed. If not, it is setting us up for failure and despondence. There can be no sense of arrogance when it is known that the Church is the product of the gifts that the Holy Spirit has distributed to it. Charismatic Christians are what the Church needs, but if they act like this, they will not be able to give the Church what is needed because egos may shadow the light of Christ. Wimber's teaching on spiritual gifts reminds us that any gift received from God is not a personal possession, but is there according to the will of God and it can be taken away if misused or ignored.

There is also a need to understand the role that the Church plays in ministry, pointing to something more than itself. As Newbigin notes, the Church and kingdom are not interchangeable and nor are they separable. The Church is a sign of the kingdom and offers a foretaste of it, pointing to what is yet to come. In this sphere, the Church ought to be enjoyed.[168] As the people of God, the Church is to minister for the coming kingdom of God and to point people to the fact that the King is returning (Rev 11:15; Matt 25:1–13). These also affect our accountability in that Christians are living and working for another kingdom, and ultimate allegiance to Christ is owed to Christ.

---

167. Wimber, *Everyone Gets to Play*, 47–48.
168. Newbigin, *Discovering Truth*, 99.

Conclusion

Introduction

I WILL NOW RETURN to the visiting alien, whom we met in the Introduction, walking the streets of Northern Ireland. Seeing the wide proliferation of Presbyterian Churches may mean that he comes across something that is different. This would not necessarily be a new denomination but a new practice within the existing structures. It would be a marriage of Reformed and Charismatic theology through the suggestions made by Wimber. The unique element would be seen in the way evangelism, discipleship and ministry are being exercised. There would be a new form of evangelism that demonstrates the power of the gospel in signs and wonders. There would be a new form of discipleship that emphasizes the power of the Holy Spirit in Christian development and growth. There would be a new form of ministry preparation in which every believer is actively encouraged to serve God, and to meet every spiritual and practical need with which they are confronted.

This is the balanced view between Word and Spirit, between intellect and experiential, and between presence and power that Bradford claims is necessary for the Church today.[1] Historically, there may have been some animosity between those who suggested a continuation of the gifts of the Holy Spirit and those who emphasized Reformed theology; although, there has been some debate whether this was the case within the framers of the Westminster Confession, the Puritans, and the Reformers. Nevertheless, as Fyall states, it is also my contention that the Church needs to endeavor to grasp the compatibility of these two streams, for its own best interest.[2] This view is also echoed by Roger S. Greenway who suggests that the witness of

---

1. Bradford, *Releasing the Power*, 15.
2. Fyall, *Charismatic and Reformed*, 2.

the Church, through words and actions, is enabled through a continuing work of the Holy Spirit.³ While he does not explicitly connect a charismatic element to such witness, it raises the issue of the need for an ongoing experience of the Holy Spirit within the Reformed tradition that goes beyond salvation.

Fyall also suggests that the means of emphasizing the need for the Holy Spirit will come through the proclamation of the Word of God, which is particularly relevant to Reformed congregations. It is only in this context that he claims "the gifts of the Spirit can be seen in their true context."⁴ Williams agrees that it is through understanding that which the Bible teaches on charismatic manifestations that the Church will be able to grasp how to minister, effectively, for Christ in the world today. This is because, in his view, the means by which Christ has elected to take ministry forward is through individuals' experience of the power of the Holy Spirit.⁵ It is this practical aim that I have sought to address through this book. I suggest that a charismatic experience may not be as incompatible with Reformed theology as sometimes assumed, and that it is necessary for evangelism, discipleship, and ministry in a Reformed congregation.

Theological Reflections

In drawing this book to a conclusion, I want to return to the theological issues, outlined in chapter 2, and address the issue of their implementation considering wider theological contexts and the specific context of the Reformed Churches and Northern Ireland, in particular.

The Implications of Implementing Wimber's Theology in PCI

Having already considered the issue of the cessation of the charismata, regarding the WCF, it may be appropriate now to consider the implications for PCI of applying kingdom theology.⁶ Historically, PCI has been an evan-

---

3. Greenway, *Go and Make Disciples*, 17.
4. Fyall, *Charismatic and Reformed*, 12–13.
5. Rodman Williams, *Renewal Theology*, 2:335–36.
6. The PCI is an all-island denomination, with churches and presbyteries in what is now the Irish Republic. O'Ferrall notes that the main location of Irish Presbyterians were historically in four of the nine counties of Ulster, Antrim, Down, Armagh, and Derry. O'Ferrall, «Daniel O'Connell and Henry Cooke," 20. O'Riordan notes that today Irish Presbyterianism is strongest in South Antrim and North Down. O'Riordan, «Protestantism in Ireland," 90. For the purpose of this reflection I will limit my focus to

gelical denomination, influenced by revivalist preaching and evangelical awakening. David W. Miller sees the influence of John Wesley, particularly on eighteenth-century Irish Presbyterianism.[7] This may suggest a willingness to learn from traditions other than those that agree, theologically, with the WCF. Andrew Holmes specifically states that Irish Presbyterianism has its own roots and development within the revivalist tradition, especially the Six Mile Water and 1859 revivals. These were accompanied by a large number of conversions, the establishment of new churches, and even "unusual phenomena and emotional behavior."[8] This revivalist tradition, right at the beginning of Irish Presbyterianism, may suggest an openness to spiritual gifts and charismatic phenomena in practice. Six Mile Water appears to have been a significant event in the history of Irish Presbyterianism. The preacher, Rev. Glendenning, had a powerful effect on his listeners, producing feelings of extreme "anxiety" about their spiritual condition.[9] David Carnduff understands his methods to be somewhat unorthodox, although he does not elaborate.[10] Taking this on board, therefore, a more emotional brand of Christianity that has been influenced by missionary contexts, which may appear to be less developed than the Western culture, may not be beyond the remit of acceptance by PCI.

A further issue regarding Wimber's theology of the kingdom may be the evangelical position prevalent within PCI, which has been associated with cessationism, as outlined in chapter 2. Holmes and Dunlop note the strong evangelical influence on early Presbyterianism, and how a commitment to Bible Societies, in particular, brought the Synod of Ulster of the Church of Scotland and the Secession Synod together in 1840.[11] The evangelical aspect of Wimber's theology could, therefore, be emphasized, something which he is keen to do himself.[12] While this may not alleviate the concerns of some regarding elements of Wimber's doctrine and practice, it may point to a possible source of convergence between the two streams, coming from a historical perspective.

Having noted the evangelical disposition of PCI, I want to consider how a generally evangelical ethos could relate to kingdom theology. To critique

---

Northern Ireland, which is the extent of my experience. It may even come through in some of my reflection.

7. Miller, "Presbyterianism and 'Modernization,'" 66.
8. Holmes, "Experience and Understanding," 361.
9. Stewart, *Short History*, 44.
10. Carnduff, *Ireland's Lost Heritage*, 25.
11. Holmes and Dunlop, *Union of Synods*, 14.
12. Wimber, *Kingdom of God*, 27.

evangelicalism, it is first necessary to define evangelicalism. Miller suggests, specifically within PCI, that this is a connection to the Wesleyan practice of evangelical mission and conversionist preaching.[13] David Bebbington notes five characteristics: the Bible reveals God to humanity in an accessible manner; Christ was incarnate to reveal God to humanity; the cross is the center of theology, offering hope to humanity; there must be a response to the gospel in conversion; and, the gospel must be demonstrated in action.[14] Christopher Catherwood adds: the unity of the Godhead as Triune; the sovereignty of God in everything; universal sinfulness; the bodily resurrection of Jesus; the work of the Holy Spirit in regeneration; justification by grace and faith alone; the indwelling of the Holy Spirit; the unity of the Church; and, the return of Christ.[15] The text of the Apostles and Nicene Creeds could also be interpreted as foundational for evangelicalism. Within PCI, the kind of evangelicalism that exists is a confessional type.

R. Albert Molher, Jr. applies the idea of the bounded and centered set, which we will consider later regarding culture, toward evangelicalism. The centered set seems to sit more with liberal evangelicalism, and the bounded with a more conservative understanding. He goes on to outline three levels of doctrine: the first is the fundamental issue, which we have already stated; the second is that of the denomination and theological distinctives, which interpret the first set; and the third relates to the issues of conviction and conscience.[16] Where kingdom theology is placed will determine the degree of its acceptance within PCI. If it is seen as a first level issue, then it may take considerable effort to implement its principles. If it is second level, then it may have to deal with challenging doctrinal subordinate standards, such as the WCF. It may be that kingdom theology is a third-level theological issue. David Hilborn suggests that some of these third-level issues are the view of creationism, and the place of Israel in eschatology.[17] Catherwood includes views on spiritual gifts, eschatological positions and the place of women.[18] This may provide a framework for the acceptance of kingdom theology, if it is carefully presented as neither changing fundamental doctrine, nor contradicting the subordinate standards. In this context it may be applicable as a third-level, non-fundamental issue of theology. The issue of boundary may also be important. Patrick Mitchel notes that, traditionally, evangelical-

13. Miller, "Presbyterianism and 'Modernization,'" 66.
14. Bebbington, *Evangelicalism in Modern Britain*, 4–8.
15. Catherwood, *Evangelicals*, 15–23.
16. Molher, "Confessional Evangelicalism," 75–80.
17. Hilborn, "Evangelicalism," 3.
18. Catherwood, *Evangelicals*, 24.

ism has been confined to a small Protestant minority in Ireland. He argues, however, that this is too narrow an approach because the boundaries have shifted to include some Roman Catholic groups, as well as new fellowships developing out of that ecclesiastical background, that are not comfortable with the Protestant designation.[19] Kingdom theology may provide an emphasis that is neither Protestant nor Catholic, neither Irish nor British, but a third voice, being molded and formed by missionary experience. To point out this aspect may well provide an alternative focus for the Christian Church, and a point of commonality around which the different aspects of the Church can unite.

Irish Presbyterianism is strongest in the north of the island of Ireland, amongst Scottish settlers. Yet, there was a historical commitment to other cultural traditions on the island. At the Union of Synods in 1840, the General Assembly of the Presbyterian Church in Ireland adopted a policy that all ministry students ought to study the Irish language.[20] While this practice may have fallen in recent years, it seems to suggest a historical pattern of seeking to apply the Christian message to the culture in which it is being ministered. Wagner speaks of the cultural mandate of the Church, which considers those to whom they are ministering, and seeks to become a "channel for the supernatural working of the Holy Spirit" as the gospel is presented.[21] In applying this to PCI, it is not taking the principles of a non-Western culture and applying them to contemporary Ireland, but it may suggest an openness to cultural relevancy. This may, in turn, support an openness to the perceived non-Western basis of kingdom theology that is being applied in contemporary Ireland by PCI. Thus, an argument from history, which may demonstrate a drifting from a previous practice, could provide a precedent for a current change of theology. Theologically, Lucas points out that such an understanding may find its support from the Presbyterian idea that the Messiah came to set up a realm as much as to effect a rule.[22] Understanding that the Messiah came to set up a realm may dovetail with the discussion of Wimber's view of the kingdom in chapter 2. This realm aspect may also seek to present kingdom theology as having a wider function within the Church than that of personal charismatic experience. This focus on the work of the Holy Spirit, to empower the Church to wit-

---

19. Mitchel, "Living with Difference," 140–41, 146–50. He outlines eight manifestations of evangelicalism in Ireland: Reformed; Charismatic; Pentecostal; Minorities in the Traditional Churches; Independents—Congregationalists and Baptists; Independent groups—the Brethren; Ethnic groups; and Evangelical Catholics.

20. Holmes and Dunlop, *Union of Synods*, 14.

21. Wagner, *Church Growth*, 21.

22. Lucas, *On Being Presbyterian*, 62.

ness and proclaim the gospel, is the ongoing connection of kingdom theology to Presbyterian practice.[23] While this may open PCI to the possibility of kingdom theology, and perhaps even the benefits of kingdom theology, it does not necessarily imply that kingdom theology will be drawn upon. There may still be the need to overcome the cultural barrier of adopting a theology influenced by non-Western cultures.

An ecclesiological issue may be that of the natural inclination of Irish Presbyterians toward conservatism, which A. T. Q. Stewart notes, especially when, as a denomination, they are placed under pressure.[24] Chapter 1 noted the apparent decline in PCI.[25] When placed under such pressure, Irish Presbyterians may react in certain ways. This may mean that, while concerned about the apparent decline, and even financial pressures, PCI will swing towards a theological conservatism that may not understand the place of kingdom theology. It may be recognized that traditional theological doctrines are out of step with that which society sees as important. The question arises, however, over whether doctrine ought to be changed for the sake of culture, or culture for the sake of doctrine. The Willowbank Report of the Lausanne Committee for World Evangelisation emphasizes the need to reconcile the gospel with the cultures in which it is proclaimed.[26] The challenge to PCI is the extent to which this is applied. To engage with the changing nature of Ulster culture, there may be a need to revisit some issues that were once significant, yet now may have become a historical hangover. The degree to which this may be needed is a further issue of debate. John Shelby Spong argues that, before new theological questions are raised, the "bankruptcy" of old solutions must be accepted.[27] Hamilton disagrees with Spong, stating that when the Church revises its doctrine without any appreciation for past theological insights, it ignores axioms that are necessary for ecclesiastical identity.[28] What I am suggesting is not a departure from what has always been believed and done, but that Wimber's theology improves the existing models, a claim he asserts himself.[29] I am suggesting that what is needed may be an appreciation of a different form of Christian theology, one that has been influenced from a missionary context, and a

---

23. Weeks, *Presbyterian Source*, 21.
24. Stewart, *Narrow Ground*, 99–100.
25. Dickinson, *Presbyterian Herald*, 10.
26. "The Willowbank Report."
27. Spong, *Why Christianity Must Change or Die*, 137.
28. Hamilton, *Erosion of Calvinist Orthodoxy*, 10.
29. Wimber, *Kingdom of God*, 27.

consideration that the culture in which PCI now exists is changing to reflect different cultural and theological traditions.

A key factor in this discussion is the role played by leaders within Presbyterianism. G.D. Henderson notes that a minister is not a delegate of a Bishop, but is the proclaimer of the Word, celebrant of the sacraments and director of public worship. This authority requires a "consecrated personality" which, though formed through an educational process, also requires dependence on the Holy Spirit.[30] This could allow for the implementation of kingdom theology from the pulpit down, if a minister is so inclined to adopt such doctrine. However, it might also mean that if a minister is theologically opposed to kingdom theology, then it is within his remit of authority to limit its implementation.

The views of a minister need also to be balanced against a long-term eldership, who Henderson notes, are often "maintainers of the status quo."[31] Lawrence R. Eyres understands their role as guarding entrance into the visible church.[32] This maintenance of a perceived status quo is further explained by Samuel Miller, who emphasizes that the elders, along with the teaching elder (minister), form a "judicial assembly" that superintends all the spiritual interests of the congregation.[33] This will be especially true if the ruling eldership is the constant, whereas the teaching elders are transitory. John M. Barkley notes, therefore, that the influence of the Kirk Session is felt throughout Irish Presbyterian Churches, and that theological debate is implied in their oversight.[34] *The Code* states the role of elders is to work with the minister in the oversight of the congregation, in "holy concord"; this does not necessarily mean agreement with all ministerial emphases.[35] A minister may take a stand for his theological convictions, which could be positive. However, it may also mean discord with the Kirk Session. If kingdom theology is to be implemented within a local Presbyterian congregation, it may stand or fall on the support of the eldership. If it is not supported by the Kirk Session, and the minister remains persuaded of the need to implement it within congregational life, then it may mean an effort to challenge and change the attitudes of the Kirk Session.

---

30. Henderson, *Presbyterianism*, 162–63.
31. Ibid., 167.
32. Eyres, *Elders of the Church*, 15.
33. Miller, *Essay on the Warrant*, 195.
34. Barkley, *Eldership in Irish Presbyterianism*, 101.
35. *Code*, para. 30 (1), 14. Dickson speaks of "warmhearted sympathy" between elders and ministers. Dickson, *Elder and his Work*, 115–16.

The issue of the Westminster Confession is also to be considered if kingdom theology is to be implemented within PCI. Barkley notes that the notion of orthodoxy is adherence to the WCF.[36] Commenting on the theological foundation of Presbyterianism, Barkley notes two characteristics. First, Reformed theology is "totalitarian," meaning that every aspect is related to every other aspect of doctrine. Second, its religion is also "totalitarian," meaning that every aspect of the Reformed Christian's life is related to God, entirely.[37] This implies that if kingdom theology is understood to contradict one aspect of wider Reformed theology, then it may be incompatible with Presbyterianism. This book has attempted to reconcile Wimber and Reformed theology by looking at evangelism, discipleship and ministry. If, however, the rectitude of such a reconciliation is rejected, according to the WCF, then applying kingdom theology to a Presbyterian context may be impossible. This may mean that not only kingdom theology is to be judged, but also the character of kingdom theologians. It may put both on trial for the validity of the doctrine. Chapter 2 attempted to show that there is a developing theological position that can see Charismatic theology and Reformed theology as complementary. It also indicated that there are also those who see the two positions as irreconcilable. This may mean that any large-scale adoption of kingdom theology may be impossible within Presbyterianism. It may only work amongst those who can hold some aspects in tension with each other.

If the issue of the WCF is connected with the evangelicalism within PCI, a further issue may arise. Kraft notes the evangelical tendency that attempts to preserve doctrinal orthodoxy by opposing anything perceived to be liberal. Kraft modified his methodology by opening himself to new avenues of practice that neither his home congregations nor the seminary had ever imagined, and became an "open evangelical."[38] In part, this change may have been due to fundamentalist influences, where a strong division between evangelical and liberal is perceived. This defines new ideas as leaning either toward evangelicalism or liberalism.[39] The implementation of kingdom theology within Presbyterianism, therefore, depends on the definition of the evangelicalism that is adopted.

Another issue is the extent to which PCI subscribes to the WCF. The ordination and installation ceremony accepts the WCF as subordinate

---

36. Barkley, *Eldership in Irish Presbyterianism*, 102.
37. Barkley, *Presbyterianism*, 12–13.
38. Kraft, *Christianity in Culture*, 8.
39. Ibid., 39.

standards to the Bible.[40] How PCI, and individual elders, understand their relationship to the WCF will determine whether it is adopted as a systematic theology, to be accepted entirely, or a system of beliefs that provide room for different interpretations and emphasizes. It is also worth noting that PCI reserves the right to "interpret and explain her standards under the guidance of the Spirit of God."[41] The denomination did this in 1988 when it concluded that the Bible did not teach that the Pope was the antichrist, yet the WCF did state this.[42] Hamilton argues that this may be to do with the theological understanding of the Bible as *norma normans,* and the WCF as *norma normata.*[43] He suggests that the conclusion of this may mean that the Church is able to redefine and reshape its confessions according to the inspiration of the Holy Spirit.[44] It may not, therefore, be beyond the realms of possibility to allow for an acceptance of kingdom theology, yet to remain true to the WCF. It was noted earlier that Charismatic Renewal and PCI's theology are not, necessarily, mutually exclusive.[45] This may also be reinforced by the fact that PCI ministers promise not to "refuse light from any quarter."[46] This seems to demonstrate a desire to reconsider traditional views about Roman Catholicism. Whether the same desire could be applied to kingdom theology is not as clearly stated. It might be that the theological challenge PCI is to face is how to deal with the issue of Charismatic Renewal, and allow for a general acceptance of its principles beyond the emphasis within local congregational life.

A further issue may be that of ecumenical relations, as kingdom theology requires a degree of interaction with those of a different theological and ecclesiastical understanding.[47] This may provide a way into kingdom theology because of the ecumenical movement within PCI. Finlay Holmes notes the contribution that PCI has made to the ecumenical movement in

40. *Code,* 212 (6), 69.

41. *Code,* 14, 11.

42. WCF 25:6; "Doctrine Committee Report 1998," 54.

43. This means that the Bible is the standard against which all other theological standards are judged, and no human creed is of the same standard as Scripture.

44. Hamilton, *Erosion of Calvinist Orthodoxy,* 10.

45. Ad Hoc Committee on Special Fellowships 1983, 188–89.

46. *Code,* 11, 10.

47. The position of PCI to the Roman Catholic Church specifically has been explained in *Agreements and Disagreements of Irish Presbyterians and Roman Catholicism.* Key are the issues of authority and the Bible (2), "exclusivist and unacceptable claims" for Catholic structures (5), and the belief that Presbyterians do not have the whole understanding of truth (12). Dunlop comments that ecumenism which seeks to ignore these divergent principles does the Church no benefit. Dunlop, *Precarious Belonging,* 36.

Ulster. Revs. Ray Davey and John Morrow, chaplains at the Queen's University of Belfast, were involved in reconciliation ministries, as well as Protestant and Catholic Encounter (PACE). While PCI withdrew from the World Council of Churches in 1980, primarily because of its opposition to liberation theology, it nonetheless retained its membership of the Irish Council of Churches, the British Council of Churches and the World Alliance of Reformed Churches.[48] Chapter 1 pointed out the high-profile ecumenical activities of some Irish Presbyterians. David Armstrong, in Limivady, outlines his own journey toward a more ecumenical praxis, which would ultimately cause him to join the Church of Ireland.[49] The ecumenical work of Very Rev. Prof. J. M. Barkley, throughout the 1970s and 1980s, is also noteworthy. It included experiences such as addressing the Fourth Congress of Jesuit Ecumenists (1972), and his continued friendship with Cardinal Tomás Ó Fiaich, reaching its zenith on 29 September 1979, when he met Pope John Paul II in Dublin.[50] Very Rev. Dr. Ken Newell cites the Charismatic Renewal as reinvigorating him in the work of ecumenism, his own background being a missionary in Indonesia.[51] This seems to link the Renewal movement with a wider appreciation for different Christian traditions and expressions.[52] This connection between Charismatic Renewal and ecumenism, according to Harper, has been championed specifically by Ireland.[53] John Dunlop, a former missionary in Jamaica, notes the improving relationships between Presbyterians and Roman Catholics, even to the extent of Irish Mission workers being welcomed into local primary schools.[54] While this has been ongoing, it must also be held in tension with the apparent conservatism

---

48. Holmes, *Our Irish Presbyterian Heritage*, 173–74.

49. Armstrong, *Road too Wide*, 99–124.

50. Barkley, *Blackmouth and Dissenter*, 163–68.

51. Wells, *Friendship Towards Peace*, 23, 30–31. Newell is stated as believing Calvinism is a good counter measure to the extremes of the Charismatic Renewal. Smith notes that missionary thinking accepts that different Churches from different cultures have much to contribute to theological reflection. Smith, *Mission After Christendom*, 110.

52 It is not a necessary connection that an openness to the Holy Spirit and ecumenical relations go together. The traditional Pentecostals Churches may be an example. Flynn notes that Roman Catholic businessperson, Frank Forte, received the Baptism in the Holy Spirit through an Elim Pastor. Flynn, *Charismatic Renewal*, 52. Dempster notes that some Pentecostals found a greater acceptance for their understanding of Baptism in the Holy Spirit amongst Roman Catholic and Easter Orthodox believers. Dempster, "Search for Pentecostal Identity," 3. Robinson notes, however, that the traditional position of Elim has been for the mass conversion of Roman Catholics, thus taking a non-ecumenical position. Robinson, *Pentecostal Origins*, 126, 307.

53. Harper, *Three Sisters*, 35.

54. Dunlop, *Precarious Belonging*, vii, 33.

that this book has noted in chapter 1, as well as the predisposition toward conservatism noted earlier. Both directions were moving at the same time within the denomination. The connection between ecumenism and the acceptance of kingdom theology is tenuous at best, apart from the reference to Newell's experience. What it does seem to show is that there is a stream of openness to different cultural traditions within PCI that may allow an engagement with kingdom theology. The context of these statements, as having come from ex-missionaries, may suggest that the missionary influence on Wimber's theology may be more acceptable to those who have missionary experience in other cultures.

The Challenge of Calvinism

Holmes places John Calvin as the founding father of Presbyterianism.[55] What is interesting is that the WCF seems to have a greater influence on the theology of PCI than Calvin.[56] Holmes notes that the real influence of Calvin on PCI has been ecclesiological: the rejection of bishops in favor of colleges of elders arranged in geographical areas.[57] While the theological influence of Calvin appears to be present, the WCF has a great influence on PCI. If, however, areas of compatibility between kingdom theology and Calvin are possible, it may provide a way in for Wimber's practices within PCI. Calvin engages with the concept of the kingdom of God in book 3, chapter 10 of the *Institutes of the Christian Religion*. He states:

> God reigns when men, in denial of themselves, and contempt of the world and this earthly life, devote themselves to righteousness and aspire to heaven.[58]

This concept of personal spiritual development, in opposition to the attractions of the world, seems to be in sympathy with Wimber's theology that emphasizes personal spiritual warfare.[59] For Calvin, the coming of the kingdom happens when the desires and demands of fallen human nature are corrected, and when our thoughts are brought into captivity to God.[60]

---

55. Holmes, *Our Irish Presbyterian Heritage*, 1.
56. Barkley, *Presbyterianism*, 11–15. Barkley notes the influence of the WCF and the Nicene Creed but not Calvin.
57. Holmes, *Our Presbyterian Heritage*, 2–3.
58. Calvin, *Institutes of the Christian Religion*, 2:189.
59. Wimber, *Power Evangelism*, 39.
60. Calvin, *Institutes*, 189. Skydsgaard notes that Calvin qualifies his theology of the kingdom as being complete only when Christ returns. Skydsgaard, «Kingdom of

This seems to agree with Wimber's concept of living between the times. Bosch sees this at work in Calvin, placing the kingdom between the ascension and parousia.[61] The kingdom is seen as authoritative, overwhelming any opposition. For Williams, this meant that he felt he could control life, the Bible, the Church and people, but this was changed because of kingdom theology.[62] The issue of control may be misunderstood here; it may be more to do with human depravity than anything else. Calvin sees the kingdom as humbling the world by taming sinfulness.[63] The role of the kingdom of God seems to function in bringing people under the authority of the King. Wimber seems to agree with Calvin, that to combat spiritual evil on the part of the kingdom of God, there is a required commitment to God.[64] Combining elements of Wimber's theology with the Calvinistic tradition, therefore, may not be radically different from the understanding of Calvin. Both appear to emphasize the pietistic element of faith, the need for personal accountability for spiritual development, and the role of the individual in waging warfare against the kingdom of Satan.[65] David B. Calhoun agrees, seeing Calvin's theology of the kingdom as arguing for a destruction of all God's enemies.[66] Wimber also sees this ongoing spiritual battle between the two kingdoms, and emphasizes the final authority of Christ over the kingdom of Satan.[67] To implement this theological principle, a precise line of demarcation between the two kingdoms may be important. For the Calvinistic Church to understand the focus of their spiritual battle, it may require an activist mentality that seeks to engage the enemy and impose the rule of the kingdom of God. Whether Calvin would have agreed with this interpretation is difficult to determine. Chapter 2 considered the WCF and the Reformers position on the Holy Spirit, noting that it was not within their remit of discussion. To argue that Calvin would support a kingdom theology, which seeks to confront the kingdom of Satan by demonstrating the power of Christ through signs and wonders, seems unlikely. It seems more likely that Calvin would point to the example of a surrendered and obedient Christian lifestyle as a symbol of Christ's kingdom's power. If kingdom theology, therefore, is to be reconciled

---

God," 386.

61. Bosch, *Transforming Mission*, 515.
62. Williams, *Signs, Wonders*, 8.
63. Calvin, *Institutes*, 189.
64. Wimber, *Kingdom of God*, 15.
65. Calvin, *Institutes*, 190.
66. Calhoun, "Prayer," 362.
67. Wimber, *Power Evangelism*, 39. He notes: Destroyer, Deceiver, Liar, the Butcher of the World.

and implemented with the theological tradition of Calvinism, this needs to be recognized as a problem.

Implementing Kingdom-Based Theology in Northern Ireland

How the principles of kingdom theology can be applied to Northern Ireland is a further issue of reflection.[68] There appears to be a trend toward identifying the culture of Ireland as something that has been imposed from the outside.[69] Declan Kiberd suggests that it may have been the English who created modern Ireland, and that the history of Irish rebellion was a backlash against that.[70] If this were the case, then any review of the Irish culture must include the English imposition of that culture upon an existing culture. It may also raise the question of what the indigenous Irish culture might look like. What is important is a respect for the Irish culture and various subcultures, and not an assumption that simply following the pattern of another culture within the British Isles is the answer. This can often be perceived as coming from the English influence in Ireland. There seems to be some suggestion of an English superiority syndrome, in which a specific worldview is deemed to be better than all other worldviews.[71] This can be seen as a degree of colonialism, in which the culture of one society is imposed upon that of another society; therefore, an inherent respect for the culture of Northern Ireland may be a prerequisite to applying kingdom theology.

Wimber does seem to want to challenge any notion of cultural superiority in any context, arguing that the Western world ought to be viewed as a potential mission field, as non-Western countries have been.[72] It was noted that Wimber understood the power of God to be necessary to "primitive peoples," so that they will believe.[73] To take, therefore, a theol-

---

68. I have identified culture as that which is specific to Northern Ireland, the unique tapestry of religious and political views that form how the world is interpreted. This is different from Niebuhr's definition which does not apply culture to one specific, but applies it to a wider culture, that of civilization. Niebuhr, *Christ and Culture*, 30–32.

69. Smith, *Mission After Christendom*, 121–22. Smith notes that missionary activity in the first instance produced the ecclesiastical structures that now represent the cultural guardians. Mission produced the culture.

70. Kiberd, *Inventing Ireland*, 1.

71. Haider, "Toward a Superior Account," 231.

72. Wright, *Mission of God*, 38–39. He further states that the Western position itself is contextual.

73. Wimber, *Power Evangelism*, 54.

ogy underpinned by such an ethos, and apply it to Northern Ireland, may require a direct confrontation between certain cultural traditions and the kingdom of God. It may also challenge the concept of what is culturally and religiously acceptable. Kraft also challenges the notion of cultural superiority by addressing how God revealed himself within culture. He notes fives aspects of revelation: God only reveals certain aspects; humanity has a finite understanding of revelation; human sinfulness obscures revelation; we are culturally conditioned to accept certain things and reject others; and we are individually conditioned through culture to accept certain things and reject others.[74] Kingdom theology, therefore, in drawing from missionary contexts and cultures that appear to be radically different from those of Northern Ireland, challenges any notion that Ulster culture is the only correct culture. It reminds the Church of its own humanity, and it challenges theological fundamentalism of the extent to which its doctrines are formed by culture rather than by exegesis.

Stanley connects the missionary activity of the nineteenth and twentieth centuries with this kind of colonialism. He argues that this applies to British missionaries as a whole, specifically those working in British colonies, who promoted Britishness and the benefits of Western society alongside the Christian message.[75] This may be of relevance to applying kingdom theology in Northern Ireland as the issue of political identity has become one of division within the province. This can be seen through institutions like the Loyal Orange Order, which connects Britishness with Protestantism. While, historically, the institution may have begun as a religious one, political identity soon took over. The challenge of kingdom theology may be a separation between Protestantism and politics, allowing for an ecumenism of interpretation in which alternative models of ministry, from different cultures, are valued. It may also require a commitment beyond that of a political ideal, to working for the kingdom of God, and to that which is beyond political kingdoms.

It is important not to homogenize PCI as one definitive position, nor Ulster society at large. Willowbank notes that there will be a number of subcultures within a given culture, and these may have different emphasizes and understandings. This may then even lead to a counterculture that will attempt to destroy the prevailing culture.[76] What needs to be grasped in the role of culture in God's dealings with humanity? Kraft suggests that God uses culture to communicate with people, and limits himself to that culture

---

74. Kraft, *Christianity in Culture*, 129.
75. Stanley, *Bible and the Flag*, 157.
76. "The Willowbank Report."

so that people may understand him.[77] The challenge is about the way in which the Church relates to any given culture, especially the culture from which is springs; whether there is acceptance, or rejection, or imposition of a subculture upon the greater culture. Kraft argues that the Church's role is to transform culture.[78] This seems similar to the position argued by Keller as the rationale for Redeemer Presbyterian Church, New York City. Keller argues that the purpose of redemption was not just so that individuals would escape the world, but so that the Church could seek to influence and change the societies in which they live. This happens through Christians forming a counterculture in which they express the values of God in their living.[79] The challenge is when a specific religious expression is identified with a specific culture to such an extent that they are perceived to be the same. Julia Neuberger believes that the answer may be identification with the wider European culture of Northern Ireland. She argues that an official recognition within Europe may ensure that religious issues are taken seriously, and that what defines people most is respected. This could further be explored as different traditions interact with each other through dialog, so bringing a revival of the best aspects of religious life.[80] The political aspect of Neuberger's statement is beyond the remit of this discussion; suffice to say that interaction between different strands, which respect differences and emphasize issues of commonality, seems to connect with a wider acceptance of kingdom theology. The beginning of this suggestion may be in ecumenical partnership. Simon Lee suggests that local Churches ought never to do alone what can be done together. This suggestion reflects upon the apparent necessity for ecumenical dialog and partnership in missionary contexts, where division over denominational differences cannot be allowed to divide in the face of an opposing culture.[81] This would not only emphasize the necessity for engagement as the Northern Irish Church moves to consider the culture as a mission field, but also the need to engage with different perspectives in mission.

Drawing on the benefits from those with experience in missionary work, such as Kraft, Wagner, Ladd, and their protégé, Wimber, may offer a practical solution. This may require a movement into the future without depending on what has already been accomplished or experienced. This is a "progressive interpretative method" that looks at the past in a different

---

77. Kraft, *Christianity in Culture*, 115.
78. Ibid., 349.
79. Keller, "Redeemer Vision Paper 6," 2.
80. Neuberger, "Religion, Culture," 61–63.
81. Lee, "Freedom from Fear," 17.

way from the traditional way.[82] This also links in the proposed need to see Northern Ireland as a missionary field, rather than the Church as being a chaplain to a specific culture. It could imply an acceptance that the past does not provide all the criteria needed for the present, and that a different perspective may be positive and effectual. Changing to consider Northern Ireland as a missionary context may mean that the Church is not identified with a specific aspect of that culture. This may necessitate the distinguishing of biblical absolutes from those beliefs that are culturally conditioned.[83] There may be some attitudes toward the missionary influences on kingdom theology that appear to be contradictory to perceived Northern Irish understanding. The issue of demonology and possession may be a possible example of this. Moving beyond a natural reaction to such views may require not only revisiting perceived theological axioms, but cultural ones also.

There may also be warrant in considering how kingdom theology will be culturally received. Mitchel notes that many Roman Catholics view evangelicalism as irrelevant to their culture because it is viewed as British. This has meant that converts are unlikely to join Protestant Churches that are financed and staffed by Unionists. To aid this, he suggests a focus upon the biblical basis for evangelicalism, rather than the cultural basis.[84] Kingdom theology may be able to do this because its formulation appears to have come from a different culture than that of Irish or British. This may divorce the Church from any political or cultural identity, thereby emphasizing a kingdom identity that is more inclusive than that of culture. Morrow suggests that in every Church there are doctrinal vestiga, even amongst those who would be unsympathetic to the Reformed position.[85] This may also connect with the rapidly growing number of ethnic Churches throughout the island.[86] This is seen with the implantation of Russian Orthodoxy, in Co. Laois,[87] and Antiochian Orthodoxy in Belfast.[88] If there is to be a common acceptance of different traditions, then understanding a cultural difference in a theological basis may sup-

82. Ellis, *Vision and Reality*, 155.

83. Smith, *Mission After Christendom*, 75.

84. Mitchel, "Living with Difference," 153–54. Morrow cites the association between Presbyterianism and Unionism as an obstacle to Roman Catholic or Nationalist listening to the Reformed position. Morrow, "Mission Ireland," 495.

85. Ibid., 498.

86. Mitchel, "Living with Difference," 149.

87. *Church of Saint Colman of Oughaval*.

88. The Antiochian Orthodox Church of St. Ignatius, Congregations have also been established in Cork, Ballydehob, Dublin and Armagh. http:// www.belfast.antiochireland.org/.

port kingdom theology. Evangelistically, it may also provide for a more acceptable form of witness to those from different traditions because it has separated religion from one specific culture.

Answering the Research Questions

The object of this book was to assess whether Wimber's theology and practice could be related to a Presbyterian congregation without ignoring its unique traditions; and, whether it would challenge its mission in the world. Having considered the three contextual applications—evangelism, discipleship and ministry training—it is my view that such a relationship may be possible. The different models that have been considered may present challenges to interpretation in a charismatic dimension. Indeed, should the underlying premise that the gifts of the Holy Spirit are contemporary be rejected, then none of this work's suggestions will be feasible. There are still issues of style to overcome between the two streams: Wimber represents a more relaxed approach; whereas, as we have seen with the discussion of the regulative principle, the Reformed Churches follow a more rigid understanding of worship. Perhaps this research highlights a perceived issue with Reformed theology: an apparent lack of connection between doctrine and practice.[89] What I have sought to do is to connect the doctrine and practice of the Reformed Churches, through Wimber, while reflecting on Reformed models and the challenge or complement that his theology makes to them.

Regarding evangelism, Wimber's theology may work alongside existing models and may complement them. This appears to be the uniqueness of his contribution: that it is not an either/or equation, but a both/and principle. Wimber expressly states that his method of evangelism is not a new form that would replace and invalidate all other forms. He remains respectful of traditional methods. He sees the fear model as implicit in the gospel.[90] He has a critical sympathy with the "incarnational model."[91]

---

89. A. Carter notes: "I'm convinced the best Reformed teaching is experiential, that it engages not only the mind, but the heart. It's not just theoretical, but practical. Reformed teaching has understood that theology is essentially practical. But it's gotten a bad rap that it's solely theoretical. But that's not historically been the case, and need not be the case.» He further relates the story telling emphasis of, particularly African American preaching, which could improve the doctrinal preaching of the Reformed Churches. Morgan, "Interview with Anthony Carter."

90. Wimber and Springer, *Power Evangelism*, 36.

91. Wimber, *Way In is the Way On*, 63, *Power Evangelism*, 36. It has been noted that there may be some confusion in Wimber's theology on this issue. Or it may be a theme that is underdeveloped, or one in which his opinion changed over the years.

Although Wimber seems to have little sympathy for "the relational model," this could fit well with his theology of powerpoints.[92] Power evangelism rests upon God's direction to specific situations, to minister with his power, which is something that would resonate with Reformed theology.[93] His approach could, therefore, find a home in the Reformed tradition without demanding too great a theological shift.

Regarding discipleship, Wimber looks for the integration of those converted through power evangelism into the local church.[94] He further notes that commitment to Church will develop only when people have a sense of their faith directing their lives.[95] In reflecting upon the behavioral model, Wimber emphasizes that fellowship is significant to spiritual growth and belonging.[96] The proclamation model is also harmonious with Wimber's theology, which desires all Christians to be under the dominance of the Bible.[97] The sacramental model, too, may be reconciled to Wimber's theology because he sees baptism and communion as integral to spiritual development, and views both as pointing toward salvation.[98] His own emphasis on spiritual fruit, as having a priority over spiritual gifts, is significant to the Reformed Churches, which place a strong emphasis on Christian character and the outworking of personal faith in action.[99] His criticism of those who emphasize experience, over the Bible, is equally applicable to Reformed thought.[100] The element of the Baptism in the Holy Spirit taking place at conversion is the same as that of the Reformed position.[101] Considering this, there appears to be little that would make Wimber's position on discipleship incompatible with that of Reformed theology.

Commenting on ministry training, Wimber believes that everyone has a position to fill in the Church; so, training for leadership or other forms of ministry was for everyone. This does change the notion of leadership in Reformed Churches that sets a minister apart from the congregation

---

92. Wimber and Springer, *Powerpoints*, 5.
93. Wimber and Springer, *Power Evangelism*, 101.
94. Wimber, *Kingdom of God*, 15.
95. Wimber, "Leadership and Followership."
96. Wimber and Springer, *Dynamics of Spiritual Growth*, 148.
97. Wimber, *Everyone Gets to Play*, 17.
98. Wimber and Springer, *Dynamics of Spiritual Growth*, 149–50.
99. Ibid., 10. "And the life of a saint is nothing but a life of faith." Watson, *Godly Man's Picture*, 29.
100. Wimber and Springer, *Dynamics of Spiritual Growth*, 43–44.
101. Ibid., 139–40.

through a unique title or unique clothing.[102] The training model was useful for Wimber as it produced those who were equipped to use the Bible in ministry.[103] He also sees that power evangelism needs this theological foundation for it to work correctly.[104] He is critical of those who were trained in the Bible, in an abstract manner, with no emphasis on the practicalities of ministry.[105] Wimber's theology is, therefore, applicable in this model, to a limited degree, and may be understood as foundational to operating in power evangelism. Wimber is sympathetic to the apprenticeship model of training.[106] This model may also be applicable to a Reformed position. If it is all that is meant by ministry training then it would be out of line with the current practice, but coupled with a college education it already is a pattern in many denominations. Wimber does seem to like the idea of leaders being trained at home, within their local congregations.[107] This model would not be applicable to many Reformed Churches at present because few leaders move to leadership in their home congregations. It may, however, be a useful form of lay preaching or eldership training. His theology of spiritual gifts is significant here because it speaks of a corporate ownership.[108] This would harmonize well with the Presbytery system of many Reformed Churches. What seems to be becoming clear is that elements of each system are applicable to the Reformed ethos, as are elements of Wimber's own theology. It would appear that this is the least developed aspect of his views, and that may be because of the emphasis of the Wimber that was power evangelism.

Viewing the follow-up questions, it is possible to be a Presbyterian minister and develop a Charismatic practice. There would be few theological hindrances to a Presbyterian congregation implementing the Wimber model. As noted in the introduction to this book, there have been some Irish Presbyterian congregations that have developed a relationship with Charismatic theology and practice. There is always a challenge to see what can be learned from any method, and the benefit is ecumenical relations with those from another tradition. This was something pursued by the World Alliance of Reformed Churches between 1996 and 2000.[109] Whether Irish Presbyterianism could attain the popularity of the Charismatic streams

---

102. Ibid., 137.
103. Wimber, *Way In is the Way On*, 30–31.
104. Wimber, *Witnesses for a Powerful Christ*, 33–34.
105. Wimber and Springer, *Power Evangelism*, 108.
106. Ibid., 191–92, 196.
107 Wimber, *Everyone Gets to Play*, 25.
108. Wimber and Springer, *Power Healing*, 201.
109. http://www.warc.ch/dt/erl1/20.html.

would also need further study. If Reformed leaders, who positively view the Charismatic models, implement these principles then it would also be worth further study in the future.

The Harmony of the Book

I want to suggest that the harmony of this book offers a method for the integration, consolidation and training of new converts into ministry. The book is linked by the common thread of Wimber's theology, and the contextual applications flow also from Wimber's own writings. The book outlined flows from Wimber's own writing; it begins with *Power Evangelism* (1985), leading to *The Dynamics of Spiritual Growth* (1990), and ending in *Everyone Gets to Play* (2008). Also included is the pattern from "Laying All Down for Jesus" which connected evangelism, discipleship and ministry.[110] The rhythm of these three models and how they interact with each other may, therefore, be viewed as a self-repeating methodology.

This book further challenges the assumptions on which the Reformed faith builds its understanding of pneumatology. Pawson suggests that Cessationist theology has its foundation in theological and historical tradition rather than biblical theology.[111] This tradition has left little space for the exercise or experience of charismatic manifestations. B.A. Gerish writes: "The usual approach to discussing the Reformed tradition is to catalog some distinctive beliefs or doctrines."[112] While Reformed theology claims to be biblical theology, there is still the emphasis on history and tradition. Lucas calls these "Presbyterian stories." They reflect on the history of what happened in the Reformation, and even upon what Europe may have been like without the Reformation.[113] Part of the method of this book was the social constructivist view that sees the world through the way in which the individuals in the world interpret that world. Reformed tradition is a mix of theology, history, and the way things have always been done and understood. I have sought to question if cessationism is a valid understanding in the light of theology and history. From a review of the literature on the subject, I have concluded that there may have been more of an openness to charismatic manifestation, historically and theologically, than previously thought.

---

110. Wimber, *Everyone Gets to Play*, 15–22.
111. Pawson, *Word and Spirit Together*, 76.
112. Gerish, "Tradition in the Modern World."
113. Lucas, *On Being Presbyterian*, 151–53.

In this book I have also sought to challenge Reformed theology with the implications of the doctrine of *semper reformata*.[114] One way in which this doctrine can be applied is to question the place of Charismatic theology and experience in the light of constant reforming. Horton notes that it has been the desire of the Reformed Churches to have every aspect of worship and life determined by the Bible, and not human whim or creativity. This is why the historical challenges to the Church were raised in the Reformation. The Church is the active part in this constant, reforming as it considers "its own doctrine, worship, and discipline in the light of ever- changing cultural contexts."[115] Considering the different culture that exists today from that of the sixteenth century, it is my contention that a reconsideration of charismatic experience may be a valid application of this doctrine. MacArthur understands the doctrine as referring to the imperfection of Christians and the need to constantly change to reflect Christ better. As such, in his view this does not mean that doctrine needs to be re-evaluated to attempt to be relevant to our culture.[116] This statement, however, does appear to allow for the possibility of charismatic experience. This would not be the Church considering how to be relevant to the culture, but the Holy Spirit working through the Church, proving in miracles, signs and wonders that the Church is relevant.

It may seem that some of the challenges that have been suggested in this work would completely transform a Church that is rich in history and tradition. The debate of what is the kernel and what is the husk of our theology and tradition is not a new one.[117] Whether this book is adopted will depend upon how the husk is understood. This does not have to be the case. Taylor notes that the richness of Christian heritage can be offered alongside new and dynamic expressions of Church that have the power of the Spirit within them.[118] This book contends that, when the power of the Holy Spirit is combined with a sense of history and belonging, a powerful contemporary witness is released. The issues with which the book is concerned: namely, the salvation, integration and release of believers into ministry, are too significant to ignore. If change is necessary, then strength is needed to take the difficult next step.

114. It may be argued that Irving began this call to another reformation. Vreeland, "Edward Irving," 1.

115. Horton, "Semper Reformanda." The roots of this doctrine seem to have come from Jodocus van Lodenstein in 1674, which argued that the Church is always in need of reforming.

116. J. MacArthur, "Semper Reformanda."

117. Stanley, "Inculturation," 22.

118. Taylor, *Out of Bounds Church*, 27.

CONCLUSION

The Application of the Book

One of the themes of this work has been how to inspire, effectively, and train Christians to make disciples. To do this, a connection has been made between evangelism that makes converts, discipleship that molds converts, and ministry that trains converts to do evangelism. In one sense, there are elements of Driscoll's understanding of "reformission." This suggests that people ought to be brought close to the Church to witness how the Church satisfies needs.[119] According to Wimber, the theology of how the Church is to operate in this Charismatic way was to be found within Evangelical theology.[120] This harmonizes with Greg Laurie who suggests that the purpose of charismatic experience is the goal of ministry and gospel transformation.[121] Taking these comments on board, the suggestions in this book could be applied to a local Reformed congregation in their work of evangelism, discipleship and ministry training to aid their effectiveness. It could also be applied to denominational structures as they seek to aid and resource their local congregations to minister effectively to their contexts.

The application of Wimber's perspective is needed for a freshness within traditional Presbyterianism. Some Presbyterian Churches are losing a significant number of members.[122] There may be many reasons for this decline, ranging from demographic changes in the parish areas to a general dissatisfaction with the ethos of Presbyterianism. To attempt to address this, there needs to be a consideration of the way in which things get done within Presbyterianism. A significant influence on the Reformed Churches has been John Calvin, whose theology comes from his own training to be a lawyer. This, W. Robert Godfrey believes, was to become "useful to him in later life."[123] Further, according to David W. Hall, Calvin's understanding of the nature of Church government was essentially "republican," in which a collegial body of local ministers govern the affairs of the local Churches. This decentralized authority, away from a ruling elite, so that the council could be free "to monitor the faith and practice of the church. "[124] These influences have led to a specific type of government within the Presbyterian Churches, specifically where theology and practice are judged through an

---

119. Driscoll, *Radical Reformission*, 69.
120. Wimber and Springer, *Power Evangelism*, 12.
121. Laurie, *Upside Down Church*, 30.
122. Dickinson, *Presbyterian Herald*.
123. Godfrey, *John Calvin*, 26.
124. Hall, *Legacy of John Calvin*, 21.

almost legal approach and graded Church courts.[125] John H. Leith writes: "all the attributes and prerogatives of the Church arise from the indwelling of the Spirit, and consequently, where He dwells, there are those attributes and prerogatives."[126] It is to those indwelling of the Spirit that the theology of Wimber emphasizes and seeks to influence the Church's practice of evangelism, discipleship, and ministry. In this sense, it could be argued that Wimber simply emphasizes the spirituality of the Reformation by emphasizing the work of the Spirit in molding and influencing Church practice.

This emphasis on the Holy Spirit may have an impact on the Reformed Churches regarding ministry, specifically. Mack and Swavely note that the work of the Spirit will inspire and motivate the Church to help others in need.[127] This begins when the Holy Spirit places a love within their hearts for those to whom the Church is ministering, which is a manifestation of charismatic experience (1 Cor 13:1–3). When people feel valued and their contribution is important, they will give, sacrificially, to see their congregation's ministry succeed. This will mean that the impact of Reformed congregations will be increased, if not by the direct effect of the Holy Spirit, then indirectly as the Spirit inspires individual members to evangelize, integrate the converts in discipleship and release into ministry.

There may also be a spiritual result of applying this thesis. Newbigin comments that, as the Church takes the gospel into every culture, so the Spirit demonstrates that every culture belongs to God; therefore, things are seen through the cosmic nature of the gospel.[128] The circular element that exists, when congregations emphasize evangelism that turns people into disciples and then trains and releases them into ministry, was the beginning of this discussion. There is also a circular element, spiritually, in that the gospel proclaims the glory of God and, as that is proclaimed, the glory of God shines brightly in the world and illuminates more of our own witness. This will encourage engagement with our communities, irrespective of whether there is any acceptance. There will be a confidence in the gospel that it will be confirmed with power.

---

125. In America the Presbyterian system grew from the congregation upward through Presbyteries, Synods to the General Assembly. In Scotland the pattern was reversed. Leith, *Introduction to the Reformed Tradition*, 147.

126. Ibid.

127. Mack and Swavely, *Life in the Father's House*, 67.

128. Newbigin, *Living Hope*, 44–45.

The New Picture of the Book

I have attempted to paint a picture in which Reformed and Charismatic theologies complement each other in a way that aids the practical work of the Church. This will encourage the Reformed Church to look beyond its own traditions for help and inspiration in its work and witness. There has been a tendency toward secession within Presbyterianism, particularly when an issue of disagreement arises.[129] Wimber notes that contemporary Christianity is more divided than ever before; yet, part of the Holy Spirit's work in him was to give him an ecumenical spirit that sees fellowship founded on common faith in Christ, not theological agreement.[130] If the Reformed Churches can begin by accepting that they may not have all the answers to their denominational needs—Churches closing, drifting members, nominal membership—then they might turn to the Charismatic model for aid.

I also suggest that this book connects Reformed Christians with the spirituality of their theological roots. This is not to say that Wimber was, in essence, Reformed, or that the roots of Reformed theology would look like Wimber. What it suggests is a recapturing of Reformation spirituality, which looks at what needs to be changed in the present Church, and seeks to do so. Alister McGrath believes that this spirituality "represented ideas with a future, possessing a high coefficient of relevance" to the sixteenth century. So the Reformation was an attempt to relate their understanding of Christianity to that era. Accordingly, this spirituality, which mingles the old and new, the transitory and the stable, is well suited for our own time.[131] Building upon the literature on the area of Charismatic and Reformed theology, the picture I have tried to paint suggests that an influence could be that of Wimber who uniquely stands in a position between Evangelical and Charismatic; namely, the radical middle. To implement these suggestions may not only be pragmatically useful for the contemporary mission of Reformed Churches, but may also rediscover something of the passionate spirituality of the Reformation tradition.

On a wider Church scale, this book paints a picture of a situation whereby the historic antagonism between Charismatics and Reformed believers gives way to détente. An example of this is the "Together for the Gospel" Movement in America where C. J. Mahaney (Charismatic), Mark Dever (SBC), Ligon Duncan (PCA), Al Molher (SBC), John MacArthur

---

129. The proliferation of Presbyterian denominations in Ireland particularly was noted in the Introduction.

130. Wimber, *Everyone Gets to Play*, 27.

131. McGrath, *Roots that Refresh*, 17. McGrath believes that this requires further study, something that I have endeavored to do in this book.

(Baptist), John Piper (ABC), and R.C. Sproul (PCA) have covenanted together to learn from each other and resource each other.[132] Banister believes this effect will be like two rivers coming together, bringing the best of the Evangelical and the Charismatic together to create Churches "anchored in the Word and alive in the Spirit."[133] The joining of these two rivers, which I would prefer to call tributaries, into one mighty flood accepts the premise that neither side has all that is needed, and what is lacking is made up from those to whom they would be traditionally antagonistic. Fyall notes some of the same issues: that a Church to be biblical must be strong in both doctrine and transformed living; reverence and celebration in worship; intellect and emotion; and, theology and practice. This moves beyond labeling a Church as Reformed and Charismatic, but addressing the fundamental identity as a biblical people.[134] A ministry philosophy of Word and Power, as that defined by Wimber, may be the answer to the needs of the Church in the twenty-first century.

The Future of Reformed and Charismatic Theological Reflection

In comparing the theology of Wimber with that of the Reformed tradition, as outlined in this book, I believe that there are a number of issues surrounding Wimber that may benefit from further consideration. These are: a comparison of Wimber's theology to Quaker theology; a comparison between power evangelism, as authenticating the gospel, with the Reformed doctrine of the sacraments as explaining the gospel; Wimber's theology of the kingdom and Peterson's theology of subversion; Wimber's theology of the kingdom and Gustavo Gutierriez's liberation theology; a comparison between Wimber's theology of the Baptism in the Holy Spirit and that of traditional Pentecostalism; a comparison between Western Reformed theology and Black Reformed theology on charismatic experience; the Charismatic style of worship and the regulative principle; and a comparison between the theology of the Vineyard and that of New Frontiers International and Covenant Ministries International. Historically, there are also a number of areas: the Reformed roots of the Pentecostal Movement in the United Kingdom;

---

132. See http://www.theopedia.com/Together_for_the_Gospel_Statement. See http://t4g.org.

133. Banister, *Word and Power Church*, 28. Banister says that this will address the hyper-emotionalism and the moral failures of many tele-evangelists that often put off postmoderns (39).

134. Fyall, *Charismatic and Reformed*, 13.

the Charismaticization of mainstream Evangelicalism (has Wimber won the Church over?); the influence of Anglicanism on the Vineyard UK, and vice versa. Statistically, it would also be interesting to see any numerical increase in Reformed Churches that have embraced the Charismatic Renewal over those who have rejected it.

Some of these areas are statistical, some are theological, and some are biblical. However, significant further study is required into conversation between Reformed theology and Pentecostal/Charismatic theology. There may also be merit in asking the same question again in a number of years' time to assess whether, at that stage, Charismatic theology can interact with Reformed theology in any meaningful way. This reflects, as Hamiliton states, the fluid nature of human relationships that form a "dynamically-moving web."[135] It may be that in the future, some theological statement of grass roots movement will develop that completely refutes or supports the relationship between the Charismatic and the Reformed.

---

135. http://acc.roberts.edu/NEmployees/Hamilton_Barry/INTRODUCTION.htm.

Bibliography

Abraham, William J. *The Logic of Evangelism, A Significant Contribution to the Theory and Practice of Evangelism.* London: Hodder and Stoughton, 1989.
"Ad Hoc Committee on Special Fellowships Report." In *Annual Reports, General Assembly of the Presbyterian Church in Ireland, 1983, Sitting in Dublin.* Belfast: Church House, 1983.
"Ad Hoc Committee on Special Fellowships Report." In *Annual Reports, General Assembly of the Presbyterian Church in Ireland, 1984, Sitting in Belfast.* Belfast: Church House, 1984.
"Ad Hoc Committee on Special Fellowships Report." In *Annual Reports, General Assembly of the Presbyterian Church in Ireland, 1985, Sitting in Belfast.* Belfast: Church House, 1985.
Adair, John. *Puritans, Religion and Politics in Seventeenth Century England and America.* Stroud: Sutton, 1982.
Adam, Peter. *Speaking God's Words: A Practical Theology of Preaching.* Vancouver, BC: Regent College, 1996.
Agreements and Disagreements of Irish Presbyterians and Roman Catholicism. Belfast: The General Assembly of the Presbyterian Church in Ireland, 1990–91.
Ahn, Che. *Spirit Led Evangelism, Reaching the Lost through Power and Love.* Grand Rapids: Chosen, 2008.
Alderson, Richard. *No Holiness, No Heaven.* Edinburgh: Banner of Truth, 1986.
Allen, David. *The Unfailing Stream: A Charismatic Church History in Outline.* Tonbridge: Sovereign World International, 1994.
Allen, Diogenes. *Theology for a Troubled Believer: An Introduction to the Christian Faith.* Louisville, KY: Westminster John Knox, 2010.
Allen, Roland. *Missionary Methods: St. Paul's or Ours?* Grand Rapids: Eerdmans, 1962.
Allen, Ronald J. "Individual and Community in Postmodernity." In *Theology for Preaching, Authority, Truth and Knowledge of God in a Postmodern Ethos,* edited by Ronald J. Allen, et al. Nashville: Abingdon, 1997.
Allen, Ronald J., et al. *Theology for Preaching, Authority, Truth and Knowledge of God in a Postmodern Ethos.* Nashville: Abingdon, 1997.
Ammerman, Nancy T. "Culture and Identity in the Congregation." In *Studying Congregations: A New Handbook,* edited N. T. Anderson, et al. Nashville: Abingdon, 1998.

BIBLIOGRAPHY

Ammerman, Nancy T., et al. *Studying Congregations: A New Handbook.* Nashville: Abingdon, 1998.

Anderson, Allan. "Varieties, Taxonomies and Definitions." In *Studying Global Pentecostalism: Theories and Methods,* edited by A. Anderson, et al. Berkley, CA: University of California Press, 2010.

Anderson, Allan, et al. *Studying Global Pentecostalism: Theories and Methods,* Berkley, CA: University of California, 2010.

Anderson, Ray S. *The Shape of Practical Theology: Empowering Ministry with Theological Praxis.* Downers Grove, IL: InterVarsity, 2001.

Andrews, Edgar H. *The Spirit has Come.* Darlington: Evangelical, 1982.

Angel, Gervais. *Delusion of Dynamite: Reflections on a Quarter-Century of Charismatic Renewal.* Eastbourne: Kingsway, 1989.

Archer, Kenneth J. *The Gospel Revisited: Toward a Pentecostal Theology of Worship and Witness.* Eugene, OR: Pickwick, 2011.

Armstrong, David, and Hillary Saunders. *A Road too Wide: The Price of Reconciliation in Northern Ireland.* Basingstoke: Marshall, Morgan, and Scott, 1985.

Atherstone, Andrew, et al. "Lloyd-Jones and the Charismatic Controversy." In *Engaging with Martyn Lloyd-Jones: The Life and Legacy of "the Doctor."* Nottingham: Apollos, 2011.

Augustine, Aurelius. *The Works of Aurelius Augustine, Bishop of Hippo.* Translated by Marcus Dods. Edinburgh: T & T Clarke, 1949.

Au, H. Yan. "Grassroots Unity and the Fountain Trust International Conferences: A study of Ecumenism in the Charismatic Renewal." PhD diss., University of Birmingham 2008.

Aulen, Gustav. *Christus Victor: An Historical Study of the Three Main Types of the Idea of the Atonement.* Translated by Albert H. Heber. New York: Macmillan, 1969.

Baille, David. "50 Years of Ministry." http://www.westchurchbangor.org.uk/ magazine/articles/davidbailie.php.

Ballard, Paul, and John Pritchard. *Practical Theology in Action: Christian Thinking in the Service of Church and Society.* London: SPCK, 2006.

Banister, Douglas. *The Word and Power Church.* Grand Rapids: Zondervan, 1999.

Banks, Robert. *Reenvisioning Theological Education: Exploring a Missional Alternative to Current Models.* Grand Rapids: Eerdmans, 1999.

Barker, William. *Puritan Profiles: 54 Contemporaries of the Westminster Assembly.* Fearn, Rosshire: Christian Focus, 1999.

Barkley, John M. *Blackmouth and Dissenter.* Belfast: White Row, 1993.

———. *The Eldership in Irish Presbyterianism.* Belfast: Privately Published, 1963.

———. *Presbyterianism.* Belfast: General Assembly of the Presbyterian Church in Ireland, 1958.

Barrs, James. "Shepherding Movement." In *New Dictionary of Theology,* edited by Sinclair B. Ferguson and David F. Wright. Leicester: InterVarsity, 1988.

Battle, John A. "Spiritual Warfare in Revelation." *The Western Reformed Journal* 5.1 (1998) 14–18.

Baxter, Richard. *The Reformed Pastor.* Basingstoke, England: Pickering and Inglis, 1982.

Beasley-Murray, George R. *Jesus and the Kingdom of God.* Grand Rapids: Eerdmans, 1986.

———. *Transform Your Church, 50 Very Practical Steps.* Leicester: InterVarsity, 2005.

Bebbington, David W. *Evangelicalism in Modern Britian: A History from the 1730s to the 1980s*. London: Unwin Hyman, 1989.
Beckett, David. "Evangelism: The Cinderella of the Church." In *Elim Life*. Carrickfergus: Elim Pentecostal Church in Ireland, 2009.
Belcher, Jim. *Deep Church: A Third Way Beyond Emerging and Traditional*. Downers Grove, IL: InterVarsity, 2009.
Bell, Judith. *Doing Your Research Project: A Guide for First-time Researchers in Education, Health and Social Science*. 4th ed. Maidenhead: Open University, 2009.
Bell, Rob. *Love Wins: At the Heart of Life's Big Questions*. London: Collins, 2011.
Benn, Wallace, and Mark Burkhill. "Power Evangelism." http://www.fows.org/index.php?option=com_content&view=article&id=57:power-evangelism&catid=40:orthos-archive&Itemid=59.
———. "A Theological and Pastoral Critique of the Teaching of John Wimber." 101.2 *Churchman* (1987) 101–13.
Bennett, Denis, and Rita Bennett. *The Holy Spirit and You*. London: Coverdale, 1974.
Beougher, Timothy K. *Richard Baxter and Conversion: A Study of the Puritan Concept of Becoming a Christian*. Fearn: Christian Focus, 2007.
Berding, Kenneth. *What are Spiritual Gifts: Rethinking the Conventional View*. Grand Rapids: Kregel, 2006.
Berends, Willem. "Prophecy in the Reformed Tradition." *Vox Reformata* 60 (1995) 30–43.
Blauw, Johannes. *The Missionary Nature of the Church: A Survey of the Biblical Theology of Mission*. Cambridge: Lutterworth, 2003.
Blomberg, Craig L. "A Response to G.R. Beasley-Murray on the Kingdom." *Journal of the Evangelical Theological Society* 35.1 (1992) 31–36.
Bloesch, Donald G. *The Church: Sacraments, Worship, Ministry, Mission*. Downers Grove, IL: InterVarsity, 2002.
———. *The Holy Spirit: Works and Gifts*. Downers Grove, IL: InterVarsity, 2000.
Boettner, Loraine. *The Millennium*. Philadelphia, PA: The Presbyterian and Reformed, 1964.
Boice, James Montgomery. *Foundations of the Christian Faith: A Comprehensive and Readable Theology*. Downers Grove, IL: InterVarsity, 1986.
Bonhoeffer, Dietrich. *The Cost of Discipleship*. London: SCM, 2010.
Bonome, Jonathan G. *Incarnation and Sacrament: The Eucharistic Controversy between Charles Hodge and John Williamson Nevin*. Eugene, OR: Wipf and Stock, 2010.
Bosch, David J. *Transforming Mission: Paradigm Shifts in Theology of Mission*. Maryknoll, NY: Orbis, 1998.
Boyce, Harold. *Personal Evangelism for Presbyterians*. Belfast, Northern Ireland: Board of Mission in Ireland, Presbyterian Church in Ireland.
Bradford, Brick. *Releasing the Power of the Holy Spirit*. Oklahoma City, OK: Presbyterian Charismatic Communion, 1983.
Branaugh, Matt. "Willow Creek's Huge Shift, Influential Mega Church Moves Away from Seeker Sensitive Services." *Christianity Today*, May 15, 2008. http://www.christianitytoday.com/ct/2008/june/5.13.html.
Bridge, Donald. *Power Evangelism and the Word of God*. Eastbourne: Kingsway, 1987.
Bridge, Donald, and David Phypers. *Spiritual Gifts and the Church*. Fearn: Christian Focus, 1995.
Brown, Raymond. *Four Spiritual Giants*. Eastbourne: Kingsway, 1997.

Brown, Steve. *Follow the Wind: Our Lord the Holy Spirit.* Grand Rapids: Baker, 1999.
Browning, Don S. *A Fundamental Practical Theology: Descriptive and Strategic Proposals.* Minneapolis, MN: Fortress, 1996.
Brueggemann, Walter. *Biblical Perspectives on Evangelism: Living in a Three Storied Universe.* Nashville: Abingdon, 1993.
Bryant, Christopher. *Reclaiming the Ground.* London: Hodder and Stoughton, 1993.
Budgen, Victor. *The Charismatics and the Word of God: A Biblical and Historical Perspective on the Charismatic Movement.* Darlington: Evangelical, 2001.
Bugbee, Bruce. *What You Do Best in the Body of Christ: Discover Your Spiritual Gifts, Personal Style and God Given Passion.* Grand Rapids: Zondervan, 2005.
Bullock, Warren D. *When the Spirit Speaks: Making Sense of Tongues, Interpretation and Prophecy.* Springfield, MO: Gospel, 2009.
Bultmann, Rudolph. *Kerygma and Myth: A Theological Debate,* edited by H. W. Bartsch. New York: Harper and Row, 1961.
Bundschuh, Rick. *The Church.* Ventura, CA: Regal, 1988.
Bundy, David. "The Ecumenical Quest of Pentecostalism." *Cyberjournal for Pentecostal-Charismatic Research.* http://www.pctii.org/cyberj/cyberj5/ bundy.html.
Bunyan, John. *The Works of John Bunyan, Vol. 2: Experimental, Doctrinal and Practical.* Edited by G. Offor. Edinburgh: The Banner of Truth Trust, 1991.
Burgess, Gary B., et al. *Dictionary of Pentecostal and Charismatic Movements.* Grand Rapids: Zondervan, 1988.
Buschart, W. David. *Exploring Protestant Traditions: An Invitation to Theological Hospitality.* Downers Grove, IL: InterVarsity, 2006.
Cain, Paul, and R. T. Kendall. *The Word and the Spirit.* Eastbourne: Kingsway, 1996.
Calhoun, David B. "Prayer: 'The Chief Exercise of Faith.'" In *A Theological Guide to Calvin's Institutes: Essays and Analysis,* edited by D. W. Hall and P. A. Lillback. Phillipsburgh, NJ: P & R, 2008.
Calian, C. Sydney. "Building a Visionary Church: An Organisational Theology for the Congregation." *Theology Today* 52.4 (1996) 485–94.
Calvin, John. *Institutes of the Christian Religion.* Vol. 2. Translated by H. Beveridge. Grand Rapids: Eerdmans, 1957.
Camp, Lee C. *Mere Discipleship: Radical Christianity in a Rebellious World.* Grand Rapids: Brazos, 2008.
Carnduff, David. *Ireland's Lost Heritage.* Newtownards: Irish Pentecostal Bible College, 2003.
Carson, D. A. "Common Errors in Understanding the Kingdom of God." *Evangelicals Now.* May 2008. http://www.e-n.org.uk/p-4197-Common-errors-in-understanding-the- Kingdom.htm.
———. *Showing the Spirit: A Theological Exposition of 1 Corinthians, 12–14.* Grand Rapids: Baker, 1996.
———. *Worship by the Book.* Grand Rapids: Zondervan, 2002.
Carter, Craig A. "Beyond Theocracy and Individualism: The Significance of John Howard Yoder's Ecclesiology for Evangelicalism." In *The Community of the Word: Toward an Evangelical Ecclesiology,* edited by Mark Husbands and Daniel J. Trier. Downers Grove, IL: InterVarsity, 2005.
Cartledge, Mark J. *Encountering the Spirit: The Charismatic Tradition.* London: Darton, Longman and Todd, 2006.

———. *Speaking in Tongues: Multi-Disciplinary Perspective*. Edited by M. J. Cartledge. Milton Keynes: Paternoster, 2006.

The Catechism of the Catholic Church. New York: Doubleday, 1995.

Catherwood, Christopher. *The Evangelicals: What they Believe, Where they Are, and their Politics*. Wheaton, IL: Crossway, 2010.

Chafter, Louis S., *Systematic Theology: An Unabridged, Original Study of Systematic Theology from a Biblical Viewpoint—Evangelical, Premillennial and Dispensational*, Vol. 7. Dallas: Dallas Theological Seminary, 1948.

———. *Grace: The Glorious Theme*. Grand Rapids: Zondervan, 1950.

Chalke, Steve, and Alan Mann. *Intelligent Church: A Journey toward Christ-Centered Community*. Grand Rapids: Zondervan, 2006.

———. *The Lost Message of Jesus*. Grand Rapids: Zondervan, 2003.

Chambers, Calvin H. *In Spirit and in Truth: Charismatic Worship and the Reformed Tradition*. Ardmore, PA: Dorrance, 1974.

Chandler, Matt. *The Explicit Gospel*. Nottingham: InterVarsity, 2012.

Chantry, Walter J. *Today's Gospel, Authentic or Synthetic?* Edinburgh: The Banner of Truth Trust, 1989.

———. *Signs of the Apostles: Observations on Pentecostalism Old and New*. Edinburgh: Banner of Truth Trust, 1993.

Chappell, Bryan. *Holiness by Grace: Delighting in the Joy that is our Strength*. Wheaton, IL: Crossway, 2001.

———. *The Wonder of it All: Rediscovering the Treasures of Your Faith*. Wheaton, IL: Crossway, 1999.

Charry, Ellen T. "Sacraments for the Christian Life." *Christian Century* (1995) 1076–79.

Chester, Tim, and Steve Timmis. *Total Church: A Radical Reshaping around Gospel and Community*. Leicester: InterVarsity, 2007.

Church Going in the UK, A Research Report from Tearfund on Church Attendance in the UK. Teddington: Tearfund, 2007.

Clark, David. *Breaking the Mould of Christendom: Kingdom Community, Diaconal Church and the Liberation of the Laity*. Peterborough: Epworth, 2005.

Clarke, R. Scott, "Letter and Spirit: Law and Gospel in Reformed Tradition." *Covenant, Justification, and Pastoral Ministry, Essays by the Faculty of Westminster Seminary California*. Phillipsburg, NJ: P & R, 2007.

———. "Who Should go to Seminary? Part 1." *The Heidel Blog*. August 12, 2008. http://heidelblog.wordpress,com/2008/08/12/who-should-go-to- seminary-1/.

———. "Who Should go to Seminary? Part 2." *The Heidel Blog*. August 13, 2008. http://heidelblog.wordpress.com/2008/08/13/who-should-got-to- seminary-s/.

Clowney, Edmund P. *The Church: Contours of Christian Theology*. Leicester: InterVarsity, 1995.

The Code: The Book of the Constitution and Government of the Presbyterian Church in Ireland. Belfast: Authority of the General Assembly, 2010.

Coggins, James R. *Wonders and the Word: An Examination of the Issues Raised by John Wimber and the Vineyard Movement*. Winnipeg: Kindred, 1989.

Coggins, James R., and Paul G. Hiebert. *Wonders and the Word: An Examination of Issues Raised by John Wimber and the Vineyard Movement*. Winnipeg, MB: Kindred, 1989.

Cohen, Louis, et al. *Research Methods in Education*, 5th ed. New York: Routledge, 2005.

Coles, Malcolm. *I Will Build My Church: The Story of the Congregational Union of Ireland 1829–1979*. Privately Published: 1979.

Conn, Harvie M. *Evangelism, Doing Justice and Preaching Grace*. Phillipsburg, NJ: P & R, 1982.

———. *Practical Theology and the Ministry of the Church, 1952–1984, Essays in Honour of Edmund P. Clowney*. Phillipsburg, NJ: P & R, 1990.

Cox, Harvie. *Fire from Heaven: The Rise of Pentecostal Spirituality and the Reshaping of Religion in the Twenty-first Century*. London: Cassell, 1996.

Craston, Colin. "Pastoral Implications of the Charismatic Movement." *Modern Churchman* 27.2 (1985) 26–38.

Creswell, John W. *Research Design: Qualitative, Quantitative, and Mixed Methods Approaches*. Los Angeles: Sage, 2009.

Crooks, Rodger M. *Salvation's Sign and Seal: What do Paedobaptists Really Believe?* Fearn: Christian Focus, 1997.

Crozier, Maurna. *Cultural Traditions in Northern Ireland*. Belfast: Queen's University of Belfast, 1991.

Dale, George M. *The Reformed Book of Common Order*. Edinburgh: National Church Association of the Church of Scotland, 1988.

Dallimore, Arnold. *The Life of Edward Irving: The Fore-Runner of the Charismatic Movement*. Edinburgh: Banner of Truth Trust, 1983.

Dart, John. "Charismatic and Mainline." *The Christian Century*, March 7, 2006. http://www.religion-online.org/showarticle.asp?title=3325.

Davies, Richard E. *Handbook for Doctor of Ministry Projects: An Approach to Structured Observation in Ministry*. Lanham, New York, London: University of America, 1984.

Dawn, Marva J. *Reaching Out Without Dumbing Down: A Theology of Worship for this Urgent Time*. Grand Rapids: Eerdmans, 1995.

Dayton, Donald W. *Theological Roots of Pentecostalism*. Grand Rapids: Hendrickson, 1987.

Deen, Lee A. "Do Evangelicals have an Image Problem? 'Manifesto' Reaffirms Doctrine and Calls for Removing Cultural and Political Baggage." *Christian Research Journal* 31.5 (2008) 1–5.

Deere, Jack. *Surprised by the Power of the Spirit*. Eastbourne: Kingsway, 1993.

———. *Surprised by the Voice of God: How God Speaks to us Today*. Eastbourne: Kingsway, 1996.

———. "The Vineyard's Response to the Briefing." In *Vineyard Position Paper 2*. Anaheim, CA: The Association of Vineyard Churches, 1993.

Dempster, M. W. "The Search for Pentecostal Identity." *Pneuma* 15.1 (1993) 1–8.

Devenish, Dave. *What on Earth is the Church For? A Blueprint for the Future for Church Based Mission and Social Involvement*. Milton Keynes: Authentic Media, 2005.

Dever, Mark. *Nine Marks of a Healthy Church*. Wheaton, IL: Crossway, 2004.

Dever, Mark, and Paul Alexander. *The Deliberate Church: Building your Ministry on the Gospel*. Wheaton, IL: Crossway, 2005.

Dickinson, John. *Presbyterian Herald*. Belfast: Presbyterian Church in Ireland, 2009.

Dickinson, Robert. *God Does Heal Today*. Carlisle: Paternoster, 1995.

Dickson, David. *The Elder and his Work*. Phillipsburg, NJ: P & R, 2004.

"Doctrine Committee Report." *Annual Reports, General Assembly of the Presbyterian Church in Ireland, 1983, Sitting in Dublin*. Belfast: Church House, 1983.

"Doctrine Committee Report." *Annual Reports, General Assembly of the Presbyterian Church in Ireland, 1988, Sitting in Belfast.* Belfast: Church House, 1988.

Dodson, Jonathan K. and Matt Chandler. *Gospel Centered Discipleship.* Wheaton, IL: Crossway, 2012.

Donnelly, Edward. "Richard Baxter—A Corrective for Reformed Preachers." *The Banner of Truth Magazine* 166.7 (1977) 1–7.

Douglass, Phillip D. *What is Your Church's Personality, Discovering and Developing the Ministry Style of Your Church.* Phillipsburg, NJ: P & R, 2008.

Downes, Martin. "Review Article: Select Works of Dr. Martyn Lloyd-Jones." *Themelios* 25.1 (1999) 1–9.

Doyle, Robert. *Signs and Wonders and Evangelicals: A Response to the Teaching of John Wimber.* Homebust West NSW: Lancer, 1987.

Drane, John. *The McDonaldization of the Church, Spirituality, Creativity and the Future of the Church.* London: Darton, Longman, and Todd, 2000.

Driscoll, Mark. *Confessions of a Reformission Rev.: Hard Lessons from an Emerging Missional Church.* Grand Rapids: Zondervan, 2006.

———. *The Radical Reformission: Reaching Out Without Selling Out.* Grand Rapids: Zondervan, 2004.

Dunahoo, Charles H. *Making Kingdom Disciples: A New Framework.* Phillipsburg, NJ: P & R, 2005.

Duncan, Ligon. *The Westminster Confession into the 21st Century.* Vol.1. Fearn: Christian Focus, 2003.

Dunlop, John. *A Precarious Belonging: Presbyterians and the Conflict in Ireland.* Belfast: The Blackstaff, 1995.

Dunlop, Robert. *Evangelicals in Ireland: An Introduction.* Dublin: Columba, 2004.

Dunn, James D. G. *Jesus and the Spirit.* London: SCM, 1975.

———. *The Theology of the Apostle Paul.* Grand Rapids: Eerdmans, 2006.

Duriez, Colin. *Francis Schaeffer: An Authentic Life.* Nottingham: InterVarsity, 2008.

Edgar, William. *The Truth in all its Glory: Commending the Reformed Faith.* Phillipsburg, NJ: P & R, 2004.

Edwards, Jonathan. "Jonathan Edwards." In *Dictionary of the Presbyterian and Reformed Traidiotn in America*, edited by D. G. Hart and M.A. Noll. Phillipsburg, NJ: P & R, 2005.

———. "Sinners in the Hands of an Angry God." http://www.jesus-is- lord.com/sinners.htm.

———. *The Works of Jonathan Edwards.* Vol. 2. Carlisle, PA: Banner of Truth Trust, 1979.

Ellis, Ian M. *Vision and Reality: A Survey of Twentieth Century Irish Inter-Church Relations.* Belfast: The Institute for Irish Studies, The Queen's University of Belfast, 1992.

Engelsma, David J. *Try the Spirits—A Reformed Look at Pentecostalism.* South Holland, IL: South Holland Protestant Reformed Church, 1998.

England, Edward, ed. *Living in the Light of Pentecost: A Selection from Renewal Magazine, 1966–1990.* Bury St. Edmunds: Highland, 1990.

Eyers, Lawrence C. *The Elders of the Church.* Phillipsburg, NJ: P & R, 1979.

Fabricus, Kenneth. "Ten Propositions on being a Theologian." *Faith and Theology.* March 28, 2007. http:// www.faith-theology.com/2007/03/ten-propositions-on-being- theologian.html.

Farley, William P. "John Bunyan: The Faithful Tinker from Bedford." *Enrichment* (2004) 92.

Fee, Gordon D. *The First Epistle to the Corinthians*. New International Commentary on the New Testament. Grand Rapids: Eerdmans, 1987.

———. *God's Empowering Presence: The Holy Spirit in the Letters of Paul*. Grand Rapids: Baker, 2009.

Ferguson, Sinclair B., and David F. Wright. *The Holy Spirit*. Leicester: InterVarsity, 1996.

———. *New Dictionary of Theology*. Leicester: InterVarsity, 1988.

Fernando, Ajith. *Crucial Questions About Hell*. Eastbourne: Kingsway, 1991.

———. *Jesus Driven Ministry*. Leicester: InterVarsity, 2002.

Firm Foundations: A Faith for Today's Church—A Study Manual on the Westminster Confession of Faith. Belfast: Board of Evangelism and Christian Training, The Presbyterian Church in Ireland, 1994.

Flynn, Thomas. *The Charismatic Renewal and the Irish Experience*. London: Hodder and Stoughton, 1974.

Fosdick, Harry E. *The Modern Use of the Bible*. London: SCM, 1924.

———. "Shall the Fundamentalists Win?" In *A Preaching Ministry: Twenty-One Sermons Preached by Harry Emerson Fosdick at the First Presbyterian Church in the City of New York, 1918–1925*, edited by David Pultz. New York: The First Presbyterian Church in the City of New York, 2000.

Fowler-White, R. "Contrary to What You May Have Heard: On the Rhetoric and Reality of Claims of Continuing Revelation." In *Whatever Happened to the Reformation?* edited by Gary L. W. Johnson and R. Fowler White. Phillipsburg, NJ: P & R, 2001.

Frame, John. *The Doctrine of the Knowledge of God: A Theology of Lordship*. Phillipsburg, NJ: P & R, 1987.

Franke, John R. *The Character of Theology: A Postconservative Evangelical Approach*. Grand Rapids: Baker, 2005.

Friesen, Albert. "Wimber, Word and Spirit." In *Wonders and the Word: An Examination of the Issues Raised by John Wimber and the Vineyard Movement*. Winnipeg, Canada: Kindred, 1989.

Frost, Michael, and Alan Hirsch. *The Shaping of Things to Come, Innovation and Mission for the 21st Century Church*. Peabody, MA: Hendrickson, 2003.

Fyall, Robert S. *Charismatic and Reformed*. Edinburgh: Rutherford House and the Handsel, 1992.

Gaffin, Richard B., Jr. "Challenges of the Charismatic Movement to the Reformed Tradition." *Ordained Servant* 7.3 (1998) 69–74.

———. *Perspectives on Pentecost: New Testament Teaching on the Gifts of the Holy Spirit*. Phillipsburg, NJ: P & R, 1979.

Gaffin, Robert B. and R. Fowler-White. "Eclipsing the Canon? The Spirit, the Word, and "Revelations of the Third Kind." *Whatever Happened to the Reformation*, Johnson, Gary L. W. and Fowler White, R. Phillipsburg, NJ: P & R, 2001.

Gee, Donald. *Concerning Spiritual Gifts*. Springfield, MO: Gospel, 1972.

Gentry, Kenneth L. *The Charismatic Gift of Prophecy: A Reformed Response to Wayne Grudem*. Eugene, OR: Wipf and Stock, 1989.

Gerrish, B. A. "Tradition in the Modern World: The Reformed Habit of Mind." http://Reformedtheology.org/SiteFiles/GerrishArticle.html.

Gerstner, John H. *The Rational Biblical Theology of Jonathan Edwards*. Vol. 2. Orlando, FL: Ligonier Ministries, 1991.

———. *Repent or Perish*. Ligonier, PA: Soli Deo Gloria, 1990.
Gibb, David. "Look Back in Wonder? Reviewing the Power Evangelism of John Wimber." *Vox Evangelica* 26 (1996) 23–42.
Gibbs, Eddie, and Ian Coffey. *Church Next, Quantum Changes in Christian Ministry*. Leicester: InterVarsity, 2001.
———. "John Wimber: A Friend who Causes me to Wonder." In *Living in the Light of Pentecost: A Selection from Renewal Magazine, 1966–1990*, edited by Edward England. St. Edmunds: Highland, 1990.
Giberson, Karl W., and Randall J. Stephens. "The Evangelical Rejection of Reason." *New York Times*, October 17, 2011.
Gibson, Andrew. "The Charismatic Movement in Northern Ireland against the background of the Troubles, the Charismatic Movement World-wide and a Selection of Movements of Enthusiasm throughout the History of the Church." MTh diss., The Queen's University of Belfast, 1987.
Gill, Robin. "The Future of Practical Theology." *Contact* 1 (1977) 17–22.
Gilley, Sheriden, and Brian Stanley. *The Cambridge History of Christianity: World Christianities, c. 1814–c.1914*. Cambridge: Cambridge University Press, 2006.
Gillquist, Peter E. *Becoming Orthodox: A Journey to the Ancient Christian Faith*. Ben Lomond, CA: Conciliar, 1990.
———. *Coming Home: Why Protestant Clergy are Becoming Orthodox*. Ben Lomond, CA: Conciliar, 1995.
Glenn, Alfred A. "Rudolf Bultmann: Removing the False Offense." *Journal of the Evangelical Theological Society* 16.2 (1973) 73–81.
Godfrey, William R. *John Calvin: Pilgrim and Pastor*. Phillipsburg, NJ: P & R, 2009.
Goligher, Liam. *The Fellowship of the King: The Quest for Community and Purpose*. Carlisle: Authentic Media, 2003.
Goodwin, John. *Wimber the Gnostic: Testing the Fruit of the Vineyards*. Cambridge: St. Matthew, 1997.
Gore, Robert J., Jr. *Covenantal Worship: Reconsidering the Puritan Regulative Principle*. Phillipsburg, NJ: P & R, 2002.
Greaves, Richard. "A Tinker's Dissent, A Pilgrim's Conscience." *Christian History* 5.3 (1986) 232–33.
Green, Lynn, and Chris Forster. *Small Church: Big Vision, How Your Church can Change the World*. London: Marshall Pickering, 1995.
Green, Michael. *I Believe in the Holy Spirit*. London: Hodder and Stoughton, 1975.
Greenway, Roger S. *Go and Make Disciples: An Introduction to Christian Missions*. Phillipsburg, NJ: P & R, 1999.
Gregson, Timothy H. "Renewal for the Called-out Ones." *New Horizons* (1989).
Greig, Gary, S. "The Purpose of Signs and Wonders in the New Testament: What Terms for Miraculous Power Denote and Their Relationship to the Gospel." In *The Kingdom and the Power, Are Healing and the Spiritual Gifts used by Jesus and the Early Church Meant for the Church Today?* edited by Gary S. Grieg and Kevin N. Springer. Venture, CA: Regal, 1993.
Grenz, Stanley J. *Renewing the Center: Evangelical Theology in a Post-Theological Era*. Grand Rapids: Baker, 2000.
Gribben, Crawford, and Andrew R. Holmes. *Protestantism Millennialism, Evangelicalism and Irish Society, 1790- 2005*. Basingstoke: Palgrave McMillan, 2006.

Grooves, John. "Spiritual Authority in the Church." *New Frontiers*. October 2007. http:// newfrontierstogether.org/Groups/101198/Newfrontiers/Resources/Articles_and_Papers/Theological_Papers/Spiritual_Authority_in_the/ Spiritual_Authority_in_the.aspx.

Grudem, Wayne. *Are Miraculous Gifts for Today?: Four Views*. Leicester: InterVarsity, 1996.

———. *The Gift of Prophecy in the New Testament and Today*. Eastbourne: Kingsway, 1992.

———. "Power and Truth: A Response to the Critiques of Vineyard Teaching and Practice by D. A. Carson, James Montgomery Boice, and John H. Armstrong in Power Religion." In *Vineyard Position Paper 4*. Anaheim, CA: Association of Vineyard Churches, 1993.

———. *Systematic Theology: An Introduction to Biblical Doctrine*. Grand Rapids: Zondervan, 1994.

Gunstone, John. *Meeting John Wimber*. Crowborough: Monarch, 1996.

Hacking, Kenneth J. *Signs and Wonders Then and Now: Miracle-working, Commissioning and Discipleship*. Nottingham: Apollos, 2006.

Hall, David W. *The Legacy of John Calvin: His Influence on the Modern World*. Phillipsburg, NJ: P & R, 2008.

———, ed. *The Practice of Confessional Subscription*. Lanham, MD: University Press of America, 2001.

Hall, David W., and Peter A. Lillback. *A Theological Guide to Calvin's Institutes: Essays and Analysis*. Phillipsburgh, NJ: P & R, 2008.

Hamilton, Barry W. "Interpretative Interactionism for Ministry-Based Research." http://acc.roberts.edu/NEmployees/Hamilton_Barry/ Interpretive.Interactionism.htm.

———. "Introduction to Action Research." http://acc.roberts.edu/ NEmployees/Hamilton_Barry/INTRODUCTION.htm.

———. "Writing the "Good" Doctor of Ministry Thesis." http://acc.roberts.edu/NEmployees/Hamilton_Barry/GOOD.THESIS.htm/.

Hamilton, Ian. *The Erosion of Calvinist Orthodoxy: Drifting from the Truth in Confessional Scottish Churches*. Fearn: Christian Focus, 2010.

Hamilton, Thomas. *The History of Presbyterianism in Ireland*. Belfast: Ambassador, 1992.

Hanh, Scott and K. *Rome Sweet Rome: Our Journey to Catholicism*. San Francisco: Ignatius, 1993.

Harper, Brad, and Paul L. Metzger. *Exploring Ecclesiology: An Evangelical and Ecumenical Introduction*. Grand Rapids: Brazos, 2009.

Harper, Michael. *Three Sisters: A Provocative Look at Evangelicals, Charismatics and Catholic Charismatics and their Relationship to One Another*. Wheaton, IL: Tyndale, 1979.

Hart, D. G. *Defending the Faith: J. Gresham Machen and the Crisis of Conservative Protestantism in Modern America*. Phillipsburg, NJ: P & R, 1994.

———. *J. Gresham Machen: Selected Shorter Writings*. Phillipsburg, NJ: P & R, 2004.

———. *John Williamson Nevin: High Church Calvinist*. Phillipsburg, NJ: P & R, 2005.

———. *Recovering Mother Kirk: The Case for Liturgy in the Reformed Tradition*. Grand Rapids: Baker, 2003.

Hart, D. G., and John R. Muether. *With Reverence and Awe: Returning to the Basics of Reformed Worship*. Phillipsburg, NJ: P & R, 2002.

Hart, D. G., and Mark A. Noll. *Dictionary of the Presbyterian and Reformed Tradition in America.* Phillipsburg, NJ: P & R, 2005.

Harvey, John D. *Anointed with the Spirit and Power: The Holy Spirit's Empowering Presence.* Phillipsburg, NJ: P & R, 2008.

Haywood, David. "A New Paradigm for Theological Education?" *Anvil* 17.1 (2000) 19–27.

Hedlund, Roger E. *The Mission of the Church in the World: A Biblical Theology.* Grand Rapids: Baker, 1991.

Heiser, Michael. "Monotheism, Polytheism, Monolatry, or Henotheism? Toward an Assessment of Divine Plurality in the Hebrew Bible." *Bulletin for Biblical Research* 18.1 (2008) 1–30.

Henderson, Gordon D. *Presbyterianism.* Aberdeen: The University Press, 1954.

Herman, Arthur. *The Scottish Enlightenment, The Scot's Invention of the Modern World.* New York: Harper Perennial, 2001.

Hilborn, David. *Charismatic Renewal in Britain: Roots, Influences and Later Developments.* Bridgewater: Group for Evangelism and Renewal, 2011.

———. "Evangelicalism—A Brief Introduction." *Evangelical Alliance Position Papers.* London: Evangelical Alliance, undated.

Hirsch, Alan, and Deborah Hirsch. *Untamed: Reactivating a Missional Form of Discipleship.* Grand Rapids: Baker, 2010.

Hocken, Peter. *Streams of Renewal: The Origins and Early Development of the Charismatic Movement in Great Britain.* Carlisle: Paternoster, 1997.

Hodge, A. A. *The Confession of Faith.* Edinburgh: Banner of Truth Trust, 1998.

Hodge, Charles. *Systematic Theology,* Vol.1. Grand Rapids: Eerdmans, 1993.

Hodges, Zane C. *The Gospel Under Siege: A Study on Faith and Works.* Dallas, TX: Rendecion Viva, 1981.

Hollenweger, Walter J. *The Pentecostals.* London: SCM, 1976.

Holmes, Andrew. "The Experience and Understanding of Religious Revival in Ulster Presbyterianism, c. 1800–1930." *Irish Historical Studies* 34.136 (2005) 215–30.

Holmes, Findlay. *Our Irish Presbyterian Heritage.* Belfast: Publications Committee of the Presbyterian Church in Ireland, 1985.

———. *The Presbyterian Church in Ireland: A Popular History.* Dublin: Columba, 2000.

Holmer, Findlay, and Ernest Dunlop. *The Union of Synods in the Context of Mid-Antrim.* Ballymena: Mid-Antrim Historical Group, 1990.

Hope, Susan. *Mission Shaped Spirituality: The Transforming Power of Mission.* London: Church House, 2006.

Horton, Harold. *The Gifts of the Spirit.* Springfield, MO: Gospel, 1975.

Horton, Michael. *People and Place: A Covenant Ecclesiology.* Louisville, KY: Westminster John Knox, 2008.

———. *Putting Amazing Back into Grace: Embracing the Heart of the Gospel.* Grand Rapids: Baker, 2002.

———. "Semper Reformanda." *Ligonier Ministries.* http://www.ligonier.org/learn/articles/ semper-reformanda/.

———. *Where in the Word is the Church? A Christian View of Culture and Your Role in it.* Phillipsburg, NJ: P & R, 2002.

Hosier, John E. *The End Times.* London: Monarch, 2000.

Hugher, R. Kent. *Set Apart: Calling a Worldly Church to a Godly Life.* Wheaton, IL: Crossway, 2003.

Hull, Bill. *The Disciple Making Church*. Grand Rapids: Revell, 1998.

———. *New Century Disciplemaking, Applying Jesus' Ideas for the Future*. Grand Rapids: Revell, 2000.

Hull, John M. *Mission-Shaped Church: A Theological Response*. London: SCM, 2006.

Hunt, Stephen. *The Alpha Enterprise: Evangelism in a Post-Christian Era*. Aldershot: Ashgate, 2004.

———. "The Anglican Wimberites." *Pnuema: The Journal of the Society for Pentecostal Studies* 17.1 (1995) 1–32.

———. "'At the Cutting Edge.' The Theme of Healing in Neo Pentecostalism with Special Reference to the Vineyard Movement and the Faith Ministries in Britain." PhD diss., University of Reading, 1998.

———. "Managing the Demonic: Some Aspects of the Neo-Pentecostal Deliverance Ministry." *Journal of Contemporary Religion* 13.2 (1998) 26–38.

———. "Were the Jesus People Pentecostals?" *PentecoStudies* 7.1 (2008) .

Huntington, Samuel P. "The West, Not Universal." *Foreign Affairs* 75.6 (1996).

Husbands, M., and Daniel J. Trier. *The Community of the Word: Toward an Evangelical Ecclesiology*. Downers Grove, IL: InterVarsity, 2005.

Hybels, Lynn, and Bill Hybels. *Rediscovering Church: The Story and Vision of Willow Creek Community Church*. Grand Rapids: Zondervan, 1995.

The Irish Presbyterian Hymnbook. Trustees of the Presbyterian Church in Ireland, Norwich: Canterbury, 2004.

Irving, Edward. *The Day of Pentecost, or, The Baptism with the Holy Ghost*. Whitefish, MT: Kessinger, 2007.

Jackson, David. *Understanding the Church: Getting Your Congregation to Work*. Fearn: Christian Focus, 1996.

Jackson, Bill. *The Quest for the Radical Middle: A History of the Vineyard*. Cape Town, South Africa: Vineyard International, 1999.

Jenkins, Thomas E. *The Character of God: Recovering the Lost Literary Power of American Protestantism*. Cary, NC: Oxford University Press, 1998.

Jensen, Peter. "Preaching the Word Today." In *Preach the Word: Essays on Expository Preaching in Honour of R. Kent Hughes,* edited by Leyland Ryken and Tom Wilson. Wheaton, IL: Crossway, 2007.

———."John Wimber Changes His Mind." In *John Wimber, Friend or Foe? An Examination of the Current Teaching of the Vineyard Ministries Movement*. Reprinted from *The Briefing*, April 1990. London: St. Matthias, 1990.

Jeseche, Marlin, *Believers Baptism for Children of the Church*. Eugene, OR: Wipf and Stock, 1983.

Johnson, Gary L. W., and R. Fowler White. *Whatever Happened to the Reformation*. Phillipsburg, NJ: P & R, 2001.

Johnson, Terry L. *The Case for Traditional Protestantism: The Solas of the Reformation*. Edinburgh: Banner of Truth Trust, 2004.

———. *When Grace Comes Home: How the Doctrines of Grace Change your Life*. Fearn: Christian Focus, 2009.

Johnstone, Patrick. *The Church is Bigger Than You Think: The Unfinished Work of World Evangelisation*. Fearn: Christian Focus, 1998.

Jones, E. Stanley. *The Unshakable Kingdom and the Changing Person*. Bellingham, WA: McNett, 1995.

Jones, R. Tudur. *The Great Reformation: A Wide Ranging Survey of the Beginnings of Protestantism*. Downers Grove, IL: InterVarsity, 1985.

Kallas, James. *The Real Satan: From Biblical Times to the Present*. Minneapolis, MN: Fortress, 2006.

Kapic, K. M., and J. Taylor, eds. *Overcoming Sin and Temptation: Three Classic Works by John Owen*. Wheaton, IL: Crossway, 2006.

Kay, William K. *Apostolic Networks in Britain: New Ways of Being Church, Studies in Evangelical Thought and History*. Milton Keynes: Paternoster, 2007.

———. *Inside Story: A History of British Assemblies of God*. Mattersey: Mattersey Hall, 1990.

Keenaway, Brian. *The Orange Order: A Tradition Betrayed*. London: Methuen, 2006.

Keller, Timothy. "Advancing the Gospel into the 21st Century." http://www.mtw.org/Pages/InVision/AdvancingtheGospel.aspx.

———. "The Gospel and the Poor." *Themelios, International Journal for Pastors and Students of Theological and Religious Studies* 33:3 (2008).

———. "The Importance of Hell." *Redeemer Presbyterian Church*. http://www.redeemer.com/redeemer-report/article/the_importance_of_hell.

———. *Ministries of Mercy: The Call to the Jericho Road*, 2nd ed. Phillipsburg, NJ: P & R, 1997.

———. "Preaching Hell in a Tolerant Age, Brimstone for the Broadminded." *Dallas Baptist University*. http://www3.dbu.edu/jeanhumphreys/deathdying/preachinghell.htm.

———. *The Prodigal God, Recovering the Heart of the Christian Faith*. London: Hodder and Stoughton, 2008.

———. *The Reason for God, Belief in an Age of Skepticism*. New York: Dutton, 2008.

———. "Redeemer Vision Paper 6—Christians and Culture." New York: Redeemer Presbyterian Church, 2005.

———. "Reformed Worship in the Global City." In *Worship by the Book*, edited by D. A. Carson. Grand Rapids: Zondervan, 2002.

Kendall, R. T. *Once Saved, Always Saved*. Belfast: Ambassador, 1992.

———. *Understanding Theology, Vol. II: The Means of Developing a Healthy Church in the Twenty first Century*. Fearn: Christian Focus, 2000.

Kiberd, Declan. *Inventing Ireland: The Literature of the Modern Nation*. London: Vintage, 1996.

King, Paul L. *Genuine Gold: The Cautiously Charismatic Story of the Early Christian and Missionary Alliance*. Tulsa, OK: Word and Spirit, 2007.

Kraft, Charles H. *Christianity in Culture: A Study in Dynamic Biblical Theologizing in Cross-Cultural Perspective*. Maryknoll, NY: Orbis, 1988.

———. *Christianity with Power: Your Worldview and Your Experience of the Supernatural*. Eugene, OR: Wipf and Stock, 1989.

———. "Culture, Worldview and Contextualisation." In *Perspectives on the World Christian Movement: A Reader*, 4th ed., edited by Ralph D. Winter and Stephen C. Hawthorne. Pasadena, CA: William Carey, 2009.

———. *Defeating Dark Angels: Breaking Demonic Oppression in the Believer's Life*. Ventura, CA: Regal, 1992.

———. "Interpreting in Cultural Context." *Journal of the Evangelical Theological Society* 21.4 (1978) 357–67.

———. *Two Hours to Freedom: A Simple and Effective Model for Healing and Deliverance*, Grand Rapids: Chosen, 2010.

Kraft, C. H., and M. G. Craft. "Communicating and Ministerign the Power of the gospel Cross Culturally: The Power of God for Christians who Ride Two Horses." In *The Kingdom and Power: Are Healing and the Spiritual Gifts used by Jesus and the Early Church Meant for the Church Today?* Edited by G. S. Grieg and K. N. Springer. Ventura, CA: Regal, 1993.

Krallmann, Gunter. *Mentoring for Mission: A Handbook on Leadership Principles Exemplified by Jesus Christ*. Hong Kong: Jensco, 1992.

Krejcir, Richard J. "Understanding and Developing Christian Accountability." *Church Leadership*, 1994. http://www.churchleadership.org/apps/articles/default.asp?articleid=42506&columnid=4542.

Kuiper, R. B. *God Centered Evangelism*. Edinburgh: Banner of Truth Trust, 1978.

Ladd, George E., *The Gospel of the Kingdom: Scriptural Studies in the Kingdom of God*. Grand Rapids: Eerdmans, 1959.

———. *A Theology of the New Testament*. Cambridge: Lutterworth, 1974.

Laurie, Greg. *The Upside Down Church*. Wheaton, IL: Tyndale, 1999.

Lee, Nigel "The Trouble with Expository Preaching." *Whitefield Briefing* 6.6 (2002).

Lee, Simon. *Freedom from Fear: Churches Together in Northern Ireland*. Belfast: The Institute for Irish Studies, The Queen's University of Belfast, 1990.

Leith, John H. *Introduction to the Reformed Tradition*. Edinburgh: St. Andrew, 1977.

Letham, Robert. *The Westminster Confession of Faith: Reading its Theology in Historical Context*. Phillipsburg, NJ: P & R, 2009.

Lewis, David, M. "An Historians Assessment." In *Wonders and the Word: An Examination of Issues Raised by John Wimber and the Vineyard Movement*. Winnipeg, Canada: Kindred, 1989.

Liethart, Peter J. *The Kingdom and the Power, Rediscovering the Centrality of the Church*. Phillipsburg, NJ: P & R, 1993.

Lim, David. *Spiritual Gifts: A Fresh Look*. Springfield, MO: Gospel, 1991.

———. "An Evangelical Critique of "Initial Evidence" Doctrine." *Asian Journal of Pentecostal Studies* 1.2 (1998) 219–29.

Lloyd-Jones, D. Martyn. *Joy Unspeakable: The Baptism and Gifts of the Holy Spirit*. Eastbourne: Kingsway, 1994.

———. *Preaching and Preachers*. London: Hodder and Stoughton, 1971.

Long, Brad, et al. *Growing the Church in the Power of the Holy Spirit: Seven Principles of Dynamic Co-operation*. Grand Rapids: Zondervan, 2009.

Lord, Andrew. *Spirit Shaped Mission: A Holistic Charismatic Missiology*. Milton Keynes: Paternoster, 2005.

Louie, Jeff. "The Holy Spirit and the Local Church." In *Who's Afraid of the Holy Spirit: An Investigation into the Ministry of the Holy Spirit Today,* edited by D. B. Wallace, B. Daniel, and Mark J. Sawyer. Dallas, TX: Biblical Studies, 2005.

Lovin, Robin. "The Real Task of Practical Theology." *Christian Century* (1992) 125–28.

Lucas, Sean M. *On Being Presbyterian, Our Beliefs, Practices and Stories*. Phillipsburg, NJ: P & R, 2006.

Lunshof, Henry. "Reformed and Charismatic: A Theology and Strategy for a Blend of the Two Streams." DMin diss., Fuller Theological Seminary, 1993.

Lutz, Uli, et al. *Wh-Scope Marking*. Amsterdam, NL: John Benjamin's, 2000.

Lyons, W. John. "The Fourth Wave and the Approaching Millennium: Some Problems With Charismatic Hermeneutics." *Anvil* 15 (1998) 169–80.

MacArthur, John. *Charismatic Chaos*. Grand Rapids: Zondervan, 1992.

———. *The Master's Plan for the Church*. Chicago: Moody, 1991.

———. *Our Sufficiency in Christ: Three Deadly Influences that Undermine your Spiritual Life*. Milton Keynes: Work UK, 1991.

Machen, J.Gresham. "Christian Scholarship and Evangelism." In *J. Gresham Machen: Selected Shorter Writings*, edited by D. G. Hart. Phillipsburg, NJ: P & R, 2004.

———. "Westminster Seminary: Its Purpose and Plan." In *J. Gresham Machen: Selected Shorter Writings*, edited D. G. Hart. Phillipsburg, NJ: P & R, 2004.

Mack, Wayne A., and Dave Swavely. *Life in the Father's House: A Members Guide to the Local Church*. Phillipsburg, NJ: P & R, 2006.

Malone, Fred. *The Baptism of Disciples Alone: A Covenantal Argument for Credobaptism Versus Paedobaptism*. Cape Coral, FL: Founders, 2003.

Mansfield, Stephen. *The Faith of George W. Bush*. Lake Mary, FL: Charisma, 2004.

Marsden, George M. *Reforming Fundamentalism: Fuller Seminary and the New Evangelicalism*. Grand Rapids: Eerdmans, 1987.

Marshall, Colin. *Passing the Baton: A Handbook for Ministry Apprenticeship*. Kingsford, NSW: Matthias Media, 2007.

Marshall, Colin, and Tony Payne. *The Trellis and the Vine: The Ministry Mind- shift that Changes Everything*. Kingsford, NSW: Matthias Media, 2009.

Masters, Peter, and John C. Whitcomb. *The Charismatic Phenomena*. London: Wakeman Trust, 1992.

Mathison, Keith A. *Dispensationalism: Rightly Dividing the People of God*. Phillipsburg, NJ: P & R, 1995.

———. *From Age to Age: The Unfolding of Biblical Eschatology*. Phillipsburg, NJ: P & R, 2009.

———. *Given For You: Reclaiming Calvin's Doctrine of the Lord's Supper*. Phillipsburg, NJ: P & R, 2002.

———. *Postmillennialism: An Eschatology of Hope*. Phillipsburg, NJ: P & R, 2000.

———. "Sola Scriptura." In *After Darkness, Light: Essays in Honour of R.C. Sproul*, edited by R. C. Sproul, Jr. Phillipsburg, NJ: P & R, 2003.

———. *When Shall These Things Be? A Reformed Response to Hyper-Preterism*. Phillipsburg, NJ: P & R, 2004.

McEvoy, Robert K. "What Can We Learn from Richard Baxter of Kidderminster?" MA diss., University of Wales, Lampeter, 2006.

McFarlane, Graham. *Christ and the Spirit: The Doctrine of the Incarnation According to Edward Irving*. Carlisle: Paternoster, 1996.

———. *Edward Irving: The Trinitarian Face of God*. Edinburgh: St. Andrew, 1996.

McGee, Gary B. "Wagner, Charles Peter (1930–)." In *Dictionary of Pentecostal and Charismatic Movements*, edited by Stanley M. Burgess, et al. Grand Rapids: Zondervan.

McGowan, Alister T. B. *Always Reforming: Explorations in Systematic Theology*. Leicester: Apollos, 2006.

McGrath, Alister. *Roots that Refresh: A Celebration of Reformation Spirituality*. London: Hodder and Stoughton, 1991.

McIntyre, John. *The Shape of Pneumatology: Studies in the Doctrine of the Holy Spirit*. London: T & T Clark, 2004.

McKnight, Scott. *The King Jesus Gospel: The Original Good News Revisited*. Grand Rapids: Zondervan, 2011.

———. "The Gospel for iGens." *Leadership Journal* (2009) 20–24.

McLaren, Brian D. *The Church on the Other Side: Doing Ministry in the Post-modern Matrix*. Grand Rapids: Zondervan, 2000.

———. *A Generous Orthodoxy: Why I am a Missional, Evangelical, Post/Protestant, Liberal/Conservative, Mystical Poet, Biblical, Charismatic/Contemplative, Fundamentalist/Calvinist, Anabaptist/ Anglican, Methodist, Catholic, Green, Incarnational, Depressed Yet Hopeful, Emergent, Unfinished Christian*. Grand Rapids: Zondervan, 2004.

———. "Interview with John Buckeridge." *Christianity* (April 2009) http://www.premierchristianity.com/Past-Issues/2009/April-2009/Profile-Brian-McLaren.

Menzies, William W. "The Reformed Roots of Pentecostalism." *PentecoStudies* 6.2 (2007) 78–99.

Merrette, Edwin J. "Company 'Doctors': Do higher academic qualifications make for "better" managers?" PhD diss., University of Birmingham, 2004.

Miller, David W. "Presbyterianism and 'Modernization' in Ulster." *Past & Present* 80 (1978) 66–90.

Miller, Donald. *Blue Like Jazz: Non Religious Thoughts on Christian Spirituality*. Nashville: Thomas Nelson, 2003.

Miller, Donald E. "Routinizing Charisma: The Vineyard Christian Fellowship in the Post-Wimber Era." *Pnuema: The Journal of the Society for Pentecostal Studies* 25.2 (2003) 216–39.

Miller, Samuel. *An Essay on the Warrant, Nature, and Duties of the Ruling Elder in the Presbyterian Church*. Dallas, TX: Presbyterian Heritage, 1987.

Milne, Garnett H. *The Westminster Confession of Faith and the Cessation of Special Revelation: The Majority Puritan Viewpoint on Whether Extra-biblical Prophecy is Still Possible*. Milton Keynes: Paternoster, 2007.

Mitchel, Peter. "Living with Difference: Evangelical Diversity." In *Evangelicals in Ireland: An Introduction*, edited by Robert Dunlop. Dublin: Columba, 2004.

Mittelberg, Mark. *Becoming a Contagious Church, Increasing your Church's Evangelistic Temperature*. Grand Rapids: Zondervan, 2007.

Moltmann, Jurgen. "What is a Theologian?" *The Irish Theological Quarterly* 64 (1999).

Moody, Josh. *The God Centred Life, Insights from Jonathan Edwards for Today*. Leicester: InterVarsity, 2006.

Moore, S. David. *The Shepherding Movement: Controversy and Charismatic Ecclesiology*. New York: T & T Clark, 2003.

Moore, Phil. "A Healthy Theology of Healing." Brighton, England: New Frontiers International.

Moore, Russell D., and Robert E. Sagers. "The Kingdom of God and the Church: A Baptist Reassessment." *Southern Baptist Journal of Theology* (Spring 2008) 66–88.

Moreland, James P. "How Evangelicals Became Over-Committed to the Bible and What can be Done about It." Paper Presented to the Evangelical Theological Society, San Diego: 2007.

Morgan, Mark. "An Interview with Anthony Carter." *By Faith Online: The Web Magazine of the Presbyterian Church in America*, June 20, 2008. http://byfaithonline.com/page/in-the-church/bringing-the-reformation- to- the-african-american-church-an-interview-with-anthony-carter.

Morphew, Derek. "Why Is the Kingdom of God so Important?" http:// www. vineyardchurches.org.uk/uploads/tttf/Why%20Is%20the%20Kingdom%20of%20 God%20so%20Important.pdf.

Morrow, Trevor W. J. "Mission Ireland: A Reformed Perspective." *The Furrow* 38.8 (1987) 498.

Muller, Richard A., and Rowland S. Ward. *Scripture and Worship: Biblical Interpretation and the Directory for Worship*. Phillipsburg, NJ: P & R, 2007.

Murphy, Nancy. *Beyond Liberalism and Fundamentalism: How Modern and Postmodern Philosophy set the Theological Agenda*. Valley Forge, PA: Trinity International, 1996.

Murray, Iain H. *Evangelicalism Divided: A Record of Crucial Change in the Years 1950–2000*. Edinburgh: The Banner of Truth Trust, 2000.

———. *Jonathan Edwards: A New Biography*. Edinburgh, Scotland, Carlisle, PA: The Banner of Truth Trust, 1992.

———. "Openness to the Holy Spirit: How Westminster Chapel Was Turned Around." A review of R. T. Kendall, *In Pursuit of His Glory: My 25 Years at Westminster Chapel*. London: Hodder and Stoughton, 2002. *The Banner of Truth Magazine* 486 (2004).

———. "Will the Unholy be Saved?" *The Banner of Truth Magazine* 246 (1984) 214.

Murray, John. *Christian Baptism*. Phillipsburg, NJ: P & R, 1980.

Naselle, Andrew D. and Colin Hanson. *Four Views on the Spectrum of Evangelicalism*, Grand Rapids: Zondervan, 2011.

Nathan, Richard. "Women in Leadership: How to Decide What the Bible Teaches?" *Joshua House*. http://www.joshuahouse.org/mediafiles/women-in- leadership-paper.pdf.

Nathan, Richard, and Kenneth Wilson. *Empowered Evangelicals: Bringing together the Best of the Evangelical and Charismatic Worlds*. Ann Arbor: Vine, 1995.

Neibuhr, H. Reinhold. *Christ and Culture*. New York: Harper and Row, 1951.

Neuberger, Julia. "Religion, Culture, What's the Difference?" *Cultural Traditions in Northern Ireland*. Crozier, Maurna. Belfast: The Institute for Irish Studies, The Queen's University of Belfast, 1991.

Nevin, John W. *The Mystical Presence: A Vindication of the Reformed or Calvinistic Doctrine of the Holy Eucharist*. Memphis, TN: General, 2010.

Newbigin, Lesslie. *Discovering Truth in a Changing World*. London: Alpha International, 2003.

———. *Living Hope in a Changing World*. London: Alpha International, 2003.

———. *Sin and Salvation*. London: SCM, 1956.

———. "The Pattern of the Ministry in a Missionary Church." October 26, 1961: Unpublished. www.newbigin.net.

Nichols, Stephen J. *J. Gresham Machen: A Guided Tour of his Life and Thought*. Phillipsburg, NJ: P & R, 2004.

Nicole, Roger. "Ecclesiology: Reformed and Reforming." In *Practical Theology and the Ministry of the Church, 1952–1984, Essays in Honour of Edmund P. Clowney*, edited by Harvie M. Conn. Phillipsburg, NJ: P & R, 1990.

Nketia, Joseph H. "The Contribution of African Culture to Christian Worship." *International Review of Mission* 47.187 (1958).

O'Ferrall, Fergus. "Daniel O'Connell and Henry Cooke: The Conflict of Civil and Religious Liberty in Modern Ireland." *The Irish Review* 1 (1986).

O'Riordan, Sean. "Protestantism in Ireland." *The Furrow* 9.2 (1958).
Odgen, Greg. *The New Reformation: Returning the Ministry to the People of God*. Grand Rapids: Zondervan, 1990.
Old, Hughes O. *Worship Reformed According to Scripture*. Louisville, KY: Westminster John Knox, 2003.
Osmer, Richard R. *Practical Theology: An Introduction*. Grand Rapids: Eerdmans, 2008.
Packer, James I. *Amongst God's Giants, The Puritan Vision of the Christian Life*. Eastbourne: Kingsway, 1991.
———. *Fundamentalism and the Word of God: Some Biblical Principles*. Leicester: InterVarsity, 1996.
———. "The Intellectual." *John Wimber: His Influence and Legacy*. Pytches, David. Guilford: Eagle, 1998.
———. *Knowing God*. Downers Grove, IL: InterVarsity, 1973.
———. "The Ministry of the Holy Spirit in Discerning the Will of God." In *Who's Afraid of the Holy Spirit: An Investigation into the Ministry of the Holy Spirit Today*, edited by Daniel B. Wallace and M. James Sawyer. Dallas, TX: Biblical Studies, 2005.
Palmer, Edwin H. *The Holy Spirit: His Person and Ministry*. Phillipsburg, NJ: P & R, 1974.
"Patton Elected as Next Moderator." *Presbyterian Ireland*. http://www.presbyterianireland.org/news/ news2008/news0626.html.
Pawson, David. *Word and Spirit Together: Uniting Charismatics and Evangelicals*. Bradford-on-Avon: Terra Nova, 2007.
Peace, Richard. *Small Group Evangelism: A Training Program for Reaching Out with the Gospel*. Downers Grove, IL: InterVarsity, 1985.
Pearson, Carlton. *The Gospel of Inclusion: Reaching Beyond Religious Fundamentalism to the True Love of God*. Tulsa, OK: Azusa International, 2006.
Percy, Martyn. *Power and the Church: Ecclesiology in an Age of Transition*. London: Cassell, 1998.
Peterson, Eugene H. *The Contemplative Pastor, Returning to the Art of Spiritual Direction*. Grand Rapids: Eerdmans, 1989.
———. *Five Smooth Stones for Pastoral Work*. Grand Rapids: Eerdmans, 1980.
Petts, David. *The Holy Spirit: An Introduction*. Mattersey: Mattersey Hall, 1998.
Pink, Arthur W. *The Sovereignty of God*. Edinburgh: The Banner of Truth Trust, 1993.
Piper, John. *Don't Waste Your Life*. Nottingham: InterVarsity, 2003.
———. "A Passion for Christ-Exalting Power: Martyn Lloyd-Jones on the Need for Revival and Baptism with the Holy Spirit." http://www.desiringgod.org/ resource-library/biographies/a-passion-for- christ-exalting-power.
———. "Signs and Wonders: Then and Now." *Desiring God*, February 1, 1991. http://www.desiringgod.org/ resource-library/articles/signs-and-wonders-then-and-now.
———. *When I Don't Desire God: How to Fight for Joy*. Wheaton, IL: Crossway, 2003.
Plass, Adrian. *An Alien at St. Wilfred's*. Grand Rapids: Zondervan, 1992.
Pointer, Richard W. "New School Presbyterians and Theology." In *Dictionary of the Presbyterian and Reformed Tradition in America*, edited by D. G. Hart and Mark A. Noll. Phillipsburg, NJ: P & R, 2005.
Poloma, Margaret. "Charisma and Institution: The Assemblies of God." *Christian Century*, (October 1990) 932–34.

Pope, Randy. *The Intentional Church: Moving from Church Success to Community Transformation.* Chicago: Moody, 2006.

Poythress, Vernon S. *Symphonic Theology: The Validity of Multiple Perspectives in Theology.* Phillipsburg, NJ: P & R, 1987.

———. *Understanding Dispensationalists.* Phillipsburg, NJ: P & R, 1987.

———. *What are Spiritual Gifts: Basics of the Faith.* Phillipsburg, NJ: P & R, 2010.

Prior, Kenneth. *The Gospel in a Pagan Society.* Fearn: Christian Focus, 1995.

Pultz, David, and J. Barrie Shepherd. *A Preaching Ministry: Twenty-One Sermons Preached by Harry Emerson Fosdick at the First Presbyterian Church in the City of New York, 1918–1925.* New York: First Presbyterian Church in the City of New York, 2000.

Pytches, David. *John Wimber: His Influence and Legacy.* Guilford: Eagle, 1998.

———. "A Man Called John." In *John Wimber: His Influence and Legacy,* edited by David Pytches. Guilford: Eagle, 1998.

Rakestraw, Robert V. "The Power of the Holy Spirit in Your Preaching." Paper presented at the Bethel Seminary Preaching Institute, St. Paul, MN, February 24, 1992. http://www.bethel.edu/~rakrob/Return to Robert V. Rakestraw HomePage.

Reed, Jeff. "Church Based Theological Education: Creating a New Paradigm." Paper presented to the North American Professors of Christian Education, October 17, 1992, http://www.bild.org/download/paradigmPapers/1_Creating%20a%20New%20Paradigm.InHouse.pdf.

Reid, Alvin L. *Introduction to Evangelism.* Nashville: Broadman and Holman, 1998.

———. *Radically Unchurched: Who They Are and How to Reach Them.* Grand Rapids: Kregel, 2002.

Reid, Harry. *Outside Verdict: An Old Kirk in a New Scotland.* Edinburgh: St. Andrew's, 2002.

Reid, Michael S. B. *Strategic Level Spiritual Warfare: A Modern Mythology? A Detailed Evaluation of the Biblical, Theological and Historical Bases of Spiritual Warfare in Contemporary Thought.* Maitland, FL: Xulon, 2002.

Reisgner, Ernest C. *Lord and Christ: The Implications of Lordship for Faith and Life.* Phillipsburg, NJ: P & R, 1994.

Richebacher, Wilhelm, I. "Missio Dei: The Basis of Mission Theology or a Wrong Path?" *International Review of Mission* 92.367 (2009) 588–605.

Riddlebarger, Kim. *A Case for Amillennialism: Understanding the End Times.* Grand Rapids: Baker, 2003.

Ridley, Diana. *The Literature Review: A Step by Step Guide for Students.* Los Angeles: Sage, 2009.

Robertson, O.P. *The Final Word: A Biblical Response to the Case for Tongues and Prophecy Today.* Edinburgh: Banner of Truth Trust, 2004.

———. "The Holy Spirit in the Westminster Confession." In *The Westminster Confession into the Twenty-first Century,* edited by Ligon Duncan. Fearn: Christian Focus, 2003.

Robinson, James. *Pentecostal Origins: Early Pentecostalism in Ireland in the Context of the British Isles.* Milton Keynes: Paternoster, 2005.

Rodman Williams, J. "A Neo Pentecostal Viewpoint." In *Perspectives on the New Pentecostalism,* edited by Russell S. Spittler. Grand Rapids: Baker, 1976.

———. *Renewal Theology.* Vols. 1–3, Grand Rapids: Zondervan, 1988.

Rollins, Peter. *Insurrection: To Believe is Human; to Doubt, Divine*. London: Hodder and Stoughton, 2011.
Rosen, David A., and Nieman, John R. *Church Identity and Change: Theology and Denominational Structures in Unsettled Times*. Grand Rapids: Eerdmans, 2001.
Ross, John. "Aspects of Dr. Martyn Lloyd-Jones' Legacy: Some Personal Observations." *Reformation 21*, March 2010. http://www.reformation21.org/articles/aspects-of-dr-martyn-lloydjones-legacy-some-personal-observations.php.
Roxburgh, Alan J., and M. Scott Boren. *Introducing the Missional Church: What it is, Why it Matters, How to Become One*. Grand Rapids: Baker, 2009.
Ruether, Rosemary R. "Redemptive Community in Christianity." *Buddhist-Christian Studies* 11 (1991) 217–30.
Ruthven, John. *On the Cessation of the Charismata: The Protestant Polemic on Post-Biblical Miracles*. Tulsa, OK: Word and Spirit, 2001.
Ryken, Leiland, and Tom Wilson. *Preach the Word: Essays on Expository Preaching in Honour of R. Kent Hughes*. Wheaton, IL: Crossway, 2007.
Ryken, Phillip G. *City on a Hill, Reclaiming the Biblical Pattern for the Church in the 21st Century*. Chicago: Moody, 2003.
Ryle, John C. *Holiness*. London: Hodder and Stoughton, 1996.
Ryrie, Charles C. *Balancing the Christian Life*. Chicago: Moody, 1994.
———. *Dispensationalism Today*. Chicago: Moody, 1999.
Sargent, Tony. *The Sacred Anointing: The Preaching of Dr. Martyn Lloyd-Jones*. London, Sydney, Auckland: Hodder and Stoughton, 1994.
Savage, Charles, and William Presnell. *Narrative Research in Ministry: A Postmodern Research Approach for Faith Communities*. Louisville, KY: Wayne E. Oates, 2008.
Savelle, Jerry. *If Satan Can't Steal Your Joy, He Can't Keep You Goods*. Tulsa, OK: Harrison, 1994.
Schaeffer, Francis. *The Complete Works of Francis Schaeffer, A Christian Worldview: Volume 5—A Christian View of the West*. Westchester, IL: Crossway, 1982.
Schmidt, John P. "New Wine from the Vineyard." *Direction Journal* 17.2 (1988).
Schneider, Raymond. "C. S. Lewis, Church Unity, and the Dynamics of the Hallway." http://people.bridgewater.edu/~rschneid/Archive/LewisChurchUnityDynamicsOfTheHallway.pdf.
Schweizer, Eduard. *Church Order in the New Testament*. London: SCM, 1961.
Scotland, Nigel, "From the 'not yet' to the 'now and not yet': Charismatic Kingdom Theology 1960–2010." *Journal of Pentecostal Theology* 20 (2011) 272–90.
Selden, Peter. "Spiritual Warfare V: Medical Reflections." In *John Wimber: Friend or Foe? Reprinted from The Briefing, April 1990*. London: St. Matthias, 1990.
Shaw, Robert. *An Exposition of the Westminster Confession of Faith*. Fearn: Christian Focus, 1998.
Shench, Louis B. *The Presbyterian Doctrine of Children in the Covenant: An Historical Study of the Significance of Infant Baptism in the Presbyterian Church*. Phillipsburg, NJ: P & R, 2003.
Shepherd, Norman. *The Call of Grace: How the Covenant Illuminates Salvation and Evangelism*. Phillipsburg, NJ: P & R, 2000.
Siekawitch, Larry D. "Calvin, Spirit, Communion and the Supper." *The Journal of the European Pentecostal Theological Association* 29.2 (2009) 14–35.
Sjogren, Steve. *Conspiracy of Kindness: A Unique Approach to Sharing the Love of Jesus*. Ventura, CA: Regal, 2008.

Skysgaard, K. E. "The Kingdom of God and the Church." *Scottish Journal of Theology* 4 (1951) 383–97.

Smail, Tom A. *Reflected Glory: The Spirit in Christ and Christians*. London: Hodder and Stoughton, 1977.

———. "A Renewal Recalled." In *Charismatic Renewal*, edited by Tom Smail, et al. London: SPCK, 1995.

Smail, Tom, et al. *Charismatic Renewal*. London: SPCK, 1995.

Smallman, Stephen. *What is Discipleship: Basics of the Faith Series*. Phillipsburg, NJ: P & R, 2011.

Smedes, Louis B. *Ministry and the Miraculous: A Case Study at Fuller Theological Seminary*. Pasadena, CA: Fuller Seminary, 1992.

Smith, Chuck. *Harvest: The Phenomenal Growth of a Church that Showed Love Where No-One Else Wanted to Know*. Eastbourne: Kingsway, 1987.

Smith, David. *Mission After Christendom*. London: Darton, Longman and Todd, 2003.

Smith, Dean R. "The "Charismatic" Scottish Presbyterians and Covenanters." Paper presented at the Evangelical Theological Society, 1996.

Smith, Gerald B. *Practical Theology: A Neglected Field in Theological Education*. Charleston, SC: Biblolife, 2010.

Smith, James K. A. "Teaching a Calvinist to Dance: In Pentecostal Worship My Reformed Theology Finds its Groove." *Christianity Today*, May 2008. http://www.christianitytoday.com/ct/2008/may/25.42.html.

Smith, Paul. *Foundations of the Faith, The Westminster Confession of Faith: Enjoying God Forever*. Chicago: Moody, 1998.

Snyder, Howard A. *The Community of the King*. Downers Grove, IL: InterVarsity, 1978.

Solomon, Robert C. "Preface." In *Existentialism*. Columbus, OH: McGraw-Hill Higher Education, 1974.

Spear, Wayne R. "Word and Spirit in the Westminster Confession." *The Westminster Confession into the 21st Century*. Vol. 1. Fearn: Christian Focus, 2003.

Spittler, Russell. *Perspectives on the New Pentecostalism*. Grand Rapids: Baker, 1976.

Spong, John S. *Why Christianity Must Change or Die, A Bishop Speaks to Believers in Exile: A New Reformation of the Church's Faith and Practice*. New York: HarperCollins, 2001.

Springer, Kevin, ed. *Riding the Third Wave: What Comes After Renewal?* Basingstoke: Marshall Pickering, 1987.

Sproul, R. C. *Essential Truths of the Christian Faith*. Amersham on the Hill: Scripture, 1992.

———. *Getting the Gospel Right: The Tie that Binds Evangelicals Together*. Grand Rapids: Baker, 2003.

———. *Truths we Confess: A Layman's Guide to the Westminster Confession of Faith*. Vol.1. Phillipsburg, NJ: P&R, 2006.

———. *Truths we Confess: A Layman's Guide to the Westminster Confession of Faith*. Vol. 2. Phillipsburg, NJ: P & R, 2007.

Sproul, R. C. *After Darkness, Light: Essays in Honour of R. C. Sproul*. Phillipsburg, NJ: P & R, 2003.

Sproul, R. C., et al. *Whatever Happened to the Reformation?* Phillipsburg, NJ: P & R, 2001.

Stackhouse, Ian. *The Gospel Driven Church: Retrieving Classic Ministries for Contemporary Revivalism*. Milton Keynes: Paternoster/ Authentic Media, 2004.

Stafford, Tim, and James Beverley. "Conversations: God's Wonder Worker." *Christianity Today*, July 14, 1997. http://www.christianitytoday.com/ct/ 1997/july14/7t8046.html.

Stanley, Brian. *The Bible and the Flag: Protestant Missions and British Imperialism in the Nineteenth and Twentieth Centuries*. Leicester: Apollos, 1990.

———. "Christian Missions, Antislavery and the Claims of Humanity." In *The Cambridge History of Christianity: World Christianities, c. 1814- c.1914*, edited by Hugh McLoed. Cambridge: Cambridge University Press, 2006.

———. "The Future in the Past: Eschatological Vision in British and American Protestant Missionary History." *Tyndale Bulletin* 51.1 (2000) 101–20.

———. "Inculturation: Historical Background, Theological Foundations and Contemporary Questions." *Transformations* 24.1 (2007) 21–27.

———. *Twentieth Century World Christianity: A Perspective from the History of Missions*. Cambridge: Currents in World Christianity Project, University of Cambridge, 1999.

Stevenson-Moessner, Jeanne. *Prelude to Practical Theology: Variations on Theory and Practice*. Nashville: Abingdon, 2008.

Stewart, A. T. Q. *The Narrow Ground: Aspects of Ulster, 1609–1969*. Belfast: Blackstaff, 1997.

Stewart, David. *A Short History of the Presbyterian Church in Ireland*. Belfast: The Sabbath School Society for Ireland, 1936.

Stonehouse, Ned D. *J. Gresham Machen: A Biographical Memoir*. 3rd ed. Philadelphia: Westminster Theological Seminary, 1977.

Storms, Sam. *Convergence: The Spiritual Journey of a Charismatic Calvinist*. Eastbourne, England: Kingsway, 2005.

Stott, John. *The Living Church: Convictions of a Life Long Pastor*. Nottingham: InterVarsity Press, 2007.

Strachan, Gordon. *The Pentecostal Theology of Edward Irving*. Peabody, MA: Hendrickson, 1988.

Sumrall, Lester. *The Gifts and Ministries of the Holy Spirit*. New Kensington, PA: Whittaker House, 1982.

Swinton, John, and Harriett Mowatt. *Practical Theology and Qualitative Research*. London: SCM, 2009.

Synan, Vinson. *The Century of the Holy Spirit: 100 Years of Pentecostal and Charismatic Renewal*. Nashville: Thomas Nelson, 2001.

———. "Discerning the Charismatic Renewal." *Theology Today* 36.3 (1979) 315–27.

———. *The Holiness Pentecostal Tradition: Charismatic Movements in the Twentieth Century*. Grand Rapids: Eerdmans, 1997.

Tanner, Kathryn. *Theory of Culture: A New Agenda for Theology*. Minneapolis, MN: Augsburg, 1997.

Taylor, Steve. *The Out of Bounds Church: Learning to Create a Community of Faith in a Culture of Change*. Grand Rapids: Zondervan, 2005.

Tchividjian, W. Tullian. *The Kingdom of God: A Primer on the Christian Life*. Edinburgh: Banner of Truth Trust, 2005.

Thomas, John C. *Ministry and Theology: Studies for the Church and its Leaders*. Cleveland, TN: Pathway, 1996.

Thomas, Scott. "Five Basics for Accountability." *Church Leaders*. http://www.churchleaders.com/outreach-missions/outreach-missions-blogs/149625-accountability_is_not_the_silver_bullet_but_it_is_a_bullet.html.

Thompson, Mark. *A Clear and Present Word: The Clarity of Scripture*. Leicester: InterVarsity, 2006.

———. "Spiritual Warfare 1: The Critical Moment." In *John Wimber: Friend or Foe, An Examination of the Current Teaching of the Vineyard Ministries*. Reprinted from *The Briefing*. St. Matthias: London, 1990.

Tomlin, Graham. *The Provocative Church*. London: SPCK, 2002.

Tomlinson, Dave. *The Post Evangelical*. London: Triangle/SPCK, 1995.

———. *Re-Enchanting Christianity, Faith in an Emerging Culture*. Norwich: Canterbury, 2008.

Tozer, Aiden W. *The Root of the Righteous*. Bromley: OM, 1995.

———. *This World: Playground or Battleground*. Camp Hill, PA: OM, 1989.

Turner, Max. "Early Christian Experience and the Theology of 'Tongues.'" In *Speaking in Tongues: Multi-Disciplinary Perspective*, edited by Mark J. Cartledge. Milton Keynes: Paternoster, 2006.

———. *The Holy Spirit and Spiritual Gifts Then and Now*. Carlisle: Paternoster, 1996.

Ufford-Chase, Rick. "Pentecostal Presbyterian Churches? This is NOT your father's Oldsmobile." *What I See Blog*. July 2005. http://what-i-see.blogspot.com/2005/07/pentecostal-presbyterian-churches-this.html.

"Union Theological College Management Committee." In *Annual Reports, General Assembly of the Presbyterian Church in Ireland, 2011, Sitting in Belfast*. Belfast: Church House, 2011.

Van Der Kooi, Cornelius. "The Wonders of God: A Reformed Perspective on Luke's Baptism in the Holy Spirit." *PentecoStudies* 7.1 (2008) 34–35.

Van Der Meer, Edwin. "The Strategic Level Spiritual Warfare Theology of C. Peter Wagner and its Implications for Christian Mission in Malawi." ThD diss., University of South Africa, 2008.

Vanhoozer, Kevin J. "On the Very Idea of a Theological System: An Essay in Aid of Triangulating Scripture, Church and World." In *Always Reforming: Explorations in Systematic Theology*, edited by Alister McGowan and T. B. Leicester: Apollos, 2006.

Virgo, Terry. *No Well-Worn Paths: Restoring the Church to Christ's Original Intention*. Eastbourne: Kingsway, 2001.

———. *The Spirit Filled Church: Finding Your Place in God's Purpose*. Oxford: Monarch, 2011.

———. "We've Not Seen Revival and I Still Pray for It." Interview with John Buckeridge, *Christianity*, July 2009.

Vlach, Michael J. "What Is Dispensationalism." *On the Wing*. http://www.onthewing.org/user/Dispensationalism.pdf.

Volf, Miroslav. "Dancing for God: Evangelical Theological Education in Global Context." Paper presented to the International Consultation for Theological Educators, High Wycombe, August 18, 2003.

Vos, Geerhardus. *The Pauline Eschatology*. Phillipsburg, NJ: P & R, 1979.

Vreeland, Derek. "Edward Irving: Preacher, Prophet & Charismatic Theologian." *Pneuma Review* 5.2 (2002) 32–53.

Vyhmeister, Nancy J. *Your Guide to Writing Quality Research Papers for Students of Religion and Theology*. Grand Rapids: Zondervan, 2008.

Wait, Eric. "Tongues and the Westminster Confession of Faith." http://www.erikwait.com/cgi-local/printer_friendly.cgi?story_id=59.

Waggoner, Berton A. "The Theology & Practice of the Kingdom of God." *Vineyard USA*. http://www.vineyardusa.org/site/about/article/theology-practice-kingdom-god-waggoner.

Wagner, C. Peter. *Church Growth and the Whole Gospel: A Biblical Mandate*. Bromley: MARC, 1981.

———. *Dominion: How Kingdom Action Can Change the World*. Grand Rapids: Chosen, 2008.

———. *Leading Your Church to Growth: The Secret Dynamic of Pastor/People Partnership in Dynamic Church Growth*. Venture, CA: Regal, 1984.

———. *Spiritual Warfare Strategy: Confronting Spiritual Powers*. Shippensburg, PA: Destiny Image, 1996.

———. *The Third Wave of the Holy Spirit: Encountering the Power of Signs and Wonders*. Ann Arbor: Vine, 1988.

Walker, Andrew. *Remembering our Future: Explorations in Deep Church*. Milton Keynes: Paternoster, 2007.

———. *Restoring the Kingdom: The Radical Christianity of the House Church Movement*. London: Hodder and Stoughton, 1988.

Wallace, Daniel B., and M. James Sawyer. *Who's Afraid of the Holy Spirit: An Investigation into the Ministry of the Holy Spirit Today*. Dallas, TX: Biblical Studies, 2005.

Wallace, Peter J. "History and Sacrament: John Williamson Nevin and Charles Hodge on the Lord's Supper." *Mid-America Journal of Theology* (2000) 171–210.

Ward, Roland S. *The Westminster Confession of Faith: A Study Guide*. Wantirna, Australia: New Melbourne, 2004.

Warfield, Benjamin, B. *Counterfeit Miracles*. Edinburgh: Banner of Truth Trust, 1986.

———. "Irvingite Gifts." The Thomas Smith Lectures for 1917–1918, Columbia Theological Seminary, Columbia, SC.

———. "The Westminster Assembly and its Word." In *The Works of Benjamin B. Warfield in Ten Volumes*. Vol. 6. Grand Rapids: Baker, 2003.

Warner, Rob. *21st Century Church: Preparing your Church for the New Millennium*. Eastbourne: Kingsway, 1999.

———. *I Believe in Discipleship: The Adventure of Living*. London: Hodder and Stoughton, 1999.

Warner, R. Stephen. *New Wine in Old Wineskins: Evangelicals and Liberals in a Small-Town Church*. Berkley: University of California Press, 1990.

Warren, Rick. *The Purpose Driven Church: Growth Without Compromising Your Message and Mission*. Grand Rapids: Zondervan, 1995.

Warrington, Keith. *Healing and Suffering: Biblical and Pastoral Reflections*. Milton Keynes: Paternoster, 2005.

———. *The Message of the Holy Spirit*. Downers Grove, IL: InterVarsity, 2009.

———. *Pentecostal Perspectives*. Carlisle: Paternoster, 1998.

———. *Pentecostal Theology: A Theology of Encounter*. London: T & T Clark, 2008.

———. "The Teaching and Praxis Concerning Supernatural Healing of British Pentecostals, John Wimber and Kenneth Hagin in the Light of an Analysis of the

Healing Ministry of Jesus as Recorded in the Gospel." PhD diss., University of London, 1999.

———. "Would Jesus have sent his Disciples to Bible College?" *The Journal of the European Pentecostal Theological Association* 23 (2003) 30–44.

Waters, Guy P. *The Federal Vision and Covenant Theology: A Comparative Analysis.* Phillipsburg, NJ: P & R, 2006.

Watson, David. *Discipleship.* London: Hodder and Stoughton, 1983.

Watson, Thomas. *The Godly Man's Picture.* Edinburgh: Banner of Truth Trust, 1992.

Weeks, Louis B. *The Presbyterian Source: Bible Words that Shape a Faith.* Louisville, KY: Westminster John Knox, 1990.

Wells, David F. *The Courage to be Protestant: Truth-lovers, Marketers and Emergents in the Post-modern World.* Nottingham: InterVarsity, 2008.

Wells, Ronald A. *Friendship Towards Peace: The Journey of Ken Newell and Gerry Reynolds.* Dublin: Columba, 2005.

Wenkel, David. "John Bunyan's Soteriology during his Pre-Prison Period (1656–1659): Amyraldian or High Calvinist?" *Scottish Journal of Theology* 58.3 (2008) 333–52.

White, James E. *Rethinking the Church: A Challenge to Creative Redesign in an Age of Transition.* Grand Rapids: Baker, 2003.

White, James R. *The King James Only Controversy: Can You Trust the Modern Translations?* Ada, MI: Bethany, 1995.

Willard, Dallas. *The Divine Conspiracy: Rediscovering our Hidden Life in God.* San Francisco: Harper San Francisco, 1997.

Williams, Don. *Signs, Wonders and the Kingdom of God: A Biblical Guide for the Reluctant Sceptic.* Ann Arbor: Vine, 1989.

———. "Theological Perspective and Reflection on the Vineyard Christian Fellowship." In *Church Identity and Change: Theology and Denominational Structures in Unsettled Times*, edited by David A. Rosen and James R. Nieman. Grand Rapids: Eerdmans, 2001.

Williamson, George I. *The Westminster Confession of Faith for Study Classes.* 2nd ed. Phillipsburg, NJ: P & R, 2004.

"The Willowbank Report: Consultation on Gospel and Culture." In *Lausanne Occasional Paper 2.* South Hamiliton, MA: Lausanne Committee for World Evangelisation, 1978.

Wimber, John. *Beyond Intolerance: Calling the Church to Love and Acceptance.* Cape Town, South Africa: Vineyard Ministries International, 1996.

———. *Everyone Gets to Play, John Wimber's Writings and Teachings on Life Together in Christ.* Boise, Idaho: Ampelon, 2008.

———. *Kingdom Come: Understanding what the Bible Says about the Reign of God.* London: Hodder and Stoughton, 1989.

———. *Kingdom Fellowship: Living Together as the Body of Christ.* London: Hodder and Stoughton, 1989.

———. *Kingdom Living: Growing in the Character of Christ.* London: Hodder and Stoughton, 1987.

———. *Kingdom Ministry: Walking in the Power of Service.* London: Hodder and Stoughton, 1987.

———. *Kingdom Mercy: Living in the Power of Forgiveness.* London: Hodder and Stoughton, 1987.

———. *Kingdom of God.* Placentia, CA: Vineyard Ministries International, 1985.

———. *Kingdom Suffering: Facing Difficulty and Trial in the Christian Life*. London: Hodder and Stoughton, 1989.

———. "Leadership and Followership." Yorba Linda, CA: Equipping the Saints, 1995.

———. *Living with Uncertainty: My Battle with Inoperable Cancer*. Anaheim, CA: Vineyard Ministries International, 1996.

———. *Prayer: Intimate Communication*. Cape Town, South Africa: Vineyard Ministries International, 1997.

———. "To Be or Not to Be a Denomination/Institution?" http://www.wimber.org/to-be-or-not-to-be-a-denominationinstitution-by-john-wimber/.

———. *The Way In is the Way On*. Eastbourne: Kingsway, 2006.

———. *Witnesses for a Powerful Christ: Strengthening the Foundation of Renewal for the 21st Century*. Cape Town, South Africa: Vineyard Ministries International, 1996.

Wimber, John, and Kevin Springer. *The Dynamics of Spiritual Growth*. London: Hodder and Stoughton, 1990.

———. *Power Evangelism*. London: Hodder and Stoughton, 1992.

———. *Power Healing*. London: Hodder and Stoughton, 1986.

———. *Power Points: Your Action Plan to: Hear God's Voice, Believe God's Word, Seek the Father, Submit to Christ, Take up the Cross, Depend on the Holy Spirit and Fulfill the Great Commission*. San Francisco: Harper Collins, 1991.

———. *Practical Healing: Practical Guide to Power Healing*. London: Hodder and Stoughton, 1987.

———. *The Way to Maturity: How to Live in the Spirit and Grow to Maturity as a Child of God*. Ventura, CA: Regal, 1993.

Winter, Ralph D., and Stephen Hawthorne. *Perspectives on the World Christian Movement: A Reader*, 4th ed. Pasadena, CA: William Carey Library, 2009.

Woodhouse, John. "Signs and Wonders and Evangelical Ministry." In *Signs and Wonders and Evangelicals: A Response to the Teaching of John Wimber*, edited by Robert Doyle. Homebust West: Lancer, 1987.

"Word and Spirit, Church and World: The Final Report of the International Dialogue between Representatives of the World Alliance of Reformed Churches And Some Classical Pentecostal Churches and Leaders 1996–2000?" *Cyberjournal for Pentecostal-Charismatic Research*. http://www.pctii.org/cyberj/cyberj8/WARC.html.

Wright, Christopher J. H. *The Mission of God: Unlocking the Bible's Grand Narrative*. Downers Grove, IL: InterVarsity, 2006.

Wright, Eric. *Church—No Spectator Sport: In Search of Spiritual Gifts*. Darlington: Evangelical, 1994.

———. *A Practical Theology of Missions: Dispelling the Mystery; Recovering the Passion*. Leominster: Day One, 2010.

Wright, James. "Profiles of Divine Healing: Third Wave Theology Compared with Classical Pentecostal Theology." *Asian Journal of Pentecostal Studies* 5.2 (2002) 271–87.

Wright, Nigel. "Restorationism and the 'House Church' Movement." *Themelios* 16.2 (1991) 4–8.

Wright, Tom. *Simply Christian*. London: SPCK, 2006.

Wright, Walter C. *Mentoring: The Promise of Relational Leadership*. Milton Keynes, England: Paternoster, 2006.

Zozzaro, J. A. "Charismatic Presbyterians?" *Ordained Servant* 6.4 (1997) 91–93.

www.ingramcontent.com/pod-product-compliance
Lightning Source LLC
Chambersburg PA
CBHW071243230426
43668CB00011B/1567